TESI GREGORIANA

Serie Diritto Canonico

— 39 —

JAMES M. OLIVER

ECUMENICAL ASSOCIATIONS

Their Canonical Status with Particular Reference to the United States of America

EDITRICE PONTIFICIA UNIVERSITÀ GREGORIANA
Roma 1999

Vidimus et approbamus ad normam Statutorum Universitatis

Romae, ex Pontificia Universitate Gregoriana

die 12 mensis maii anni 1999

Prof. GIANFRANCO GHIRLANDA, SJ
Prof. MICHAEL HILBERT, SJ

ISBN 88-7652-837-7

GREGORIAN UNIVERSITY PRESS
Piazza della Pilotta, 35 - 00187 Rome, Italy

INTRODUCTION

In his Apostolic Exhortation, *Christifideles Laici*, Pope John Paul II speaks of a new era of group endeavor. The contemporary lay groups which exist alongside the traditional groups are very diverse from one another but at the same time have the common goal of sharing in the Church's evangelical mission[1]. Some of these new groups are ecumenical. The status of these ecumenical associations, that is associations in which baptized non-Catholics are inscribed, is the focus of this study[2].

The theme of this dissertation is particular as it addresses a number of questions from a unique perspective, considering the history of ecumenism as it affects associations in the Catholic Church. Secondly, a number of associations which may be considered ecumenical are studied. Lastly, the thesis turns to the canons themselves looking for the means by which the *CIC* 83 recognizes the right of Catholics to inscribe non-Catholics into their associations.

The question will be addressed on a practical as well as a theoretical plane. Besides the historical and canonical research a search for associations which may be considered ecumenical was undertaken. A survey with follow-up research was done of the 176 Latin dioceses in the United States of America[3] and a perusal of the list of addresses of associations in relation with the PCL revealed a number of examples. The in-depth canonical study of nineteen actual associations in the dissertation brings a very real dimension to the study of associations of

---

[1] JOHN PAUL II, apost. exh. *Christifideles Laici, AAS* 81 (1989) 444.

[2] Since the *CIC* 83 does not bar non-Christian non-baptized their status will also play a part in the work.

[3] There was a 70 % response rate to the questionnaire. Of the dioceses which responded to the survey less than five reported having ecumenical associations in their dioceses. Most of the information in the dissertation was gathered in other ways. Much was gained through networking.

the faithful which have or are open to having non-Catholics as members. Such a wide, intense study has not as yet been undertaken.

The thesis undertakes new work in the field of associations. A unique synthesis is utilized for the ecumenical study. Original research concerning associations in the United States of America and in other parts of the world is herein published. The legal section treats associations differently than they are handled elsewhere. Most often the ecumenical question is a subsection of an overall treatment of associations of the Christian faithful; here the ecumenical/interreligious question is the center of the study.

This study addresses a number of questions. What is the development which led to the present ecumenical situation in the Catholic Church? What is the present praxis of bishops and the PCL in relating to associations of the Christian faithful which inscribe non-Catholic members? What do the canons reveal as far as non-Catholic participation in associations is concerned?

The question is topical as a number of associations are now desiring an official relation with the Catholic Church. It is hoped that the dissertation will prove fruitful, as the application of theory to actual practice is often difficult. The new synthesis, documentation and praxis which are surfaced by this work will bring clarity to the practical questions and issues which surround the membership of non-Catholics in associations of the Christian faithful.

CHAPTER I

Historical Development of the Ecumenical Movement

1. Introduction

This chapter is a study of the development of ecumenical relationships, as they affect canonical Catholic associations of the faithful, from *CIC* 17 to the ED93. As *CIC* 17 did not permit non-Catholics to belong to canonical Catholic associations, the development providing the possibility of their entrance will be the main focus of the chapter. The participation of the Roman Catholic Church in the ecumenical movement was a carefully considered process. She moved from participating in her own Catholic ecumenism to participation in the ecumenical movement begun by her separated brethren. Non-Catholics are now able to enter Catholic associations of the Christian faithful in ways which had not been possible.

CIC 17 will be considered in light of its presentation of the relations between Roman Catholics and non-Catholics. After selected canons are studied, pertinent information from documents of the Holy See which shaped ecumenical policy will be examined. These affect the universal Church. Another section of this work will be dedicated to the unique situation in the United States of America and the development of the relationship between the Holy Roman Catholic Church and ecumenism in that country. This unique relation lends to the possibility of ecumenical associations in a particular way.

Where there were, and are, possibilities for interaction and sharing the Church becomes involved; where these possibilities do not exist she does not become involved. The relationship between the Church and the WCC gives good example of this. The Catholic Church's relationship with the WCC is considered the first time it is discussed in the dissertation. Pope John Paul II said that the commitment on the part of the Roman Catholic Church to the ecumenical movement as expressed at the Second Vatican Council is irreversible[1]. The call *ut unum sint* is always to be kept in mind.

Documents of the Pontiffs as well as the Apostolic See will be the lampposts which will guide the work. By way of these documents it is possible to view the changes that took place within Church policy along the road to ecumenical relations with separated brethren. Just as important, the study of these documents manifests the dogmas which do not change. The fact of a visible Church established by Christ, the sacraments and the role of the bishop are examples of these unchangeable truths.

Ecumenical associations are not at the center of any of the documents to be reviewed. However, the call of Christ for unity cannot be ignored by the Church. As she moves toward unity, the doors to ecumenical associations have also opened. The basis for these associations is developed through Roman Catholic ecumenical involvement.

2. Ecumenical Relations in the 1917 Code of Canon Law

The *CIC* 17 addresses the participation of non-Catholics within associations of the faithful directly. C.693,§1 concerns membership of persons in associations of the faithful. Specifically, it concerns those who cannot be members. Its location is in title XVIII, «Associations of the Faithful in General» (cc.684-699), which is found in part II, «The Laity» (cc.682-725), of book II, «Concerning Persons» (cc.87-725). With the exception of c.693,§1, non-Catholics are not mentioned, in title XVIII or in title XIX, «Associations of the Faithful in Particular» (cc.700-725).

This section of chapter one will investigate the possibilities of non-Catholic members of associations of the faithful in the *CIC* 17. It will also study the position of non-Catholics in the *CIC* 17.

One commentator, Augustine, made an interesting comment as he reviewed the canon relating to the participation of non-Catholics in associations. While listing examples of associations which were considered secret, or condemned as seditious or suspected, interconfessional associations were mentioned. He stated that, «Interconfessional associations are almost compelled to shirk the restraints imposed by eccle-

---

[1] JOHN PAUL II, «To the Delegates of Other Christian Churches», 22 October 1978, in SHEERIN, J.P. – HOTCHKIN, J.F., ed., *Addresses*, 1.

siastical authority»[2]. He was well aware of difficulties that may be caused by having persons of different religions as members of the same association. The presence of non-Catholics could often put undue pressure on Catholics to ignore Catholic regulations and teaching in order to help all to feel welcome. Any encounter with non-Catholics involves a certain risk. A weakening or loss of the faith is always a possibility. The task for the Church is to see that all her members are solidly grounded in the faith she teaches.

2.1 *Non-Catholic Members of Associations of the Faithful*

C.693,§1 *CIC* 17 specifically states[3], «Non-Catholics and those inscribed in condemned sects as well as those notoriously punished by censor and in general public sinners are not able to be validly received»[4].

Non-Catholics include the following persons: the unbaptized and baptized apostates, heretics or schismatics. A baptized person who has not defected from the Church in any way is validly received into an association. Examples of condemned sects include: The Freemasons, communists, anarchists, cremation societies, and those which conspire against the Church or against lawful civil authority. The category of public sinners includes those persons who are living publicly, notoriously, and habitually in the state of mortal sin[5]. The use of *acatholici* in c.693 §1 *CIC* 17 makes it very clear that non-Catholics were not able to be members of associations at that time.

Conte a Coronata defined non-Catholics as those people erring in faith or positively doubting. These include apostates, heretics and schismatics. However those who err in matters of faith in assent of the mind only, may be received into associations. It is presumed that this assent has not been manifested externally. Also, those non-Catholics who have erred in faith or have positively doubted and have returned to the faith can be validly received[6].

---

[2] C. AUGUSTINE, *A Commentary*, III, 429.

[3] All translations are our own except those of official Church documents with official/accepted translations: A. P. FLANNERY, ed. *Documents of Vatican II*, Grand Rapids, MI 1978; *ChL*; and *CIC* 83 or unless otherwise indicated.

[4] C.693,§1 *CIC* 17. Acatholici et damnatae sectae adscripti aut censura notorie irretiti et in genere publici peccatores valide recipi nequeunt.

[5] J. ABBO – J. HANNAN, *The Sacred Canons*, 697-698.

[6] M. CONTE A CORONATA, *Institutiones Iuris Canonici*, I, 898.

2.2 *Concerning Non-Catholics in Particular*

At the time of the writing of the *CIC* 17, it was forbidden for Catholics to mix with non-Catholics in religious settings. The following two canons make this very clear.

2.2.1 *Canon 1258 CIC 17*

Canon 1258 states:

§1 It is by no means licit for the faithful to actively assist in any manner whatsoever or to have a part in the sacred services of non-Catholics. §2 The passive or merely material presence of Catholics at the funerals and weddings of non-Catholics can be permitted on account of civil duty or honor, because of a grave reason which, in case of doubt, must be approved by the bishop provided that the danger of perversion or scandal be absent[7].

The canon concerns *communicatio in sacris activa cum acatholicis*, active communion with non-Catholics in sacred things. *CIC* 17 was direct about what was, and was not, permitted. It was clear in its call for a certain distance between Catholics and those of other faiths in religious matters.

Blat often used scripture to underline his points. In support of c.1258 *CIC* 17 he cited the second letter of John, «If anyone comes to you and does not bring this doctrine, do not receive him into your house or even greet him; for whoever greets him shares in his evil works»[8]. Using the words of the canon Blat makes four divisions which affected the prohibition: a) in any way at all, even the mere appearance of participating in another religion, b) the active assistance, in so far as one's external actions exhibit, for example the religious modesty of attention, c) or how to take part, for example participating in those things which are done in consideration of worship in their gatherings, and d) in sacred things, namely in rites of ceremonies of divine worship of non-Catholics. They may worship a false god or they may worship the true God by their own judgment in a heretical or schis-

---

[7] C.1258,§1 *CIC* 17 «Haud licitum est fidelibus quovis modo active assistere seu partem habere in sacris acatholicorum. §2 Tolerari potest praesentia passiva seu mere materialis, civilis officii vel honoris causa, ob gravem rationem ab Episcopo in casu dubii probandam, in acatholicorum funeribus nuptiis similibusque sollemniis, dummodo perversionis et scandali periculum absit».

[8] 2 John 10-11.

matic sect or apart from that sect in worship professing heresy or schism or finally by the worship of the old law[9].

The four points highlighted help to distinguish what is acceptable and not acceptable for Catholics approaching non-Catholic services. They clarify the canon and should be kept in mind as the canon is discussed. Examples used by commentators will also be considered.

The prohibition of this canon has its origins in natural and divine law. The Church is the one true and only religious society existing by divine law. Jesus said to Peter, «On this rock I will build my Church»[10]. As we believe that there is one God alone so therefore there will be one truth, one faith and one Church. This one Church strives to live out the faith and follow the truth as presented to it by the Holy Spirit. It is within this Church that it is right to give God due worship. Participation in other sects and communities which were not the one true Church was not accepted[11].

The commentary by Bouscaren and Ellis is very clear in its organized description of *communicatio in sacris activa cum acatholicis*. They use the terms «active participation» and «passive presence» to describe types of *communicatio in sacris*. The terms come directly from c.1258,§§1-2. They described active participation as the physical presence of a Catholic at a non-Catholic worship service. Some positive act of worship in common with the non-Catholics who are worshipping was also considered active participation. Active participation is either formal or material. If one wished to truly take part in the worship, the active participation is formal. If one took part for other reasons, for instance, merely civil or for friendship, the active participation would be considered merely material. However the commentators note that all active participation is forbidden according to c.1258,§1. For Bouscaren and Ellis it does not matter if the active participation is formal or material[12].

Passive presence of a Catholic at a non-Catholic service takes place when a person is present without committing any positive act of worship. He has decided to be present but does not engage in any positive action. Bouscaren and Ellis explain that an internal intention to approve, assent or to encourage the non-Catholic worship would be formal cooperation in an evil act, and forbidden by the natural law. This

---

[9] A. BLAT, *Commentarium II*, 165.

[10] Matt. 16,18.

[11] M. CONTE A CORONATA, *Institutiones Iuris Canonici*, II, 159.

[12] T.L. BOUSCAREN – A. ELLIS, *Canon Law*, 639.

situation was not assumed and passive presence was viewed as merely material. Catholics were not to attend non-Catholic services. The presence of a Catholic at a non-Catholic service was permitted under special circumstances. Weddings and funerals are two examples given in the canon. Even though it may not be intrinsically wrong by reason of the act, presence in a non-Catholic church is likely to be wrong by reason of its circumstances or consequences[13]. In the conclusion of their commentary on this canon, reference is made to an article written by Bouscaren which treats the matter as a theological issue. He believes that further applications pertain to moral theology[14].

The view of Woywod allows for what he calls indirect cooperation. This involves the work of a particular Catholic in the participation of non-Catholic affairs. Catholic architects and workman would be allowed to work on the construction of a non-Catholic building, unless this cooperation for circumstantial reasons would be an insult to the Catholic faith. Persons were not permitted to become directly involved, that is, to donate money, building materials or give a free will offering of work toward the construction of a non-Catholic worship building[15].

Before further review of this canon by way of specific examples it would be worthwhile to consider Augustine's reasons for the prohibition. His pastoral approach adds depth to the prohibitions in three ways. First, the quasi-approval of non-Catholic worship which lies in a Catholic's participation is hard to avoid. One does not usually attend gatherings which represent and promote that which one does not believe to be true. Mere presence can represent an external profession of faith. Secondly, the mere presence of Catholics at non-Catholic gatherings or services can lead to scandal which may be given to Catholics who see the mixture of worship and the deference paid to non-Catholic ministers and functions. And thirdly, the danger of religious indifference which may arise after the faithful freely and indiscriminately participate in heretical religious services. It should not be necessary to mention it, but he adds that even the simulation of false religion is incompatible with the purity of the Catholic faith[16].

Certain situations, especially those involving witnessing marriages, receive different views from different commentators. Some have been brought before the Holy Office as doubts to which rescripts have been

---

[13] T.L. BOUSCAREN – A. ELLIS, *Canon Law*, 639.
[14] T.L. BOUSCAREN, «Cooperation with non-Catholics».
[15] S. WOYWOD, *A Practical Commentary*, II, 59.
[16] C. AUGUSTINE, *A Commentary*, VI, 193.

written[17]. As the goal is to view the relationship between Catholics and non-Catholics, that is ecumenism, in the *CIC* 17 several examples will be considered.

It is not forbidden for a Catholic to visit a non-Catholic church as a sightseer. However, to be present at a non-Catholic church for prayers, services, or sermons in a church or elsewhere is forbidden. Catholics are not to act as sponsors at the baptism of Protestants or schismatics by their own minister. Priests who attend non-Catholic funerals were not to vest or take part in any way in the proceedings performed by a non-Catholic minister. Woywod states that to be a best man or bridesmaid at a wedding in the United States is a sign of friendship and honor and not an official witness of the marriage contract. For this reason Woywod feels it is allowable[18]. Other commentators were not so free in their interpretation of the canon regarding witnesses at weddings. Recognizing passive attendance meant one could attend the wedding or funeral of a friend or public official who was not Catholic. It also meant that for one to assist as a bridesmaid or witness at the wedding of a friend was to be discouraged[19]. What actually happened regarding Catholics acting as witnesses at non-Catholic weddings depended on the pastor's or bishop's interpretation of the law. Other points concerning Catholics and non-Catholics participating in each other's religious services were to be brought to the bishop when situations were not clear.

Besides those that have already been listed, there are other prohibitions which affect Catholics. The following list is drawn from Conte a Coronata.

[1] It is never licit to offer children of Catholics for baptism by non-Catholics. In no case but danger of death is it licit to confess one's own sins to a heretic or schismatic; however, in case of death it is licit while another Catholic priest is not present and scandal is avoided and there is not danger of perversion and it is probable that the heretical minister is going to administer the sacrament according to the rite of the Church.

[2] It is never licit to receive holy orders from a heretic. Nor is it permitted for Catholics to call a heretical minister on behalf of a heretic who is in danger of death. The commentator hinted that there were

---

[17] One such list can be found in A. BLAT, *Commentarium II*, 166, another in P. GASPARRI, *Codicis Iuris Canonici Fontes*, IV, N. 978, p. 250.

[18] S. WOYWOD, *A Practical Commentary*, II, 60.

[19] P.J. LYDON, *Ready Answers in Canon Law*, 148-149.

ways to get around this situation. An example was conversing with the pastor concerning some other matter and merely mentioning the situation as an aside.

[3] It is illicit for a Catholic organist to play in a non-Catholic Church on the occasion of sacred functions. The admittance of non-Catholics to Catholic churches can be permitted or tolerated, as long as the sacraments are not administered to them, neither should they communicate in divine things with Catholics nor should they be invited to do so.

[4] Catholics are not to hear Mass in the church of schismatics with the schismatic minister celebrating. A Catholic can be sworn before a non-Catholic minister, if he is not acting as a non-Catholic minister, but as a minister of civil society, nor is it absolutely prohibited to swear an oath on the Bible of non-Catholics. It is never permitted for a Catholic party to accept a nuptial blessing from a non-Catholic minister, however the non-Catholic party may receive a blessing from the non-Catholic minister[20].

The Church was very careful to protect the flock from what might draw them from the true faith. Even as regulations may seem to constrain, they open their followers to receive as much grace as possible.

One situation that hasn't been mentioned is the participation of non-Catholics at Catholic services. Here the *CIC* 17 is silent. However their active and public participation was always forbidden. To allow it would have given the impression that there was no essential difference between the errors of the sects and Catholicism. This would promote indifferentism[21]. The Holy Office was clear when it stated that non-Catholics may not receive sacramentals, palms, blessed ashes or rosaries, etc. in Catholic public services or processions[22].

For Catholics to be involved with non-Catholics in a non-sectarian charitable cause is not forbidden by the *CIC* 17. This behavior would not involve presence at liturgical services of other Churches or ecclesial communities. Caring for the needy and assisting in charitable causes of non-Catholics may be the occasion of virtue[23]. Allowing non-Catholics to participate with Catholics when the purpose of the work is the care for he basic needs of others is commended. This cooperation between Catholics and non-Catholics is called *communicatio in di-*

---

[20] M. CONTE A CORONATA, *Institutiones Iuris Canonici*, II, 159-160.
[21] J. ABBO – J. HANNAN, *The Sacred Canons*, II, 513.
[22] P. GASPARRI, *Codicis Iuris Canonici Fontes*, IV, N. 978, p. 250.
[23] T.L. BOUSCAREN, «Cooperation with non-Catholics», 475.

vinis[24] and apart from positive prohibition is encouraged. C.693,§1 *CIC* 17 prevented associations from accepting non-Catholics as members but not from cooperating with them in the divine call to love of neighbor and living the corporal works of mercy. The fundamental law of charity demands that all people help one another toward their common destiny[25].

All of the situations and examples that have been mentioned only reinforce the situation as it existed at the time of the *CIC* 17. C.1258 *CIC* 17 further emphasizes the separation of Catholics and non-Catholics when it came to religious gatherings and services. For a canonical association to have both Catholic and non-Catholic members would have been forbidden by this canon.

C.1325,§3 *CIC* 17 will now be discussed. It concerns dialogue between Catholics and non-Catholics. The permission for Catholic participation was in the hands of the hierarchy.

As one follows the history of the ecumenical movement the careful entrance of the Catholic Church can be observed. Ecumenical associations would possibly be involved in the situations discussed in the commentaries of these canons. Therefore the study of these canons is important to the development of the possibility of ecumenical associations in the Catholic Church.

2.3 *Canon 1325,§3 CIC 17*

C.1325,§3 states:

Catholics should beware of disputations or meetings with non-Catholics especially public ones without the permission of the Apostolic See or, if the case is urgent, of the local ordinary[26].

These conferences or public debates concerned with dogmatic questions were not a forum into which Catholics were to enter to discuss their faith. Catholics have always been encouraged to study their faith and to share the truth with others and be proficient in their ability to respond to others. Under this same canon Lydon noted that the World Conferences of Religion would not have a Catholic representative. The Church will not compromise doctrine nor debate dogmas[27].

---

[24] T.L. BOUSCAREN, «Cooperation with non-Catholics», 475.

[25] T.L. BOUSCAREN, «Cooperation with non-Catholics», 475.

[26] §3 «Caveant catholici ne disputationes vel collationes, publicas praesertim, cum acatholicis habeant, sine venia Sanctae Sedis aut, si casus urgeat, loci Ordinarii».

[27] P.J. LYDON, *Ready Answers*, 215.

From the time following the Protestant Reformation organized discussions or conferences, especially those considered public, between Catholics and non-Catholics were forbidden. However c.1325,§3 *CIC* 17 was written in a way that the Apostolic See could tolerate, if she saw fit, certain gatherings. This relaxation of the law took place when it seemed that a greater good would come from the encounter. Catholics were not always permitted to attend these meetings. With time the Church became continually more open to Catholic attendence and participation in such meetings. The transition from being restrictive to becoming more open to participating in ecumenism with the other denominations is seen through the documents of the popes and the Holy Office (Congregation for the Doctrine of the Faith). These documents are highlighted throughout the remainder of this chapter.

A distinction needs to be made as to whom the canon addresses. For those who have a simple faith, these disputes and conferences could be a dangerous enterprise. A wise, knowledgeable and discerning mind is needed. Those with simple faith may become prey to heretics, infidels or pagans who have rejected the true faith and may encourage others to do the same. It may at times be necessary to dispute or defend the true faith in private settings. Catholics should know the teachings of the Church so that they can answer questions and present the beliefs of the Church clearly. Situations in which Catholics defend their faith well will strengthen those of simple faith who are present when these impromptu discussions take place[28].

In Paul's second letter to Timothy he discourages senseless arguing. «Remind people of these things and charge them before God to stop disputing about words. This serves no useful purpose since it harms those who listen»[29]. Someone who doubts the faith but still persists in disputes and various arguments sins[30]. The Church was strong in her resolve not to compromise doctrine. Many times religious conferences with the aim of unity eventually involved the compromise of doctrine.

Discussions of theology and belief among various religious groups with the goal of union began among Protestants. Examples which relate to the canon will be given here. Examples will concentrate on situations that involve groups or associations.

At times the individual churches and persons who were involved in discussions or conferences formed a society. The WCC (1948) grew

---

[28] A BLAT, *Commentarium,* 278.
[29] 2 Tim 2,14.
[30] A. BLAT, *Commentarium,* 278.

out of the groups «Life and Work» and «Faith and Order". The latter began as a result of debates and conferences held among Protestants at the World Missionary Conference at Edinburgh (1910). Roman Catholics were often invited to these conferences but declined.

At this point it is opportune to give a brief explanation of the present relationship between the WCC and the Roman Catholic Church. Even though local Catholic parishes and dioceses may be members of councils of churches this is not possible for the universal Roman Catholic Church. However relations between the two do exist.

As the Roman Catholic Church is not a member Church of the WCC, the desire for unity has prompted a link between the two bodies in the form of the Joint Working Group. It was established by mutual agreement in May 1965. The purpose of the twenty-four member group is «to explore possibilities of dialogue and collaboration, to study problems jointly, [and] to report to the competent authorities of either side»[31]. Another area in which Roman Catholics take an active role in the WCC is the Faith and Order Commission. Twelve Roman Catholic theologians, out of the one hundred twenty member commission, have held full voting membership since 1968.

Collaboration between the WCC and the Roman Catholic Church takes place within the framework of the Joint Working Group. Other areas besides Faith and Order in which the Roman Catholic Church is involved are: 1) an on-going missiology study, one sister works in this area and five other persons are appointed as consultants, 2) collaboration in the social field, which is exploratory, involving the Pontifical Council for Justice and Peace and the Pontifical Council, «Cor Unum», 3) bilateral relations, including joint studies, exchanges of visits and mutual invitations to meetings, and 4) Faith and Order which has been mentioned[32].

The differences over ecclesiology continue to be the largest obstacle toward membership of the Roman Catholic Church in the WCC. The understanding of Church for Roman Catholics is a dogma of the faith. The WCC continues to debate the issue of the definition of church as is evidenced by the current discussion, «Towards a Common Understanding and Vision of the WCC»[33]. To ask for membership in the WCC would admit of a question of the dogmatic beliefs of the Catholic Church and call into question the beliefs of any number of the member

---

[31] «Joint Working Groups», 4.
[32] «Report on the Plenary Meeting», 45-49.
[33] M. Van Elderen, «Editorial», 303.

churches of the WCC. At this time, as in the past, it is not possible for the Roman Catholic Church to seek membership in the present WCC.

In 1919 a *dubium* was placed before the Holy Office as to whether Catholics were allowed to attend meetings organized by non-Catholics for the purpose of Christian unity. The instruction of the Holy Office of 16 September 1864 had forbidden Catholics from becoming members of a certain London society established to procure the unity of Christians. The Holy Office had recourse to the earlier declaration and said that Catholics were not to attend the meetings[34].

Another example of Catholics being barred from ecumenical associations also involves a situation which went before the Holy Office. This *dubium* arose on the occasion of the Lausanne Conference in Switzerland in 1927. Again the question involved the possibility of Catholics gathering with non-Catholics for purposes of unity and specifically to form one religious federation. The response was in the negative and stood on the reply of 4 July 1919[35].

All three declarations refuse Catholic participation in the ecumenical movement that was sweeping the non-Catholic world at that time. Commentators relate these rescripts to c.1325,§3 *CIC* 17[36]. The *dubia* concerned not only participation in disputes and conferences with non-Catholics but also gathering in a type of association. The reply of the Holy Office on 8 July 1927 involved the discussion of a union of all who call themselves Christians into one religious federation. The reply of the Holy Office of 16 September 1864 regarded the involvement of Roman Catholics in the London society to procure the union of Christendom.

The requests involved more than just disputes and conferences; belonging to associations described as societies and federations was also involved. At that time the Holy Office was clear in its response that Catholics would not be allowed to be involved in such a way with non-Catholics. The involvement in the associations was in a way a mute issue as it would come into direct conflict with c.1325,§3 *CIC* 17 and would most probably involve Catholics in non-Catholic worship violating c.1258 *CIC* 17. In his encyclical, *Mortalium animos* (1928), concerning the promotion of true Christianity, Pius XI states that it is evi-

---

[34] SUPREMA SACRA CONGREGATIO S. OFFICII, «*De participatione catholicorum*» *AAS* 11 (1919) 309.

[35] SUPREMA SACRA CONGREGATIO S. OFFICII, «*De Conventibus*», *AAS* 19 (1927) 278.

[36] P.J. LYDON, *Ready Answers,* 619.

dent that the Holy See can in no way take part in these meetings, and that Catholics are not permitted to favor or to cooperate in such under-takings[37]. The Church held to the view that the return to the true fold, the Catholic Church, was the sole means of reunion. Any mixing of Catholics with heretics, apostates, or schismatics was either not al-lowed or closely monitored.

The possibilities of any type of ecumenical association developing did not exist at the time of the Pio-benedictine Code. There are several reasons for this situation. The canons themselves did not allow non-Catholics to join Catholic associations. This was forbidden by c.693,§1 *CIC* 17. Cc.1258 and 1325,§3 *CIC* 17, severely limited the spiri-tual/religious contact between Catholics and those considered heretics, apostates, and schismatics. The commentaries on the canons gave spe-cific examples of situations that were and were not allowed by canons. These were strict, but, as the twentieth century was unfolding, the ecumenical movement within the non-Catholic Christian churches was developing. Communication between the Catholic Church and this movement was one of courteous recognition. Even though invitations were received, the Church did not send delegates to conferences. For the Catholic Church to send participants to a conference whose aim was to search for truths that the Church held as doctrine was just not possible.

Thus far the canons of the *CIC* 17 have been the means by which ecumenical relations have been explored. The viewpoint of the Roman Pontiffs will now be considered concerning the ecumenical situation by following papal documents that were written during and after the pon-tificate of Leo XIII. The first documents to be considered, concerning the London society, were previously used as examples in this section. By following the highlights of the Church's reaction to the ecumenical movement, starting at the end of the nineteenth and moving up to the latest documents, insight will be gained regarding the status of con-temporary canonically approved ecumenical associations. Setting the historical stage for the possibility of these associations is an important step in the study of their existence in the Church.

3. Ecumenical Developments up to the Second Vatican Council

The purpose of this section is to present an overview of the chang-ing position on the part of the Roman Catholic Church toward ecu-

---

[37] PIUS XI, enc. lett. *Mortalium animos, AAS* 20 (1928) 11.

menical interaction with the Reformation communities. The Church's view of Orthodoxy will also be considered. Without this development, ecumenical associations would not be a possibility. The canons would not have changed. During the pontificates that spanned the years 1894 to 1949 a number of documents were written concerning Church unity. The United States had a particularly interesting situation arise at the Parliament of Religions at Chicago. Involving ecumenical dialogue at a national level, the case was brought to the attention of the Apostolic See. The situation in the United States will be considered along with that of the universal Church.

3.1 *Encyclicals and Pronouncements – Towards a Dialogue*

3.1.1 The Holy Office Pronouncements of 1864 and 1865

One of the earliest encounters with Protestant ecumenical movement groups occurred during the reign of Pius IX. This would mark the end of an era of no, or at best, negative communication which was replaced by the ecumenical awakening that took place under Leo XIII. A group in London, the «Association for the Promotion of Christian Unity» was courting Catholics to become members. This situation has been cited earlier in this work but will be considered now in more depth. A letter, *Ad omnes Angliae Episcopos,* of 16 September 1864 from the Holy Office condemned participation in the association[38]. Another letter, *Ad Quosdam Puseistas Anglicos,* also addressing the issue was signed by Cardinal Patrizi on 8 November 1865[39]. At the time the communications were not intended to set policy or precedent for the universal Church but were to address a certain situation in a certain locality[40]. When referring to separated brethren as well as their societies the terms, «heretical» and «schismatic» were not used again in this manner in official Church documents. They would be used to refer only to those who were willful and therefore sinful in their separation from the Church[41]. The letters of 1864 and 1865 made it clear that Catholics were not to belong to associations that had reunion as their goal. The «Association for the Promotion of Christian Unity»

---

[38] SUPREMAE S. ROMANAE ET UNIVERSALIS INQUISITIONIS, «*Epistola ad omnes Angliae Episcopos*», *AAS* 11 (1919) 310-312.

[39] SUPREMAE S. ROMANAE ET UNIVERSALIS INQUISITIONIS, «*Ad Quosdam Puseistas Anglicos*», *AAS* 11 (1919) 312-316.

[40] G. TAVARD, *Two Centuries of Ecumenism*, 68.

[41] G. BAUM, *That They May Be One*, 152.

taught that Eastern Orthodoxy and Anglicanism were two forms of the Christian religion in which members were able to please God in the same way as in the Catholic Church[42]. The Holy Office stated that both the beliefs of the group and the possibility of Catholic membership were not acceptable. The adjectives used to describe our separated brethren would not be so sharp in the dialogue which would take place during the pontificates which were to follow. The change in the words used to describe the Reformation communities was significant concerning relations between these communities and the Catholic Church.

3.1.2 Towards Better Communication – Pope Leo XIII

It can be said that steps have been made towards the unity of Christian churches during the past century. With this in mind one can describe the pontificate of Pope Leo XIII as one in which leaps towards unity were made. Baum in his study of papal doctrine concerning Christian unity lists thirty-five documents of the Holy See, that mention church unity, which were written while Leo was Pope[43]. He truly set a foundation for Catholic Ecumenism.

a) *A Foundation for Catholic Ecumenism*

At the time hope for reunion was just that, hope. The Pope realized this even as he strove for reunion. There would be many steps before reunion could become a reality. Leo XIII desired that the separated brethren would return to their mother and that the Church would be united with those who had left her. He did much for scholarly investigation of ecumenism and possibilities of reunion. Invitations were made to separated brethren to come home to their Mother the Church[44]. Leo always set forth the truths held in the teachings of the Catholic Church. He was the initiator of prayers for Christian unity. He made, the Call for Church Unity, a reality within the Catholic world.

Leo XIII was instrumental in the change in usage of words like «heretic» and «schismatic» to «dissidents» or even their proper name for those born into Orthodoxy, Protestantism or Anglicanism. This did not indicate a change in doctrine, but a step towards better communi-

---

[42] SUPREMAE S. ROMANAE ET UNIVERSALIS INQUISITIONIS, «*Epistola ad Omnes Angliae Episcopos*», *AAS* 11 (1919) 311.

[43] G. BAUM, *That They May Be One*, 172.

[44] LEO XIII, apost. lett. *Amantissimae Voluntatis*, *ASS* 27 (1894-95) 590.

cation[45]. Much of the Pope's work in the ecumenical arena was to effect a change in attitude towards the separated brethren. He set into place the underpinnings for Catholic ecumenism which focused on points of contact between Protestants and Catholics, such as scripture and love of Christ. He held the need to return to the sources, for without these there could be no true Catholic ecumenism. The underpinnings of scripture and Christ's love are cited as common areas of praxis in the encyclical, *Caritatis Studium* (1898) written to the Scottish Presbyterians in the hope for union[46].

The situation of the church of England was given special attention during Leo's pontificate. The Anglican church was always seen as a step closer to Rome than her Protestant cousins. The nineteenth century was a time of much activity concerning reunion between Rome and Canterbury. Even after many disappointed Anglicans gave up hope of reunion following the definition of papal infallibility at the Vatican Council, others rallied and continued to move towards reunion. The thrust at the time of Leo's pontificate was fueled by an Anglican, Charles Lindley Wood, better known by his title, Lord Halifax, who was joined by a French Vincentian priest, Abbé Fernand Portal. Even though Portal fervently desired to see a Catholic Ecumenism develop as well as an Anglican - Roman reunion, he realized that these were not possible at the time. His goal became laying the groundwork for the future. If any unity were to come about in the future, Portal believed that Catholics and Anglicans had to know one another first[47]. This Vincentian is known as the father of Catholic ecumenism for his work in bringing about a mutual exchange where esteem and friendship prevailed. For him Catholic ecumenism was the reunion of all Christian churches in the unity of the Catholic hierarchy[48]. The belief that today's dreams become tomorrow's realities was held by both Portal and Pope Leo XIII[49].

b) *Theological Investigations*

Leo XIII did much by way of investigation into the separated communities. A special study was conducted to determine the validity of

---

[45] G. TAVARD, *Two Centuries of Ecumenism*, 69.

[46] LEO XIII, enc. lett. *Caritatis Studium*, *ASS* 31 (1998-99) 8, 11.

[47] G. TAVARD, *Two Centuries of Ecumenism*, 50.

[48] G. TAVARD, *Two Centuries of Ecumenism*, 51.

[49] LEO XIII, apost. lett. *Amantissimae Voluntatis,* 592.

Anglican holy orders. Theological studies were also conducted to shed light on common ground that may have already existed. The encyclical, *Tametsi Futura,* which Leo XIII penned in 1900, illustrates the nature of the Church's ecumenical witness. Here the Holy Father is so concerned with the return to Christ of those who call themselves Christians but live without faith or the love of Jesus Christ that he concentrates on those areas that are held in common with Protestants and leaves unaccented that which separates[50].

In the encyclical, *Annum Sacrum,* (1899) the Pope wrote, «Those who have been validly baptized certainly belong to the Church, from the viewpoint of law even if erroneous opinion has led them astray or disagreement severs them from fellowship»[51]. In other words our separated brethren who are baptized using proper matter and form and with the same intention as the Church receive some incorporation into the Catholic Church. In baptism they receive the indelible mark of the sacrament and the living gifts of Christ, as long as they do not set up an obstacle. The sacramental reality is mediated, at least materially, by the Protestant churches which insist on Christian baptism. This mediation takes place by an element inherited from the Catholic Church, not by anything proper to the Protestant churches themselves[52].

As has been shown, there is common ground in the sacrament of baptism. The fact ought to be remembered that so-called Protestant baptism is truly the sacrament of the Catholic Church. Other examples where separated brethren are in some way united to the Church and indeed to God himself are by means of revelation, the Bible and faith.

The Church testifies to the revelation of God, but is not the revelation itself. God's revelation comes to His people through His Church. Even if someone is not fully incorporated into the Church, God's revelation comes to him through the Church.

That God has intervened in the history of the world is evident in the Bible. Through reading and hearing the gospel account of the life, death and resurrection of Jesus, persons «can discover sufficient credibility for the Word of God so that the act of faith becomes possible and reasonable. We must conclude that rational credibility which *ex parte subiecti* is the necessary condition for the gratuitous gift of faith can be

---

[50] Leo XIII, enc. lett. *Tametsi Futura, ASS* 33 (1900-1901) 273-385.

[51] Leo XIII, enc. lett. *Annum Sacrum, ASS* 31 (1898-99) 647. «[Ii] qui sacro baptismate rite abluti [sunt] utique ad Ecclesiam, si spectetur ius, pertinent, quamvis vel error opinionum devios agat, vel dissensio a caritate seiungat».

[52] G. Baum, *That They May Be One,* 40.

obtained outside the Catholic Church, even if not completely independent of her testimony»[53].

Aquinas makes a distinction in his *Summa Theologica* between undeveloped and developed faith. Undeveloped faith believes some articles of the faith explicitly and others only implicitly, while a fully developed faith accepts the divine message in the explicit form of the full Catholic creeds[54]. Children normally grow into believing by means of undeveloped faith. The uneducated often fall into this category. The faith of past generations of Catholics might be considered as having an undeveloped faith when compared to what is known of certain articles of the creed today. Faith whether it is developed or undeveloped believes all that God has revealed. As the faith of some of the separated brethren may be undeveloped still it can be said that they share in some small way and that they participate in the one faith of the Church.

Even as Pope Leo XIII strove to begin a movement towards reunion he always held fast to the truth contained within the Catholic Church and the fact that the Church is the Body of Christ on Earth. In the opening paragraphs of his apostolic letter, *Praeclara Gratulationis Publicae,* (1894) the Pope expresses his concern for those who are in complete ignorance of the gospel as well as those who have left the right path and moved away from the true Church. He expresses his affection for those separated in the Eastern churches in particular as well as those separated by the Reformation[55]. This was an important papal document dedicated to ecumenism. It truly was a call to Catholic unity[56]. The Pope felt that true Catholic unity, that is among those Catholics in union with Rome, must serve as an example to «all those who adore Christ but are separated from the Roman Church, so that they must be but one flock and one shepherd»[57].

Along with his call for restored communion among all Christians the Pope frankly points out difficulties. Leo XIII believed that if those outside the Church as a result of the Protestant Reformation would look at their own communities and compare these to the Church of Rome they would see that their communions were drifting and splintering from the novelty of many errors. These communions could deny

---

[53] G. BAUM, *That They May Be One*, 42.

[54] T. AQUINAS, *Summa Theologiæ*, II-II, 2, 6, p. 79.

[55] LEO XIII, apost. lett. *Praeclara Gratulationis Publicae, ASS* 26 (1893-94) 705-717.

[56] G. TAVARD, *Two Centuries of Ecumenism*, 71.

[57]R. AUBERT, *Le Saint-Siège*, 45.

that a patrimony of truth existed. To this end there is hardly an article of faith that is certain and supported by authority.

It was noted that the divine nature of Jesus Christ had come into question as had the inspiration of the Holy Scriptures. The acceptance of individual conscience as the sole guide and rule of conduct can lead to doctrines such as Naturalism and Rationalism. Christians who are not united with Rome as a result of the Reformation find themselves in a situation where certain differences cannot be resolved and so they recommend and proclaim a union of brotherly love. It is proper that we should all be united by a bond of mutual charity; this was the wish of our Lord and Savior Jesus Christ. But, Leo questions, «But how can perfect charity unite souls if faith has not made minds one?» Leo XIII was very artfully creating the basis for a Catholic Ecumenism[58]. The Church was certainly concerned with unity, but any ecumenical activity was done by the Church in her own way. Her ecumenical involvement was to be on her own terms, a Catholic ecumenism.

Even among the Reformation communions some were closer to Rome than others. The Church of England had much in common with the Roman Catholic Church and great interest was taken in investigating possibilities of reunion. Leo XIII had spoken with Portal and Halifax. He addressed the Anglicans as a group in his letter, *Amantissimae Voluntatis* (1895). It was addressed, «To the English who seek the kingdom of Christ in the unity of faith». The Pope dreamed of reunion. Debates on the validity of Anglican holy orders were followed very closely by the Supreme Pontiff. He had asked to have a study conducted concerning the situation. When it was found that the orders of the Anglicans were not valid in the eyes of the Roman Catholic Church he wrote the apostolic letter *Apostolicae Curae* (1896). In the letter he made it clear that the orders of Anglican priests were null and void:

> Therefore, unreservedly agreeing in this matter which all the decrees of the Pontiffs Our predecessors, and confirming them completely and, as it were, renewing them by Our authority, of Our own incentive and certain knowledge, We pronounce and declare that Ordinations carried out according to the Anglican rite have been and are absolutely null and utterly void[59].

---

[58] LEO XIII, apost. lett. *Praeclara Gratulationis Publicae*, 710. «Verum qui potest copulare animos perfecta caritas, si concordes mentes non effecerit fides?».

[59] LEO XIII, apost. lett. *Apostolicae Curae*, ASS 29 (1897) 202. «Itaque omnibus Pontificum Decessorum in hac ipsa causa decretis usquequaque assentientes, eaque

He knew that some Anglicans would feel alienated by the Church's pronouncement. Nevertheless the Pope continued preparations for reunion.

What some would see as setbacks Leo XIII recognized as truths and did not let them stand in the way of his goal of preparing the Church for unity. He saw the restless seeds of Protestant theology bear bad fruit through the formation of sects, instability of doctrine and a tendency towards rationalism. Most difficult was the misinterpretation of the divine substance of faith by the separated brethren. What the reformers had introduced into Christianity was not a theology but the principle of private judgment. Leo XIII knew this principle to be in direct contradiction to the vision of Christianity which Catholics held[60]. Self interpretation of revelation is not compatible with a God who is creator of all. One creator God means one truth. Scriptures cannot be interpreted by different persons to have meanings which are at odds with one another. So even in the areas of love of Christ and scripture, where much is found to be in common between the Protestant communions and Catholic Church, there were divisions. Leo did not waver from the truths held by the Church.

c) *Prayer for Christian Unity*

Besides theological investigations into the validity of Anglican orders Leo addressed the issue of unity on a spiritual plane. On May 5, 1895 he issued an apostolic letter entitled *Provida Matris*. The reunion of Christendom was the far-reaching goal of the letter as it provided and encouraged prayer, in particular a novena, in preparation for Pentecost. The Pope felt that the time between the Ascension and Pentecost was most appropriate for prayer for unity. Pentecost marks the celebration of the birth of the visible Body of Christ, the Church, and Good Friday celebrates the mystery of His Body given for us on the wood of the cross[61]. He again mentions the prayers for Christian unity in his encyclical on the Holy Spirit, *Divinum Illud* (1897). The Pope decreed that the novena take place each year in all parish churches. The attached indulgences were also explained in the encyclical. The nove-

---

plenissime confirmantes ac veluti renovantes auctoritate Nostra, motu proprio certa scientia, pronunciamus et declaramus, ordinationes ritu anglicano actas, irritas prorsus fuisse et esse, omninoque nullas».

[60] G. BAUM, *That They May Be One*, 53.

[61] LEO XIII, apost. lett. *Provida Matris*, ASS 27 (1894-95) 645-647.

nas, prayed in every Catholic parish, certainly would have heightened the awareness of many Catholics as well as non-Catholics to the Pontiff's concern for Christian unity[62].

d) *Call to the One True Church*

During his pontificate Leo XIII gave much thought, care and concern to those Christians who found themselves outside the Catholic Church. He desired that these sheep return to the fold. He pointed out in his encyclical on the Unity of the Church, *Satis Cognitum*, (1896) that his chief consideration in relations with these communities was unity.

> It is very well known to you that a great part of Our thoughts and cares is devoted to Our endeavor to bring the sheep that have strayed back to the *fold*, placed under the guardianship of Jesus Christ, the Chief Pastor of souls. Bent upon this We have thought it most conducive to this salutary end and purpose to describe the exemplar and, as it were, the lineaments of the Church. Among these the most worthy of Our chief consideration is the *Unity* that the Divine Author impressed on it as a sign of truth and of unconquerable strength forever[63].

The purpose of this section concerning the pontificate of Leo XIII has been to present an overall view of his desire for unity and his activity in the beginning stages of Catholic Ecumenism. The goal was not to outline every ecumenical detail which took place during this period. For the purposes of this study it is important to note that the pontificate of Pope Leo XIII marked a beginning of ecumenism in which the Catholic Church would take part. Still the Church held to her beliefs. She did not enter into the mainstream of ecumenism with separated brethren but continued to invite them to be one with, that is, within the Catholic Church. Even as she searched for unity with the Church of England, Anglican orders were declared to be null and void by the Roman Church. In the search for unity Pope Leo did not disregard the truths held by the Roman Catholic Church. A phrase used on a number

---

62 LEO XIII, enc. lett. *Divinum Illud, ASS* 29 (1896) 657-658.

63 LEO XIII, enc. lett. *Satis Cognitium, ASS* 28 (1895-96) 708. «Satis cognitum vobis est, cogitationum et curarum Nostrarum partem non exiguam illuc esse conversam, ut ad ovile in potestate positum summi pastoris animarum Iesu Christi revocare devios conemur. Intento hac in re animo, non parum conducere salutari consilio propositoque arbitrati sumus, Ecclesiae effigiem ac velut lineamenta describi: in quibus praecipua consideratione dignissima unitas est, quam in ea, velut insigne veritatis invictaeque virtutis, divinus auctor ad perpetuitatem impressit».

of occasions by Leo XIII, *ad maturandum Christianae unitatis bonum*, towards the growing goodness of Christian unity, expresses his overall concern for the movement. During his pontificate the Church indeed moved toward better communications with the non-Catholic Christians of the world.

3.1.3 Pius X and Benedict XV

The pontificates of Pius X and Benedict XV were not as ecumenically significant as had been that of their predecessor Leo XIII. Pius X began the work on the Code of Canon Law and almost saw it to completion. As has already been seen, the *CIC* 17 did not allow non-Catholics to belong to canonically recognized associations of the faithful and did not allow for *communicatio in sacris*. He does clarify some acceptable gathering in his letter to the German bishops. A good amount of his time was spent fighting Modernism which he called the synthesis of all heresies.

a) *Pius X and the Labor Unions of Germany*

In his encyclical *Singulari Quadam* (1912), written to the German bishops, Pius X gives complete approbation to Catholic workers' societies or unions. However it was not permitted for Catholics to take part in unions which touch on the sphere of religion or morality. After praising the strictly Catholic unions the Pope stated:

> However, in saying this we do not deny that Catholics have a right, in their efforts to improve the worker's situation, more equitable distribution of wages, or for any other just advantage, to collaborate with non-Catholics for the common good provided they exercise due caution. For such a purpose, however, We prefer to see Catholic and non-Catholic associations unite their forces through that appropriate institution known as the *cartel*[64].

Pius continues and assigns to bishops the duty to watch especially those trade unions with Catholic members. The Catholic members themselves should also watch that no teaching or action would be car-

---

[64] PIUS X, enc. lett. *Singulari Quadam*, *AAS* 4 (1912) 659-660. «Verumtamen, hoc cum dicimus, non negamus fas esse catholicis — ut meliorem opifici fortunam, aequiorem mercedis et laboris conditionem quaerant, aut alia quavis honestae utilitatis causa — communiter cum acatholicis, cautione adhibita, laborare pro communi bono. Sed eius rei gratia, malumus catholicas societates et acatholicas as iungi inter se foedere per illud opportunum inventum, quod Cartel dicitur».

ried out which is in opposition to the teaching of the Roman Catholic Church[65]. Even though there was not a lot of ecumenical action during the pontificate of Pius X he did much for associations and their membership. In his concern for the Catholics in the workplace the Pope approved any mix of Catholics and non-Catholics in an association known as a labor union or society. His idea concerning Catholic and non-Catholic unions gathering in a cartel would be imitated by the Holy See when Catholic associations known as fellowships would be part of a larger ecumenical community. Charging the bishops with watching the unions with Catholic members was a foreshadowing of the bishop's position in ecumenism and concerning canonical associations.

b) *Benedict XV Encourages Protestant Ecumenists*

Benedict XV was sympathetic to the Protestant ecumenists, but did not allow the Catholic Church or her members to participate in their groups or meetings[66]. To attend meetings of those seeking unity was not possible for Catholics when topics included what type of unity Christ wanted for His Church. Attending conferences of this nature would bring into question the Church's own doctrine on unity. As far as the Pope was concerned the only way to approach doctrinal agreements would be in the truth that was found in the Catholic Church.

Of the various conferences that were taking place at the time among Protestant and Orthodox ecumenists one that particularly stands out is the Edinburgh Conference of 1910. It had been decided beforehand that this conference would discuss action and similarities, and not doctrinal differences. A most important result of the conference was the eventual birth of the «Faith and Order» movement. As only common ground was discussed at Edinburgh it was decided that a committee ought to be formed to study differences. Later that same year the General Synod of the Protestant Church in the United States proposed a resolution which constituted the beginning of the Faith and Order movement[67]. The goal of the organization, was to begin the next step

---

[65] PIUS X, *Singulari Quandam*, AAS 4 (1912) 661.

[66] Cf. SUPREMA SACRA CONGREGATIO S. OFFICII, «*De participatione catholicorum*», AAS 11 (1919) 309. It was during Benedict XV's eight year reign that the Supreme Holy Congregation of the Holy Office on 4 July 1919 issued a decree forbidding Catholics to participate in gatherings of any kind for the promotion of Christian unity.

[67] L. VISCHER, *A Documentary History*, 8.

toward unity[68]. The hope was to create a world conference on Faith and Order through prayer and independent commissions which would meet and make final plans and arrangements for the conference[69]. The goal would be met through dialogue and discussion, that by a better understanding of differences the communions would grow in their desire for union[70].

At the same time another ecumenical movement was growing. With the idea that «doctrine divides and service unites» the movement called «Life and Work» developed. Its goals were practical. Work was undertaken in areas which required no previous dogmatic discussions. Efforts were made toward social service. An insistence on the use of gospel principles was made when considering contemporary social problems[71]. The political situation of the First World War and later the post-war economic situation were fuel for much discussion[72].

The two groups were not in competition. In fact quite a number of the members of «Faith and Order» also joined «Life and Work». Eventually, in 1948 at Amsterdam, the two became the WCC. An international council of churches had been the dream of the founder of «Life and Work», Lutheran Bishop Söderblom. Now it was a reality[73].

While the Catholic Church would not send delegates to attend conferences she did encourage the Protestants and Orthodox to meet and dialogue. In 1910 at the Missionary Conference of Edinburgh a letter was read from Bishop Bonomelli of the Diocese of Cremona in Italy. He encouraged the participants, making the point that Christianity should be spread as a world religion and that the unity present at the conference warranted further discussion[74].

A correspondence was begun between Cardinal Gasparri, the cardinal secretary of state under Benedict XV and Pius XI, and Gardiner an organizer of «Faith and Order». Gasparri, himself interested in Christian unity, expressed Benedict XV's support at the opening of the Malines Conversations[75].

---

[68] L. VISCHER, *A Documentary History*, 199.
[69] L. VISCHER, *A Documentary History*, 200-201.
[70] G. TAVARD, *Two Centuries of Ecumenism*, 78.
[71] G. BELL, ed., *The Stockholm Conference 1925*, 1.
[72] G. TAVARD, *Two Centuries of Ecumenism*, 83 and G. BELL, ed., *The Stockholm Conference 1925*, 3.
[73] J. HARDON, *Christianity*, 421.
[74] R. ROUSE – S. NEILL, *A History*, 361-362, 680-681.
[75] G. TAVARD, *Two Centuries of Ecumenism*, 93.

The Malines Conversations were five unofficial discussions between Anglicans and Roman Catholics at Malines, Belgium. These
took place over a period of five years. The first lasted from December
6 -8, 1921 and the fifth and last from October 11 - 12, 1926. What had
started as peaceful dialogue, noting common beliefs, became unpro-
ductive by the fifth session when differences were the topic of discussion. All present agreed that conditions were no longer conducive to
continue the talks. Both Portal and Lord Halifax, whose support of
unity was noted earlier in this work, were key participants at the Malines Conversations[76].

Pope Benedict XV also supported the gathering of «Practical Christianity» in the Scandinavian countries but sent no representative[77]. The
Pope did not support official meetings between Roman Catholics and
those of faiths resulting from the Protestant Reformation. The Holy
Father's position was made clear by the 4 July 1919, decree of the
Holy Office which barred Catholics from participating in conferences
discussing Christian unity[78]. There was support on the part of the Roman Pontiff for the meetings of the Protestants themselves, but attendance at gatherings by Catholics was not allowed.

c) *Possibilities Clarified*

Pope Benedict XV encouraged the Protestants and those who attended their meetings in their search for unity and truth. He would not
however send delegates to any of these meetings. His pontificate was
truly a realistic reminder of just what the Church could and could not
do ecumenically. To participate in these types of ecumenical conferences would be to question her own doctrine on unity. The only possibility of approaching doctrinal agreements would have to be in truth[79].

Pope Benedict XV did much to support the Eastern Rites within the
Church. He founded the Pontifical Institute of Oriental Studies as an
autonomous institution in 1917, since 1862 it had been a department of
the Propagation of the Faith. The Congregation for the Oriental
Churches was erected by Benedict XV in 1917. His desire for unity is

---

[76] R. AUBERT, «Stages of Catholic Ecumenism», 186., and W. FRERE, *Recollections of Malines*, 7.

[77] G. TAVARD, *Two Centuries of Ecumenism*, 93.

[78] SUPREMA SACRA CONGREGATIO S. OFFICII, *«De participatione catholicorum»*,
AAS 11 (1919) 309.

[79] G. TAVARD, *Two Centuries of Ecumenism*, 49.

manifest in his work with the Oriental Catholic Churches as well as his encouragement of the separated brethren.

3.1.4 Pius XI

Benedict XV's successor, Pius XI, had doctorates in philosophy, theology and law. He was an academician and approached the ecumenical situation in a scholarly manner. Oriental theological study was encouraged, and the Oriental Institute which his predecessor had begun was reorganized. Scholarship and his interest in Eastern Orthodoxy were the two characteristics that affected Pius XI's policy toward ecumenism.

a) *Eastern Churches*

+ Eastern Rite Catholics

Reunion with the Orthodox has always been seen as a possibility. It could come about much more swiftly as their sacraments are all recognized as valid and their bishops have apostolic succession. Pius XI, true to his academic background, viewed Oriental study as very important. He encouraged Catholic faculties to introduce courses in Eastern Studies into their curricula. In his encyclical *Rerum Orientalium* (1929), the Holy Father ordered the introduction of similar courses into the curriculum of all major seminaries[80]. The Pope desired the establishment of Benedictine monasteries of the Byzantine Rite. The monastery at Amay in Belgium was the first which was devoted to the cause of union.

Much was done by Pius XI for better relations between the Oriental and Latin Churches. The study of the culture, practices and beliefs of the Orientals was very important to him. To achieve the goal of unity the Pope encouraged people to pray for unity and to undertake works which would move the Church towards unification[81].

+ Orthodox

The work that the Pope had done in collaboration with Eastern Rite Catholics was seen as a hope for better understanding and relations with the Orthodox. He urged the cardinals to work for unity with the East. In an allocution delivered to the Italian University Catholic Fed-

---

[80] Pius XI, enc. lett. *Rerum Orientalium, AAS* 20 (1928) 284.
[81] R. Aubert, *Le Saint-Siège* 111.

eration on 10 January 1927 Pius XI said that most necessary to reunion is for people to know one another and to love one another[82]. He recognized this call as one that would be shared in the relations with those separated during the Reformation[83].

b) *The Reformation Communities*

The encyclical *Mortalium Animos* (1928) was written six years into Pius XI's seventeen year pontificate. His predecessor, Benedict XV, had forbidden Catholics to attend gatherings of those seeking unity. This was reemphasized by the Holy Office shortly before the World Conference on Faith and Order which took place at Lausanne Switzerland in 1927 and once again in *Mortalium Animos*[84]. Pius XI in his encyclical encouraged the Protestants to return to the Apostolic See. He was very clear in stating that he was not happy with the direction that the ecumenical movement was taking. He noted that a good number of those involved in these meetings deny a visible Church, that is a Church which appears as a body of the faithful, agrees on one and the same doctrine, and is under one teaching authority and government. They saw the church as a federation of communities of Christians. These may even be incompatible one with another[85]. Those who believed that they could hold such diverse beliefs and come together in loose unity of a church were called *pan-Christians* by the Pope[86]. He very clearly stated that when our Lord said, «I pray not only for them, but also for those who will believe in me through their word, so that they may all be one, as you, Father, are in me and I in you, that they may be one in us, that the world might believe that you sent me»[87]. This unity exists within the Roman Catholic Church.

The Pope invited all the separated children to draw close to the Holy See:

Unfortunately the children left the paternal home, but it did not for this reason perish, for it was supported by God's perpetual defense. Let them therefore return to the common Father, who will forget the insults previ-

---

[82] PIUS XI, Allocution to the Italian University, 20.

[83] G. TAVARD, *Two Centuries of Ecumenism*, 96.

[84] PIUS XI, enc. lett. *Mortalium Animos*, *AAS* 20 (1928) 11.

[85] PIUS XI, enc. lett. *Mortalium Animos*, *AAS* 20 (1928) 8.

[86] PIUS XI, enc. lett. *Mortalium Animos*, *AAS* 20 (1928) 7.

[87] John 17,20-21.

ously imposed on the Apostolic See, and will receive them most lov-ingly[88].

He both welcomed the separated brethren and clearly stated what was and was not possible for Catholics regarding dialogue with non-Catholic Christians concerning theological differences and unity.

3.1.5 Pius XII

As Leo XIII made leaps towards unity by the beginning of the de-velopment of the Catholic ecumenical movement, it has been said that a turning point of the Church's attitude towards the ecumenical move-ment was made during the pontificate of Pius XII. The instruction from the Holy Office, *Ecclesia Catholica*, (1949) marks the turn in the prac-tice of the Apostolic See. Two other documents written by Pius XII which are of significant importance to ecumenism are: *Mystici Corpo-ris Christi* (1943) and *Humani Generis* (1950).

As Pius XII addressed *Mystici Corporis* to the bishops of the Church he gives highest praise to the act of belonging to the Holy, Catholic, Apostolic and Roman Church, with the Vicar of Christ at its head and the heavenly bread as its food[89]. He notes well that there are separated brethren who in fact look to the Church as the only haven of salvation. The truths he will present in the encyclical he set before all[90]. The Pope states that the one Church is both visible and a body which is made up of individuals, with Christ's vicar on earth. He re-minded the bishops that doctrine concerning the Church as the Body of Christ was not accepted by all. The separated brethren in particular re-jected the Roman Catholic Church as the visible body of Christ on earth. Those who rejected Church teaching were in error.

As *Mystici Corporis* was very concise about members of the Body of Christ, the Instruction of the Holy Office, *Ecclesia Catholica*, out-lines the Catholic Ecumenical Movement. Here was set forth the «offi-cial charter» of Catholic Ecumenism. Three areas of importance were distinguished.

First, it was recalled that:

---

[88] PIUS XI, enc. lett. *Mortalium Animos, AAS* 20 (1928) 15. «Recesserunt heu filii a paterna domo, quae non idcirco concidit ac periit, perpetuo ut erat Dei fulta prae-sidio; ad communem igitur Patrem revertantur, qui, iniurias Apostolicae Sedi ante inustas oblitus, eos amantissime accepturus est».

[89] PIUS XII, enc. lett. *Mystici Corporis, AAS* 35 (1943) 237-238.

[90] PIUS XII, enc. lett. *Mystici Corporis, AAS* 35 (1943) 194.

In many parts of the world, as a result of various external events and changes of attitudes, but especially as a consequence of the common prayers of the faithful, through the grace of the Holy Spirit, in the minds of many separated from the Catholic Church there has constantly grown the desire for a return to unity on the part of all who believe in the Lord Christ[91].

Second, so that those seeking true unity would not follow a false path the Holy Office recommended:

Since the above-mentioned «reunion» is a matter which especially concerns the authority and office of the Church, it is necessary that the bishops «whom the Holy Spirit has installed to rule the Church of God (Acts 20:28)» give it special attention. They should, therefore, not only diligently and effectively watch over all this activity, but also prudently promote and direct it, both to help those who seek the truth and the true Church, and to defend the faithful from the dangers which easily result from the activity of this «movement»[92].

To achieve these goals the bishops were to: 1) Appoint priests to be involved in the movement who would report to them. 2) Watch, with special care, materials published by persons involved in the ecumenical movement. 3) Provide services to non-Catholics as well as Catholics seeking to learn more about the faith[93]. The bishops were to ensure that the purity of Catholic doctrine was protected so that its true meaning would not be obscured. The whole Catholic doctrine was to be presented and explained to those interested[94].

---

[91] SUPREMA SACRA CONGREGATIO S. OFFICII, instruction *Ecclesia Catholica, AAS* 42 (1950) 142. «Vero in pluribus Orbis partibus, quum ex variis externis eventibus et animorum mutationibus, tum maxime ex communibus fidelium orationibus, aflante quidem Spiritus Sancti gratia, in multorum animis ab Ecclesia Catholica dissidentium desiderium in dies excrevit ut ad unitatem omnium redeatur, qui in Christum Dominum credunt».

[92] SUPREMA SACRA CONGREGATIO S. OFFICII, instruction *Ecclesia Catholica, AAS* 42 (1950) 143. trans. T.L. BOUSCAREN, *Canon Law Digest,* III, 537. «Quum praefata "reunio" ad Ecclesiae munus et officium potissimum pertineat, speciali cura Episcopos, quos "Spiritus Sanctus posuit regere Ecclesiam Dei (Act., XX, 28)" eidem attendere oportet. Ipsi igitur non solum diligenter et efficaciter universae huic actioni invigilare debent, verum etiam prudenter eam promovere et dirigere, tum ut adiuventur qui veritatem veramque Ecclesiam exquirunt, tum ut arceantur a fidelibus pericula, quae actionem ipsius "Motionis" facile consequuntur».

[93] SUPREMA SACRA CONGREGATIO S. OFFICII, instruction *Ecclesia Catholica, AAS* 42 (1950) 143.

[94] SUPREMA SACRA CONGREGATIO S. OFFICII, instruction *Ecclesia Catholica, AAS* 42 (1950) 144.

And third, the possibility of assembling with non-Catholics was addressed:

> «As regards the case of *assemblies and associations of Catholics and non-Catholics,* which in recent times have been held in many places to promote "reunion" in the faith, there is need for a very special vigilance and control on the part of Ordinaries»[95].

The permission of the Ordinary was required for the events to take place. *Communicatio in sacris* was prohibited. Certain prayers, such as the Our Father, could be recited. And, at the close of the year a report was to be sent to the Holy Office concerning meetings held and benefits gathered from them[96].

The guidelines of the instruction opened new possibilities for dialogue between Catholics and non-Catholic Christians. At the same time they called bishops and priests to involvement. These decisions would affect the future of the Catholic ecumenical movement.

Humani Generis addressed false opinions that would undermine the foundations of Catholic doctrine. The areas in question were philosophical and theological in nature. Pius XII spoke out against the ideas without singling out any one group of offenders. Discussion toward the truth was encouraged by experts in the field especially concerning the doctrine of evolution[97]. This is another example of the Church allowing serious discussion, but always upholding the truth.

Under Pius XII the Catholic Church was officially represented at a number of ecumenical meetings. A number of the Protestants were ecumenically organized now that the WCC was a reality. The possibilities for dialogue certainly increased during the pontificate of Pius XII.

These meetings are on the periphery of ecumenical associations which are the topic of our study. Ecumenical associations were not yet a possibility. Still, the mixing of Catholic priest-theologians and non-Catholics that was allowed in certain assemblies and conferences can be seen as another step towards their realization. The faithful were for-

---

[95] SUPREMA SACRA CONGREGATIO S. OFFICII, instruction *Ecclesia Catholica, AAS* 42 (1950) 143, trans. T.L. BOUSCAREN, *Canon Law Digest,* III, 539. «Quod mixtos in specie catholicorum cum acatholicis conventus et collationes, quae multis in locis ad fovendam in fide "reunionem" recentioribus temporibus haberi coepta sunt, singulari prorsus Ordinariorum vigilantia et moderamine opus est».

[96] SUPREMA SACRA CONGREGATIO S. OFFICII, instruction *Ecclesia Catholica, AAS* 42 (1950) 142-147.

[97] PIUS XII, encyclical letter *Humani Generis, AAS* 42 (1950) 575.

bidden to attend unless they had obtained special permission from ecclesiastical authority[98]. Until dialogue was able to take place between Catholics and non-Catholics the mixing of non-Catholics with Catholics in associations of the faithful would not be possible.

3.2 *The American Situation*

The American situation regarding ecumenical development was unique. Because of its novel government, guarantee of religious freedom and Protestant beginnings the United States presented a situation that was ripe for Catholic Ecumenism. While Catholic beliefs could be followed without being corrupted, service and action within the ecumenical movement could exist.

3.2.1 Bishop John England

A young bishop at thirty-three years of age coming from Ireland in 1820 England rode horseback as he made the rounds of his Diocese of Charleston which encompassed the states of North and South Carolina and Georgia. His own Catholic flock was a minority in the territory covered by the diocese and England was not opposed to preaching to gatherings of Protestants who were glad to have anyone speak to them of God.

As a mode of organizing his diocese and at the same time fighting trusteeism[99] England set up an assembly of clergy and laymen which met once a year. Their main task was the temporal administration of the diocese. This organization was much like that of the Anglicans[100]. It was effective while England was guiding the diocese but the assembly was not held in place by his successor. This experiment which gave lay Catholics a say in the financial concerns of the diocese was the only one of its kind in the United States. It gave the people representation in the running of the diocese without the danger of trusteeism.

---

[98] SUPREMA SACRA CONGREGATIO S. OFFICII, instruction *Ecclesia Catholica*, *AAS* 42 (1950) 145.

[99] A system of parish adminstration operating in the United States mostly during the first half of that country's existence. Lay parishioners acting as trustees sought, on the basis of civil law, to control adminstrative decisions of the parish. Included in these decisions was the right to approve and dismiss pastors. Persons supporting trusteeism viewed their position as one in which they were living the democracy of the infant nation.

[100] G. TAVARD, *Two Centuries of Ecumenism*, 53.

Clancy, coadjutor to England, asked persons of all faiths to serve in the fight against the cholera epidemic that ravaged the Carolinas in 1836. He called Catholics, Episcopalians, Methodists, Presbyterians, Universalists, Baptists and all other denominations to learn, even at the eleventh hour, to look on each other as brothers of one common social family. He encouraged them to work together in serving those burdened by the epidemic and to strive to do mutual good, and avoid all moral and physical evil[101].

England was a tireless worker for the Church and the people he served. At times his ways and ideas were questioned, even by his fellow bishops. However he was always respected. He drew the hierarchy together at the Council of Baltimore. His openness to non-Catholics left a lasting impression. His care and concern for non-Catholics was a practical foreshadowing of the ideas of Leo XIII forty years before that Pontiff would reign.

3.2.2 American Hierarchy

An interesting statement appeared in the joint pastoral letter of the Bishops of the United States in 1884.

> The spirit of American freedom is not one of anarchy or license. It essentially involves love of order, respect for rightful authority, and obedience to just laws. There is nothing in the character of the most liberty-loving American, which could hinder his reverential submission to the divine authority of Our Lord, or to the like authority delegated by Him to His apostles and His Church. Nor are there in the world more devoted adherents of the Catholic Church, the See of Peter, and the Vicar of Christ, than the Catholics of the United States[102].

A rather bold statement indeed, but the Church in the United States had weathered years of immigrants entering a country where the political atmosphere was open to all religions and pluralism was in the air. Religious pluralism was a challenge to the Roman Catholic Church. Some would see it as a problem, others as an opportunity. With so many Protestant communities splintering into smaller groups with beliefs that were just a bit different from their neighbors, the Catholic Church would stand as a pillar of orthodoxy and constancy.

---

[101] P. GUILDAY, *The Life,* II, 340-341.

[102] J. GIBBONS, Pastoral Letter issued at the Third Plenary Council of Baltimore, #15. As found in H. NOLAN, ed., *Pastoral Letters,* I, 216.

It was the task of the bishops to hold the people, particularly the immigrants, together and give them direction. England had done this in Charleston. Archbishop John Ireland served in St. Paul from 1884 until 1918. Cardinal James Gibbons was at Baltimore from 1877 until 1921. These prelates were much involved in the American situation. They were considered by Archbishop Corrigan of New York among others to have liberal tendencies, this rift in the American hierarchy was noticed by Rome. Even as they strove to shepherd their flocks these Americanizing prelates would help a Catholic ecumenism to begin in the United States.

Ireland had written an introduction to the English edition of *The Life of Father Hecker*. The Ireland agreed with Hecker's thought recognizing the democratic and social needs of the time. Hecker, a convert to Catholicism from agnosticism, viewed the Roman Catholic Church as the crown of religious pluralism in the United States. In Hecker's mind the Catholic Church was the providential end towards which all the churches of the United States were moving. Hecker wanted to show Americans that the Catholic Church was based on the foundation of a freedom of belief. Here Hecker offered the underpinning for a theological justification for religious pluralism that would contain the ideas of an ecumenical program[103]. Ireland realized that some of the views that he and Hecker held in common might be criticized. He did not realize the uproar that would be caused, which would only be put to rest by an Apostolic Letter of the Holy Father. The book was translated into French and quite a stir was caused by Hecker's ideas which came to be included in the term Americanism[104]. After a dispute between those who questioned these ideas and those who supported them, Pope Leo XIII condemned Americanism in his apostolic letter, *Testem Benevolentiae* (1899) which was addressed directly to Gibbons. In the letter the Holy Father identified the basis of the problems as a softening of the faith for those who do not believe.

> That, in order to bring over more easily to Catholic wisdom those who dissent, the Church ought to adapt herself somewhat to the culture of an advanced age, and, relaxing her ancient rigor, show some indulgence to recent popular theories and methods. Many think that this is to be understood not only with regard to the rule of life, but also to the doctrines in which the deposit of faith is contained[105].

---

103 G. TAVARD, *Two Centuries of Ecumenism*, 54.

104 J. MOYNIHAN, *The Life*, 108.

105 LEO XIII, letter *Testum benevolentiae*, *ASS* 31 (1898-99) 471. «quo facilius qui dissident ad catholicam sapientiam traducantur, debere Ecclesiam ad adulti sae-

In closing the letter the Holy Father said:

So, from what We have said so far, it is clear, Beloved Son, that We cannot approve all those opinions which some intend by the name of Americanism[106].

Even with the clarification by the Pontiff, 1899 marked the end of one chapter in the American contribution to the beginnings of Catholic ecumenism[107].

3.2.3 Parliament of Religions

Testem Benevolentiae was not the first letter to be addressed to the American hierarchy which questioned the activities of members of the Catholic Church in the United States. On 15 September 1895 Pope Leo XIII sent a letter to the Apostolic delegate, Archbishop Satolli. The letter concerned the presence of Catholics at the Parliament of Religions that had taken place at the time of the World's Fair in Chicago in 1892.

The Parliament of Religions was to be a chance for all forms of religion to stand against all forms of non-religion. Gibbons was a member of the advisory committee. Twenty Catholics gave talks at the parliament. Each day a talk was given by a Catholic. Six bishops, nine priests and four laymen gave presentations. The themes ranged from «The Existence of God», to, «The Incarnation Idea in All History and in Jesus Christ». The involvement of the Catholics meant that they would not only participate with Protestants and schismatic groups but also with Buddhists, Shintoists and other Asian sects[108]. Bishop Keane of Richmond who was also rector of the Catholic University of America at Washington, DC wrote a summary of the Parliament in the *Catholic Family Annual* of 1894. It seemed as if he were preparing for criticism. In his conclusion he stated:

---

culi humanitatem aliquanto proprius accedere, ac, veteri relaxata severitate, recens invectis populorum placitis ac rationibus indulgere. Id autem non de vivendi solum disciplina, sed de doctrinis etiam, quibus fidei depositum continetur, intelligendum esse multi arbitrantur».

[106] Leo XIII, letter *Testem benevolentiae*, *ASS* 31 (1898-99) 479. «Ex his igitur, quae huc usque disseruimus, patet, dilecte Fili Noster, non posse Nobis opiniones illas probari, quarum summam Americanismi nomine nonnulli indicant».

[107] G. Tavard, *Two Centuries of Ecumenism*, 54.

[108] T. McAvoy, *The History,* 310-311.

They will consider the Church degraded, because she stood there in the midst not only of her own truant children but even of heathens. But the dear Lord, who has said that his Church must bring forth from her treasure «*new* things and old», and who has made her, as St. Paul says, «a debtor» to all outside wanderers and gropers, will be sure to view the matter differently. For him alone was the work undertaken and carried on; to His honor and glory may all its results redound[109].

Pope Leo XIII wrote to His delegate in the United States, Satolli, advising that Catholics organize their own conferences separately from the others. The Pope noted that admittance should be open to all including separated brethren[110]. The parliament had not been undertaken as an ecumenical endeavor, but to recognize the pluralism of religion that existed in the United States. The Catholics who supported and participated in the parliament wanted a Catholic voice, not silence. By means of the parliament Catholics were able to present themselves to the citizens of the United States and at the same time participate in a manifestation of American pluralism[111]. The participation of Catholics did help the American public to have a better knowledge of Catholics and their faith.

3.2.4 The Boston Letter

Another important piece of the American-Catholic experience that led to a better understanding of relationships between Catholics and Protestants and other non-Catholics was what has come to be known as the Boston Heresy Case. The question of salvation outside the Church is the central theme of the document. It was sent from the Holy Office on 8 August 1949 to Archbishop Cushing of Boston.

The letter refuted the statements made by Father Leonard Feeney, S.J. and his followers. The issue was the interpretation of the Church teaching *extra ecclesiam nulla salus*, that outside the Church there is no salvation. Feeney insisted on a rigorous interpretation of the teaching and taught that only Catholics could be saved and achieve heaven. The Holy Office put the question to rest even though Feeney and his followers continued in their error. What is of interest is the response of the Holy See which clarified Church teaching.

---

[109] The Illustrated Catholic Family Annual for 1894 (New York, 1893): 140. as found in: T. McAVOY, *The History*, 311.

[110] J. MOYNIHAN, *The Life*, 43.

[111] G. TAVARD, *Two Centuries of Ecumenism*, 54.

The Holy Office restated the teaching that there is no salvation out-side the Church. This teaching would not change. However the dogma was to be understood as it was by the Church herself and not by those making private judgments[112].

Jesus commanded that all should enter the Church. And also that the Church would be the means of salvation without which no one could enter the Kingdom of Heaven. To attain salvation it is not always nec-essary that one be actually incorporated into the Church as a member. If a person was united to the Church by a true yearning and desire, sal-vation may be theirs. This reference to a yearning and desire was taken from the encyclical *Mystici Corporis*. To avoid confusion the letter clarified that not any yearning and desire would assure salvation. Per-sons must respond to and accept supernatural grace, which comes to humans through Christ and His Church[113].

The Church teaches that those who may not be incorporated mem-bers may still in good faith be united to her. This may have come as a surprise to many Catholics. Even though the Boston Letter was not a new teaching of the Church as a response to the statements of Feeney it was an important document, especially in the United States. With the beginning of the second half of the twentieth century the sometimes popular idea that Protestants would miss out on the glory of Heaven could no longer be held. Yet another door had been opened for better understanding and cooperation between the Roman Catholic Church and the separated communities. As Feeney had been a popular speaker, both in public and on the radio, many American Catholics were af-fected by the happenings surrounding his excommunication. The re-sponse of the Roman Catholic hierarchy in the Boston Heresy Case brought clarity to the status of non-Catholic Christians and salvation. Even though Christendom is not a united body there is a definite rela-tionship in faith between Catholics and those other Christians who be-lieve, as Catholics do, in the Trinity, Baptism and salvation in Christ. All this led to a certain openness on part of Catholics toward their separated brethren at the dawn of the Second Vatican Council.

The religious situation in the United States was certainly unique. The number of denominations and religions represented within one country was great. The situation was truly ripe for Catholic ecumen-ism.

---

[112] H. DENZINGER – P. HÜNERMANN, ed., *Enchiridion Symbolorum*, 1382.
[113] H. DENZINGER – P. HÜNERMANN, ed., *Enchiridion Symbolorum*, 1384.

4. Ecumenism and the Second Vatican Council

The Second Vatican Council made a great impact on the ecumenical movement as far as Catholic involvement was concerned. The conciliar documents concerning ecumenism are pertinent to the present work. *Unitatis Redintegratio*, and *Orientalium Ecclesiarum* will be studied as another facet which relates to the openness leading to the eventual possibility of ecumenical associations. Changes which occurred by way of these documents were significant.

4.1 *Unitatis Redintegratio*

UR will be considered in two stages, the first its development relating to the wider ecumenical movement and the second six specific areas: theological underpinnings, initiatives and activities, the Holy Spirit and spiritual ecumenism, bishops, Eastern churches, and the separated churches and ecclesial communities in the West.

4.1.1 Development of *Unitatis Redintegratio*

On 25 January 1959, the Feast of the Conversion of St. Paul and the last day of the octave of prayer for Christian unity, Pope John XXIII announced an ecumenical council. It could have been taken as a sign that the council's sole aim would be Christian unity. The ecumenical movement outside the visible boundaries of the Catholic Church had reached a fever pitch with so many of the non-Catholic Christian churches and ecclesial communities involved. The creation of the WCC only ten years before was also a source of great hope. However these hopes were not met as the Church and her own condition in modern times and her call to make disciples of all the nations was to be the principal thrust of the Council. Still, his care for ecumenism was manifest as he established the Secretariat for Promoting Christian Unity in article 9 of his *motu proprio*, «*Superno Dei Nutu*» on 5 June 1960[114].

Pope Paul VI, in his opening address to the second session of the Second Vatican Council on 29 September 1963 declared, «What should the Council think or what should it do that concerns the huge masses of brothers separated from us and the possible varieties of union? The situation is quite clear. It is for this reason that the special convocation of this council has taken place»[115].

---

[114] JOHN XXIII, apost. lett./*motu proprio Superno Dei Nutu, AAS* 52 (1960) 436.
[115]*AS*, II/I, 193. «Quid sentiat, quidve agat Concilium, quod attinet ad haec ingen-

Paul VI made it clear that the ecumenical aspects of the Council were to continue. During the early days of the Council, under John XXIII, work on ecumenical statements to be included in the documents had already begun.

Work on *UR* included much editing and many changes. 1 December 1962 is a red letter date in the development of the Decree. Until that time there had been three *coeti* working on related topics: 1) Chapter XI, «On Ecumenism» of the schema for *Lumen Gentium,* and 2) *Unitatis Redintegratio* prepared by the Secretariat for Christian Unity and 3) *Ut omnes unum sint* prepared by the commission for the Eastern Churches. It was at the discussion of *Ut omnes unum sint* that a resolution was made to have only one text on the problem of ecumenism instead of the three which had been proposed[116]. The Council Fathers approved this by a vote of 2068 to 36 with 8 invalid votes[117]. This decision was another indication of the ecumenical concern at the Council.

As the decree went through various stages of development, the meaning of the term «ecumenical» became clearer. The word «ecumenical» had always been used by the Catholic Church to refer to her universal councils which had taken place. Only with the movement towards unity on the part of so many separated groups was the term used in this new manner to refer to all the baptized belonging to the one Body of Christ.

The title of the first chapter of the decree originally was «Principles of Catholic Ecumenism». This was later changed to be «Catholic Principles of Ecumenism». The unity of the Church would no longer be described within the limits of a Catholic ecumenism. It would be seen within the larger context of the fulfillment of the Christian inheritance. The introduction to the decree notes that a movement for the restoration of unity among all Christians was taking place among the separated brethren. The Holy Spirit is instrumental in fostering this movement. *UR* identifies God's grace at work within the ecumenical movement among separated brethren. The first chapter sets forth principles by which Catholics are encouraged to respond to the grace of the divine call toward unity. No more would there seem to be two ecumenical movements, one of non-Catholics and one of Catholics. The Catho-

---

tia agmina seiunctorum a Nobis Fratrum, et ad possibiles varietates in unitate? Res prorsus patet. Etiam hanc ob rationem singularis evadit huius convocatio concilii».

[116] *AS* I/IV, 9.
[117] *AS* I/IV, 141.

lic Church would participate in the movement according to her own principles.

4.1.2 *Unitatis Redintegratio* – the document itself

The document itself is a guideline for Catholics in order that they be able to respond to God's call that all may be one. *AT* would be published later to aid the Church in putting into practice the theology and guidelines of *UR*. In general the decree would be more theological while the directory more practical.

a) *Theological Underpinnings*

+ «Where two or three are gathered»

One of the principle concerns of the Council was the restoration of unity among all Christians[118]. The involvement of non-Catholic Christians in the movement who believed in the Trinity and confessed Jesus as Lord and Savior was acknowledged by the Roman Catholic Church. «[They do this] not merely [only] as individuals but as members of the corporate groups in which they have heard the Gospel, and which each regards as his Church and indeed God's»[119]. Ecumenical involvement was viewed as existing both among individuals and between groups. At an official level, the groups would be of higher concern, but still the individuals are mentioned and are important. As the situation of non-Catholics is discussed in *UR* the separated brethren are recognized either as individuals or as communities and churches[120]. Again individuals are mentioned. Even from these statements it is possible to acknowledge that the ecumenical movement is not only for churches and communities but also includes individuals. So a community that welcomes even one separated brother or sister into their congregation in the spirit of ecumenism is in fact working toward unity.

All are called to be involved according to their state in life. The whole Church is to have a concern for restoring unity. Each ought to use his own talent to contribute to the movement[121]. When one person is involved ecumenically with another person Jesus is present. Jesus told his disciples that where two or three gathered in His name he

---

[118] *UR*, in *AAS* 57 (1965) 90.
[119] *UR* 1. «nec modo singuli seiunctim, sed etiam in coetibus congregati, in quibus Evangelium audierunt quosque singuli Ecclesiam dicunt esse suam et Dei».
[120] *UR* 3.
[121] *UR* 5.

would be in their midst[122]. Even the involvement of two separated brothers as individuals would find Jesus present and His call for unity being answered.

+ Salvation and the Church

UR identifies the more important ways that God works in both building up and vivifying the Church itself, including: the written Word of God; the life of grace; the theological virtues; and the other interior gifts of the Holy Spirit, as well as visible elements. These the decree says can also be found outside the visible boundaries of the Catholic Church. *UR* also teaches that God's grace, which may be at work outside the Church[123], flows through the Church to those non-members who are believers. Indeed the Holy Spirit has used the separated communities as a means of salvation. Later in the same article it is noted that it is through Christ's Catholic Church alone that the fullness of the means of salvation can be obtained[124].

+ The Sin of Separation

As *UR* defined the relationship between the separated brethren and the Catholic Church it spoke of responsibility for the rifts and divisions of the past. The decree clearly states that those now born into separated churches (the Orthodox) or separated communities (Protestants) cannot be held responsible for the separation that has already occurred[125]. They are not responsible for the history of the ecclesial community into which they were born. As persons brought up in the faith of Christ the Catholic Church accepts them with respect and affection as brothers[126].

+ Baptism as Incorporation into the Crucifixion and Glorification of Christ

UR presents Baptism as the sacramental bond of unity among all who receive it and are born again through its reception[127]. This in-

---

[122] Matt 18,20.

[123] *LG* 8; Chapter III, section 4.3.2.

[124] *UR* 3; *LG* 15.

[125] This book calls the Orthodox «church» because they have valid apostolic succession and the full valid sacramental system; it calls the other separated brethren «ecclesiastical community» or «Protestant church» because they do not possess them. Cf. *AS* III/I, 205.

[126] *UR* 3, 4.

[127] *UR* 22, LG, in *AAS* 57 (1965) 1; the same thing is said in *LG* 15; and LEO XIII, apost. lett. *Praeclara Gratulationis Publicae, ASS* 26 (1893-94) 707.

cludes all who receive the sacrament in the way the Lord meant for it to be received and as well the way it was meant to be conferred. In this incorporation into the crucifixion and glorification of Christ Catholics are at one with all who have been baptized. However, Baptism is only the beginning: it is the gateway to the fullness of life in Christ. This fullness involves: an orientation toward a complete profession of the faith, total incorporation into the system of salvation as Christ willed it, hierarchical communion and movement to a complete integration into Eucharistic communion[128]. This movement toward the fullness of life in Christ is not shared by all, so that even as Baptism is a sign of unity when it is lived out as Christ willed it, a certain disunity is manifest among the baptized. Those who do not accept all the means of salvation given to the Church, and follow their own way, are not fully incorporated into her. So even with the bond of Baptism full incorporation is not always present[129].

b) *Initiatives and Activities, Encouraged and Organized*

Five points are presented in *UR* as ways of promoting Christian unity according to the various needs of the Church. These initiatives and activities include: 1) avoiding expressions, judgments and actions which do not represent the truth concerning the separated brethren and which only strain the relationship with them, 2) dialogue between experts of different churches each explaining his own faith in greater depth with the goal of better understanding, 3) carrying out duties for the common good of humanity, 4) common prayer when and where it is permitted, and 5) self-examination of faithfulness to the will of Christ for His Church. The Christian faithful are called to live these initiatives and activities in their lives.

c) *The Work of the Holy Spirit and Spiritual Ecumenism*

The fact that the Holy Spirit is mentioned in *UR* not less than twelve times, many of these being found in the first chapter which set the ecclesiological principles governing the ecumenical movement, reinforces the churches' belief that Christian unity is God's will. *UR* states: «Today in many parts of the world, under the influence of the Holy Spirit, many efforts are being made in prayer, word and action to attain

---

[128] *UR* 22.
[129] *LG* 14.

that fullness of unity which Jesus Christ desires»[130]. Toward the end of the article, «Nor should we forget that anything wrought by the grace of the Holy Spirit in the hearts of our separated brethren can contribute to our own edification»[131]. The Catholic Church certainly perceives the ecumenical movement to be the work of the Holy Spirit working from within and outside of the visible boundaries of the Church.

The Council encourages Catholics aware of the signs of the times to take an active and intelligent part in the work of ecumenism. Catholics are called to an increase in fidelity to their own vocation as members of Christ's Church. They are also called to interior conversion while striving to practice ecumenism[132].

By way of «spiritual ecumenism»[133], which is the soul of the whole ecumenical movement, Catholics were called to pray both in private and in public for the unity of Christians. In addition to prayer with other members of their own Church, Catholics are in certain circumstances to participate in prayer services for ecumenism with separated brethren. Besides public and private prayer for unity, «spiritual ecumenism» calls for a change in heart and holiness of life[134]. UR recognized the renewal which was taking place in the Church. Seeing renewal as an increase in fidelity to her own calling, the desire for unity was noted as a natural result[135]. Often it happens that when renewal occurs within the Church others are interested in unity. The work of the Holy Spirit within one church or ecclesial community or association certainly attracts others. When a certain vibrancy is present others will most certainly want to participate in such a movement.

All Christians are called to express their faith in the triune God and in our savior Jesus Christ. Cooperation of Christians in social justice matters is highly encouraged. Every possible way to lighten the burdens of our times caused by poverty, natural disasters and illiteracy should be engaged[136]. Working with separated brethren on various

---

130 UR 4. «Cum hodie in pluribus orbis partibus, afflante Spiritus Sancti gratia, oratione, verbo et opere multi conatus fiant accedendi ad illam plenitudinem unitatis, quam Iesus Christus vult».

131 UR 4. «Neque est praetereundum, quaecumque Spiritus Sancti gratia in fratribus seiunctis efficiuntur, eadem ad nostram quoque aedificationem conferre posse».

132 UR 7.

133 The expression, «spiritual ecumenism» is attributed to Fr. P. Couturier (1881-1953), cf. G. CURTIS, «P. Couturier», I, 347-53.

134 UR 8.

135 UR 6.

136 UR 12.

projects and toward certain goals will enable Catholics to become familiar with the outlook of their separated brethren[137]. This ought to be accompanied by study. The particular situation would determine the amount and type of study needed.

Worship in common, *communicatio in sacris*[138], was not to be seen as an indiscriminate method for the restoration of unity among Christians. While the action of praying in common with separated brethren could present a false unity, still the grace to be attained at times would commend it. Participation in *communicatio in sacris* can occur at different levels. Examples are: intercommunion and sharing in sacraments, praying the same liturgical prayer together as one body, and each community praying its own separate prayer as two or more communities are gathered together. The decree leaves the decision to the local bishop following due consideration of the circumstances of time, place and persons, unless the Episcopal conference or Apostolic See had already made decisions concerning particular situations[139]..

d) *The Role of Diocesan Bishops*

The local ordinary is mentioned three times in *UR*[140]. The context is always one of guidance and, except in the case of *communicatio in sacris*, promotion. Dialogue and other involvement on the part of Catholics in the ecumenical movement is to be encouraged by the bishop and subject to his supervision.

e) *Separated churches*

UR in its third chapter entitled, «Churches and Ecclesial Communities Separated from the Roman Apostolic See», concerns the special position of the separated churches of the East and the churches and ecclesial communities in the West. Both differences and commonalities are identified in this section. In both situations dialogue and interaction when possible are helpful.

The recognition of the validity of sacraments of Orthodoxy, especially Eucharist and Ordination by way of apostolic succession, put these churches into a special relationship with the Catholic Church.

---

[137] *UR* 9.
[138] *UR* 8.
[139] *UR* 8.
[140] *UR* 4, 8.

Communicatio in sacris, under certain conditions is encouraged[141]. The situation is different for the western ecclesial communities separated at the time of the Reformation. They differ substantially from the Catholic Church and also among themselves. Their confession of Christ and the Trinity[142], love for Sacred Scripture[143] and belief in Baptism[144] constitute the bonds by which an ecumenical relationship is possible. But, much theology and interpretation of scripture is not held in common. While the differences between the Catholic Church and Orthodoxy are hierarchical and jurisdictional, concerning church governance, the differences resulting from the Reformation are doctrinal as well.

Depending on their geographic location, Catholics find themselves in contact with more persons affected either by the Eastern or Western Schism. This situation reinforces the need for the local bishop to care for the ecumenical activities in his diocese. Each diocese has its own religious history, and will require different attention.

The conclusion to the Decree encourages the faithful to involve themselves in ecumenical activity as approved and encouraged by the Catholic Church. The faithful were encouraged to always be mindful of the fullness to which Christ calls His Church.

4.2 *Orientalium Ecclesiarum*

Included among the conciliar documents is a decree on the *sui iuris* Churches in union with Rome. Their situation is reviewed at this point because of their ritual and liturgical relationship with Orthodoxy. Each of the particular Churches or rites have their own tradition coming from the apostles through the fathers. The rites in union with the Holy See have Orthodox counterparts not in full union with Rome. The diversity of liturgical rites, ecclesiastical traditions and disciplines of Christian life among the Eastern Catholic Churches does not diminish the unity in the Holy Roman Catholic Church but in fact serves to emphasize it[145].

OE clarifies any question concerning division between the Oriental and Latin Rites. Latin and Oriental Catholics normally attend their own

---

[141] *UR* 15.
[142] *UR* 20.
[143] *UR* 21.
[144] *UR* 22.
[145] *OE,* in *AAS* 57 (1965) 76; *OE* 2; *LG* 13c.

Churches and receive the sacraments there, thereby preserving the heritage of the Eastern Churches[146], however nothing prevents them from receiving the sacraments in a different ritual Church. The various rites exercise the right to govern themselves[147] as the *CCEO* evidences. Each rite has its own liturgy, ecclesiastical discipline and spiritual tradition yet all are under the pastoral governance of the Roman Pontiff[148].

OE charges all to pray for unity especially between Orthodoxy and Catholicism. The various levels of union with Rome are a sign of hope for full communion. Those rites in full communion with Rome are certainly an example to those Eastern Christians who do not yet enjoy full union with the Holy See.

5. After the Second Vatican Council

5.1 *Ad Totam Ecclesiam*

To put *UR* into practice, an instrument was needed. This came in the form of a directory. On Pentecost Sunday 14 May 1967, two and one-half years after *UR* was presented to and approved by the thirty-first general assembly of the Second Vatican Council, the directory *AT* was promulgated. Pope Paul VI had approved *AT* in audience with the Secretariat for the Promotion of the Unity of Christians[149], which had prepared the directory. This, as well as its revision «The Directory for the Application of Principles and Norms on Ecumenism», will now be considered. They are the branches of the trunk of the tree which was *UR*. It is hoped that from these directories the fruit of Jesus' call, «*ut unum sint*» will be realized.

Associations are not specifically mentioned in *AT*. The purpose of the directory is to provide the tools for putting into practice what was promulgated by the conciliar documents, in particular *UR*. This indicates that *AT* was built on *UR*. Throughout the sixty-three articles which comprise *AT*, *UR* is cited not less than twenty-four times. It is interesting to see that associations are mentioned in the ED93. This is twenty-six years after *AT* and ten years after the *CIC* 83 which gave attention to associations both public and private. In *AT* the practical

---

146 *OE* 5.

147 *OE* 5.

148 *OE* 3.

149 SECRETARIATUS AD CHRISTIANORUM UNITATEM FOVENDAM, «*Directorium*», *AAS* 59 (1967) 592.

directives for living the call for unity continue to open the possibilities for ecumenical associations.

5.1.1 Moving Toward a Concern for Associations

As *AT* is reviewed the theological themes which will lend to the development of ecumenical associations will be identified. Three areas will be studied: *communicatio in spiritualibus*, ecclesiology/the role of the Apostolic See and bishops, and future associations. In the study attention will be paid to the development of ecumenical relations between the Roman Catholic Church and other churches and ecclesial communities. To the extent which the Church becomes gradually more open to dialogue and to *communicatio in spiritualibus*, as the principles she brings to the ecumenical movement allow, ecumenical possibilities for associations will be present.

a) *Communicatio in Spiritualibus*

While *UR* had spoken of spiritual ecumenism and *communicatio in sacris, AT* also speaks of *communicatio in spiritualibus*[150]. After restating that conversion of heart and holiness along with prayer for unity in public and private make up spiritual ecumenism which is the soul of the ecumenical movement, a list of fixed and suggested reasons for prayer for unity were offered and all were encouraged to remember to pray for unity whenever possible. At least half of the directory is dedicated to, «Sharing of Spiritual Activity and Resources with our Separated Brethren». It is in this section that the new term, *communicatio in spiritualibus* is found. *AT* states,

> Fraternal charity in the relations of daily life is not enough to foster the restoration of unity among all Christians. It is right and proper that there should also be allowed a certain *communicatio in spiritualibus*-i.e., that Christians should be able to share that spiritual heritage they have in common, in manner and to a degree permissible and appropriate to their present divided state[151].

---

[150] *AT* 25.

[151] *AT* 25. «Ad redintegrationem unitatis inter omnes Christianos fovendam non sufficit ut Christiani inter se fraternam caritatem exerceant in quotidiano vitae commercio. Decet quoque quandam communicationem in spiritualibus permitti seu Christianos communem partem habere illorum bonorum spiritualium quae ipsis communia sunt, idque eo modo et ratione quae in praesenti divisionis statu licita esse possunt».

Quoting *UR* 3, that elements and endowments which go to build up the Church can be found outside the Church, *AT* makes the point that in diverse Christian communities these spiritual endowments are found in different ways[152]. Remembering this diversity, further definitions and guiding principles are proposed:

> The term, sharing of spiritual activity and resources (*communicatio in spiritualibus*) is used to cover all prayer offered in common, common use of sacred places and objects, as well as all sharing in liturgical worship (*communicatio in sacris*) in the strict sense.

> There is *communicatio in sacris* when anyone takes part in the liturgical worship or in the sacraments of another church or ecclesial community.

> By «liturgical worship» is meant worship carried out according to the books, prescriptions or customs of a church or community, in his capacity as minister of that community[153].

Communicatio in spiritualibus is a new term used in *AT*. The document had stated that living the golden rule is not enough on the part of separated brethren in their desire for unity[154]. The Church's openness to new forms of common worship are based in *UR*. Approved prayer in common, in which all are encouraged to take part, involves prayer services specifically for unity and in ecumenical gatherings. Other intentions and themes of mutual concern may be the topic of prayer[155]. However movement toward Christian unity is to underpin other prayer for the common intentions of those attending such prayer sessions. These prayer services should be organized and the place carefully chosen. A church or oratory is appropriate[156].

The principles concerning *communicatio in sacris,* that the lack of unity forbids communication while the grace available encourages it, are reiterated. Even with the guidelines there is room for sharing in

---

[152] *AT* 26.

[153] *AT* 29, 30, 31. «Nomine communicationis in spiritualibus intelleguntur omnes precationes communiter faciendae, usus communis rerum vel locorum sacrorum, et omnis communicatio in sacris quae proprie vereque dicitur.(29) Communicatio in sacris habetur cum quis quemlibet cultum liturgicum vel etiam sacramenta alicuius Ecclesiae vel Communitatis ecclesialis participat.(30) Voce "cultus liturgici" intellegitur cultus ordinatus secundum libros, praescriptiones vel consuetudines alicuius Ecclesiae vel Communitatis, celebratus a ministro vel delegato eiusmodi Ecclesiae vel Communitatis, prout hic eiusmodi munere fungitur»(31).

[154] *AT* 25.

[155] *AT* 33.

[156] *AT* 35.

some liturgical worship depending on the situation and with the approval of the competent authority. The final subsections of the directory set forth what is possible in praxis rather than that which concerns the ecclesiological relationship between Roman Catholics, the Orthodox and other separated brethren.

5.1.2 The Role of the Apostolic See and Bishops

AT reminds its readers that it is the task of the Apostolic See and the bishops in their dioceses, after considering all circumstances, to adopt ecumenical policy[157]. The directory was formed specifically to be of service to the bishops as they exercise their role as shepherd of the flock entrusted to their care[158]. The hierarchy is reminded to be open to future inspirations of the Holy Spirit[159]. The bishop, for those subject to him, makes decisions that form the ecumenical endeavors in his diocese. This task can be the charge of the diocesan ecumenical council, commission or secretariat, whose establishment is mandated in *AT*, to apply the conciliar decisions on ecumenical affairs and promote ecumenism in the diocese. A group of bishops representing their own bishop's conference will comprise a territorial commission. A list of the functions of both these bodies is found in *AT*[160].

The diocesan ecumenical commission is to promote ecumenical activity within the diocese. By this means the bishop is able to implement the conciliar teachings on ecumenism. Contact will be made with the territorial commission so that bishops can be assisted in their task of seeking unity by both commissions.

In the subsection of the directory covering other separated brethren the bishops' authority in deciding cases concerning *communicatio in sacris* is clarified. Since sacraments are signs of unity and sources of grace they may under certain circumstances, as in danger of death, be shared with baptized Christians not in full communion with the Catholic Church. Recourse can be had to the bishop in cases which are not clearly presented in the directory[161].

---

[157] *AT* 2, *UR* 4, 8.
[158] *AT* 2.
[159] *AT* 2, *UR* 24.
[160] *AT* 3-8.
[161] *AT* 55.

5.1.3 Future Associations

AT does not mention associations specifically, however the document does call for and point out possibilities of involvement. The opening line of *AT* is taken from *UR* 5 reminding that all Catholics are called to strive for unity with others who believe in Christ in a way that is wholly and totally Catholic[162]. The two commissions outlined in the directory are not associations but are groups chosen by the bishop or conference of bishops to serve the cause of ecumenism in the diocese or territory respectively. Often groups are able to accomplish more than a single person. This is certainly an advantage to an association. They have by their statutes a clear goal and have some recognition by their bishop. Two situations which may lend to associations considered ecumenical will now be explored.

a) *Institutions and Enterprises*

«This commission should cooperate with such ecumenical institutions and enterprises as already exist or may be launched, making use of their help where occasion offers»[163]. *AT* here recognizes the presence of groups with an ecumenical thrust. Depending on the ends, governance and membership of these groups they may have the capacity to be erected or recognized by the competent ecclesiastical authority as canonical associations. Institutions and enterprises were also recognized at the level of the conferences of bishops. Much research would have to be done before a decision could be taken. The goal here is to point out the possibility that has been identified in the directory.

b) *Communicatio in Spiritualibus*

The section of the directory covering the «Sharing of Spiritual Activity and resources with Our Separated Brethren» does not specifically mention groups or movements. It does seem to have a place where associations will fit nicely. The directory states that, «Fraternal charity in the relations of daily life is not enough to foster the restoration of unity among all Christians»[164]. Something deeper is needed, but *Communi-*

---

[162] *AT* 1.

[163] *AT* 4. «Huiusmodi commissio mutuae excolat necessitudinis rationes cum institutis operibusque oecumenicis vel iam existentibus vel erigendis eorumque auxilio pro opportunitate utatur».

[164] *AT* 25. «Ad redintegrationem unitatis inter omnes Christianos fovendam non sufficit ut Christiani inter se fraternam caritatem exerceant in quotidiano vitae commercio».

catio in sacris is not to be the means to be used as a quick fix answer[165]. The directory speaks of what can take place between the two ideas of *Communicatio in sacris* and fraternal charity. The first is only permitted under special circumstances and the second is the gospel call required of all Christians; however, union requires interaction, charity must be put into action. Prayer for unity offered in common is the most discussed example. This prayer must be supervised and planned. A stable group or association will be a great benefit for the *Christifideles* who are involved ecumenically by means of this prayer which *AT* calls «Prayer in Common»[166]. Dialogue and consultations are also recommended by *AT*. The diocesan ecumenical commission will also have a part in these activities. That business of ecumenism, which is the recognition of full communion between separated brethren, is ultimately entrusted to those who govern the Church while not diminishing the importance of the interaction which takes place among those who believe in Christ.

As the human body has both a skeleton and flesh which cannot exist separately so the ecumenical movement needs an organizing structure and a spiritual and human dimension. The directory recognizes the helpfulness of institutions and enterprises in advancing the cause for unity. Called to cooperate with the diocesan ecumenical commission, these organizations would have both a structure or skeleton and a vibrant life or flesh. *AT* does not define institutions and enterprises, nor is it clear as to all the types of actions that Catholics involved in the life of the movement should undertake. When the directory lists examples for common prayer and cooperation it includes: peace, social justice, mutual charity among men, the dignity of the family, and concludes the list with the words, «and so on»[167]. There is room for interpretation here. Are marriage and the support of married couples, knowledge of the scriptures and scripture study, and the gifts of the Holy Spirit[168] charismatic prayer groups and gatherings part of the, «things similar to these» of *AT* 33 or not? It seems that they are and each is a prime candidate to gather as an association of the faithful and even have non-Catholics interested in becoming members. The associations of the *CIC* 83 certainly can bring some clarity to the undefined institutions and enterprises and also to the *hisque similia* of *AT* 33. Associations

---

[165] *UR* 8.
[166] *AT* 32-35.
[167] *AT* 33. «hisque similia».
[168] 1 Cor 12, 4-11.

have a relationship in place between the local ordinary and the association itself which can also interact with the diocesan ecumenical commission. Ends, governance and membership are all included in the statutes of the associations so that persons belonging and those interested will know the reason for the association's existence. In their statutes, associations contain the structure or skeleton of their group. In the members' lived out work is contained the flesh; here the goals of the association will be seen in action.

5.2 Codex Iuris Canonici 1983

The *CIC* 83 fits in the chronological scheme of the development of the ecumenical movement at this point. The principles and doctrines by which Catholics participate in the movement will be a strong support of ecumenical associations. As John XXIII called for both an ecumenical council and a new code of canon law it was obvious that the code would be affected by what happened at the council. Pertinent canons affecting the involvement of Catholics in the ecumenical movement will now be studied.

The preface to the *CIC* 83 lists ten principles which were to guide the writing of the *CIC* 83. Of particular importance is the principle of subsidiarity which is to be applied to the office of bishops. A certain «decentralization» was to take place. Particular laws and executive power not absolutely required for the unity of the universal Church were to be placed under the jurisdiction of the local bishop[169].

The *CIC* 83 is different than the *CIC* 17, because it is not a compilation of extant laws but is built on the Pio-benedictine Code and the theology of the conciliar documents. The work on the new code would not be able to begin until the Council was over. Especially the teaching on ecumenism and the Church found in the *CIC* 83 was developed during the years of the Council. As the *CIC* 83 explains the role of bishops in their position as members of the college with the Holy Father at the head and as shepherds in their dioceses the principle of subsidiarity is manifest. A number of the canons concerning ecumenism support the bishop's role.

5.2.1 C.755 – Fostering and Directing the Ecumenical Movement

§1 It pertains especially to the entire College of Bishops and to the Apostolic See to foster and direct among Catholics the ecumenical movement,

---

[169] JOHN PAUL II, *Prefatio* [Preface to CIC83], *AAS* 75 (1983) XXII.

the purpose of which is the restoration of unity between all Christians which, by the will of Christ, the Church is bound to promote.

§2 It is a matter likewise for Bishops and, in accordance with the law, for Bishops' Conferences, to promote this same unity and, in line with the various needs and opportunities of the circumstances, to issue practical norms which accord with the provisions of the Church[170].

Perhaps the strongest canon concerning ecumenism in the *CIC* 83, it charges the hierarchy with the task of fostering and directing the ecumenical movement. The first paragraph appoints the entire College of Bishops and the Apostolic See with the task of promoting Christian unity so that «all may be one». The Church is bound to promote this goal of Christian unity, *ut unum sint,* by the will of Christ. This mandate of the divine law is very strong. C.755,§2 puts the same charge within the competence of bishops and bishops' conferences noting the particular circumstances of regions. The local bishop is charged with promoting and directing the ecumenical movement in his own diocese according to the norms of law. Formerly decisions concerning ecumenical involvement were made at the level of the Holy See[171]. This is a major shift in the ecclesiological approach the Roman Catholic Church took toward ecumenism. The principle of subsidiarity is invoked as the bishop has the mandate to promote ecumenism in his own diocese. C.755,§2 will be discussed later as it is cited by the ED93.

5.2.2 C.383 The Bishop's Pastoral Role

§1 In exercising his pastoral office, the diocesan bishop is to be solicitous for all Christ's faithful entrusted to his care, whatever their age, condition, or nationality, whether they live in the territory or are visiting there. He is to show an apostolic spirit also to those who, because of their condition in life, are not sufficiently able to benefit from ordinary pastoral care, those who have lapsed from religious practice.

---

[170] C.755,§1 *CIC* 83. «Totius Collegii Episcoporum et Sedis Apostolicæ imprimis est fovere et dirigere motum œcumenicum apud catholicos, cuius finis est unitatis redintegratio inter universos christianos, ad quam promovendam Ecclesia ex voluntate Christi tenetur. §2. Episcoporum item est, et, ad normam iuris, Episcoporum conferentiarum, eandem unitatem promovere atque pro variis adiunctorum necessitatibus vel opportunitatibus, normas practicas impertire, attentis præscriptis a suprema Ecclesiæ auctoritate latis»

[171] SUPREMA SACRA CONGREGATIO S. OFFICII, instruction *Ecclesia Catholica,* *AAS* 42 (1950).

§2 If he has faithful of a different rite in his diocese, he is to provide for their spiritual needs either by means of priests or by an Episcopal vicar.

§3 He is to act with humility and charity to those who are not in full communion with the Catholic Church; he should also foster ecumenism as it is understood by the Church.

§4 He is to consider the non-baptized as commended to him in the Lord, so that the Charity of Christ, of which the Bishop must be a witness to all, may shine also on them[172].

The canon concerns the pastoral role of the bishop. He has care for all in his diocese. Besides his own flock he is to provide for the needs of faithful of different rites who reside within the boundaries under his jurisdiction. The bishop is to treat separated brethren not in full communion with the Catholic Church with charity and foster ecumenism as it is understood by the Church[173]. As he is called to be a witness before all, the bishop is also to consider the non-baptized as if they were committed to his care.

5.2.3 C.204 *CIC* 83 Christifideles

C.204,§1. Christ's faithful are those who, since they are incorporated into Christ through baptism, are constituted the people of God. For this reason they participate in their own way in the priestly, prophetic and kingly office of Christ. They are called, each according to his or her own particular condition, to exercise the mission which God entrusted to the Church to fulfill in the world.

---

[172] C.383,§1 *CIC* 83. «In exercendo munere pastoris, Episcopus dioecesanus sollicitum se præbeat erga omnes christifideles qui suae curae committuntur, cuiusvis sint aetatis, condicionis vel nationis, tum in territorio habitantes tum in eodem ad tempus versantes, animum intendens apostolicum ad eos etiam qui ob vitae suae condicionem ordinaria cura pastorali non satis frui valeant necnon ad eos qui a religionis praxi defecerint».

§2. «Fideles diversi ritus in sua dioecesi si habeat, eorum spiritualibus necessitatibus provideat sive per sacerdotes aut paroecias eiusdem ritus, sive per Vicarium episcopalem».

§3. «Erga fratres, qui in plena communione cum Ecclesia catholica non sint, cum humanitate et caritate se gerat, oecumenismum quoque fovens prout ab Eclesia intelligitur».

§4. «Commendatos sibi in Domino habeat non baptizatos, ut et ipsis caritas eluceat Christi, cuius testis coram omnibus Episcopus esse debet».

[173] C.383,§3 *CIC* 83. *CD* 16, in *AAS* 58 (1966) 681.

§2. This Church, established and ordered in this world as a society, subsists in the catholic Church, governed by the successor of Peter and the
Bishops in communion with him[174].

The *Christifideles* are defined in this canon as those who have been
incorporated into Christ through baptism. The canon also calls them to
fulfill the mission which God has given to the Church and in its second
paragraph recognizes the Church as subsisting in the Catholic Church
with the pope at its head and the bishops in union with the pope. The
Christian faithful are those who are faithful to the truth of the baptismal call. The second paragraph makes clear that the way to live out the
call is in the Roman Catholic Church. So the Christian faithful are Roman Catholics. But what of the baptized non-Catholic? Through Baptism they are incorporated into Christ but are not in full communion
with the Roman Catholic Church[175].

5.2.4 C.844 *CIC* 83 Communicatio in Sacris

C.844,§1. Catholic ministers may lawfully administer the sacraments only
to catholic members of Christ's faithful, who equally may lawfully receive
them only from catholic ministers, except as provided in §§ 2, 3 and 4 of
this canon and in can. 861 § 2.

§2. Whenever necessity requires or a genuine spiritual advantage com-
mends it, and provided the danger of error or indifferentism is avoided,
Christ's faithful for whom it is physically or morally impossible to approach a catholic minister, may lawfully receive the sacraments of penance, the Eucharist and anointing of the sick from non-Catholic ministers
in whose Churches these sacraments are valid.

§3. Catholic ministers may lawfully administer the sacraments of penance,
the Eucharist and anointing of the sick to members of the eastern Churches
not in full communion with the catholic Church, if they spontaneously ask
for them and are properly disposed. The same applies to members of other
Churches which the Apostolic See judges to be in the same position as the
aforesaid eastern Churches so far as the sacraments are concerned.

---

[174] C.204,§1 *CIC* 83. «Christifideles sunt qui, utpote per baptismum Christo incorporati, in populum Dei sunt constituti, atque hac ratione muneris Christi sacerdotalis, prophetici et regalis suo modo participes facti, secundum propriam cuiusque
condicionem, ad missionem exercendam vocantur, quam Deus Ecclesiae in mundo
adimplendam concredidit».

§2. «Haec Ecclesia, in hoc mundo ut societas constituta et ordinata, subsistit in
Ecclesia catholica, a successore Petri et Episcopis in eius communione gubernata».

[175] For further discussion of c.204,§1 *CIC* 83 cf. Chapter III, section 5.1.3.

§4. If there is danger of death or if, in the judgement of the diocesan Bishop or of the Bishop's Conference, there is some other grave and pressing need, catholic ministers may lawfully administer these same sacraments to other christians not in full communion with the catholic Church, who cannot approach a minister of their own community and who spontaneously ask for them, provided that they demonstrate the catholic faith in respect of these sacraments and are properly disposed.

§5. In respect of the cases dealt with in §§ 2, 3 and 4, the diocesan Bishop or Bishops' Conference is not to issue general norms except after consultation with the competent authority, at least at the local level, of the non-catholic Church or community concerned[176].

The first paragraph of the canon forbids Catholic ministers from administering the sacraments of Eucharist, Penance, or Anointing of the Sick to non-Catholics and Catholics from receiving the sacraments from ministers of separated Churches. In this paragraph itself the other paragraphs are sighted as they will note the exceptions to c.844,§1. §§2 and 3 allow for *communicatio in sacris* when indifferentism or error will not arise, and necessity requires or genuine spiritual advantage suggests. This sharing is to take place between members of the Roman Catholic and Orthodox churches. Only in the danger of death or grave

---

[176] C.844,§1 *CIC* 83. «Ministri catholici sacramenta licite administrant solis christifidelibus catholicis, qui pariter eadem a solis ministris catholicis licite recipiunt, salvis huius canonis §§ 2,3 et 4, atque can. 861, § 2 praescriptis».

§2. «Quoties necessitas id postulet aut vera spiritualis utilitas id suadeat, et dummodo periculum vitetur erroris vel indifferentismi, licet christifidelibus quibus physice aut moraliter impossibile sit accedere ad ministrum catholicum, sacramenta paenitentiae, Eucharistiae et unctionis infirmorum recipere a ministris non catholicis, in quorum Ecclesia valida exsistunt praedicta sacramenta».

§3. «Ministri catholici licite sacramenta paenitentiae, Eucharistiae et unctionis infirmorum administrant membris Ecclesiarum orientalium quae plenam cum Ecclesia catholica communionem non habent, si sponte id petant et rite sint disposita; quod etiam valet quoad membra aliarum Ecclesiarum, quae iudicio Sedis Apostolicae, ad sacramenta quod attinet, in pari condicione ac praedictae Ecclesiae orientales versantur».

§4. «Si adsit periculum mortis aut, iudicio Episcopi dioecesani aut Episcoporum conferentiae, alia urgeat gravis necessitas, ministri catholici licite eadem sacramenta administrant ceteris quoque christianis plenam communionem cum Ecclesia catholica non habentibus, qui ad suae communitatis ministrum accedere nequeant atque sponte id petant, dummodo quoad eadem sacramenta fidem catholicam manifestent et rite sint dispositi».

§5. «Pro casibus de quibus in §§ 2, 3 et 4, Episcopus dioecesanus aut Episcoorum conferentia generales normas ne ferant, nisi post consultationem cum auctoritate competenti saltem locali Ecclesiae vel communitatis non catholicae, cuius interest».

necessity are Catholic ministers to administer these sacraments to members of other Christian churches or ecclesial communions. A number of requirements must be met before any of the three mentioned sacraments may be received by these non-Catholics. The final paragraph forbids the diocesan bishop or conference of bishops from enacting any general norms until after the local competent authority from the non-Catholic Church is consulted.

5.2.5 Other Ecumenical Canons

At least five other canons make reference to non-Catholics or ecumenism. C.528 *CIC* 83 charges the pastor with the aid of the Christian faithful to bring the gospel message to those who have stopped practicing the faith and also persons who do not profess the true faith. C.933 *CIC* 83 allows the priest to celebrate the Mass in a space belonging to separated brethren which is usually used by them for worship. This may be done when just cause is present and the approbation of the local ordinary has been obtained. Seminarians are to be instructed diligently, according to c.256,§2 *CIC* 83, in the art of personal interaction. This is to include relations with non-Catholics and even non-believers. Ecumenism underpins this line of the paragraph. With the approval of the bishop's conference c.825,§2 *CIC* 83 permits Catholics to prepare with non-Catholics editions of the Sacred Scriptures which may include a commentary. When a diocesan synod takes place those to be present and invited are listed in c.463,§3 *CIC* 83. After listing those whose presence is required and mentioning those who can be called, ministers and members of non-Catholic churches and ecclesial communities, if it is deemed opportune, may be invited by the diocesan bishop to observe at the synod.

The great difference in the ecumenical approach of the two codes of canon law are simply manifest here. Some of the changes had begun before the Second Vatican Council, but most were a result of it. Some of the further developments in the new directory are the effects of the *CIC* 83. The new directory will now be reviewed.

5.3 *Directory for the Application of Principles and Norms on Ecumenism*

It had been twenty-six years since *AT* had been published. During this time both the *CIC* 83 and *CCEO* (1990) were promulgated. The disciplinary situation for the Roman Catholic Church was partly new as a result of the two codes[177]. Furthermore, an ecumenical dimension is included in «The Catechism of the Catholic Church». Since the Council, ecumenical relations between the Roman Catholic Church and separated churches and ecclesial communities had broadened. Meanwhile, involvement of the Roman Catholic laity in ecumenical matters had grown. The topic chosen for the plenary session of the Secretariat for the Promoting Christian Unity (1988) was a revised directory:[178] a new directory, to serve the new conditions[179].

5.3.1 Doctrine and Theology

The doctrine and theology of the ED93 are rooted in the conciliar documents. The new directory continually refers to *LG*, *UR*, *AT* and the Sacred Scriptures. It is in the Scriptures and the conciliar documents that one finds the basis of the ecumenical commitment of the Roman Catholic Church.

In at least three instances the ED93 reminds its readers of Jesus' call «that they all may be one». The Church is diligently working toward answering this prayer of Jesus, desiring and praying for its fulfillment. It is a part of her mission to preach the message of the Gospel of the Kingdom to the ends of the earth[180]. The Father's answer to the prayer for unity is a grace, which grace comes to us in the form of the ecumenical movement.

As Catholics respond to the universal call to holiness they ought to be able to recognize it outside the boundaries of their own Church[181]. A true desire for unity among all the baptized requires a «change of heart and holiness of life, along with public and private prayer for the unity of Christians»[182]. This «spiritual ecumenism» is based in *UR* 8 and continues to be the heart of the ecumenical movement.

Realizing that God's grace works outside the visible boundaries of the Catholic Church, she still holds that for Roman Catholics ecumenism is lived out within the visible boundaries of the Church: ED93 restates that the ultimate goal of unity or full communion between the Roman Catholic Church and any other body lies in the hands of the

---

[177] PONTIFICIUM CONSILIUM AD UNITATEM CHRISTIANORUM FOVENDAM, «*Directoire*», *AAS* 85 (1993) 1039.

[178] JOHN PAUL II, allocution/address *Ad eos qui*, *AAS* 80 (1988) 1202.

[179] Cf. G. SEMBENI, *Direttorio Ecumenico 1993*.

[180] ED93 15.

[181] ED93 25, *UR* 3.

[182] ED93 25, *UR* 8.

College of Bishops and the Apostolic See. It is up to them to decide the requirements of full communion[183]. A certain tension is present between what is common to the churches and ecclesial communities and what is not. As the Council states the Catholic truth that the one Church of Christ subsists in the Catholic Church «which is governed by the successor of Peter and by the Bishops in communion with him»[184] continues to be held firmly she is aware that other churches and ecclesiastical communities are not in full communion with her. The ED93 reiterates these truths of the Catholic faith from the former ecumenical documents as it renews Christ's call for unity.

Another doctrine continually clarified by the new directory is the communality shared through Baptism. Still the differences in the ways that the sacrament is lived out by those who have been incorporated into Christ manifest the divisions which are present. Similarities and differences among Christians are presented where the ED93 studies Baptism.

Diverse ecumenical situations found in different geographic areas call for various approaches to answer the call for unity among Christians. The type of ecumenical involvement will be the choice of the bishop of the local diocese. As each region can have a very different mix of Christians, more or less Catholics, Orthodox, or ecclesial communities resulting from the Reformation, decisions at a local level can tailor the ecumenical practice to the needs of a particular region[185]. The ED93 confirms the episcopal power of the local bishop in his own diocese. Associations which are approved or erected by their bishop can also be diverse in each diocese. An ecumenical accent in an association will depend on the local ecumenical situation. The circumstances of bishops and associations in the ED93 will now be studied.

5.3.2 The Bishops and their Dioceses

The position of the bishop regarding the ecumenical movement in his own diocese is mentioned not less than seventeen times in the ED93. The movement for unity in each particular Church is put directly into his hands. *UR* 4 entrusts the ecumenical movement, «to the bishops everywhere in the world for their diligent promotion and prudent guidance». C.755 *CIC* 83 also affirms this diligent promotion of

---

[183] ED93 29; c.755,§1 *CIC* 83; cc.902, 904,§1 *CCEO*; *AT* 2; *UR* 4, 8.
[184] *LG* 8b.
[185] ED93 30-34.

the ecumenical movement as the bishops' position, along with that of the College of Bishops and the Apostolic See[186].

Here the *CIC* 83 supports the ecumenical movement by instructing the Church hierarchy to promote unity. The canon points out that this unity is the will of Christ. The provisions and norms set forth by the Apostolic See are to be directed by the hierarchy.

The bishops bring a certain ecclesiology to Catholic involvement in the ecumenical movement as they shepherd their own particular Churches and at the same time follow the directives of the universal Church as outlined in the conciliar documents and the ecumenical directories of 1967 and 1993. The episcopal power plays a key role in the life of the ecumenical movement as it does for associations. In his call as priest, prophet and king the bishop will stand as a sign of unity among the churches and ecclesial communities[187]. This triple image is alluded to by *CIC* 83 which speaks about profession of faith (prophet), the sacraments (priest) and ecclesaiastical governance (king)[188]. The laity insofar as they participate in these episcopal functions are in full communion with the Catholic Church here on earth because they are joined with Christ in His visible body[189]. In his role as king he governs within his diocese. As priest he stands as a symbol of the unity brought about through the sacrament of Baptism. At the same time in his sacerdotal role he is a sign of the differences between the Christian churches and ecclesial communities as they do not share in the other sacraments especially the sacrifice at the altar, the duty of the priest. As prophet there are also signs of unity and division. The Scriptures which we share show unity. However, the teaching of the Magisterium of the Church often is not accepted by others, becoming a sign of the differences between Christians. Probably most clear role of the bishop in the ED93 is that of king. Here he governs and serves his own Church and her members.

The role of king or governing puts the bishop in a position of decision making. He will direct those new efforts in ecumenism which are according to the teachings of the Church and encourage those who run into difficulties to follow Catholic teachings on ecumenism and to be aware of the obstacles to reunion[190].

---

[186] Cf. c.755,§§1,2 *CIC* 83.
[187] Cf. c.375,§1 *CIC* 83.
[188] C.205 *CIC* 83.
[189] Cf. C.205 *CIC* 83.
[190] ED93 30.

5.3.3 Associations

Associations are highlighted, three times in the ED93. As their members live out the ends of the association, as listed in the statutes, an ecumenical dimension can be brought to the association which can do much for unity among all Christians. Also, organizations of the Catholic faithful and a number of other groupings of *Christifideles* are encouraged as having the potential to aid the ecumenical movement. While the ED93 is not specifically concerned with the membership of these groups of *Christifideles,* their relations with the ecumenical movement are discussed. Associations in the ED93 will be examined in their relation to their bishop[191] and the initiatives of the associations themselves[192].

a) *The Role of the Bishop*

Associations at the diocesan level exist under the care of the bishop, who in communion with the other bishops make up a college, with the pope, as successor of Peter, at the head. The bishop guarantees that the particular Church to which he ministers remains connected to and makes present the one Church of Christ founded on the apostles. He is to coordinate the spiritual energies and works of the associations and their members in their desire to see the upbuilding of the Church and its mission in action[193].

The unity of association members themselves and the union of associations with other groups and members of the Church is present as all Catholics gather around their bishop looking to him as chief shepherd[194]. The relationship between the associations and the diocesan ecumenical commission is important as it will bring unity, the purpose for the ecumenical movement, to the foreground[195]. As the bishop is to shepherd his own and is called to apply the Church's ecumenical teaching he will call associations forth to live out the call of Jesus, «that they all may be one».

b) *Encouraged Initiatives and Associations*

The ED93 specifically supports the faithful in their own ecumenical initiatives. «The situations being dealt with in ecumenism are often un-

---

[191] ED93 4; c.755 *CIC*83; cc.902, 904 *CCEO*.
[192] ED93 30.
[193] ED93 14.
[194] ED93 27.
[195] ED93 43.

precedented, and vary from place to place and time to time. The initiatives of the faithful in the ecumenical domain are to be encouraged»[196]. Within the directory a number of styles of organization for the service of Christian Unity are identified, including: the diocesan ecumenical officer, the diocesan ecumenical commission or secretariat, the ecumenical commission of synods of Eastern Catholic Churches and episcopal conferences, ecumenical structures within other ecclesial contexts, institutes of consecrated life and societies of apostolic life, organizations of the faithful and The Pontifical Council for Promoting Christian Unity. Because of the large number of various movements and groupings of *Christifideles* in the Church they are at times difficult to organize. The goals and position in the Church of the persons and groups listed certainly manifest a diversity within the underlying unity of the Roman Catholic faith. Those which may be fitted into the canonical status of associations of the faithful will be considered now. Associations, a canonical structure and key to organizing lay movements and groups, will be considered after the others.

+ Supranational Bodies

These groups, often international, have as their aim the cooperation and sharing of helpful knowledge among episcopal conferences. As they aid the conferences in assisting one another, structures ought to be set up that ensure an ecumenical dimension to the work of the supranational bodies[197]. The statutes and procedures of each supranational body will determine its potential and specific aim.

ICO are mentioned in the section covering cooperating toward unity in social and cultural life[198]. They are similar to the supranational bodies as both work globally and also have their own statutes to guide them. ICO often may have an ecumenical dimension as they seek to work in areas where there is no specific Catholic presence. They may bring this presence. One example would be the International Catholic Association for Radio and Television which cooperates with non-

---

[196] ED93 30. «Les situations dont l'œcuménisme s'occupe sont très souvent sans précédent, elles varient de lieu en lieu et d'époque en époque. Aussi les initiatives des fidèles dans le domaine de l'œcuménisme sont à encourager» (PONTIFICIUM CONSILIUM AD CHRISTIANORUM UNITATEM FOVENDAM, «*Directoire*», *AAS* 85 [1993] 1050-1051).

[197] ED93 48.
[198] ED93 218.

Catholic organizations who have an interest in radio and or television[199].

+ Organizations of the Catholic Faithful

ED93 points out the existence of organizations within the Church which are actively contributing to the Church's apostolate life. These are not a part of the official diocesan structure concerning ecumenism as the diocesan ecumenical officer and the diocesan ecumenical commission or secretariat. These organizations are encouraged to develop an ecumenical dimension to their activities. As the organizations have statutes they can include the ecumenical dimension[200].

The term «organizations» is generic as it is. The meaning becomes less specific as it is used rather loosely in the ED93: «Among these communities and organizations are found institutes of consecrated life and societies of apostolic life and various organizations of Catholic Faithful». ICL and SAL are very specific types of organizations described in the *CIC* 83. «Organizations of Catholic faithful» is not a canonical term and therefore does not have the clarity that the other two hold.

+ Other Generic Terms

Like the term organizations and even supranational bodies the ED93 uses other non-canonical terms which only tell the reader that a group of persons is gathering who my have governing statutes. Among these are, «various groups and communities»[201] and «groups of lay people»[202]. The terms make sense as they stand in their sentences while at the same time they remain general.

No reference was made in ED93 to associations of the Christian faithful as they appear in the *CIC* 83. Associations are mentioned, but it is not clear if these are those of the *CIC* 83 or not. Since the terms ICL and SAL are used instead of the more generic, «religious orders» the proper terminology for associations ought to be used. Proper terminology for associations includes terms such as: public associations of

---

[199] UNDA, the Catholic Association for Radio and Television, is open to Catholic individuals or organizations working in radio or television and accept the goals of UNDA.

[200] ED93 49, 52.

[201] ED93 27.

[202] ED93 174.

the faithful or private associations of the faithful. The proper canonical status for the vast majority of these groups are associations of the faithful as listed in the cc.298-329 *CIC* 83. The canons outline the structure of the associations of the faithful. These, however are not referred to when ED93 mentions associations. The use of such varied terms when associations of the faithful are in place in the *CIC* 83 leaves the ED93 less clear than it ought to be.

+ Associations

The last style of organization is the association itself. In most situations the term is used generically. Still these are all excellent examples of situations where canonical associations of the faithful could be recognized or erected.

As noted earlier the spiritual energies and gifts of the faithful and their associations were to be coordinated by the bishop[203]. The diocesan ecumenical commission is to have a relationship with the parishes and parish organizations by way of the ICL, SAL, movements and associations of lay people[204]. Besides these relationships associations were commended as places for ecumenical formation to take place. Here the term «associations» was listed along with other places of formation: the family, parish, school, different groups, associations and ecclesial movements[205]. Associations are encouraged, but still the term is not clarified. The associations may be generic, any group of persons as families or a school, or specifically canonical as ICL and SAL. They are included in both lists. Comparing the lists does not help to decipher whether the document is referring to canonical associations or associations in general.

Even if the terms are in question it is clear that the ED93 has broken new ground in calling Catholic groups to have an ecumenical dimension. The letters of the Holy Office of 1864 and 1865 had forbidden Catholics from having anything to do with the London group concerned with church unity, now the Church encourages her own groups to be involved. Catholic principles are to be followed, the Church encourages her own members to relate spiritually with separated brethren more than ever before.

---

[203] ED93 14.
[204] ED93 43.
[205] ED93 65, 69.

The associations of the faithful as found in the *CIC* 83 are truly the best structure for many of the movements and groups who are doing apostolic works in the Church. The different types of associations can accommodate the various groups, communities, organizations, initiatives, and supranational bodies listed in the ED93. All will benefit from this status. As an association of the Christian faithful the group defines clear ends and has a relation with the local bishop. If these groups are to have an ecumenical dimension what better way than to have it included in their statutes.

Formation of persons in ecumenism will truly bring about a desire, on the part of those formed, for unity. Associations are identified as one of a number of suitable settings for ecumenical formation to take place. These persons would be filled with a solid ecumenical spirit. Formation goes beyond book learning to a lived experience which transforms the person being formed. This can certainly take place in a person who is a member of or participates in an association. If the association lives out its call for unity, all the better.

The attention given to associations/organizations in the ED93 is in great contrast to what had been said about them in *AT* and *UR*. The *CIC* 83 brought them to a position of prominence. The ecumenical challenge is not going away. Initiatives are welcome. The competent authority will guide and direct the Christian faithful as needed.

Before the presentation of the associations in the next chapter a review the roots of the term «ecumenical association» and the possibility of non-Catholics inscribing in canonical associations of the Christian faithful as presented in the schemata to the *CIC* 83 will take place.

6. The Post Synodal Apostolic Letter: Christifideles Laici

6.1 *Christifideles Laici 31 and its Roots*

ChL 31 states:

The PCL has the task of preparing a list of those associations which have received the official approval of the Holy See, and at the same time, of drawing up, together with the Pontifical Council for the Union of Christians, the basic conditions on which this approval might be given to ecumenical associations in which there is a majority of Catholics, and determining those cases in which such an approval is not possible[206].

---

[206]JOHN PAUL II, apost. exh. *Christifideles Laici*, *AAS* 81 (1989) 449. «Ad Pontificium Consilium pro Laicis autem munus delatum est redigendi elenchum earum

Article 31 of *ChL* presents the conditions for non-Catholics to in-scribe in officially reviewed or approved associations. In his Post-Synodal Apostolic Exhortation the Supreme Pontiff names associations of this nature «ecumenical associations». The roots of this terminology and concept are found in the propositions on which the synod delegates voted and then presented to the Supreme Pontiff at the close of the Synod. The fact that the propositions were presented to John Paul II after having been approved by the vote of the synod delegates mani-fests the approval of this document by the delegates themselves. The particular paragraph of article 31 of *ChL* which is of interest to this study is footnoted in the apostolic exhortation. The citation is to confer proposition fifteen[207]. The paragraph of article 31, concerning ecu-menical associations, is practically the same as paragraphs b) and c) found in the *Origins* printing of the Propositions. Differences are found in the first half of paragraph b). Instead of using the more general yet canonically precise term «associations» as found in *ChL* 31 the propo-sition uses the terms international Catholic organizations and spiritual and apostolic movements. The Apostolic Exhortation has honed the verbiage to bring a more precise and canonical meaning to the state-ment by using the word «associations» which is found in the *CIC* 83 and in fact includes some international Catholic organizations and spiritual and apostolic movements. The second clause in the one sen-tence paragraph is again almost identical to the proposition. Concern-ing the possibility of ecumenical associations *ChL* uses the canonical term «approved» while the proposition had used the words, «positive judgment». It is apparent that the Apostolic Exhortation was carefully written to clearly state that ecumenical associations exist and ought to be canonically recognized under specified conditions.

The propositions presented to the Roman Pontiff by the synodal delegates cover the major areas of the discussions at the synod. Of fifty-four propositions presented, thirty-one were cited in *ChL*. It is not by mistake that proposition fifteen was included in the Apostolic Ex-hortation. The concept of ecumenical associations as presented in the

---

associationum, quae officialem habent Sanctae Sedis approbationem, et simul de-finiendi, cum Pontificio Consilio ad Unitatem Christianorum Fovendam, quibus con-ditionibus approbari possit *consociatio oecumenica* cuius maior pars membrorum catholica est, minor autem pars acatholica, et in quibus casibus iudicum positivum dari nequeat». Emphasis added.

[207] Synod 1987: The Synod Proposals, *Origins* 17, no. 29 (31 December 1987), 504.

propositions is not found in the *Lineamenta* nor the *Instrumentum La-boris*. Father Giovanni Caprile's, *Il Synodo dei Vescovi 1987*[208]. does not contain the term, «ecumenical associations». However, the concept of ecumenical associations or non-Catholic participation in Catholic associations is found in the index under the heading «associative forms» and the subheading «Mixed associations of Catholics and non-Catholics or non-Christians»[209]. Three references are under the sub-heading relating to mixed associations. Two are interventions and one the work of a smaller circle (the Latin language group). The Arch-bishop of Bombay, Pimenta, made the first intervention concerning non-Catholics and associations. After reminding his listeners that sixty percent of the Asian population is between the ages of fifteen and twenty-four he added that the students among these young people often find themselves in schools with a number of religious groups repre-sented. Catholics are often in the minority. Students would very much like to have non-Catholics as members in their associations and even to allow them to serve in positions of responsibility within the associa-tions. Pimenta noted that having non-Catholics in Catholic student as-sociations may in fact at times be difficult, but that the bishops do and will supervise the associations[210]. The associations involve not only ecumenism, but interreligious relations, since non-Christians including Buddhists, Moslems and Hindus are the majority of the persons to be considered for membership in these associations. While *ChL* refers to ecumenical associations, its concern is for non-Catholic Christians more than non-Christians. Pimenta in his intervention to the synod touches the topic of non-Catholic members. He encourages and asks those present to consider the possibility of non-Catholic membership in associations.

The second intervention was made by Bishop Perrot of the Diocese of San in Mali, Africa. Catholics in his diocese make up only one per-cent of the overall population which includes sixty to seventy percent Muslims. He spoke of lay apostolic movements in his diocese and

---

[208] G. CAPRILE, *Il Sinodo dei Vescovi 1987*; Father Caprile has compiled works covering the synods. In these volumes are found the interventions made at the par-ticular synod on which he is writing. If the term «ecumenical associations» was coined during the interventions at the synod, «The Vocation and the Mission of the Laity in the Church and in the World Twenty Years after the Second Vatican Coun-cil» it would be in Father Caprile's book.

[209] G. CAPRILE, *Il Sinodo dei Vescovi 1987*, 766.

[210] G. CAPRILE, *Il Sinodo dei Vescovi 1987*, 115-6.

stated that Catholics always direct these. However, Christians are often involved and give spiritual care and other types of assistance as participants in the movements. This interaction helps to bring about a situation of peaceful tolerance between different Christian denominations and religions. In closing this section of his intervention, he asked if anyone had a monopoly on the Holy Spirit[211]. This is the second intervention where the associative element and ecumenism or interreligious activity were brought together.

In the report on the language groups, discussion by the Latin group is of particular interest. At one point the discussion focuses on lay women and their vocation and mission in ecclesial communities in the Church and in the world. The group was positive about Catholic women working with women of other religions and cultures to defend their common dignity[212]. This point is removed from associations, but it is easy to see that the line of thinking: laity working together with members of other denominations and religions may lead to questions about and demands for ecumenical associations.

Proposition fifteen has some of its roots in these interventions and discussion. It would have been formulated by those who prepared the propositions for the Holy Father in preparation for his writing of the Apostolic Exhortation. More important than how these or other ideas became a part of the propositions which were presented to the Supreme Pontiff is the fact that they were in fact included in Pope John Paul II's Post-Synodal Apostolic Exhortation itself.

6.2 Task of Christifideles Laici 31

With the identification of ecumenical associations in *ChL* 31 came a charge to two councils of the Roman Curia. The charge involves the formation of three documents. The documents are: 1) A list of those associations which have received the official approval of the Apostolic See, (to be compiled by the PCL); 2) the basic conditions under which approval might be given to ecumenical associations, in which the majority are Catholics; and 3) the cases in which it is not possible to give approval to ecumenical associations. The final two lists are to be compiled by the PCL in conjunction with the PCPCU[213]. In fact, none of these charges has yet been completed.

---

[211] G. CAPRILE, *Il Sinodo dei Vescovi 1987*, 253.
[212] G. CAPRILE, *Il Sinodo dei Vescovi 1987*, 437.
[213] Cf. JOHN PAUL II, apost. const. *Pastor Bonus*, *AAS* 80 (1988), 865.

The PCL does maintain an address list. This list of the International Associations of the Faithful with whom the PCL is in relation[214] contains associations which have the official approval of the Apostolic See as well as a number which do not. Examples of groups which are on the list but do not have official approval of the PCL are l'Arche as well as the People of Hope, the Sword of the Spirit, Worldwide Marriage Encounter, Cooperators of Opus Dei, Madonna House and Chemin Neuf. Official approval refers to canons 298-329 of the *CIC* 83 which outline the requirements for private associations of the faithful to be reviewed, approved, or to be given juridic personality, or in the case of a public association of the faithful, erected a public association of the faithful which makes it a public juridic person. The address list is not of associations which have official approval of the Apostolic See through the PCL but those who have some relationship with the PCL. Therefore, the address list is not the list of *ChL* 31.

The charges to list the basic conditions when ecumenical associations are acceptable or not, have not been completed. However, ecumenical associations recognized by the PCL do exist. Example associations and their particular praxes will be studied later in this chapter.

6.3 *Canonical Ecumenical Associations of the Christian Faithful as found in* ChL *31*

The term «associations» is used to refer to movements or communities within the Church which are established according to cc. 298-329 *CIC* 83. However when used alongside terms like «movements» and «groups» the meaning can take on a wider context than that set forth in the canons. The right of persons to form associations is recognized by the Second Vatican Council and the *CIC* 83[215]. Important to the topic of this dissertation is whether the Holy Father in *ChL* is referring to structured associations of the *CIC* 83 or a more general understanding. If reference is to associations of cc. 298-329, then ecumenical associations also are to be recognized and structured according to the *CIC* 83. In an attempt to manifest the fact that ecumenical associations are to be organized and canonically acknowledged according to the *CIC* 83 the following areas will be investigated: 1) associative terminology of the

---

[214] PONTIFICIUM CONSILIUM PRO LAICIS, *Liste d'adresses (mailing list)*, August 1997.

[215] Cf. *AA*, in *AAS* 58 (1966) 854; C.215 *CIC* 83.

CIC 17, 2) ecumenical associations as an association type, and 3) shared fonts of *ChL* and the *CIC* 83.

6.3.1 Terminology Concerning Associations in the *CIC* 17

It might be said that John Paul II's charge to determine in which situations ecumenical associations are permissible does not refer to associations which can be recognized canonically[216] by the Catholic Church, but to any organizations which come together according to the right of association[217]. This would be a wider interpretation of the term association. By reviewing the terms used in one of the preceding articles of the Exhortation the use of the word «associations» can be better interpreted. In article 29, as the Supreme Pontiff encourages group forms of participation for the laity, he speaks of a *«nova quadam aggregationum temperies»* (a new era of group endeavors) for the lay faithful. He points out new group forms of lay participation in the life of the Church. These include *associationes, coetus, communitates et motus* (associations, groups, communities, movements). The Roman Pontiff compares these forms of participation to other groups which have been present in the history of the Church: *Confraternitates*[218], *tertii ordines*[219] *et sodalitia*[220] are specifically identified. Sodalities which were approved by ecclesiastical authority were often labeled pious unions[221]. Pious unions undertook some work of piety or charity[222]. Confraternities were erected by competent ecclesiastical authority for the promotion of public worship. Members of third orders live in the world but under the direction of a first order. All three particular types of associations of the Christian Faithful presented in title nineteen of book two of the *CIC* 17, *«De fidelium associationibus in specie»*[223] are ecclesiastical[224]. Ecclesiastical associations in the *CIC* 17 were erected or at least approved by the competent authority. Other associations were only commended[225] and did not have the rights or duties *coram*

---

216 Cf. cc.298-329 *CIC* 83.
217 C.215 *CIC* 83.
218 Cc.707-719 *CIC* 17.
219 Cc.702-706 *CIC* 17.
220 C.707,§§1,2 *CIC* 17.
221 Cc. 707-719 *CIC* 17.
222 C.707,§1 *CIC* 17.
223 Cf. cc.700-719 *CIC* 17.
224 C.686,§1 *CIC* 17.
225 C.684 *CIC* 17.

ecclesia. The Pontiff singles out only associations which are ecclesiastical and are either approved, as pious unions, or erected juridic persons, as confraternities, in the Church. As John Paul II draws a comparison between the terminology used in the *CIC* 17 and in *ChL* it would seem that the second newer set would like the first be sanctioned by the Church. This point is small but adds to the belief that the Holy Father meant that these associations of which he spoke were to be or have the possibility of being approved or erected by the Church as those which he mentioned from the *CIC* 17. These are the associations which he will identify in paragraph 31 as having at least a majority of Catholics and he names ecumenical associations.

The older terminology for associations (confraternities, sodalities and pious unions) is much more apt to have a connotation connected to religious life than the new terms as found in *ChL* 29. The newer terminology for associations is not canonical except the word «associations» itself. The use of these newer terms (groups, communities and movements) can bring confusion into the discussion of canonical versus non-canonical associations. In popular Latin and English dictionaries the older terms almost always have a religious sense connected to their definition. The newer terms do not[226]. The use of the term «associations» spans both codes, but has lost a bit of its connotation relating to canonical corporations of persons. The recognition of the natural right of persons to gather in associations has allowed a certain confusion to come to the meaning of the word[227]. Each time reference is made to an association in the Church, it does not follow that the association is canonically recognized, having received a letter of recognition or decree from the bishop. However, the Pope meant canonical associations in *ChL* 31. Two further arguments will prove this point.

6.3.2 Ecumenical Associations as One Type of Association

The Supreme Pontiff recognizes ecumenical associations when he instructs the appropriate pontifical councils to draw up guidelines for Church approval of such associations. This groundwork is ecclesiological, because the pope invites all baptized Christians to participate in associations. He then hones this invitation with a list of criteria. Ecumenical associations are one type of association which fit into the

---

[226] Cf. L. STELTEN, *Dictionary of Ecclesiastical Latin*; H. WOOLF – *al.*, ed., *Webster's New Collegiate Dictionary*.
[227] *AA* 19; c.215 *CIC* 83.

ecclesiology and criteria presented by the Roman Pontiff. In *ChL* 28 John Paul II writes about forms of participation in the life of the Church. Since *Christifideles* refers to all baptized[228] he affirms that the laity as well as priests and religious compromise the one people of God and Body of Christ[229]. Each *Christifidelis* must be fully aware of being a member of the Church[230]. All the Christian faithful are incorporated into the Church through Baptism[231]. Even though not fully incorporated into the Church, baptized non-Catholic Christians indeed have a bond with the Roman Catholic Church[232]. This short but direct ecclesiological explanation of participation in the life of the Church opens the path for the Holy Father's reference to ecumenical associations[233].

After reinforcing the freedom of the laity to associate in groups within the Church[234], the Holy Father suggests «criteria of ecclesiality» for lay groups. «*(Si) primae dantur partes vocationi cuiusvis Christifidelis ad sanctitatem*» (The primacy given to the call of every Christian to holiness)[235] is addressed to all Christians: the universal call to holiness. Group participation ought to help persons become more holy. A second criterion provides for professing the Catholic faith: «*Responsabilitas confitendi fidem catholicam*» (The responsibility of professing the Catholic faith)[236]. Besides professing the Catholic faith the criterion calls participants in associations to be in communion with the Pope as well as the local bishop. Other criteria include living out the Church's apostolic goals and a solicitude for health and needs of human society. The Catholicity of group participation is reinforced in *ChL* 31. Some new groups and movements are encouraged to receive official recognition and explicit approval from competent authority[237]. The variety of types of associations is recognized by the Supreme Pontiff; and no

---

[228] Cf. C.204,§1 *CIC* 83. The presentation of the term, «*Christifideles*» which includes all the baptized, even non-Catholics is taken from a theological point of view. However in a canonical context the term signifies only Catholics; see G. GHIRLANDA, *Il Diritto nella Chiesa*, 247. For further discussion see Chapter III, section 5.1.3.

[229] *ChL* 28.

[230] *ChL* 28.

[231] *LG* 11.

[232] LG 15.

[233] The discussion of the «*Christifideles*» continues in Chapter III, section 5.1.3, «Canon 204,§1 *CIC* 83» of this.

[234] *AA* 19; c.215 *CIC* 83.

[235] *ChL* 30.

[236] *ChL* 30.

[237] *ChL* 31.

groups are urged to be recognized in the same manner or in fact to be officially recognized at all.

It is this theology based on ecclesiology[238] in which all the baptized, being lay faithful and members of the Church, coupled with the suggested criterion of ecclesiality for lay groups that the Holy Father makes his charge to draw up conditions in which ecumenical associations might be approved and those in which they may not. The canons of the *CIC* 83 which relate the laws on associations are not cited in *ChL*. However the legal terminology used for associations and competent authority is present in the Apostolic Exhortation. When the document calls for official recognition and explicit approval (*ChL* 31) for some new associations it uses the terms, «*agnosco, agnoscere*»[239] (to acknowledge or to recognize) and «*probatio, probationis*»[240] (approval). This terminology, appearing in *ChL* 31 and the *CIC* 83 concerning associations, reinforces the desire that these ecumenical associations are to be viewed canonically.

Before completing article 31 with a call for unity in the wounded body of Christ, pastors are encouraged to form stronger bonds among the various types of associations. The previous paragraph of *ChL* 31 called for ecumenical associations. Is it possible to say that the Holy Father was not referring to associations as recognized in canons 298-329 of the *CIC* 83? The call to ecumenical unity is further reinforced by the last paragraphs of article 31 which call for Church communion, overcoming temptation toward division and the Church to be a sign for all the world and a strength that will lead persons to faith in Christ[241].

6.3.3 Shared Fonts

It is intriguing that the pertinent articles (28-31) of *ChL* relating to group participation in the life of the Church and in particular ecumenical associations do not cite canons 298-329 of the *CIC* 83 which is title five of book two, «Associations of the Christian Faithful». However the articles and canons share the same fonts: articles 19 and 24 of the decree *AA* are cited by both the canons and *ChL*. The right of the laity to associate in a variety of types of associations and to join those associations which are already existing is presented in *AA* 19. The relation-

---

[238] *ChL* 29.
[239] C.299,§3 *CIC* 83.
[240] C.322,§2 *CIC* 83.
[241] *ChL* 31.

ship between the association and the hierarchy is the topic of *AA* 24. The article acknowledges different types of relationships between the various associations and Church authorities. One reason for the variety is the freedom on the part of the laity to choose to run and join associations.

7. The Development of Ecumenical Possibilities in Associations of the Faithful

7.1 *Canon 307,§4 sch 82*

Canon 307,§4 sch 82 which dealt specifically with the membership of non-Catholics in associations of the faithful was deleted just before the *CIC* 83 was promulgated. The paragraph had stated:

> Non-Catholics cannot be enrolled in public associations of the faithful i.e., Catholics; but neither may they be enrolled in private associations unless in the judgment of the ordinary it can be done without detriment to the activity of the association itself and no scandal arises[242].

The development of the canon which never became law is interesting and aids in building the case for ecumenical associations. During the sessions of the study groups of the *PCCICR* and up until and including the sch 82, the *CIC* 83 had been open to the possibility of non-Catholic members in canonically recognized associations of the faithful. Initially, the paragraph was completely open to non-Catholic inscription in public and private associations, and became progressively restrictive until only a small window was left for non-Catholic membership.

A closer look at the development of c.307,§4 sch 82 will bring the thoughts and opinions of the individual consultors and also their collective presentation into focus. Even though these thoughts and opinions are not law, they represent the opinion of learned experts. The *mens legislatoris* is also very telling since this question was left open when the *CIC* 83 was promulgated.

The acceptance of non-Catholics into associations of the Christian faithful was a reality before the *CIC* 83. The Second Vatican Council

---

[242] C.307,§4 sch 82 «Non-catholici christifidelium consociationibus publicis adscribi non possunt; consociationibus vero privatis ne adscribantur, nisi, iudicio Ordinarii, id fieri possit sine detrimento actionis associationis propriae et nullum oriatur scandalum». PCCICR, *Codex Iuris Canonici: Schema Novissimum*, Città del Vaticano 1982, 53.

made these ecumenical associations a theological possibility by means of its support of ecumenism[243] as well as the right of association[244]. The development of what would have been c.307,§4 *CIC* 83 begins with the sessions of study which predated the *schemata* of the *CIC* 83. The result of the sessions was positive for ecumenical associations. With the completion of the first session of the Second Vatican Council, Pope John XXIII constituted the *PCCICR*. Forty cardinals made up the membership of the commission which had its first plenary session on 12 November 1963[245].

Just over two years after the first plenary session of the newly constituted *PCCICR,* ten study groups were created. By the end of the year the group of study *De Laicis* met in its own first session from 28 November - 3 December 1966. As the meeting opened it was announced that associations of the faithful would not be discussed at the session. However, one topic for discussion was whether there should be treatment in the *CIC* of catechumens and other non-Catholics[246]. This question was followed by a discussion of the rights and obligations of all the Christian faithful[247]. These became the two topics for discussion at the first session. The discussion on the two topics was not concluded at the first session. It was noted that the consultors thought that the rights and duties of all the Christian faithful should be clarified before those of individuals were discussed[248].

Of particular interest at this early stage of development in the *CIC* 83 is its openness to or lack of a definitive stance regarding baptized non-Catholics and their rights and duties in the Church. The position of baptized non-Catholics was broached generally and at the same time more specifically. In reality the terminology «baptized non-Catholics» and «Catholics» is not found in the report of the first session of the groups of study concerning the laity[249]. The terminology used by the consultors was instead, «Christian faithful», and «Catechumens and other non-baptized». Often when referring to the Christian faithful the adjective «all» is attached, so as to read «all the Christian faithful»[250].

---

[243] Cf. *UR* 8.
[244] Cf. *AA* 19.
[245] *Comm.* 1 (1969) 36.
[246] *Comm.* 17 (1985) 166.
[247] *Comm.* 17 (1985) 167.
[248] *Comm.* 17 (1985) 187.
[249] Cf. *Comm.* 17 (1985) 164-195.
[250] Cf. *Comm.* 17 (1985) 165.

The question of the juridical position of baptized non-Catholics is an obvious one. It was brought to the forefront of the discussion by two consultors who reminded the *coetus* that *AG* 14 called for the new *CIC* to make clear the juridical status of catechumens[251]. The Roman Catholic Church recognizes as persons in the Church of Christ all non-Catholics who are validly baptized; such people are part of all the Christian faithful, although they may be limited in the exercise of their rights and the fulfilment of their obligations[252]. Since they are baptized and the Catholic Church does recognize the validity of their baptism, they are in some way joined to the Church[253]. In general, the group of study seems to accept baptized non-Catholics as part of all the Christian faithful.

More specifically Rev. Onclin, assistant secretary to the commission who also exercised the duty of office moderator, identified the question of treatment of catechumens and other non-baptized in the code as difficult. He cited c.87 *CIC* 17:

> By baptism a person is constituted as a person in the Church of Christ with all the rights and duties of Christians, unless, in so far as rights are concerned, there is some obstacle that impedes the bond of ecclesial communion, or a censure inflicted by the Church[254].

and noted that the question is greatly disputed by the doctors[255]. One consultor argued positively quoting the Second Vatican Council.

> All men are called to this catholic unity which prefigures and promotes universal peace. And in different ways to it belong or are related: the Catholic faithful, others who believe in Christ, and finally all mankind, called by God's grace to salvation[256].

Then he postulated that if canon law is the complex of divine and human norms which regulate the social relations of ecclesial activity, it is necessary that it be consistent to this variety of situations by which

---

[251] *Comm.* 17 (1985) 167); cc. 206, 788, 1170, 1183 *CIC* 83.

[252] Cf. *LG* 15; *UR* 3; c.96 *CIC* 83.

[253] *LG* 15.

[254] C.87 *CIC* 17. «Baptismate homo constituitur in Ecclesia Christi persona cum omnibus christianorum iuribus et officiis, nisi, ad iura quod attinet, obstet obex, ecclesiasticae communionis vinculum impediens vel lata ab Ecclesia censura».

[255] *Comm.* 17 (1985) 166.

[256] *LG* 13. «Ad hanc igitur catholicam Populi Dei unitatem, quae pacem universalem praesignat et promovet, omnes vocantur homines, ad eamque variis modis pertinent vel ordinantur sive fideles catholici, sive alii credentes in Christo, sive denique omnes universaliter homines, gratia Dei ad salutatem vocati».

the intimate life of the Church thrives[257]. Another consultor contradicted the opinion that non-baptized cannot have true rights and duties. He added that it might happen that the progress of the Second Vatican Council could lead to a new scope of canon law. This would have to be discussed by the coordinating commission[258].

The first session seemed, more than anything else, to clarify the fact that there was an ecumenical question. The canonical role of baptized non-Catholics or the non-baptized was not clarified at the session. The view of the commission would be most clearly manifest in the canons as they were presented to be promulgated by the Supreme Pontiff.

Ecumenical discussion again took place at the second session which was held 16-20 October 1967. The discussions of the *coetus* concerning the laity would affect the final presentation of the *PCCICR* before the promulgation of the *CIC* 83 by Pope John Paul II. The topics chosen to guide the second session were: 1) the fundamental juridical law of the Christian faithful and 2) the legislation concerning associations of the faithful in general[259]. The work which was specifically ecumenical has the title, «*Statutum Iuridicum Generale Omnium Christifidelium*»[260]. A few paragraphs were presented as possible canons but these did not appear later. However, the ecumenical ideas contained in these paragraphs would be clearly visible as the possibility of non-Catholic participation in associations of the Christian faithful is manifest. The paragraphs encouraged Catholics to promote ecumenical activity in daily life or study, to abstain from anything which could injure the progress of unity, and moved by the leadership of pastors and the humanity and love of Christ, to nourish a fuller ecumenical action with non-Catholics in activities for the common good which are required by every right conscience[261]. After discussion in which fathers commented that the ideas were without a juridical character and that at least the second point would be more appropriate for an ecumenical directory, a canon was proposed which encouraged individuals to foster peace and unity among Christians according to the norms of competent authority[262].

---

[257] *Comm.* 17 (1985) 167.
[258] *Comm.* 17 (1985) 167.
[259] *Comm.* 17 (1985) 197.
[260] *Comm.* 17 (1985) 208.
[261] *Comm.* 17 (1985) 226.
[262] *Comm.* 17 (1985) 226.

The ecumenical issue continued to challenge the commission and it was presented in a concrete fashion at the third session which lasted from 26-30 March 1968. Canons which had been prepared for the session were presented and discussed[263]. C.7,§3 *ses* III stated:

Baptized non-catholics may belong only to those associations of the faithful whose particular end and method of action they can accept according to their own conscience and as long as in the judgement of the ordinary of the place no danger arises from it which would put the faith of the catholics in danger[264].

Discussion of this «ecumenical canon» ensued.

The changes made were the following:

1) Instead of «*iudicio loci ordinarii*» a reference was made to c.5,§2 *ses* III which gave the Apostolic See vigilance over universal and international associations, and conferences of bishops over regional associations and the local ordinary over associations located in his own diocese. This change was made and is reflected throughout the development of this paragraph during the groups of study[265]. Eventually this concept of vigilance was moved to its present location in c.312,§1 *CIC* 83.

2) Because freedom of conscience is always presupposed, the cardinal presider, pointing out that the contrary would be odious, supported the consultor who asked that the phrase, «Only (those associations) whose particular end and method of action they can accept according to their own conscience»[266]. be removed and it was.

3) A most unsettling change took place during the discussion:

It is the most excellent consultor who pointed out that it is not logical that enrolling in these associations be limited to batized non-catholics. Therefore it would be more fitting to say «non-catholic persons or simply non-catholics». This observation was acceptable to everyone[267].

---

[263] *Comm.* 18 (1986) 216.

[264] *Comm.* 18 (1986) 219. C.7,§3 *ses* III. «Personae baptizatae non-catholicae adscribi possunt illis christifidelium consociationibus tantum quarum finem proprium et agendi rationem secundum propriam conscientiam admittere possunt, et dummodo iudicio loci Ordinarii nullum exinde oriatur periculum ne catholicorum fides in discrimen vocetur».

[265] *Comm.* 18 (1986) 219.

[266] *Comm.* 18 (1986) 219-220. «tantum quarum finem proprium et agendi rationem secundum propriam conscientiam admittere possunt».

[267] *Comm.* 18 (1986) 219. «Est Exc.mus Consultor qui animadvertit congruum non esse ut possibilitas dandi proprium nomen his associationibus limitetur ad perso-

The omission of the word, «baptized» might move these associations from the category ecumenical to interreligious. The consultors did not discuss the ramifications of such a change or at least it is not reported in *Communicationes*. Without a distinction between baptized non-Catholics and the non-baptized there is less respect for ecclesiology. The baptized certainly have a link to the Catholic Church even though they are not fully incorporated. To determine the rights and duties of the non-Catholic baptized Christians concerning associations of the Christian faithful is made more difficult by the openness on the part of the commission.

4) The last change concerned c.7,§4 *ses* III. It is minor but is telling for the dissertation. The paragraph presented was:

> Proof of reception into an association takes place according to the norm of the statutes; nevertheless if the association has been erected into a canonical person, inscription in the list of the association is necessary for the validity of the reception (of the member's name) (cfr. 694)[268].

It was suppressed because, as one of the consultors noted, signing on the list of an association is not always required. The observation was accepted and the paragraph was dropped[269]. The question of who is a member of an association is unclear at this point. If signing or similar form of enrollment is not always required, how is membership achieved? This question was not answered by the satisfied consultors.

The amended text of c.7,§3 *ses* III read:

> Non-catholics may be enrolled in associations of the faithful as long as according to the judgement of the authority in c.5 §2, no danger arises that would place the faith of catholics in jeopardy[270].

The proposed canon allowed non-Catholics to become members of Catholic associations with the approval of the appropriate competent authority. By allowing non-Catholics to join associations of the faith-

---

nas non catholicas baptizatas. Aptius ergo diceretur: "personae non catholicae" vel simpliciter "non catholici". Animadversio omnibus placet».

[268] *Comm.* 18 (1986) 219. «Probatio receptionis in consociatione fit ad normam statutorum; attamen si consociatio in personam canonicam erecta fuerit, inscriptio in albo consociationis ad validitatem receptionis necessaria est» (cfr. Can. 694).

[269] *Comm.* 18 (1986) 219-220.

[270] *Comm.* 18 (1986) 220. «Non-catholici adscribi possunt christifidelium consociationibus, dummodo iudicio auctoritatis de qua in can. 5 § 2 nullum exinde oriatur periculum ne catholicorum fides in discrimen vocetur».

ful, Roman Catholics fulfill the call of the Second Vatican Council toward ecumenism.

Session four lasted from 25 February to 1 March 1969. An addition was made to the paragraph. One consultor felt that not enough was done to avoid danger to the faith of Catholic members. Other consultors agreed and after adjusting the use of the phrase «danger to the faith» and adding a reference to the phrase which followed it, c.7,§3 *ses* IV appeared:

> Non-catholics may be enrolled in associations of the faithful as long as, according to the judgement of the authority in c.5 §2, lest the ends of the association be compromised[271].

The change is based on the fear that if non-Catholics become the majority and want to change the statutes then the association itself will be in danger. It was observed that this danger could be avoided in the very formulation of the statutes of the association[272].

Only minor changes took place at sessions five (28-31 January 1970) and six (7-11 April 1970). At session five the word, «*dummodo*» was changed to «*nisi*»[273]. In the sixth session references to the Second Vatican Council, which had been present, were removed. The canon's number was changed from seven to eight. With these changes the paragraph was put into the sch 77 as c.46,§3.

The discussion of c.46,§3 sch 77 took place on 20 November 1979. A dicastery of the Roman Curia had made an observation concerning the paragraph. The Monsignor Secretary presented the concern. The dicastery saw little reason for non-Catholics to become members of Catholic associations with all the effects of membership. It was suggested that they might become invited members or guests without power of suffrage. As invited members or guests these non-Catholics would not participate *pleno iure* nor could they be considered «full members». The Monsignor Secretary, «proposes to suppress the paragragh and to accept that the norm may be defined in the individual statutes of the associations»[274]. Suppression does not take place at this

---

[271] *Comm.* 18 (1986), 290. «Non-catholici adscribi possunt christifidelium consociationibus, dummodo iudicio auctoritatis de qua in can. 5 § 2 ne fines consociationis in discrimen vocentur».

[272] *Comm.* 18 (1986) 290.

[273] *Comm.* 17 (1986) 340.

[274] *Comm.* 12 (1980) 101. Propone di sopprimere il § e di lasciare che la norma sia definita nei singoli statuti delle associazioni.

time; however, it is the ultimate fate of the paragraph. This proposal of the Msgr. Secretary is important especially as he presents the practical opinion that norms be enunciated by the statutes of the individual associations themselves.

The dicastery of the Roman Curia did not oppose the paragraph on the grounds that it was *contra legem* or even *praeter legem*. It was only recorded that the monsignor secretary emphasised an observation to the canon made by

> a Dicastery of the Curia. He declared that it seems hardly reasonable for non-catholics to become members in all the effects of catholic associations: at most they can become invited members or guests (as an episcopal conference desires) without deliberative power[275].

Non-Catholic membership was never termed, «impossible» or «wrong», nor were non-Catholics categorized as *non-capax* or *inhabiles*. It is surprising that no comment was made concerning differences between baptized non-Catholics and non-baptized physical persons. After the discussion at the first session and the third session where terminology was changed from «baptized non-Catholic» to «non-Catholic» little else was said. As he presented these comments to the committee charged with reviewing the schema the Monsignor Secretary proposed suppression[276] which leaves the decision in the hands of the associations themselves.

The responses to the comments of the bishops' conferences were varied. One consultor highlighted the proposal of an episcopal conference which stated, «It remains permissible for associations to enroll non-catholics who are willing and able to collaborate in carrying out the ends of these associations»[277]. A second consultor voiced his disagreement with non-Catholic membership and his support of the secretary's position. He thought the non-Catholics would have the potential to damage or even disintegrate the associations. Three possibilities were proposed:

a) to suppress the paragraph

---

[275] *Comm.* 12 (1980) 101. un Dicastero della Curia, dichiara che sembra poco ragionevole che non-cattolici possano diventare membri a tutti gli effetti di associazioni cattoliche: al massimo possono essere membri invitati o ospiti (come vuole una Conferenza Episcopale) senza facoltà deliberativa.

[276] *Comm.* 12 (1980) 101.

[277] *Comm.* 12 (1980) 101. integrum est consociationibus adscribere non-catholicos qui ad fines ipsarum prosequendos collaborare possunt et volunt.

b) to say, «non-catholics cannot be enrolled unless it can be done without damage...»

c) to say that they can be admitted as invited or as guests, etc.

After divided discussion on the possibilities the Monsignor Secretary proposed:

> Non-catholics cannot be enrolled into public associations of the faithful. But they may not belong to private associations unless in the judgement of the competent authority it can be done without danger to the action proper to the association and no danger arises»[278].

Discussion obviously took place since the proposal was so different from the earlier perceived possibilities. The distinction between public and private associations and their membership was introduced here for the first time. The text was pleasing to all and appeared as above in the sch 80. The paragraph was numbered c.681,§4 sch 80 because it was inserted into the proposed *CIC* 83 after the sections on religious life found in book two, People of God.

Emendations to sch 80 were discussed at a plenary meeting of the *PCCICR* which was held from 20-28 October 1981[279]. Changes to the c.681,§4 sch 80 were minimal. Besides its change in location in the sch 82[280], there was a change in terminology, from «*iudicio auctoritatis competentis*» to «*ordinarii*». By using the more specific term «*ordinarii*» in the paragraph with respect to private associations it was thought that the integrity of the private association would be protected. The possibility of membership *pleno iure* by non-Catholics is recognized:

> 1. The norm which is given in the paragraph for private associations does not seem prudent unless it is further clarified, because: a) if non-catholics are members with full rights in the association the right of voting must be

---

[278] *Comm.* 12 (1980) 101. a) sopprimere il paragrafo; b) dire, «adscribi nequeunt non catholici, nisi fieri possit detrimento..». c) dire che possono essere ammessi come invitati, ospiti, ecc.

After a discussion about the possibilities the Msgr. Secretary proposed:

«Non-catholici christifidelium consociationibus publicis adscribi non possunt; consociationibus vero privatis ne adscribantur nisi iudicio auctoritatis competentis id fieri possit sine detrimento actionis associationis propriae et nullum oriatur periculum».

[279] *Comm.* 15 (1983) 55.

[280] The canons on associations of the faithful had been grouped with ICL and SAL in part III of Book II and were moved to the introductory part of Book II, part I, *De Christifideles* .

given to them. If in fact non-catholics constitute the majority of the association. In practice this could lead to the governing of the association by non-Catholics b) it would also be necessary to specify what is the competent authority in question, the bishop, the religious superior, the parish priest or directors of the association. (a priest)

Response. The observation is partially accepted. Namely, the text is amended as follows: «...unless in the judgement of the ordinary it can be done...» and thus it is left up to the prudence of the ordinary to apply the means necessary to ward off the dangers[281].

The specification of the competent authority in the case of each association would be necessary. This final draft of the sch 82 was approved by the plenary session. With this approval the *PCCICR* presented the sch 82 to the Holy Father for promulgation. It seemed that ecumenical associations, as well as interreligious, would now have a positive presence in the *CIC* 83.

It was between the presentation of the schema to the Pontiff (22 April 1982) and the promulgation of the *CIC* 83 on 25 January 1983 that c.307,§4 sch 82 was deleted. The conclusion can be that the Holy Father did not want c.307,§4 sch 82 to become law. Without a law positively permitting or restricting the inscription of non-Catholics in associations of the faithful various interpretations abound and the path is open for praxis to vary in different dioceses. This variety is to be expected in associations of the faithful as they strive to foster a more perfect life, promote public worship or Christian teaching[282].

The silence on the part of the *CIC* 83 and the charge of the Holy Father in *ChL* 31 both open the door for the development of ecumenical associations. Indeed a number of associations of this nature are in existence. These will be presented after a review of non-Catholics in associations of the Christian faithful in the *CCEO* 90. The suppression

---

[281] *Comm.* 15 (1983) 84. «1. Norma quae in § datur quoad consociationes privatas non videtur prudens nisi ulterius clarificetur, quia: a) si non-catholici sint membra pleno iure consociationis, ius suffragium ferendi eis tribueretur, quod in praxi, si nempe non-catholici maiorem consociationis partem constituant, ducere potest ad gubernationem ipsius consociationis a non-catholicis; b) oporteret quoque ut specificetur quaenam sit "auctoritas competens" in casu: Episcopus, Superior religiosus, parochus vel directores consociationis (Aliquis Pater)».

«R. Animadversio recipitur iuxta modum, nempe textus sic emendatur: "[...] nisi iudicio Ordinarii id fieri [...]", et ita prudentiae Ordinarii relinquitur media adhibere quae pericula arceant».

[282] *AA* 19; cc.298,§1-329 *CIC* 83.

of c.307,§4 sch 82 means the acceptance or rejection of non-Catholics is to be determined entirely by the statutes.

7.2 Development of Ecumenical Associations in the CCEO

The history of non-Catholic participation in associations of the faithful as found in the *CCEO* 90 is similar to its development in the *CIC* 83. First, there was open acceptance, then questions arose, and in the end, cc. 307; 316 *CIC* 83 were used as a basis for cc. 578; 580 *CCEO* 90 and, like the *CIC* 83, a lacuna was left in the *CCEO* 90. The question remains: may non-Catholics become members of associations of the Christian faithful or not? Paul VI announced the inauguration of the work of the *PCCICOR* to draft the *CCEO* in the allocution, *Duc hic praesentes*, on 18 March 1974[283].

The first specific work on associations of the Christian faithful by *PCCICOR* which was reported in *Nuntia* was open to having non-Catholic members inscribe in associations. The group of study concerning the laity numbered the c.7,§2.

> Non-Catholics can be validly admitted into associations if the statutes that have been properly approved explicitly allow it ltgaccording to the proper nature of each association[284].

This proposed canon would allow for the valid acceptance of non-Catholics while the apostolic letter, *CS*[285], had not.

> §1. Concerning associations of the faithful:

> 1° Non-Catholics cannot be validly admitted, nor those enrolled in condemned associations, nor those who are under public censure[286].

The next consultation on the question of non-Catholic inscription in associations of the faithful in the *CCEO* 90 was reported in the 1981 edition of *Nuntia*. The consultors pointed out that opening membership

---

283 PAUL VI, allocution *Duc hic praesentes, AAS* 66 (1974) 743-749.

284 *Nuntia* 5 (1977) 46. «Acatholici valide admitti possunt in Consociationes, si Statuta, legitime adprobata, id explicite determinent iuxta naturam uniuscuiusque Consociationis propriam».

285 Four times Pope Pius XII issued apostolic letters *motu proprio* of sections of what would later be used to form the *CCEO*. Out of necessity these sections were promulgated by the Supreme Pontiff. *CS* is the fourth. For more on this topic see V. J. POSPISHIL, *Eastern Catholic Church Law*, 66-68.

286 *CS*, in *AAS* 49 (1957) 595. «§1. In fidelium consociationes: 1° Valide admitti nequeunt acatholici et damnatae sectae adscripti aut censura notorie irretiti».

in associations of the Christian faithful to non-Catholics had been questioned by the special assembly for study which had taken place in November 1980, significantly following similar discussion by the plenary session of *PCCICR* in November of the previous year. The assembly felt that such a situation would bring disharmony[287]. At the same time it was decided that if non-Catholics were not positively welcomed by the canons because of possible disharmony, for ecumenical reasons the prohibition of c.541§1 *CS* was not to be held[288].

Nuntia reports one other discussion of non-Catholics in associations of the faithful[289]. Recalling the special assembly for study of November 1980, some consultors held that in the statutes of single associations with juridic personality of a *sui iuris* Catholic Church, as long as the integrity of the faith is safeguarded and the supervision of the competent authority is present, non-Catholic members may be accepted[290]. Other consultors did think that it was necessary for the *CCEO* 90 to make an explicit prohibition against non-Catholics. One consultor stated, « There should be a separate canon on membership, which should also state whether baptized Eastern non-Catholics can be members of such associations»[291]. Finally the consultors adopted c.307,§§1-3 *CIC* 83 for use in the *CCEO* 90[292]. In this way a direct prohibition is avoided and the statutes of the individual associations themselves define possibilities for non-Catholic membership.

Two important points can be drawn from the work of the *PCCICOR* which is reported in *Nuntia*. Both of these points support the recognition, approval and erection of ecumenical associations. The first point is that, of the discussions which took place non-Catholics were more often than not to be accepted into associations of the faithful. The question of disharmony within a juridic person[293] and of retaining the prohibition against non-Catholic membership of c.541,§1,1° *CS* [294] were the positions against the enrollment of non-Catholics. However, from the beginning of the discussion the possibility of non-Catholic membership was always an acceptable position. It was never claimed

[287] *Nuntia* 13 (1981) 91.
[288] *Nuntia* 13 (1981) 91.
[289] *Nuntia* 21 (1985) 33.
[290] *Nuntia* 21 (1985) 33.
[291] *Nuntia* 21 (1985) 32.
[292] *Nuntia* 21 (1985) 33.
[293] *Nuntia* 13 (1981) 91.
[294] *Nuntia* 21 (1985) 33.

that non-Catholics were not *capax* to be enrolled in associations of the Christian faithful. They had been *inhabiles* according to c.541,§1,1° *CS*. This prohibition could be changed by law, especially in light of the Second Vatican Council. The first point is simply that in the discussions the possibility of inscription of non-Catholics was always present and that any prohibition was not accepted.

The second point was more specific. It appears twice in *Nuntia*,

> if the admission of non-Catholics to public associations is not maintained the prohibition expressed in the actual canon, for ecumenical reasons, is *not* in force[295].

A prohibition against non-Catholics was not to be put into law for ecumenical reasons. Changes in the way the Roman Catholic Church approached the ecumenical movement reinforce the decision of the consultors. This abrogation of c.541,§1 *CS* leaves the opening for non-Catholics to become members. The law as it was promulgated, with the adoption of c.307 *CIC* 83, reinforces this openness.

8. Conclusion

The topic of the dissertation is ecumenical associations. The vast portion of the study of ecumenical documents undertaken in this chapter did not uncover any direct reference to ecumenical associations or even reference to associations that would be considered canonical according to cc.298-329 *CIC* 83. The research on *ChL* 31 is the only area where ecumenical associations were clearly discussed. These possibilities will be researched further from a purely canonical viewpoint in chapter three. Still it is surprising that ecumenical documents, especially when they speak of associations, do not clarify whether these associations are generic or specifically canonical. This was apparently not among the goals of the authors of the documents.

The purpose of this chapter was an historical review of ecumenism, using the documents of the Church as a guide. It identified situations which led to evidence for the approbation of ecumenical associations canonically recognized (by those with competent authority) in the Roman Catholic Church. As has been seen, Leo XIII initiated the Catholic ecumenical movement. This aided the Church in studying possibilities

---

[295] *Nuntia* 21 (1985) 33; *Nuntia* 13 (1981) 91. «si admissio acatholicorum in publicis consociationes non sustinetur, prohibitionem in iure vigenti expressam (*CS* can. 541 §1), oecumenismi ratione, *non* retineri». Emphasis added.

for unity, considering areas where her theology could be clarified and honing her own doctrines which would not change. This historical review has shown that there is room for ecumenical associations, or associations which allow a number of non-Catholic members, within the guidelines of the ecumenical movement.

Until the pontificate of Pius XII the official response of the Church to Catholic involvement in public discussions of the faith sponsored by separated brethren toward the purpose of reunion was negative. The Holy Office's 1949 «Instruction to Local Ordinaries about the "Ecumenical Movement"» directed that priest experts be sent to colloquia attended by Catholics and non-Catholics alike. The instruction was another step toward the changes of the Second Vatican Council. Still working from within her own Catholic ecumenism, the Church was engaging the wider ecumenical movement.

By changing the title of the first chapter of the conciliar document *UR* from «Principles of Catholic Ecumenism» to «Catholic Principles of Ecumenism» a significant shift was symbolized. The Church would no longer have a separate ecumenical movement, she would participate in the larger movement according to her own principles. This change in wording is representative of the development which occurred in the Church's ecumenical relations. She would be a part of the overall ecumenical movement, hoping and pressing for the unity that is the prayer of Christ. At the same time she would hold to the doctrinal truths she possesses as the one, holy, Catholic, and apostolic Church founded by Jesus Christ on the rock who is Peter.

Thus change would come, but the truth holds fast. For example, where previously both persons standing as witnesses for children at baptism were to be Catholics, now only one of them need be a Catholic. The bond between all of those baptized by use of the Trinitarian formula and pouring of water along with the same intentions of the Church is held today as it had been by Leo XIII in *Annum Sacrum* and in *LG* 15. There is no longer a legal restriction of non-Catholics in a Catholic choir. At the same time and on a different level the Church held to her fundamental teaching on *communicatio in sacris* except in special cases for example Orthodoxy and the danger of death for Protestants.

The points made concerning Catholic/non-Catholic relations in associations, even if not canonical, would include non-Catholic membership in Catholic canonical associations of the faithful. Pius X, in his letter to the German bishops gave more encouragement to strictly

Catholic unions, but he did accept the presence of mixed unions when the faith of the Catholics stood in no danger of harm and bishops were vigilant in their care for such groups. The union of these workers was not of a religious nature and so did not threaten the faith of the Catholic members.

The principle of subsidiarity, including the governing power of bishops and the decisions made by the Church, universal or local, which were a part of the Second Vatican Council and the *CIC* 83 had a profound effect on the possible membership and participation of non-Catholics in canonical Catholic associations of the faithful. Bishops were given the charge, following the directives of the Apostolic See, to guide and implement the ecumenical movement in their dioceses. This would include ecumenical associations. After considering the statutes of an association, as well as the specific needs and situation of the diocese, the bishop is to make the decision to approve or not to approve the statutes of a group which may include non-Catholic members. By this action he can provide approbation to an ecumenical association.

By reviewing a section of the ecumenical history of the United States of America the dissertation has shown that the Protestant and pluralistic beginnings of that country lead to a real desire for unity. The use of the principle of subsidiarity in the United States by her bishops, coupled with the decision-making power concerning issues ecumenical that they received through ecumenical documents and the *CIC* 83 put them in a position to support ecumenical associations. Each bishop in his own diocese must discern whether an ecumenical association would be appropriate. At times the presence of non-Catholics can harm the faith of Catholics. This also must be considered by the bishop as he does or does not give approbation to the statutes of a particular canonical association.

The directories of both 1967 and 1993 encourage ecumenical involvement for groups of Catholics. Without directly stating that membership should be open to those not fully initiated in the Catholic faith the directories encourage ecumenical participation. ED93 particularly points out a variety of groupings called to be formed ecumenically and to add to the cause. *AT* in its discussion of *communicatio in spiritualibus* calls for ecumenical activity as possible between those persons who share the same spirituality. A number of possibilities, among them marriage encounter groups and charismatic prayer groups, have been mentioned. The field for ecumenical work in canonical associations of the faithful is large. Much work for the Catholic Church and her ecumenical call can be done by these canonical disciplines. What c.693,§1 *CIC* 17 had forbidden, the writings of the Popes and Apostolic See were now supporting.

The final section of the chapter covered the more specific history of ecumenical associations. This specific history includes: ChL 31 and its development, the growth of c.307,§4 sch 82 and its ultimte removal, and ecumenical associations in the CCEO. Research on the particular history of ecumenical associations is a good starting point for the study of some of the actual associations which exist universally and in the United States of America.

CHAPTER II

The Rise and Development of «Ecumenical Associations»:
Identification of Associations Recognized by the Apostolic See
and the Dioceses of the United States of America

1. Associations Under Consideration

1.1 *Introduction*

This chapter will study the nineteen different associations under review in this disseration. In accordance with the title of the thesis, international groups will be studied followed by a number which are located in the United States of America. Another division will be made between those approved in the United States and those existing in the United States without official approval. Each of these three overall sections will be divided into either two or three other subsections. Each of the three will include a subsection covering ecumenical associations with non-Catholic members according to *ChL* 31 as well as a subsection covering interconfessional associations or communities[1]. Two other subsections are specialized. Under the section covering international associations a subsection will investigate ecumenical associations that participate in larger interconfessional communities. Members of these associations (or fellowships) are strictly Catholic. The second subsection is located under the section which includes ecumenical associations existing in the United States without official approval. Atypical ecumenical associations, not recognized by Church authority, are the topic of this subsection. The dissertation covers associations recognized by the Apostolic See to those of particular dioceses in the

---

[1] The designation «interconfessional» means that non-Catholics hold leadership positions and they may have a larger representation in the Association than Catholics.

United States of America, as well as those which are not recognized. With this method a wide variety of possibilities will be studied.

A summary to the presentation will categorize the various types of associations which have been studied. The praxis of relationships between the associations and Church authority will also be examined.

The majority of the associations involved in the study were contacted directly, usually by post. Most, willingly offered a copy of their statutes and decree or letter of recognition or approval for use in the dissertation; others chose not to do so. Some information gleaned also came by way of personal letters. These letters were in response to specific questions posed for use in the study.

1.2 *International Associations Approved by the Apostolic See or in Direct Connection with It*

1.2.1 Ecumenical Associations with Non-Catholic Members According to *ChL* 31

a) *Opera di Maria (Focolare)*

The *Opera di Maria* (Work of Mary) or *Focolare*[2], as the group is often called, is the oldest and largest association to be considered in this study. Begun by the laywoman Chiara Lubich in Trent during the Second World War, it first received official diocesan approval in 1947 from Carlo Di Ferrari, Archbishop of Trent[3]. The Sacred Congregation for the Council approved by decree the Work of Mary, as a pious union on 5 December 1964[4]. In 1990 Focolare received status as a universal private association of the faithful of pontifical right[5] with juridic personality[6]. A revised edition of the statutes was approved in 1994[7].

---

[2] The terms «Work of Mary» and «Focolare» as titles are synonomous and will be used interchangeably.

[3] J. GALLAGHER, *A Woman's Work*, 47.

[4] PONTIFICIUM CONSILIUM PRO LAICIS, 900/90/S-61/A-23, Rome.

[5] The term «pontifical right» is most often used to refer to institutes of consecrated life (c.589 *CIC* 83) and societies of apostolic life (c.732 *CIC* 83). In these instances the institutes and societies which are public juridic persons have been established or approved, by means of a formal decree, by the Apostolic See. When this terminology is used to describe Associations of the faithful it is not to be inferred that such Associations have public juridical personality, but only that they are established or approved by the Apostolic See.

[6] PONTIFICIUM CONSILIUM PRO LAICIS, 900/90/S-61/A-23, Rome.

[7] OPERA DI MARIA, *Statuti Generali*, 1995, 4.

Focolare with its focus on unity and the love of Jesus as found in the gospel has appealed to many persons. Simple explanations of the Blessed Virgin Mary as the Mother of God and the mother of us all has drawn many non-Catholics to desire to be a part of the Work of Mary. A popular contemporary biography of the Focolare and its founder, explains that the Work of Mary has had to seek to find a legal framework for non-Catholic participants (whom the book calls «members») within their statutes which are in accord with the canon law of the Catholic Church. It is reported that non-Catholics are able to be fully integrated into the life of the movement; being referred to as «associate members»[8]. All who are interested in the Work of Mary are able to participate in the movement in some way. The mode in which Focolare welcomes non-Catholics who wish to participate in its activities begins our study of actual groups which can be considered ecumenical. This study of Focolare and its desire for unity will manifest its ecumenical activities. The praxis for relations between Church hierarchy and associations wishing to be ecumenical with regard to activity and in particular membership will highlight the theme of the dissertation.

+ Ends

The first article, of the one hundred and forty-four articles which make up the statutes of the Work of Mary, describes the status of Focolare just as it had been described in its decree of approval. It then makes the general statement that the statutes contain the norms of life and governance for all persons who are a part of the Work of Mary. An explanatory footnote attached to article one of the statutes qualifies certain other articles which apply differently to persons who participate in Focolare through different modes of belonging.

> These statutes in their application to the persons who are a part of the Work of Mary take account of the various ways of participating in the Work (cf. artt. 15 ss).

> Only the persons who are a part of the Work as members or as adherents (cf. artt.16 e 17) are able to fully live the articles that regard the spirituality (cf. artt. 1-12 e 21-63).

> The brothers and sisters of other Churches and ecclesial communities live the spirituality as associates in the measure in which the differences in faith allow it (cf. artt. 18 e 130).

---

[8] J. GALLAGHER, *A Woman's Work*, 127.

The faithful of other religions participate in the Work as collaborators they sense a bond to be united on the basis of a religious sense and they live the spirit of the Work in some way (cf. artt. 19 e 135).

The persons of good will who do not have a religious faith respect the Work for its moral and spiritual goods and they desire to participate as collaborators to share the ends of the Work according to their conscience (cf. artt. 20 e 136), (stat. 95 art. 1, fn. 1)[9].

Different modes of belonging is the principal method which the Work of Mary uses to address the issue of non-Catholics in its midst.

Even though these points of application of the statutes to non-Catholics also concern membership in Focolare, and so will be reviewed later in that light, they are important to the nature and ends of the association, particularly the ecumenical involvement of the Work of Mary. Even as the footnote to article one states that only Catholic participants (*membri* - members and *aderenti* - adherents) in Focolare can fully live the statutes regarding spirituality it further states that brothers and sisters of other Christian churches and ecclesial communities (*aggregati* - associates) live the spirituality of Focolare in the measure in which the differences in faith permit them (stat. 95 art. 1, fn. 1).

The name Work of Mary itself carries with it the idea of unity which is part of the make up of the nature of the movement. All persons are sons and daughters of the mother of Christ (stat. 95 art. 2). Its bond with Mary and its resemblance to the Church meet in the reestablishment of unity among all Christians and the orientation of all of humanity. The statute states that unity is the point of Focolare. This

---

[9] «Questi statuti, nella loro applicazione alle persone che fanno parte dell'Opera di Maria, tengono conto dei loro vari modi di appartenenza all'Opera» (cf. artt. 15 ss).

«Possono vivere integralmente gli articoli che riguardano la spiritualità (cf. artt. 1-12 e 21-63), solo le persone che fanno parte dell'Opera come membri o come aderenti» (cf. artt. 16 e 17).

«I fratelli e le sorelle di altre Chiese e comunità ecclesiali vivono la spiritualità quali aggregati, nella misura in cui le differenze nella fede lo permettono» (cf. artt. 18 e 130).

«I fedeli di altre religioni, in qualità di collaboratori aderiscono all'Opera, si sentono legati ad essa accomunati sulla base del senso religioso, e ne vivono in qualche modo lo spirito» (cf. artt. 19 e 135).

«Le persone di buona volontà che non hanno una fede religiosa stimano l'Opera per i suoi beni spirituali e morali e desiderano, in qualità di collaboratori, condividerne le finalità secondo la loro coscienza (cf. artt. 20 e 136)». (stat. 95 art. 1, fn. 1) .

unity furthers the spirit, ends, structure and government of the Work of Mary (stat. 95 art. 4). Unity as a goal of the nature of Focolare clearly encompasses not only the Catholic members and adherents but also all Christians, non-Christians, persons of good will and in fact all of humanity.

The «ends» are presented under the subheadings of general and specific. 1) Perfection of love and 2) to live the evangelical spirituality of the Work of Mary in its fundamental points and various aspects which are expressed in the statutes and in the rules of the sections, branches and movements are two points listed as the general ends of Focolare (stat. 95 art. 5).

Specific ends are based on unity. The specific ends include working toward an ever deeper unity among the faithful of the Catholic Church and also to establish with other Christians communal fraternity and testimony, in all ways possible, with the desire of the re-establishment of full union. These ends of Focolare include dialogue and activities of common interest with persons of other churches and religions as a means to help them know Christ. Persons of good will are also included as a specific aim of the Work of Mary. Participants in Focolare are called to dialogue and work toward universal brotherhood in the world. One hope is that persons of good will open their hearts to Christ (stat. 95 art. 6).

The nature and ends found in the statutes of the Work of Mary clarify its own ecumenical experience. Three points clarify the ecumenical experience of Focolare: 1) the participation of non-Catholics in the Work, 2) the possibility for these persons to be actively involved to the extent that their own faith permits them, and 3) the call for unity which Focolare has embraced. The name Work of Mary, is a subtle reminder that the association is Catholic and is canonically rooted in the Catholic Church. In the quest for unity, the statutes recognize a desire for non-believers to know Christ and open their hearts to Him.

+ Members

The manner in which the Work of Mary incorporates all those who wish to be a part of the movement is organized by assigned titles. Some of these categories have been mentioned as they manifest the nature of Focolare. Here a more detailed consideration of the modes of participation will be undertaken.

The Titles and their Meanings

Even though the *CIC* 83 does not specifically forbid non-Catholics from being members of associations of the faithful, the statutes of the Work of Mary make a distinction. The praxis seems to be that a different label for non-Catholics is used to address the question of non-Catholic membership and involvement in the group. The different ways that persons can be a part of the Focolare speak of its openness to the participation of non-Catholics. Among these modes of participation are: Catholics as members and adherents, non-Catholic Christians as associates, and persons of other religions as well as persons of good will as collaborators.

Considering each of the ways of taking part in the movement and of the levels of involvement in the Work of Mary as described in the statutes will help to clarify the differences persons of various faiths and religions experience in the movement. The members, that is Catholics, are a part of one of the divisions[10] or *diramazioni* of Focolare. They take on a certain responsibility within Focolare suitable to their vocation (stat. 95 art. 16). The divisions are three: 1) Sections, of which there are one for men and one for women. These are further broken down into categories of common life and married life. 2) Branches, of which there are twenty-two, are for persons of all walks of life and ages who wish to take part in the Work of Mary. Some of the branches are: diocesan Focolarini priests and deacons, diocesan volunteer priests and deacons, men and women lay volunteers, «gen» male and female branches («gen» are youth groups which exist for young adults, teenagers and children), «gens» for those considering a vocation to the priesthood, and men and women members of institutes of consecrated life as well as societies of apostolic life. 3) Movements within the Work of Mary are: the new families movement, the new humanity movement, young adults for a united world movement, teenagers for unity, and the parish movement (stat. 95 art. 13). Each of the sections, branches and movements have their own rules and regulations approved by the general assembly of the Work of Mary.

Besides being diverse ways of participating in Focolare the three different divisions are levels of commitment into which persons are

---

10 The word «divisions» is the author's translation of the Italian term *diramazioni*. The translation was chosen for clarity. The word «branch» is a more literal translation but could be confused with its use by the Work of Mary for one of the three *diramazioni*.

able to enter. The sections make up the principal component of the Work of Mary. They are the load-bearing structure of the movement, having foundational control of Focolare. Here are found the Focolarini men and women, married and celibate, all of whom have committed themselves to full time commitment to the Work by means of an act of consecration. This consecration is of a private nature and is to be differentiated from the consecrated life canonically recognized in *CIC* 83 (Cf. stat. 95 art. 11, fn. 1). The branches are made up of persons who are radically committed while those who take part in the movements are less committed (stat. 95 art. 12, fn. 2). While the activity by which persons participate in the Work of Mary is different, the level of commitment is also diverse allowing persons who would like to be a part of the unity which exists for those belonging to the Work to do so.

Thus far the ways of involvement in Focolare have been explored for persons of different beliefs and also for the divisions, that is sections, branches and movements of Focolare. These two mesh as those who take part in the Work of Mary participate in the divisions. Levels of involvement which might seem to restrict a person's commitment in the Work of Mary in actuality open the way for as much participation as possible.

Restrictive Yet Open

The description of non-Catholic participation in focolare might seem to restrict their participation in the Work of Mary. Nothing could be farther from the truth because subjectively non-Catholics have a full participation «in so far as it is possible for them». This is true even though Catholics have a fullness of participation that is both objective and subjective. Even though the statutes state that only persons who take part in the Work as members and adherents (therefore Catholics) are able to completely live the articles regarding spirituality, they can still participate (stat. 95 art. 1, fn. 1). It is evident that non-Catholics would not live out their spirituality in the same way as Catholics. That non-Catholic Christians are normally not able to partake in the sacraments of Eucharist and Reconciliation is one example. The articles, which concern the spirituality of Focolare and which only Catholics are able to live fully, themselves at times also refer to the persons that take part in the Work of Mary (cf. stat. 95 arts. 1, 8, 21, 22, 23, 43, 47, 49, 50, 54, 56 and 58). This is a reference to all who participate in Focolare: members, adherents, associates and collaborators. They do, in fact, live many of the points of the spirituality.

A number of articles in the statutes are particularly concerned with the relationship of Catholic Focolare with members of other churches and ecclesial communities. These often reinforce the possibilities of non-Catholic Christians participating in the Work. Persons who live the spirituality of Focolare as associates (stat. 95, art. 1, fn. 1) share the spirit, which attracts them, and work towards its ends to the measure that the differences in belief allow them (stat. 95, art. 130).

The statutes seem to imply that the fullness of the truth is found in the Catholic Church. Catholics have this truth. Non-Catholics participate in it as possible. That non-Catholics participate «as their faith allows them» or «as is possible» is a key point. The more an individual Christian is able to follow the magisterium and the canon law of the Roman Catholic Church and the spirituality of Focolare the more they can be involved in the divisions of the Work.

New Terms

The revision of the statutes from 1990 to 1995 saw an interesting change in the use of the term «members». The change from «members» (membri) to «persons who are a part of the Work» (*Le persone che fanno parte dell'Opera*) widens the aperture to persons entering into relationship with and the activities of the Work of Mary. Article 18 of the 1990 statutes stated that, «Christians of other Churches and ecclesial communities are able to participate in the life and the initiatives of the Work of Mary not as members but as collaborators (stat. 90 art. 18)[11]. The term members was used in the 1990 statutes not less than fifteen times, many of these were located in the sections concerning the spirituality of the Work. In contrast, «members» is rarely found in the 1995 edition. This terminology was restricting. This meant that these areas of the spirituality of Focolare were only open to Catholics. The new terminology: is more inclusive, has a wider audience «all who make up a part of the Work of Mary». Thirteen articles in the text of the statutes make reference to persons who «take part in the Work of Mary;» (stat. 95 arts. 1, 8, 21-23, 32, 43, 47, 49, 50, 56 and 58) replacing the term «member» which had been used in the 1990 edition of the statutes. Most of the references to persons who take part in the Work of Mary are found in the third part of the statutes which covers

---

[11] «Possono partecipare alla vita e alle iniziative dell'Opera di Maria, in qualità non di membri ma di collaboratori, anche cristiani di altre Chiese e comunità ecclesiali». (stat. 90 art. 18)

concrete aspects of the life of the Work of Mary. Even though non-Catholics are not able to become members they in fact are involved to the fullest extent without breaking Church law or taking positions of leadership which might put them in compromising situations as non-Catholics. The way the statutes are now written more persons are welcomed to take a greater part in Focolare, and the use of the term member remains the same.

In Focolare the non-Catholic Christian associates (*aggregati*) are able to participate in many ways similar to their Catholic counterparts. The fact that they are not Catholics and are participating in a Catholic organization has inevitable consequences. These include the fact that 1) they are not able to fully participate in the sacraments of the Catholic Church (stat. 95 art. 46)[12]; these sacraments are the heart of the fullness of the spirituality in which the non-Catholics are not able to partake. The unity which is such a key to the movement cannot be lived out among the persons of different churches because they are not able to receive the Eucharist together. This is one glaring example where unity is just not possible. The unity is lived as possible with those who take part in Focolare centering around Jesus who is love and is at the center of the Work of Mary. 2) Only those considered members, thereby excluding non-Catholics, are able to participate in the General Assembly, a governing body in the Work of Mary (stat. 95 art. 69). Still non-Catholics obviously receive the benefits of participation in Focolare as so many are a part of the Work of Mary. One example which concretizes the abundance of non-Catholic Christian participation is in England where about one third of those who are a part of Focolare are members of the Anglican Communion[13]. This statistic speaks of the openness of the Work and the success of its ecumenical endeavors. Members of the Anglican Communion are joined to Focolare as associates. As such they may participate in all of the divisions to the point that their faith allows them. The statutes do not limit persons who are a part of the Work of Mary from being active in the different divisions. Thus, non-Catholics are able to take part in the sections, the principal component of the Work of Mary, as Focolarini and Focolarine. This includes consecration and full time work for Focolare and living the community lifestyle with community members.

---

[12] Cf. c.844,§1 *CIC* 83.
[13] J. GALLAGHER, *A Woman's Work*, 127.

+ Rights and Duties

The third part of the statutes of Focolare, including articles 21-64, have as their concern some concrete aspects of the association. It is here that the rights and duties of those who take part in Focolare can be found. Certain activities mentioned in the statutes are only open to members, who must be Catholics. This continues to reinforce the distinction between Catholics and non-Catholics who are a part of the Work of Mary and at the same time manifest the participatory possibilities for non-Catholics who are not able to be called members. The areas of rights and duties addressed are: 1) the communion of temporal goods, and economy, and work, 2) the apostolate, 3) union with God and prayer, 4) health and sickness and death, 5) attire and dwelling, and 6) wisdom and study and 7) unity and means of communication. These rights and duties continue to manifest unity and Jesus-Forsaken which are central to the spirituality of the Work of Mary.

The Communion of Temporal Goods, and Economy, and Work

According to circumstances and vocation all practice the communion of goods according to the example of the primative Christian community (stat. 95 art. 24). The Holy Family of Nazareth is the model of how the Focolarini should work (stat. 95 art. 24).

The Apostolate

The statutes call participants to live unity within the Catholic Church itself and seek the unity of all Christians. The quest for unity ought to be a catalyst for persons of other religions and people of good will to find Jesus (stat. 95 art. 38). Producing and offering conventions and meetings which are open to the public or tailored for specific groups is one of the principal forms of apostolate of the Work of Mary. Participation in these conferences may be a right or duty of those who are a part of the Work. According to the statutes members, therefore Catholics, of Focolare may live in «strongholds of witness»[14] or «cities on a mountain». In these communities they live the gospel, pray, work, study and live out other aspects of the life of the Work (stat. 95 art. 41). It is article forty-one of the statutes, which uses the term «members» and would make it seem that only Catholics are able to live in these «strongholds of witness». This particular restriction does not

---

[14] Author's translation of «città delle testimonianza».

make sense. The «strongholds of witness» would be an ideal spot for non-Catholics to participate in the Work of Mary. They would not participate in the governance of the Movement or enter into *communicatio in sacris*. Examples will show that the use of the word «members» in article forty-one is not as restricting as it might seem. It might be possible that the term was not changed to «those who make up a part» with the updating of the statutes from 1990 to 1994. A center for ecumenical life started at Ottmaring, near Augsburg, Germany in 1968, developed into what is referred to as a «little town» inhabited by both Catholics and Lutherans[15]. These Lutherans and Focolarini live and work together. In this situation the Lutherans have their own fraternal community life called *Bruderschaft vom gemeinsamen Leben* (the brotherhood of common life).

All are citizens of the «little town» which has developed into a Mariapolis. The Mariapolis is a center of formation and meetings (stat. 95 art. 57). Here it becomes obvious that the terms «Mariapolis», «little town» and «strongholds of witness» all have the same meaning, representing the same types of city - community. At present there are nineteen Mariapoli in the world found on each of the five global regions[16]. The presence of non-Catholics at the centers is in line with the statutes; only Catholics are able to live the spiritual life of the Work of Mary completely but non-Catholics may participate as their faith allows them. As persons who make up the Work of Mary, as members, adherents, associates, or collaborators, live the apostolate, it is always to be centered on Jesus the Savior of all (stat. 95 art. 42). Living the charisms of «unity», the presence of «Jesus in the midst» of the community (cf. stat. 95 art. 132) and «Jesus Forsaken» are all certainly possible for non-Catholic Christians. The Mariapolis at Tagaytay in the Philippines gives importance to dialogue between Christianity and the major Asian religions[17]. Again, non-Catholics are to live the spirituality and ends of Focolare as possible. This will obviously be different for non-Christians and persons of good will who have no religious faith as compared to non-Catholic Christians. The accepted terminology of ecumenism and interreligious dialogue also draw these distinctions. Trinitarian Baptism and belief in Jesus Christ as Savior bring all

---

[15] J. GALLAGHER, *A Woman's Work*, 123 and 157.

[16] Global regions refer to continents, however the Vatican and other European nations exclude Antarctica and combine North and South America making the number of continents five and not seven.

[17] J. GALLAGHER, *A Woman's Work*, 157.

Christians into a much closer relationship than with persons of other religions. Still with the goal of unity Focolare is open to all interested persons. Without calling them official members, non-Catholics are involved to the fullest extent possible as official associates and collaborators.

Union with God and Prayer

Rights and duties of those who take part in Focolare also include striving toward union with God and prayer. They all are called to an ever increasing and profound relationship with God and specifically to live the life of the resurrected Christ. They are to embrace the cross and to live the life of Jesus abandoned on the cross when pains are encountered. Constant prayer, love of God and neighbor, and a recognition of life in the Trinity add to the depth of the call. A right and duty specifically addressed to Catholics is the reception of the sacraments; Reconciliation and Eucharist ought to be received frequently by them (stat. 95 art. 46). The Work of Mary accepts as its own right and duty the personal and community care of all those who participate in the spiritual patrimony (stat. 95 arts. 43-48). Again each person who participates in the Work of Mary participates as they are able. This particularly affects the non-Christians and non-Catholics.

Health and Sickness

Also in this section of the statutes, health is addressed. As persons who are a part of the Work of Mary are able, they view «Jesus present» as their true health. He is their salvation whether they are in good health or in bad. This attitude is for all persons who participate in Focolare, a call for Catholics and non-Catholics alike, to a deeper trust in Jesus. Catholics are specifically addressed regarding the importance of the Eucharist: it is re-emphasized as the Sacrament of the Divine Love and the enduring bond of unity among all the living and the dead brothers and sisters. Care for the body in terms of good health and physical fitness is a concern for all; however all who make up a part of the Work of Mary also accept sickness and death (stat. 95 arts. 49-51).

Attire and Dwelling

In regard to dress, clothes are to be simple and at the same time according to fashion. Homes also are to be simple and clean and neat. The Work wants its followers to blend easily with the world and likewise to be attractive to it (stat. 95 art. 55). These duties and rights, concerning dress and dwelling of those persons who take part in the Work of Mary can certainly be engaged by Catholics and non-Catholics alike. Simple but fashionable dress might not be at the center of Focolare Spirituality, but it is seen as important to them as they strive to live in the world and be appealing to the world, while not being of the world.

Wisdom and Study

Formation for Focolare includes a desire for wisdom and study. The search for true Christian wisdom culminates in Jesus, the cross, the resurrection and living out the gifts of the Holy Spirit. There will be a foundational formation in catechism. This should touch all areas of the lives of all those who take part in the Work of Mary, Catholics and non-Catholics alike. The Work provides and funds courses, and catechetical and theological schools of formation. Cultural and professional topics are also presented depending on the person's tasks in the Church and in society (stat. 95 arts. 58-60). These courses may be opened to non-Catholics. For example Anglican priests involved with the non-Catholic Christian Focolarini in England may spend time at the Mariapolis outside Florence, Italy at Loppiano one of the first Mariapoli.

Unity and Means of Communication

Unity is to be promoted by means of spiritual communication. Conversations are to involve useful information. Idle talk and talk that is not necessary are not encouraged by the Work of Mary.

As the duties and rights of those who make up a part of the Work of Mary have been studied a number of the vast possibilities of involvement have come to light. There is a web of possibilities for persons who would like to participate in the Work. Since Focolare is Catholic it is obvious that some restrictions may be present for persons wishing to participate in Focolare who are not Catholics. Non-Catholics and non-Catholic Christians in particular are able to share in the rights and duties of Focolare as their faith allows. They participate in the three divisions.

The particular situation of members and adherents who must be Catholic versus that of non-Catholics is the overriding question of this study. Areas which concern sacraments and catechetics again manifest the issue of membership. The sacraments are for Catholics. Catechetics seem to be open to all as are experiences at the Mariapoli. That Focolare is open to non-Catholic participants in its activities but not as members continues to be a point clearly made. Again membership is only open to Catholics, but all others who make up a part of the Work of Mary are able to participate as their faith allows them. It has been stated that following Church law non-Catholics who make up a part of the Work do not share in the Eucharist or in the other sacraments. Community living situations, prayer, meetings, and convocations are all able to be engaged by persons who make up a part of the movement meaning non-Catholics. The term «members» speaks of persons, that is Catholics, who do have more rights and duties in Focolare than others. As far as we have seen rights and duties in which non-Catholics do not share are the same for Focolare as found in the Roman Catholic Church. The rights and duties or possibilities for persons who make a part of Focolare are also manifested in its government. A study of the governance will help to further understand the participation of non-Catholics in the association of faithful which is Focolare. Here rights and duties are limited by the Work itself and through its relations to the Apostolic See.

+ Governance

External Governance

From the history of the Work of Mary as given above, it is clear that there has always been a relationship between Focolare and the proper ecclesiastical authority. This continues to be true. The section of the statutes covering the organs of the general government states that when a new person enters the posts of president and vice-president/vicar they must be confirmed by the Apostolic See (stat. 95 art. 70).

The last section, part eleven, of the statutes has as its specific concern the rapport with ecclesiastical authority. Focolare, in all of its initiatives which further its ends through the Work of Mary's various organs and statutes places itself under the direction of the Apostolic See. (stat. 95 art. 139) The president, as head of the juridic person, is entrusted with the task of representative to the Apostolic See (stat. 95 art. 140). Focolare conforms itself to the teaching of the Pope and bishops. It looks to the Apostolic See for its activities which regard the whole of the Work and to the diocesan bishop for those which involve the Work of Mary in a particular diocese (stat. 95 art. 141). The Work of Mary has a relationship with the local ordinary and diocesan organizations. It is subject to the canonical vigilance or supervision of the competent authority. Focolare informs the diocese of its presence and asks before setting up living arrangements or undertaking apostolic activity (stat. 95 art. 142). In the zones, delegates are assigned to set up relations with local ecclesiastical authority (stat. 95 art. 143-144). On the basis of this we conclude that Non-Catholic associates who are part of Focolare may at times have to conform to the directives of the local bishop. These non-Catholic associates are not directly under his jurisdiction, but as part of the Focolare Movement under the local bishop they may be affected by his directives. But their participation in the movement or the supervision by the bishop does not seem to put these non-Catholics in a compromising situation. Whoever joins Focolare as an associate or collaborator, realizes that he is joining a Catholic association of the faithful and will follow its statutes as his faith permits.

Allowing non-Catholics to join the association will not endanger its Catholic character. This might be the fear of some who would prefer that non-Catholics be prohibited from entering canonical associations of the faithful. The faith of the individual members and adherents would not be compromised by the presence of Christians of various denominations or followers of other religions. The relationship of the Work of Mary with the local bishop ought to further safeguard the integrity of the Focolare Movement as a canonical association which can be considered ecumenical since it is possible for non-Catholic Christians to join as associates and persons of other religions to participate as collaborators.

Internal Governance

The internal governance of Focolare is highly developed. Besides the divisions (sections, branches and movements) and those persons who are a part of the Work (members, adherents, associates and collaborators), the Work is divided geographically into sixty-six zones or determined territories throughout the world[18]. The zones have their own government. In this consideration of internal governance, the zones will be examined as well as the organs of the general government.

The praxis of Focolare is to limit government positions to members only. This limits the rights of adherents (Catholics), associates (non-

---

18 F. ZAMBONINI, *Chiara Lubich*, 73.

Catholic Christians) and collaborators (non-Catholics from other religions and persons of good will). In general they do not hold leadership positions. Still it is understandable that certain positions of leadership be reserved for members in order to keep the Catholic integrity of the Work of Mary.

Zones

The governance of the zones has a two-fold goal: unity within the zone itself, and a bond between the zone and the center of the Work of Mary located in the Alban Hills outside Rome. Two delegates, a Focolarino and a Focolarina, both in perpetual vows, represent the Work of Mary in the zone. They are nominated by the president and approved by the General Council. Delegates are among the list of persons who make up the General Assembly which is to be made up of Catholics as will be seen in the section covering the General Assembly. Each is assisted by a council. The council is comprised of members that represent the territorial subdivisions of the Work of Mary in the zones, and also the sections, the branches and the movements (stat. 95 art. 112). It is key to recognize that the zone advisors are to be members of the Work of Mary and, therefore, Catholics. As was seen in the study of the internal governance, virtually all leadership positions are reserved to members of the Work of Mary only; therefore, non-Catholic associates do not exercise these roles.

Organs of the General Government

The organs of general government include: the General Assembly, the Center of the Work, the president of the Work, the vice-president/vicar, the central delegates and the general councilors. Organs of the general government will be studied as they add insight into the ecumenical situation of Focolare. Any restrictions imposed on those who make up a part of the Work of Mary as to their participation in the government of the Work will be the first building block in the development of the praxis of non-Catholic participation in associations of the faithful which are universal and recognized by the Holy See.

General Assembly

Not all who make up a part of the Work of Mary have the right to occupy a seat in the General Assembly. The Assembly has charge of the elections of the president, vice-president, vicar and general advisors and is convoked when the president is to finish her term or when she deems it necessary or advantageous (stat. 95 art. 69). Only Catholics can be elected to these positions in the government of Focolare.

In their capicity as members of the Work the following participate in the general assembly,
– The president, the vice-president/vicar, and other outgoing members of the general council;
– the two outgoing secretaries of the general council;
– those holding central responsibility for specific tasks within the secretariat and those responsible for activities and works dependent on the center of the Work.
– the delegates of the zones, see art. 105 and 107
– the men and women focolarini elected by the zone assemblies (cf. art. 116).
– the members of the central councils of the sections, branches and of the movements according to the regulations[19].

These governing positions which handle the transition from one president to the next are filled by members of the Work of Mary; therefore non-Catholics are not able to fill these positions. But according to the statutes (stat. 95 art. 134), the opinion of non-Catholics will be asked with regard to matters that concerns them. At this time of change for Focolare it is important that its ends remain intact. As the Work of Mary is a Roman Catholic movement, it is natural that its integrity as Catholic be protected in its statutes. The guarantee of Catholics in the government will protect the Catholicity of Focolare.

Center of the Work

The Center of the Work strives to: express unity, aid the accomplishment of the ends, coordinate activities and determine which ac-

---

[19] «All'Assemblea generale partecipano, in qualità di membri dell'Opera:
– Il Presidente, il Copresidente e Vicario, gli altri membri uscenti del Consiglio generale;
– i due segretari uscenti del consiglio generale;
– i responsabili centrali delle segreterie per gli scopi specifici e quelli delle attività ed opere dipendenti dal Centro dell'Opera;
– i delegati di zona di cui agli art. 105 e 107;
– i focolarini e le focolarine eletti dalle assemblee zonali (cf. art. 116) delle zone costituite;
– i componenti dei consigli centrali delle sezioni, delle branche, e dei movimenti, previsti nei rispettivi regolamenti». (stat. 95 art. 66)

tivities must depend directly on the Center. The Center is comprised of the president, vice-president/vicar, the two central delegates, the general advisors elected by the general assembly and representatives of the sections, branches, and movements. The president is assisted by a General Council whose posts are filled by members of the Work. This is clear from the statement, «In their capacity as members of the Work they make up part of the general council» (stat. 95 art. 76)[20]. The list which follows in the statutes is identical with the list of persons who are the Center of the Work (stat. 95 arts. 72 and 76). It follows that the constituents of the Center of the Work of Mary as well as the General Council are *de facto* Catholics.

The President

The position of president is unique in Focolare. It is the highest position of leadership and service in the Work. Mary is the model which the president is to follow making the president a true mother to the Work of Mary (stat. 95 art. 88).

On one occasion in audience with the Holy Father (23 September 1985), Lubich asked if it would be good that the presidency of the Work of Mary be reserved to women. John Paul II responded in the affirmative, citing Hans Urs von Balthasar whose four profiles of the Church include one which is Marian (stat. 95 art. 73, fn. 1). As a consequence Focolare will always have a woman as its president. This brings into question the rights of members and in fact of all who make up a part of the Work. Does the prohibition of men from the office of president in Focolare restrict their rights in the association? It is possible for men and women Catholics to participate fully in all of Focolare's divisions as either members or adherents. However it is only possible for women to become the president of the Work. This decision was made after Lubich's audience with John Paul II. This is not a divine law as the male priesthood but a human law which could be changed. In a way the prohibition of men from serving Focolare as president restricts their rights as members of the association, yet they are fully members. They can be considered members without full rights. For females also there are positions in which they are not able to serve. This leads to the last areas of governance to be covered.

---

[20] «Fanno parte del Consiglio generale, in qualità di membri dell'Opera». (Stat. 95 art. 76).

Other Organs

Among the other organs listed by the General Statutes are the vice-president and vicar, the central delegates, and the general councilors. The duties and position of these persons does not affect the ecumenical aspects of Focolare, yet the situation of the vice-president/vicar is interesting in relation to the president who is always to be a woman. «The vice president/vicar is chosen from among members of the focolarini section who have made perpetual vows» (stat. 95 art. 73)[21]. He must also be a priest because of the notable presence of priests in the Opera di Maria. This may be viewed as providing a balance to an exclusively female presidency. Because the vice-president and vicar hold seats in the general assembly they have the active right of participation in the election of the president as the president for the vice-president and vicar. Being elected is a passive right and is considered as such. In fact, because of the different positions which are to be held by women or men (priests), it cannot be said that anyone in Focolare has full-rights, that is able to serve in all of the positions possible. This is true for Catholics, in the situations of president, vice-president and vicar and for non-Catholics who are not able to participate in the government of Focolare. So no one taking part in Focolare is able to claim full-rights in the Movement.

The situation of the internal governance of the Work of Mary clarifies the praxis within Focolare itself and the praxis of the Apostolic See since it, through the PCL, has established the Work of Mary as a private juridic person. Even though non-Catholics participate in the Work of Mary as associates and collaborators they are not able to enter into the government of the Work of Mary. Moreover, neither Focolari (men) nor Focolarine (women) are able to hold all of the positions within the government. While holding to its charism Focolare has welcomed everyone to share in its unity as possible.

+ Conclusion

In conclusion, it is important to review the possibilities for non-Catholic associates and collaborators in Focolare, the actual structural organization of the many methods of participating in Focolare and the rights of those who make up a part of Work of Mary. These three areas

---

[21] «Il Copresidente e Vicario, scelto tra i sacerdoti membri di voti perpetui della sezione dei focolarini». (stat. 95 art. 73)

each have an impact on the over all praxis of allowing non-Catholics to join Focolare. This praxis which has been used by the Apostolic See and Focolare as it has grown and been canonically recognized by the Holy See as a private association of the faithful which is universal, that is, of pontifical right and enjoys juridic personality, is important to other ecumenical associations since they may seek to be canonically recognized by the Apostolic See.

In Focolare it is not possible for non-Catholic associates and collaborators to be called, classified or named members. Non-Catholics are not able to serve in the governing bodies. These points are made in the statutes[22]. Church law concerning non-Catholics is followed. The ruling of the Church as promulgated in the *Directory for the Application of Principles and Norms on Ecumenism* concerning non-Catholics and reception of the sacraments are honored[23]. Because of the Catholicity of Focolare it would not be logical that non-Catholic persons would be treated as if they were Catholic simply because they are taking part in the Work.

The division between non-Catholic Christians and non-Christians is wide. An example is the suffering of Christ abandoned. Catholics and all baptized Christians are called to live this fundamental reality of the faith in their lives. Even though non-Christians may be able to imagine or even ponder this ideal they cannot live it out as those who have died and risen with the Lord Jesus Christ in baptism. Non-Christians may live their lives for others and even suffer for others, but the particular fundamental change that takes place for the Christian is not present for the non-baptized. Because of the common belief in Jesus of non-Catholic Christians and Catholics, these associates would be able to share in the spiritual life of the Work of Mary in more ways than followers of other religions or persons of good will. Non-Catholic Christians are able to share in prayer to Jesus and the Trinity. Jesus' presence when two or three are gathered in His name is important to Christians, Catholic and non-Catholic. They may recognize Mary as the Mother of God and in turn as the Mother of all.

The structural organization of The Work of Mary is complex. Through the different modes of belonging persons can take part as members, adherents, associates and collaborators in the various divisions and the approximately thirty possibilities within the divisions.

---

22 Cf. c.307,§4 *CIC* 83.
23 ED 93, 129.

The sixty-six zones which divide the globe into geographic areas for the Work are yet another angle of participation. Each of the zones, divisions and modes of belonging have representation in the government of the Work of Mary. The beauty in the complexity of possibilities of participating in Focolare is that so many in fact can participate in a variety of ways. This is true for Catholics and non-Catholics alike.

Even with different beliefs all persons who desire may take part in all of the divisions of Focolare as their own faith allows them. This opens them to the four different sections, and many of the twenty-two branches. These few ways that non-Catholics are not able to enter the divisions are small compared to the over thirty possible ways to join Focolare.

Beyond simple membership in the Work, the question of rights of members and non-members is an issue. To be a member of Focolare signifies that a person is Catholic and is engaged at some level of responsibility in the Work. As has been seen it is not possible for any one person to fill every position in the Work of Mary: only women may fill the presidency and only a priest may serve as vice-president/vicar. This limits possibilities.

As concerns non-Catholics in Focolare what is most important is to recognize that they can join the Work, but not as members or adherents. Rather, non-Catholics, are aggregated to the Work as «associates». Since associates can take part in the Work as their faith allows them, it is obvious that some non-Catholics can be more involved and committed to the Work than Catholics. Focolarini who have made perpetual vows are mentioned in the statutes but the way that they become consecrated members is not clearly spelled out; neither is the way that a person becomes a member, adherent, associate or collaborator. But although not determined by the statutes much seems to be determined by the regulations, which unfortunately were unavailable for consultation. Because of these limitations we can only suppose that it should be possible that some baptized non-Catholics pronounce private vows as Focolarini and that the modality of this vow taking is established by the regulations. Even within the organization there is much freedom for participation. Under the title «associates» the non-Catholics who make a part of the Work of Mary are able to be involved as their faith enables them in all the benefits which make up the nature and purpose of the Focolare. Even though they are not members in the vast majority of the means of participation they can act like members, with whom they share many of the rights and duties of the Work.

b) *Communauté de l'Emmanuel*

The spiritual roots of the Emmanuel Community are in the Catholic Charismatic Renewal. Some of the first members of what would eventually become Emmanuel made a retreat on the weekend of 12-13 February 1972 at the residence of Father Caffarel in Troussurres, France[24]. Thirty persons spent their time in prayer and sharing. One couple shared their experiences of the Charismatic Renewal in the United States. At the end of the weekend many asked for prayer for the Baptism in the Holy Spirit. The founders of Emmanuel, Pierre Goursat and Martine Catta, who attended the retreat had known each other through their work at a prayer school in Paris. After experiencing this retreat they began to meet for prayer each evening. Others joined them. Because of increasing numbers, within a year over five hundred persons were involved, the group split. Three weekly prayer groups began to meet in local Catholic churches and a Catholic center[25].

Two other developments, besides the increase in participants, brought about the birth of the Emmanuel Community. It was felt that the prayer groups themselves were not providing enough in the way of religious growth for the participants so weekend retreats, catechism teachings and other instructional methods were engaged[26]. The third development which moved these prayer groups in the direction of a community was a shared living situation into which Goursat entered with two other men[27]. By living under the same roof they felt they were more easily able to serve the Lord together. It was through these developments that the leaders invited those participating in the prayer groups to enter into a committed community life of prayer, service and evangelization. Approximately fifty persons responded to this call which was made in June 1977[28]. By 1988 there were three thousand five hundred members in the Community and presently there are approximately five thousand members. Emmanuel is present in forty-four countries in all five of the global regions[29].

---

24 F. LENOIR, *Les Communautés Nouvelles* 137.
25 F. LENOIR, *Les Communautés Nouvelles*, 142.
26 F. LENOIR, *Les Communautés Nouvelles*, 142.
27 F. LENOIR, *Les Communautés Nouvelles*, 142-143.
28 F. LENOIR, *Les Communautés Nouvelles*, 144.
29 «I Movimenti e le Nuove Comunità», 14.

+ Ends

The nature and ends of the Emmanuel Community manifest it as a Catholic association. However, it is obvious that the group could have appeal to Christians who are not Catholic as the association's purpose is Christ centered. The possibility of living community life with other committed Christians certainly can have an appeal for persons who are looking for more ways to live out their faith. All who join the Community rely on grace and the Catholics in particular on the graces which are poured forth from the sacraments especially the Eucharist and Reconciliation. Emmanuel takes the Blessed Virgin Mary as its mother, adding to its Catholic character. The Community, with its headquarters in Paris, gathers together faithful from all walks of life. These persons desire to engage in a life which is both contemplative and apostolic as well as being at the heart of the Church (stat. I, 1, 2).

Continuing to examine the nature and ends of the Catholic association, goals are identified which are fundamental to all Christian faiths. All members, lay or clerical, see each other as brothers and sisters in Jesus Christ with the same call to sanctity and to announce the gospel. This call is to be lived by members according to their state in life and ministry. They are to engage in forming one community and are to bring to the Community an active role of assistance, materially, fraternally and spiritually. They promise to God and to each other to live a life of holiness and of announcing the Kingdom of God (stat. I, 1).

Even as the Community desires to participate in the life of the Church it is open to the participation of all baptized Christians. Doing apostolic work side-by-side with other Catholics: lay, religious and priests draws persons of faith. When Christ's work is done in a vibrant manner it draws others. They also hear the call of God's Spirit. Evangelization is an important part of Community life. Believers and non-believers are targeted both as individuals and culturally. The Community strives to serve the sick and poor and to promote family and social life. All evangelical activities of the Community, even those which are cultural, charitable or social are done explicitly in the name of Jesus Christ and are accompanied by the announcement of the Good News. Activities are in line with Church teaching and a trusting submission to the magisterium prevails in the Community (stat. I, 3).

The Emmanuel Community is recognized as a universal private association of the faithful with juridic personality by both the PCL and the Archdiocese of Paris. This status only reinforces the Church's support of the association. The rights and duties of members and governance which are affected by this status will be reviewed.

As outlined by the proper statutes the nature and ends of the Emmanuel Community are Catholic. Participation by non-Catholic Christians in the Community is possible as will be set forth in the next section concerning members.

+ Members

Non-Catholics are not able to become members of the Emmanuel Community. They are however able to participate in the work of the association. Catholic membership will be reviewed followed by a review of non-Catholic participation. The statutes include a wide range of life-styles and methods by which Catholics may enter the Community. Membership is open to all Roman Catholics who are baptized and confirmed. To be eligible for membership, Catholics must have reached the age of majority according to both canon and civil law. A probation period of two years is undertaken by all who desire to become members. An interesting sentence found in the statutes concerning members makes the point that none of the commitments spoken of in the statutes bind members under the pain of sin (stat. II, 5). A list of those eligible for membership includes: married, lay persons, men and women bound to celibacy for the kingdom, permanent deacons, transitional deacons, priests and religious men and women. These will fit into different states of membership (stat. II, 6). The types of membership include: members in probation, committed members, associate members (these are Catholics who cannot make a full commitment to the Community or Fraternity), associate brothers and consecrated members in the Fraternity (stat. II, 10).

Non-Catholics may participate in the Emmanuel Community as associate brothers. They cannot be accepted in the ordinary work or commitment of the Community as members of any type. As associated brothers non-Catholic men and women participate in the life and graces of the Community to the measure in which: 1) they recognize in the Emmanuel Community a call from God for them, 2) they declare themselves willing to respect the Catholic Church in her mystery, her identity, her teachings and her sacramental practice; and 3) they can participate significantly in the graces of the Community, its life, and its demands in a way compatible with the respect and loyalty due to the ecclesial community to which they belong (stat. II, 9).

Associate brothers undergo a probation period similar to that of Catholics entering the Community. This lasts approximately two years. An agreement is then made with the moderator and the council on a particular commitment which specifies the participation of the associated brother in the Community and respect for their bonds with their own ecclesial community. Non-Catholics do not participate in the government of the Community and will have no responsibilities for the formation of members (stat. II, 9).

As has been seen, much of the life of the Community is centered around the sacraments of the Roman Catholic Church. Nevertheless the common living arrangements and desire for a community lifestyle seem to attract baptized non-Catholics. The zeal of members of a new community in itself often attracts others toward participation. Here we see the praxis of the Apostolic See regarding non-Catholic membership in associations of the faithful. Baptized non-Catholics are not to be members, but may participate under another title, which brings with it some sense of belonging. The associate brothers participate in the activities of the Community save those which ecclesial differences in belief do not allow. To safeguard the Catholic integrity of the association, non-Catholics are not to hold positions of authority in the Community. This point which seen in the statutes of the Community is part of the general praxis of the Apostolic See in these situations involving associations which may be considered ecumenical. This same praxis has been seen for the associates and collaborators of Focolare.

+ Rights and Duties

The rights and duties of the members of the Emmanuel Community involve prayer and community life. Catholics and non-Catholics alike may engage in many of these opportunities for sanctification. Some situations in which non-Catholics are not able to share fully are very apparent as these involve sacraments.

Under the section entitled rights and duties, the statutes list types of prayer and sacraments which in a particular way make up the life of the Community members. Long periods of adoration, before the Blessed Sacrament when possible, are encouraged. Members make a commitment to daily periods of adoration as they are able. Daily attendance at Holy Mass and frequent confession are the norm for laity, religious, deacons and priests. Small gatherings of persons living in proximity of one another offer prayer of praise which is celebrated joyously (stat. III, 15).

The ways, rights and obligations of members also includes a commitment to community life. Many modes for community living are available. Priests and deacons often find housing together as they strive to live out the life and spirit of the Community. Singles may live with families, but those committed to celibacy do not live in coed environments. Some members and participants in Emmanuel may live outside of a community setting; all, however, are expected to take part in Community activities. Once a month the whole Community gathers as a body. This is a duty as well as a grace since the Community is made manifest. All benefit from the prayers of the brothers and sisters who are involved in the Community. Thus, it is possible for the associate brothers to receive benefits from their association with the Community.

The duties which have been decided between the associated brothers, and the moderator and council might include attendance at monthly Community gatherings, daily prayer of praise and living in Community residence situations for the brothers associated with the Community. Even though non-Catholics are not permitted to be members they share in a number of the rights and duties which are a part of membership in the Community.

Other means by which participants engage in the benefits of the Emmanuel Community are formation and missionary activity. Formation includes: Biblical studies, theology, spirituality (in particular spirituality of the Second Vatican Council) and Church teaching. Formation in the Community aims at deepening the mystical life of contemplation and action as well as conforming to the particular charisms of Emmanuel (stat. III, 22). Being totally committed to evangelization and being missionaries in the world, certain members of Emmanuel are sent to foreign countries to carry out the ministry of the Community. Thus the Community's international work is manifest by its presence in mission countries. Its international standing is confirmed by its recognition by the PCL.

This review of the rights and duties of the Community helps to clarify the areas in which non-Catholics might participate in the life of the Community and also areas where this may be difficult. At this international level the general praxis of the Apostolic See is not to grant membership to non-Catholics. Similar to Focolare Emmanuel has another possibility for joining the Community. Associate brothers, men and women, participate in the communal prayer of the Community, its formation, and missionary activity. Following Church law they do not receive sacraments. Neither do they have responsibility for the formation of Community members.

+ Governance

External Governance

Emmanuel has an agreement with a bishop before the association is established in his diocese. Besides approving their presence, the ordinary decides in cooperation with the Community what type of apostolic service they will provide in the diocese. The statutes require that the agreement be in writing and include time limits. The bishop's approval is also needed to found or use houses of formation or of religious study in his diocese. As candidates for ordination to the priesthood, seminarians are to have a diocese into which they will be incardinated. These candidates for ordination must be presented to the bishop issuing their dismissorial letters (stat. VI, 45). Priests who work with the Community in mission sites are incardinated into the diocese in which they are working (stat. III, 24). A relationship is also maintained with the Archbishop of Paris, in whose jurisdiction the Community headquarters are located[30]. These statutes set a good relation with the local bishop, it should be kept in mind that a relation with the Apostolic See is also present at the PCL[31].

External governance does not affect non-Catholics save that they realize that the Community is Catholic and answers to the Catholic hierarchy. The formation and prayer life of the Community follow the magisterium. *Communicatio in spiritualibus* will be engaged according to law as will the restrictions of *communicatio in sacris*.

Internal Governance

The review of the internal governance will be two-fold. Attention will be given to the Fraternity of Jesus, a community within the Emmanuel Community, as well as the internal system of government in the whole of the Community. Men, women, couples and priest members of Emmanuel consecrate themselves totally to the Emmanuel Community when they join the Fraternity of Jesus[32]. Only Catholics are permitted to become members of the Fraternity as their consecration is specifically to Jesus present in the Eucharist. This prohibition is

---

[30] The relationship between the Archbishop of Paris and Emmanuel was one of vigilance and pastoral ministry. The archbishop's responsibilities were assigned during the five year experimental period for the statutes.

[31] PONTIFICIUM CONSILIUM PRO LAICIS, 1560/92/S-61/B-45/b, Rome.

[32] F. LENOIR, *Les Communautés Nouvelles* 147.

clearly stated in the statutes. «Among the Catholic members of the Emmanuel Community some may receive a more radical call» (stat. II, b)[33]. The praxis of only allowing Catholics to enter the consecrated life of the Fraternity of Jesus parallels the praxis of the Apostolic See in limiting the participation of non-Catholic Christians in governing roles of in associations canonically recognized. The consecration is an affirmation of Baptism as depicted in *LG* 10. Persons see themselves consecrated as temples of the Spirit and a holy priesthood.

Catholic members of other similar communities may also join the Fraternity of Jesus. Here the Catholicity of the Fraternity is accentuated. They participate in the graces and spirit without submitting to or participating in the government.

> Certain people not members of Emmanuel, but Catholics involved in communities of similar spirit may be admitted into the Fraternity of Jesus. These people will participate in the graces and spirit of the Fraternity without participating in or being subject to its government (stat. II. c)[34].

This openness on the part of Emmanuel is not surprising. Since graces of evangelization along with adoration and compassion[35] are the basis of their lifestyle it is natural that Emmanuel would welcome others to share in their lifestyle as possible. Yearly gatherings at Paray-le-Monial in France draw over twenty thousand persons[36]. Members of other charismatic communities would certainly be present and they may be called to the personal consecration of the Fraternity of Jesus.

The Emmanuel Community is governed by a moderator who is assisted by an international council. A consultative committee is convened when situations warrant. A college of prayer and election is responsible for electing the international council. The moderator is elected by the international council (stat. VI, 33).

The globe is divided into provinces whose borders are defined by the international council (stat. VI, 34). Each province has a coordinator assigned by the moderator with the approval of the international council. The coordinator with a bureau and an apostolic committee who as-

---

[33] «Parmi les membres catholiques de la Communauté de l'Emmanuel, certains peuvent recevoir un appel plus radical». (stat. II, b).

[34] «Certaines personnes non membres de la Communauté Emmanuel, mais catholiques engagées dans des communautés d'esprit analogue, peuvent être admises dans la Fraternité de Jésus. Ces personnes participeront aux graces et à l'esprit de la Fraternité sans participer ni être soumises à son gouvernement». (stat. II, c).

[35] F. LENOIR, *Les Communautés Nouvelles*, 137.

[36] «I Movimenti e le Nuove Comunità», 14.

sist him is responsible for community life and apostolic activities in the province (stat. VI, 35).

The international council of twelve to sixteen members in coordination with the moderator set the general orientation of the life, the apostolate and formation of the Community in conformity with its proper charisms (stat. VI, 39). Seats in the international council are occupied by consecrated members of the Fraternity of Jesus (stat. VI, 38). The moderator keeps the Community on course towards using the basic foundations of the Community, adoration, compassion and evangelization. He or she[37] represents the Community in relations with religious and civil authorities. As a community within a community the Fraternity of Jesus is also governed by the same moderator as Emmanuel (stat. VI, 48). However the Fraternity does have its own council of fifteen members (stat. VI, 49) which assists the moderator in his responsibilities toward the Fraternity. The governmental structure of the Community and Fraternity certainly are able to serve the needs of both organizations.

All persons who serve in the government of Emmanuel and the Fraternity of Jesus must be Roman Catholics. This is obvious for the Fraternity because only Catholics can belong to it (stat. II, b). Regarding baptized non-Catholics participating in the government of Emmanuel the statutes are clear. «They do not participate in the government of the Community and do not have responsibilities in formation (program)» (stat. II, 9)[38].

+ Conclusion

As was stated in the section covering membership, non-Catholics do not enter into the governance of Emmanuel. The Fraternity is another body into which non-Catholics are not able to enter. Nevertheless, non-Catholics can play an important role as they participate in the Community as associate brothers.

The Emmanuel Community, by means of its governance, and rights and duties certainly is able to attain its ends. By way of group living situations the ideal to live fraternally in community is possible. Docility to Church hierarchy and teaching are within reach as those who join community life are aware of these goals. Love of the sacraments and

---

37 F. LENOIR, *Les Communautés Nouvelles*, 146.

38 «Ils ne participent pas au governement de la Communauté et n'ont pas de responsabilités dans la formation». (stat. II, 9).

frequent reception along with daily prayer of praise (charismatic) is very important to Community participants. A dedication to evangelization as well as the proclamation of the Good News in a vibrant community is attractive to believers. The Community is well organized in its openness to non-Catholic participation as is seen in the steps leading to belonging as an associate brother. Non-Catholics are not officially members but certainly are involved in the life of the Community. Even if they do not receive the sacraments, do not serve in the government and are not involved in the Fraternity their presence is certainly felt by the whole Community. Here as in Focolare the praxis of the Apostolic See is manifest in its concern for non-Catholic participation in associations of the faithful.

c) *La Fraternité Chrétienne Intercontinentale des Personnes Malades Chroniques et Handicapées Physiques*

Two of the communities to be studied are both at the service of handicapped persons. Communities which have been the subject of this paper so far, have all had some type of household or community living as a part of their structure. This lifestyle is helpful to the communities to achieve their ends and live out their apostolate. What makes these communities who serve the handicapped different is that their living situation is their apostolate. What they do is what they are. Being a community and providing community for the handicapped is the work of the communities. This added dimension of challenge for these persons ought to lead to a praxis which is conscious of the special needs of these persons.

+ Ends

The Intercontinental Christian Fraternity of Chronically Sick and Physically Handicapped Persons has its headquarters in Verdun, France. It is a private international association of the faithful having juridic personality and is recognized by the Apostolic See. The Intercontinental Fraternity desires the well being of all people and bears the gospel message of a God who is love and life. For the Fraternity, God is particularly at work through the actions and words of Jesus when He says, «Get up and walk»[39]. On this spiritual basis the Fraternity puts its mission into action. To reach its goals, the Fraternity seeks to promote:

---

[39] Mt. 9,5.

the development of a fraternal life for members and their communities, attention to the life of individual persons, and attentive listening to the word of God which becomes the source of transforming actions (stat. 1.4).

The evangelization of man is the main objective of the Fraternity. The sick and handicapped are of particular concern. Development of the person through a personal and community context lead toward: the transformation of the world, the coming of a new society founded on the dignity of man, the evangelical transformation of the Church, and a universal Fraternity (stat. 2.1.A). As an intercontinental Fraternity, the association establishes ties with persons and communities among the sick and handicapped themselves (stat. 1.12). This allows the goals of the Fraternity to be reached in the most effective ways possible.

The ends, purpose, objective and nature of the Fraternity in themselves do not exclude non-Catholics. Indeed with the objective of transformation of the world and a universal Fraternity all mankind is targeted. As will be seen, the Fraternity has a strong Catholic structure. For the Fraternity, the denominator of service to and with needy persons open to the love of God in Jesus brings Christians and other believers together.

+ Members

Membership of the Fraternity encompasses the sick and handicapped themselves as well as co-workers. While the Fraternity opens itself to non-Catholics, it also roots itself into the life of the Church.

A movement of the Church, the Fraternity places itself within the pastoral [ministry] of the Roman Catholic Church, acting in communion with its pastors at all levels — local Church, the Conference of Bishops, the universal Church — and in fidelity to the teaching of her magisterium. In the spirit of the conciliar decree on Ecumenism [the Fraternity bears the concern of the decree] and accepts people of other confessions on condition that these respect the freedom of conscience the spirit and identity of the movement (stat. 1.3)[40].

---

[40] «Mouvement d'Eglise, la Fraternité s'inscrit dans la Pastorale de l'Eglise Catholique, agissant en communion avec ses pasteurs à tous les niveaux — Eglise locale, Conférence des Evêques, Eglise universelle — et en fidélité à l'enseignement de son magistère. Dans l'esprit du Décret conciliaire sur l'oecuménisme, elle porte le souci de celui-ci et accepte les personnes des autres Confessions, à condition que celles-ci respectent la liberté de conscience, l'esprit et l'identité du Mouvement». (stat. 1.3).

Non-Catholics who would be a part of the Fraternity must respect the identity of the movement, which means that they recognize and respect that the Fraternity follows the Magisterium of the Church. These non-Catholics are members of the community. They are not able to serve in all the positions of the Fraternity and thus cannot be considered members with full rights. Still, they are considered members. The statutes do not carefully define the term «member» and do not have an alternative term for non-Catholics who participate in the Fraternity. Both Focolare and Emmanuel have specially designated terms for non-Catholics who participate in their associations. No special terminology of this nature is found in the statutes of the International Christian Fraternity of Chronically Sick and Physically Handicapped Persons. Even its name lends to its ecumenical character. Other restrictions that apply to the participation of non-Catholic members of the Fraternity will be identified in the sections which follow.

+ Rights and Duties

Members of the Fraternity are to be enabled to participate in the Church as is possible, even if this involves problems because of social or religious beliefs (stat. 1.8). The sick and handicapped themselves as well as co-workers will work to see that rights are respected including the duties of the Catholics involved as well as the respect of the non-Catholics toward the Church. The Fraternity assures the human, Christian, and spiritual formation of the members starting with the circumstances of their lives. Members will be helped progressively to organize themselves and then in mutual interaction to walk toward meeting Jesus Christ (stat. 1.10). Aware of the situation of each of the chronically ill and physically handicapped members, the Fraternity works toward the total development of its members. It strives to give value to the qualities that each person possesses. By drawing forth the potential in each person, the Fraternity realizes its evangelical mission. Personal potential is drawn forth by putting persons in charge of their own lives and aiding them in being conscious of their mission in society and in the Church (stat. 2.1.B). All that is done for the members and all that is asked of them is done within Church guidelines. What is done for the betterment of society is also to be done with the Church's evangelical goals in mind: namely, that all would come to know the truth and that all would be one. Members' rights and duties are the opportunity to participate in this great vocation as participants of the Fraternity.

+ Governance

The Fraternity is comprised of an intercontinental committee, an intercontinental council, an intercontinental team and continental assemblies (stat. 3.1). Each has various tasks to make the goals of the movement realities. The ecumenical dimension of the Fraternity is determined by governance in two ways: approval of appointments and religious requirements. Further, statutory requirements place restrictions on two positions in the Fraternity: that of Intercontinental Coordinator and Intercontinental Chaplain. «The intercontinental coordinator must be a *Catholic* (stat. 3.2.5)[41]. This person is the highest ranking officer in the Fraternity. Having a Catholic in this position affects the whole Fraternity as the Intercontinental Committee of which he is a member has responsibility for all of the Fraternity. This requirement reinforces the position of non-Catholics as members. If only Catholics could be members and non-Catholics had another title the statutes could state that only members have the position of Intercontinental Coordinator. This not being the case the term «Catholic» becomes all important. The candidate for chaplain of the Fraternity must be approved by the Apostolic See (stat. 3.3.3). This gives the Church a specific voice in the spiritual role which plays a major influence on the Fraternity. Because the Apostolic See approves the chaplain it seems that this position will be occupied by a Catholic. The statutes do not limit the role that non-Catholics can play in the government of the Fraternity; only the positions of International Coordinator and chaplain have any restrictions or requirements attached. The statutes allow non-Catholic members to government positions on the Intercontinental Committee, the Intercontinental Council, the Intercontinental Team and the Continental Assemblies, since they do not forbid it. The Church's right of supervision will protect the Catholicity of the Fraternity[42].

The Apostolic See also is given the task of approving the statutes and amendments which are proposed by the Intercontinental Committee (stat. 3.2.5). One of the tasks of the Intercontinental Team is to represent the Fraternity in the meetings of the movement itself and in meetings with the Roman Catholic Church and in meetings with other Christian Churches (stat. 3.4.6). The Catholicity of the Fraternity is

---

[41] «Le Coordinateur Intercontinental doit être *Catholique*». (stat. 3.2.5). Emphasis in the original.
[42] c. 305,§1 *CIC* 83.

reinforced by the power that the Church has over the formation of its statutes. At the same time the ecumenical dimension of the Fraternity is manifest as the team represents the movement at meetings with other Christian Churches.

+ Conclusion

The relationship which the International Christian Fraternity has desired with the Apostolic See is presented in its statutes. Persons of different faiths are called to respect one another. The statutes do not restrict non-Catholics from membership in the Fraternity or place them in a category other than that of member. According to the statutes non-Catholics must recognize and respect the fact that the Fraternity follows the Magisterium of the Roman Catholic Church. They are restricted from holding some government positions, but do enjoy most all of the rights and duties of the «Catholic» members of the Fraternity. The Fraternity has been able to draw up statutes which are acceptable to the Apostolic See and at the same time their aims as an ecumenical Christian association with canonical recognition as a juridic person.

d) *Communauté et Communion du Chemin Neuf*

Chemin Neuf is a large international French community. Even though its official canonical approval is not from the Apostolic See nor a diocese of the United States of America it is an excellent example of an ecumenical association and for this reason is used in the present study. It has been erected a public association of the Christian faithful by the Archbishop of Lyon where the Community was founded and has its headquarters. The association is diocesan right. Relations do exist between Chemin Neuf and the PCL as the association does appear on the Council's mailing list. It may be that the praxis for approval of ecumenical associations is different at the Apostolic See and at the individual dioceses. Two theories of praxis are addressed by the founder of Chemin Neuf. These points of view will be presented later in this section. The study will also explore the three dimensions: Religious Institute, Community, and Communion, of Chemin Neuf.

Chemin Neuf emerged from a prayer group of the Catholic Charismatic Renewal which had been meeting in Lyon, France since 1971. Seven persons who attended the group, after receiving the baptism in the spirit and dedicating themselves more deeply to their faith and to worship, began to live in community at Lyon. Presently there are approximately five hundred members of the Community and four thousand who are members of the Communion of Chemin Neuf[43]. When all who are associated with or serve the communion either in training or on mission are gathered their number reaches over six thousand[44]. Erection as a public association of the faithful in the Archdiocese of Lyon took place on 20 April 1984[45]. The association, ecumenical in both aim and membership, has a particular relationship with the Apostolic See as the Community's youth service (service jeunes) is recognized by the PCL (youth section) as an international movement[46]. A study of the ends, membership, and governance of the Community will shed more light on this association which has a relationship at both the diocesan and pontifical levels. Chemin Neuf is an example of a community which as a public association of the Christian faithful incorporates non-Catholic members.

+ Ends

Chemin Neuf describes itself as an apostolic community striving to serve mankind and the church. Evangelization, proclaiming the Good News that Jesus has come to proclaim liberty to captives, recovery of sight to the blind, and to set the oppressed free[47], is the foundation to the method of evangelization undertaken by the Community. The division which exists among Christians is viewed by the Chemin Neuf Community as the greatest obstacle to evangelization. It is for this reason that they feel called to work for unity; within the person, in couples, and in the Church of Christ. This evangelical call draws the Community toward ecumenism. This does not mean it abandons its Catholicity. Their spiritual life is influenced by such spiritual masters as St. Ignatius of Loyola and St. Theresa of Avila. They strive to live a spirituality that is both contemplative and active and involves them in charismatic renewal and Ignatian Spirituality[48].

What has been said so far about the ends of the Community center around evangelization and spirituality. These are complimented by the Community's fellowship and mission. Viewing itself as a small cell

---

[43] THE CHEMIN NEUF COMMUNITY AND COMMUNION, *Tychique*, 88, November 1990, 5.

[44] O. TURBAT, *Spending the World Youth Day*, 11.

[45] A. DECOURTRAY, *Decree of erection*, 20 April 1984.

[46] O. TURBAT, *Spending the World Youth Day*, 8.

[47] Lk 4,18.

[48] THE CHEMIN NEUF COMMUNITY AND COMMUNION, *Tychique*, 103, 3.

within the larger body of the church Chemin Neuf does not have an end in itself but takes strength from the Spirit of Jesus as He opens it to the dimensions of the Father's love. This fellowship that the Community shares among its members, only in and with the Trinity, leads it to its mission. Evangelization and service are the only way that the Community has meaning. This is the Community's mission. Community members believe that if they are together it is only because of Christ and the gospel[49]. The ends, rooted in the Catholic faith, are wide enough that they can be met by non-Catholics Christians as well.

+ Members

With its evangelical/ecumenical outlook the Community is open to non-Catholic members. Father Laurent Fabre, head of Chemin Neuf, shared his insights.

> In that which concerns the non-Catholic members we live exactly that which is said in canon 316 §1, §2. We know that this text may be interpreted in two different ways and we hope that the next code of canon law will take away a little more of the ambiguity[50].

He added two interpretations of the canons: The first is that non-Catholics may not canonically constitute part of a public association of the faithful; the second, that Protestants and Orthodox who are not in public opposition to the Catholic faith may be members of a public association of the faithful. He cites Msgr. Passicos, the vicar general of the Archdiocese of Paris and a consulter to the Pontifical Council for the Interpretation of Legislative Texts, who gave the interpretation of the texts to Fabre advising that the Community receive persons of other Christian churches as long these do not become the ones principally responsible for the Community[51]. This is amazing as the group has connections with the Holy See at the PCL and the PCPCU. The group is international but still has a decree of erection as a public association from, and therefore juridic personality within, the Archdiocese of Lyon. The Community says of itself:

---

[49] THE CHEMIN NEUF COMMUNITY AND COMMUNION *Tychique*, 103, 5.

[50] L. FABRE, *Personal letter*, 2 August 1997. «En ce qui concerne les membres non catholiques, nous vivons exactement ce qui dit Canon 316, §§ 1 et 2. Nous savons que ce texte peut être interprété de deux manières différentes et nous espérons que le prochain code de droit canonique lèvera un peu plus l'ambiguité».

[51] L. FABRE, *Personal letter*, 2 August 1997.

La Communauté du Chemin Neuf — communauté catholique à vocation oecuménique — accueille des membres d'autre églises (réformée, évangélique, orthodoxe). Plusieurs parmi nous exercent un ministère ordonné dans l'Eglise catholique (diacre, prêtre) ou de pasteur de l'Eglise Réformée[52].

It is clear that the Chemin Neuf Community has followed the less restrictive interpretation of c.316,§§1 and 2 *CIC* 83. The Community is a good example for this study. Besides having an ecumenical outlook non-Catholic Christians are able to be members of the Community. Found among the members there are even pastors of other faiths. This is with archdiocesan approval.

Chemin Neuf manifests itself in three different forms: the Community, the religious institute and the communion. The Community includes all members of Chemin Neuf. The Chemin Neuf Community is a Catholic Community with an ecumenical vocation[53]. Within the Community there is a religious institute for priests and laymen who have taken a vow of celibacy. Parallel to this but not forming a part of it is the communion which consists of persons who have specific apostolates. The religious institute, erected by the Archdiocese of Lyon, is at the center of the association. As the heart of the Community it strives to respect the various denominations of the members and at the same time to maintain its Catholic character.

The religious institute which is at the heart of the Community consists of Catholics[54] and brings with it the possibility for male members to enter religious life and priesthood within the Community of Chemin Neuf. At the same time it reinforces the specifically Catholic dimension of the canonical public association of the faithful which is Chemin Neuf while living an ecumenical lifestyle and accommodating non-Catholic Christian members. Non-Catholic Christians may freely join the Community and communion as members. However it can be said that they are not members with full rights because they are not to be in

---

52 THE CHEMIN NEUF COMMUNITY AND COMMUNION *Tychique*,103, (May 1993) supplement, 3. Translation from English edition. The Chemin Neuf Community, a Catholic Community with an ecumenical vocation, welcomes members of other churches (French Reformed, Evangelical, Lutheran, Orthodox...). Many of us are ordained ministers in the Catholic Church (deacon, priest) or in the Reformed Church (pastor).

53 THE CHEMIN NEUF COMMUNITY AND COMMUNION, *Tychique*, 103, 3. and L. FABRE, *Personal letter*, 2 August 1997.

54 Cf. Cc.597,§1; 645; and 663 *CIC* 83.

a position to be principally responsible for the Community. It would seem that the pastors of the French Reformed church would have the respect of their own denomination as well as others simply because of their position as a pastor. Even though every member may not enjoy the possibility of engaging every right, that is having full rights, they are still full members.

An example may help to make this point. Persons who are naturalized citizens of the United States of America, who are not citizens from birth but later receive citizenship, are full citizens. They are just as much citizens as persons who are born in the United States or are born abroad of parents who are citizens. Naturalized citizens are not able to serve the country as president, but still are full citizens. It may be said that the naturalized citizen does not have all of the rights which the citizen from birth has, but both are still full citizens of the United States. The same can be said concerning members of associations of the faithful. Non-Catholics are full members of Chemin Neuf even though they may not be able to participate in all of the rights of the association.

Members of the Community enjoy its structured lifestyle. In France and abroad, approximately forty fraternities of seven to twelve people are in existence. Fraternities are of two types: neighborhood fraternities which consist of persons living in the same area and household fraternities which consist of persons living in the same house. Presently, about fifty percent of Community members live in neighborhood fraternities and fifty percent live in household fraternities[55]. Scheduled prayer times exist for those living in the fraternities, persons are also expected to set aside time for personal prayer. Community prayer times include a daily office and a weekly fellowship meeting. Several times each week members share a meal with their fraternity. All Community members are expected to work. A few work full time for the Community, some for the Community missions (student hostels, Christian training centers, bookstores, and audiovisual operations) and others have jobs outside the Community. In the household fraternities the Community takes responsibility for the material needs of members while in the neighborhood fraternities persons are to be responsible for their own needs. Simplicity of life is a goal for all Community members. With prayer at the center of communal life members learn a deep trust in God. This trust in God is lived out by listening to one another,

---

[55] THE CHEMIN NEUF COMMUNITY AND COMMUNION, *Tychique*, 103, 4.

accepting truth about self and sharing of oneself. As persons trust in God they are led to reconciliation and deeper freedom in their lives. Each fraternity member is to have a spiritual guide with whom they meet regularly aiding them to live the challenges of the spiritual life. Several times a year the entire Community gathers. They reflect on where they have been and seek God's direction and celebrate together[56].

«The Communion of Chemin Neuf is an apostolic body which participates in the mission alongside the Community and has specific prayer and sharing requirements»[57]. Members of the communion participate in one of a number of special fraternities which have a life and mission separate from the Community. Participants in these fraternities work with married couples, young people, medical professionals, artists and other persons. Although remaining distinguished from the Community, communion members by their apostolic work have some kind of association with the Community. Those who are members of the fraternities may participate in the apostolate of the Community by committing themselves to the Chemin Neuf Communion. Through the communion a certain link is made between the fraternities and the Community. Members of the Community add to this link as they often work in the fraternities[58].

+ Governance

The Chemin Neuf Community has a canonical relationship with the Archdiocese of Lyon. However a certain rapport does exist with the Apostolic See. As has been seen presence on the mailing list of the PCL does not mean that the group or association is canonically recognized by the Council. In preparation for World Youth Day in Paris 14 - 24 August 1997 the Chemin Neuf Community, at the invitation of the PCL, organized two international youth gatherings at two of its community sites in France at Hautecombe and Tigery. Programs included a presentation on St. Thérère of Lisieux, world peace and ecumenism[59]. The work for World Youth Day brought the Community into a working relationship with the youth section of the PCL.

The Community and its religious institute have been charged with the care of at least five parishes in Europe and Africa. The archbishops

---

[56] THE CHEMIN NEUF COMMUNITY AND COMMUNION, *Tychique*, 103, 4-5.
[57] THE CHEMIN NEUF COMMUNITY AND COMMUNION, *Tychique*, 103, 6.
[58] THE CHEMIN NEUF COMMUNITY AND COMMUNION, *Tychique*, 103, 6.
[59] O. TURBAT, *Spending the World Youth Day,* 3, 5 and 6.

of Paris and Berlin, among others, have invited the Community to work in the churches of Saint-Denys-la-Chapelle and Sacred Heart respectively[60]. The Community continues to operate as an association of «diocesan right»[61]. This terminology balances with «pontifical right» which was used to describe the Work of Mary. The label does not limit the association to work only in its own diocese any more than for institutes of consecrated life with the same title are thus limited. Associations are always subject to the supervision of the bishop in whose diocese they reside or work[62].

+ Conclusion

Chemin Neuf is a powerful example for this study. Non-Catholic Christian members and an ecumenical vocation define it as an ecumenical association. As a canonical public association of the Christian faithful the Community, as an aggregate of persons or a corporation acts in the name of the Church. The founder and leader, Fabre, recognizes the different interpretations concerning non-Catholic membership in canonical associations. He sees a need for clarification, yet follows the law as it is written. The interpretation which he follows, like the canons[63], does not restrict non-Catholic Christian membership for those who have not publicly rejected the Catholic faith.

As the association is in the process of erecting a religious institute, the possibility for non-Catholic Christians to enter canonical associations comes into focus. Canons concerned with institutes make it clear that those desiring membership in an institute must be Roman Catholic. 1) Catholics with the right intention according to universal Church law and the law of the institute may be admitted[64]. 2) Baptismal and Confirmation certificates are to be presented. 3) Members of religious institutes are to receive Holy Eucharist daily if possible[65]. No such statements concerning Catholics or the need to receive the sacraments is present in the canons on associations.

The distinction between full members and members with full rights is important as it is impossible for a non-Catholic to have full rights in a Catholic organization. If non-Catholics were to have leadership of a

---

[60] O. Turbat, *Spending the World Youth Day*, 11.
[61] Cf. C. 594 *CIC* 83.
[62] C.305,§2 *CIC* 83.
[63] C.316,§§1 and 2, and c.307,§1 *CIC* 83.
[64] C.597,§1 *CIC* 83.
[65] C.663 *CIC* 83.

Catholic organization its direction would certainly come into question. Still without full rights non-Catholics can be full members. This is the praxis of the Archdiocese of Lyon and would seem to be acceptable to the dioceses which engage their services, including the Apostolic See. The question of praxis will be visited again later. Chemin Neuf has certainly brought an interesting situation to light which involves both the individual diocese and the Apostolic See.

1.2.2 Ecumenical Associations Comprised of Only Catholic Members that Participate in Interconfessional Communities

a) *The Catholic fraternity of Covenant Communities and Fellowships*

A unique situation is found in the Catholic Fraternity of Covenant Communities and Fellowships. Members of the Fraternity are not physical persons but associations describing themselves as either communities or fellowships. These associations are world wide, found in twelve countries, spanning four of the continents. With this international character from its beginning, it is appropriate that the Fraternity have a relationship with the Apostolic See by way of the PCL. Each member community and fellowship is also to have a relationship with their own diocesan bishop (stat. 3.1(a)).

+ Ends

The Catholic Fraternity of Covenant Communities and Fellowships will be studied because of its specifically ecumenical ends as well as its ecumenical dimension lived out through its constituent fellowships. Two of these fellowships will be studied along with the Fraternity itself. The ecumenical situation of the fellowships is rather novel, as they involve Catholic participation in an ecumenical community. The ecumenical involvement on the part of the Fraternity itself, as well as the fellowships, allows them to fit into the «category of ecumenical associations». As associations of the Christian faithful the member communities and fellowships of the Fraternity strive to foster a more perfect life, promote public worship or Christian teaching or undertake other works of the apostolate[66]. Answering the call of the «Directory for the Application of Principles and Norms on Ecumenism»[67] the Fraternity has ecumenism among its ends. The Fraternity is to

---

[66] C.298,§1 *CIC* 83.
[67] Cf. ED93, 30.

foster both an authentic ecumenism in the hope of perfect unity and form member communities of the Fraternity in ecumenism in accordance with the teachings, orientations and norms of the Catholic Church (*UR* 8); and (stat. 1.6(i))

encourage its member communities to participate in spiritual ecumenism (*UR* 8) and other ecumenical activities, when circumstances permit, under the guidance of the local Church[68]. Ecumenical activities of an international nature will proceed only after consultation with the PCL (1.6(j)).

The statutes themselves cite *UR* and the document on ecumenical collaboration (1975) published by the *quondam* (at one time) Secretariat for Promoting Christian Unity. The Fraternity follows the magisterial teaching of the Church found in *UR* 8 which all individual members and associations within the Church are challenged to follow. Comments on the development of the Fraternity under the heading «Members» will clarify their ecumenical tendencies. The fellowships which are a part of the Fraternity fit into the broad understanding of ecumenical associations. Because the fellowships fit the definition, the Fraternity of which they are constitutive also is considered ecumenical.

+ Members

The Fraternity was formed with the goal of creating a body whose member communities and fellowships would be Catholic. Church identity was important to a number of Catholic groups which were members of the International Brotherhood of Communities. The Brotherhood was an ecumenical grouping of communities which included a large Catholic membership[69]. The Fraternity developed as an organization which would give a Catholic foundation to the identity of the International Brotherhood of Communities. A formal link between the communities and the Catholic Church was also to be formed[70]. The

---

[68] The statutes cited the document: Secretariat for Promoting Christian Unity, *Ecumenical Collaboration at the Regional, National and Local Levels*, Città del Vaticano 1975, sections 3 and 7.

[69] In the appendix to the 1990 Statutes of the Catholic Fraternity of Covenant Communities and Fellowships the Charter of the International Brotherhood of Communities states, «The International Brotherhood of Communities (IBOC) is an Association of charismatic communities. These communities are equal, autonomous, independent and joined together by a bond of charity».

[70] Information can be found at: http://ourworld.compuserve.com/homepages/emmcovcom/ When information is available through the internet it is listed in the footnotes for the convenience of the reader. The statutes of the communities which

actual status of the Fraternity will be considered after the types of members are presented. The reason for different types of members is so that groups who had strong ties with Protestant/interdenominational communities could retain these.

The covenant communities are described in the statutes:

> In various places throughout the world, members of this one, holy, catholic and apostolic Church have expressed their desire to support one another in following Christ and in responding to His call by forming covenant communities. A covenant is a formal commitment to enter into relationship with members of a community and to participate in their lifestyle and mission. At the heart of such a commitment is the desire to grow in holiness and to be involved in apostolic work in service to the Church's mission (stat. 1.3).

These Catholic communities make up close to ninety percent of the Fraternity with the remainder made up of fellowships. The fellowships are defined as:

> a constituted group of Catholics who live a covenant community lifestyle and maintain a bond of charity, prayer and witness with Christians or groups of Christians belonging to other confessions within a broader ecumenical community (stat. 1.3; fn. 6).

Fellowships are of a special interest as they participate in an ecumenical situation different from those previously discussed in which non-Catholics participate to some degree in a Catholic association.

Even the Fraternity itself is a special situation as its members are not so much physical persons as they are communities and fellowships, or corporate persons. The corporate persons are to be Catholic (stat. 1.5; fn. 9) while having an ecumenical outlook.

+ Governance

External Governance

The Catholic Fraternity of Covenant Communities and Fellowships received status as a private association of the Christian faithful, of pontifical right, endowed with juridical personality by decree on 30 November 1990. The statutes were approved on an *ad experimentum* basis for five years[71]. With completion of the trial period the statutes

---

are the subject of this study have been received from the Associations themselves or their constituents.

[71] PONTIFICIUM CONSILIUM PRO LAICIS, 1585/90/S-61/B-50, Città del Vaticano.

were confirmed on 30 November 1995[72]. The relationship is ongoing since «The Fraternity maintains relations of faithful listening, dialogue and collaboration with the Holy See, particularly the PCL» (stat. 4.1).

The relationship between the Fraternity and the Apostolic See is also maintained by the ruling body of the Fraternity. 1) A spiritual advisor takes part in meetings of the governing bodies of the Fraternity. He is appointed by the PCL from a list of three candidates presented by the executive committee of the Fraternity (stat. 6.1) 2) The president of the council of the Fraternity is to act as liaison with the PCL. (stat. 5.5(b)) These are two of the ways in which external governance plays a role in the relationship between the Fraternity and the Apostolic See. Governance either external or internal does not involve the particular ecumenical aspect of the Fraternity which is found in the fellowships. Still the position of the Fraternity in relation to the Apostolic See as a private juridical person of pontifical right clearly shows the respect and position of the ecumenical association in the eyes of the Roman Catholic Church.

Internal Governance

The Fraternity itself is not an ecumenical body. Non-Catholics communities are not a part of it. If any ecumenical involvement is to take place this will be discussed by the council of the Fraternity.

> The Council provides a means by which member communities and fellowships may formulate their ideas, plans and concerns and be involved in decision making, facilitating and implementing the living out of the aims and objectives of the Fraternity (stat. 5.3).

One representative from each community or fellowship makes up the council which meets at least every other year. A non-voting consultant may accompany the representative to meetings.

An executive committee to the counsel may have up to two representatives from each of the continents. Other regions and realities may be represented as deemed necessary by the council (stat. 5.2). The executive committee ensures the observance of the statutes, cares for admission requests, draws up and implements the Fraternity's plan of activities and cares for relations with other organizations (stat. 5.4). Members of the executive committee are elected as president, vice-president, treasurer and secretary. These serve both the executive committee and the council.

---

[72] PONTIFICIUM CONSILIUM PRO LAICIS, 1266/95/S-61/B-53, Città del Vaticano.

+ Conclusion

The Fraternity, by way of its governance and members, ought to be able to achieve its ends. Its ecumenical goals are especially addressed through the Catholic fellowships which are full members of the Fraternity while also holding full membership in another community which is ecumenical. Two of the constituent fellowships will be studied.

b) *The Alleluia Catholic Fellowship*

The Alleluia Catholic Fellowship is a member of the Catholic Fraternity of Charismatic Covenant Communities and Fellowships. It is also a member of the Alleluia Community, an ecumenical Christian community. After considering its unique ecumenical situation as a member of the Alleluia Community, the ends, members, rights and duties and governance will be reviewed. Ecumenical involvement in these areas, as always, will be the goal of this investigation.

+ Link with the Alleluia Community

To consider only the relationship between the Fellowship and the competent Church authority which recognizes or approves it would be to leave out an important link in the life of the Fellowship and its members. The bond with other Christians, who may belong to Fellowships of their own, in the context of a larger Christian community is at the heart of the ecumenical experience of the Catholic Fellowship. This interaction which takes place within the formal link between the ecumenical Christian Community and the Catholic Fellowship is what in fact provides for the definition of the Fellowship as an ecumenical association of the faithful. The following is a description of Christian community as outlined by the Alleluia Community.

A Christian community exists when people who have accepted Jesus Christ as their Lord and Savior join together in a very committed way. They place above other values their mutual faith in Jesus Christ and their common life in supporting and nurturing Christian values and ideals. It involves committing their whole lives and resources to one another to carry out their common mission. It means accepting whatever is necessary to live in a Godly way, including such things as mutual correction, accountability and authority to bring order to their common life and mission. Christian community can only be sustained where everyone seeks to place

God first in every area of their lives and where the «Golden Rule» (loving your neighbor as yourself) is put into practice by all on a daily basis[73].

This description of the life in which the members of the Alleluia Catholic Fellowship participate involves basic Christian values in which all baptized Christians can participate. While they strive to live this life along with other Christians the relationship is truly ecumenical. The covenant and descriptions of the Community are important to envision the call to which these Catholic members of Alleluia are called. The Community itself has a number of ellowships. Members include a number of Protestant denominations including United Methodist, Southern Baptist, Episcopal, Church of Christ, Pentecostal, Anglican, Presbyterian, Church of God, and Independent Charismatic. Some of these have their own denominational fellowships, but this is not required. All are to be faithful to their own churches or ecclesial communities and their doctrines, while at the same time striving for ecumenical unity within Alleluia[74]. All are called to live *communicatio in spiritualibus*.

+ Ends

Even without non-Catholic members, the Alleluia Catholic Fellowship has ecumenical priorities woven into its statutes. The link with the Alleluia Community is certainly supported by the statutes as are the relations with the diocesan bishop and the Apostolic See through the Fraternity.

The manner in which the statutes were written at times combines governance and the ends and membership. These will be separated for the sake of organization. The statutes themselves make numerous references to ecumenism and at the same time to the diocesan bishop.

Besides living out c.298,§1 *CIC* 83 the nature of the Fellowship includes relating, first, to other Catholic groups[75] — an obvious reference to the Fraternity — and, second, to Protestant bodies and groups — an obvious reference to the Alleluia Community (stat. I.A.3.4). The statutes state that one of the purposes of the Fellowship is:

---

[73] ALLELUIA COMMUNITY, *Frequently Asked Questions (FAQs)*, http://www.csra. net/alleluia/

[74] ALLELUIA COMMUNITY, *Alleluia Protestant Fellowships*, http://www.csra.net/ alleluia/

[75] C.298,§2 *CIC* 83.

To form members of the Fellowship in the mind of the Church regarding ecumenism with a view to possible collaborations with non-Catholics in grass roots ecumenism if local circumstances permit. This collaboration would be primarily to make the work of ecumenism more effective (*Ecumenical Collaboration at the Regional, National, and Local Levels* [7] and *Evangelii Nuntiandi* [77]). (Alleluia Community, as an ecumenical body, provides a practical living out of this grass roots ecumenism envisioned above) (stat. I.B.4).

The ends of the Fellowship are without a doubt ecumenical even if only Catholics can be members. It is the link with the Alleluia Community by the Alleluia Catholic Fellowship which solidifies the ecumenical dimension recognized here. This continues to be reinforced throughout the statutes.

+ Members

«Membership in the Fellowship is open to baptized Roman Catholics who are active members of the Alleluia Community. Individuals must seek membership which must be confirmed by the moderator of the Fellowship» (stat. II.A). The statutes are very clear about the fact that only baptized Roman Catholics who are also members of the Alleluia Community may be members. This clarity is helpful when considering the possibility of inscribing non-Catholics as members of associations of the faithful. Here the importance of clearly stating in the statutes who are and who are not to be admitted to membership in a particular association is underlined. This is not always clear in the statutes of some associations and can lead to confusion.

Begun in 1973, the Alleluia Community in general and the Catholic members in particular have had time to develop their organization to the point that they are able to make a very clear presentation of themselves. Membership in the Fellowship is open to all Catholics. Three levels of membership are noted, 1) full membership, 2) associate membership, and 3) underway membership. The underway or prospective members pass through a period of formation where they learn about Community life and follow courses offered in the Fellowship formation program. After this period of formation persons become full members by making a personal commitment in writing and proclaiming the commitment publicly at a gathering of the Fellowship. Associate members of the Catholic Fellowship and Christian Community are persons not able to make a full commitment for some reason. They participate in the life of the Fellowship and Community as possible. Membership in the Fellowship does not involve taking vows (stat. II.C;

D; G). Even though non-Catholics are not members of the Fellowship, they are members of the ecumenical Alleluia Community.

Membership in the Fellowship and Community parallel one another. Members of the Fellowship who are full members, associate members or underway members are also members of the Alleluia Community. Members hold the same status in both the Fellowship and the Community. To become a member of the Fellowship one must be an active member of the Community. The taking of vows is not involved in membership. A personal commitment is made and proclaimed vocally at a gathering of the Fellowship, which simultaneously affects membership in both the Fellowship and the Community.

At the other end of the spectrum from entering into the Fellowship is departure. If someone is dismissed from the Community they are automatically dismissed from the Fellowship. Repeated violation of Christian doctrine or morality which involves an unrepentant offender, public dissent from Church teaching, or non-compliance with the requirements for membership in the Fellowship are all reasons for loss of membership in the Fellowship and Community. After a waiting period a terminated member may have recourse to the diocesan bishop. (stat. II.H) The connection between the Fellowship and the Community are very close. The parallel situation for members of the Fellowship certainly confirm its ecumenical situation.

+ Rights and Duties

The rights and duties which one enjoys as a member of the Fellowship include all rights and duties of a member of the Alleluia Community. Persons are able to participate in the activities of both the Community and Fellowship. Prayer for each other and acceptance of legitimate authority in both the Fellowship and Community are duties of membership. All are to live according to the Community covenant and the statutes of the Fellowship. Prolonged and insistent failure to do so can lead to termination from the Fellowship and Community (cf. stat. II.H).

+ Governance

External Governance

The ecumenical history of the Alleluia Community[76] and the desire of the Catholic members to have a closer relationship with the compe-

---

[76] Members of the Alleluia Community accept responsibility for Community order and recognize the headship of the coordinators and agree to obey correct and pray

tent authority within the Roman Catholic Church have lead the way to a succinct and well-established relationship with the local bishop. The statutes further clarify this relationship: Of the seven sections which make up the Alleluia Catholic Fellowship Statutes the diocesan bishop is mentioned in each one; and in five sections he is mentioned more than once. This only manifests the desire of the Fellowship, like the Catholic Fraternity of Charismatic Covenant Communities and Fellowships of which it is a member, to develop their own Catholic identity and to form a closer bond with the hierarchy of the Roman Catholic Church.

As the Fellowship strives to live out its ends it stays in close contact with the local bishop. The liturgical and sacramental needs of the members are most often taken care of by the local parish; however, the bishop is consulted at times when particular needs are present (stat. I.B.6). In accord with c.755,§2 *CIC* 83 the Fellowship engages in «informal and formal ecumenical contacts and relationships with Protestant bodies and groups when» approved by the diocesan bishop» (stat. I.A.4). Further development is envisioned for the future (cf. stat. V.F). The stable relationship between the Alleluia Catholic Fellowship and the Alleluia Community is clearly approved by the bishop. Other ecumenical endeavors or projects are to be presented for the bishop's approval before such activities take place. Outside the ecumenical sphere, the Fellowship commits itself to supporting diocesan and parochial activities (stat. I.B.5).

Supporting and reinforcing this relationship with the local hierarchy is the concern of the section of the statutes which specifically describes the Fellowship's relation with the diocesan bishop. The Alleluia Catholic Fellowship invites the bishop or his delegate to visit and experience the life into which the members have entered (stat. VI.D)[77]. At the same time the Fellowship periodically reports developments in its life to the diocesan bishop (stat. VI.C). These general guidelines set up a praxis of open lines of communication between the bishop and the Fellowship and in particular its ecumenical agenda.

---

for them. (Alleluia Community, *Alleluia Community Covenant*, (http://www.csra.net/alleluia/):1, 3). Leadership positions in the Alleluia Community are held by both men and women. «The government of the Community is headed by three Elders and a Governmental Council. In addition, there are councils of men and women who oversee particular groupings of people as well as the Alleluia School, Outreach and the Pastoral and Formation Center». (ALLELUIA COMMUNITY, *Frequently asked Questions*, (http://www.csra.net/alleluia/) 8).

[77] C.305,§1 *CIC* 83.

Spiritual formation which takes place within the Fellowship is to have the approval of the bishop. The elders, who govern the Fellowship, in consultation with the diocesan bishop choose a spiritual director for the Fellowship (stat. III.D)[78]. The same is true for the moderator who acts as liaison in relations between the Fellowship and the bishop, and as the «stand-up leader of the Fellowship at gatherings» (stat. IV.A.5). A basic course in Catholic doctrine is given to new members. The outline used in the course is developed in consultation with the bishop (stat. III.B).

Through the choice of spiritual director and syllabus for the course in Catholic doctrine the bishop is able to have his finger on the implementation of the formation of Alleluia Catholic Fellowship members.

Other areas of the life of the Fellowship in which the bishop is involved by way of governance are membership and the governance of the Fellowship itself. These will be treated in the next section. To complete the well-rounded relationship between the Bishop of Savannah and the Alleluia Fellowship it is noted that the Fellowship may be dissolved by the elders only after consultation with the diocesan bishop (stat. VII.A). The importance of the ecclesiastical authority in the life of the Fellowship is reinforced by the last statute. «The Alleluia Catholic Fellowship is recognized in the Diocese of Savannah and may not function in any other diocese without the recognition of the competent authority» (stat. VII.C). This requirement only continues to reinforce the positive relationship between the Fellowship and the competent Church authority and respect for the rule of its law.

Internal Governance

Internal governance in the Alleluia Catholic Fellowship is simple. The organization consists of a moderator and elders. The internal governance of the Fellowship is related to that of the Community.

If a Catholic is appointed an elder to the Community, he is automatically an elder of the Catholic Fellowship. The elder's role in the Fellowship is approved by the diocesan bishop (stat. IV.A.2). Other internal governance which includes the diocesan bishop and is also ecumenical involves the Catholic elders. The removal of an elder of the Fellowship by the Body of Elders needs the consultation of the diocesan bishop before a removal can take place (stat. IV.A.4). The removal of a Catholic elder needs previous consultation with the bishop while

---

[78] C.324,§2 *CIC* 83.

removal of a Catholic member does not. The diocesan bishop is also to be consulted before an elder is appointed moderator of the Fellowship, the highest position in the association (stat. IV.A.5). The importance of an ecumenical presence and the role of the bishop are both manifest throughout the statutes of the Fellowship.

+ Conclusion

The Alleluia Catholic Fellowship is a fine example of a canonically recognized association of the Christian faithful. It has recognition at the Apostolic See[79] as well as in the Diocese of Savannah, where its headquarters are located. The ends of the Alleluia Catholic Fellowship can be met through its neighborhood/Community lifestyle.

The relationship between the Alleluia Catholic Fellowship and their bishop is well founded. Ecumenical interaction, support of diocesan activities, invitation to the bishop or his delegate to visit the Fellowship, periodic reports on development in the Fellowship and his approval of the instruments used for spiritual formation are some of the modes identified and studied regarding the Fellowship's relation with its bishop. Open channels of communication and checks and balances as found in the statutes of the Alleluia Catholic Fellowship are an excellent example of a structure which is a stepping stone to good relations between a bishop and an association of the Christian faithful. The ecumenical involvement of the Fellowship warrants this relationship. An association with non-Catholics would do well to follow suit.

c) *Lamb of God Catholic Fellowship*

The Lamb of God Catholic Fellowship, approved in the Diocese of Christchurch in New Zealand, fits the broad understanding of the definition of ecumenical associations. It is the promised second fellowship of the Catholic Fraternity of Charismatic Covenant Communities to be studied. The Lamb of God Catholic Fellowship is a constituent of the Fraternity and at the same time the Lamb of God Covenant Community, an ecumenical Christian community. The membership of the Fel-

---

[79] The Alleluia Catholic Fellowship is recognized by the Apostolic See as it is a member of the Catholic Fraternity of Charismatic Covenant Communities and Fellowships. As studied above in Chapter II, section 1.2.2.a the Fraternity is an international private Association of the faithful, recognized by the PCL. As a member Association of the Fraternity the Alleluia Catholic Fellowship is recognized by the Apostolic See.

lowship in the larger ecumenical Christian covenant Community places it into the category, «ecumenical associations» as defined by this dissertation. The Fellowship is a canonical association of the Christian faithful as it is approved by the bishop in the diocese of Christchurch[80] as well as three other dioceses in New Zealand[81] where branches of the Fellowship and Community are located. Since there are six dioceses in the country, the Fellowship is canonically recognized in more than sixty percent of New Zealand. The history and statutes of the Catholic Fellowship witness to the Lamb of God as an ecumenical association of the Christian faithful.

Formed in 1979, the Lamb of God Covenant Community is committed to advancing ecumenism by following the teaching and principles of the Roman Catholic Church. Throughout its history the Community has emphasized the charismatic gifts, Christ at the heart of the life of members, support of families and singles in living their Christian vocation and bringing persons of all ages and situations together. (stat. Introduction) The historical context is certainly one in which *communicatio in spiritualibus* is able to thrive.

By adopting a statement of nature in 1981, it was made clear that «the Community is not a church and requires its members to be practicing Christians in their own denominations» (stat. Introduction). This point of the statement of nature recognizes that the Community is not meant to fulfill all of the spiritual needs of all of its members. They are to be rooted in their own churches or ecclesial communities.

In 1983 an informal fellowship was formed at Christchurch where a branch of the Community was located. Its aims were instruction in the Catholic faith and aid to Catholics who have been away from the Church or persons with no Church allegiance. The Fellowship aids Catholics in living out their identity. The full Catholic practice of their faith is a goal of the Fellowship. Absolute truthfulness is the first prerequisite of any genuine ecumenical undertaking according to the statutes of the Fellowship (stat. Introduction). This strong statement rein-

---

[80] B. MEEKING, *Decree* [giving approval to the Lamb of God Catholic Fellowship and its statutes], 11 August 1989.

[81] D. BROWNE, *Decree* [giving permission for the Lamb of God Catholic Fellowship to function as an approved body under its statutes] (15 February 1996). P. DUNN, *Decree* [formally recognizing the Lamb of God Catholic Fellowship as a private Association of the Christian faithful] (29 November 1996). T. WILLIAMS, *Decree* [granting approval to Lamb of God Community to develop Lamb of God Fellowship according to statutes], (19 November 1990).

forces the forthrightness of the Fellowship and the authentic ecumenism undertaken by the whole Community. No false irenicism will be able to creep into the relations between members of the various denominations of the Community.

Since 1980 the Community has worked internationally with a number of groups and other covenant communities. The fruit of this work was the development of the International Brotherhood of Communities which in turn led to the development of the Catholic Fraternity of Charismatic Covenant Communities and Fellowships. The Lamb of God Catholic Fellowship is a founding member of the Fraternity and has a representative on the Fraternity's council.

The history of the Fellowship reached a high point when its statutes were approved by the Bishop of Christchurch in 1989. The statutes manifest the developing history of the Fellowship in particular as well as the covenant Community. The status as a private association of the faithful and membership in the Fraternity are the results of a Catholic group desiring to live «life in the spirit» and to be at one with their Church.

+ Ends

The Fellowship strives to:

a. Help its members live a fervent Christian life and witness in the ordinary situations of their lives, families and occupations,
b. To carry out a work of direct evangelism particularly in de-Christianized environments.
c. To form members of the Fellowship in the mind of the Church regarding ecumenism.
d. To be of service and to work in harmony with the overall pastoral plan of the Diocese, contributing to the animation of diocesan and parochial activities where appropriate (stat. art. (1) 4.a).

This first article of the statutes concerning the nature and purpose of the Lamb of God Fellowship directs members to the ends of Christian lifestyle, evangelism, ecumenism, and cooperation with the pastoral plan of the diocese and parochial activities. This private association of the faithful, as a member of the Fraternity, also has the ends of the Fraternity as its own. The ecumenical ends of the Catholic Fellowship are expressed in the larger Lamb of God Covenant Community where each member is to live out the faith of his own denomination. Catholics do this in the Lamb of God Catholic Fellowship, whose statutes call members to practice their Catholic faith to the fullest in submission to the teaching authority of the Church (stat. art. (3) 1).

+ Members

Membership in the Lamb of God Catholic Fellowship includes: only Catholics, a parallel membership in both the Covenant Community and the Fellowship, a personal commitment and a termination policy. The strength of the members as true followers of the Roman Catholic faith is important to the life of the Catholic Fellowship in relation to the ecumenical covenant Community. To be truly ecumenical, Catholics must be strong in their own faith, live a sacramental life and be docile to Church teaching, and at the same time be respectful of the beliefs of others.

Members of the Catholic Fellowship are *de facto* members of the larger Community. After passing through the entrance process, which includes attending courses and groups of formation, persons become full members after demonstrating that they can and want to live the life of the Fellowship. To quote the statutes, «Members will need to have completed teaching courses, retreats and be able to demonstrate an active prayer and sacramental life» (stat. art. (3) 3). The link between the Fellowship members and the Church is summarized in the section of the statutes which covers nature and purpose.

> Its membership may consist of baptized persons, who are fully in communion with the Roman Catholic Church, and are joined with Christ in visible structure by the bonds of profession of faith, of the sacraments and its ecclesiastical governance (stat. art. (1) 3).

The life to which the members are called is much more involved than for example Magnificat, a women's group in the United States which asks members to agree with the aims of the association and to pray for its intentions[82]. This can be done by women without leaving their homes. Lamb of God is a bit more involved.

The Fellowship and Community require their members to make a personal public commitment. No taking of any type of vows is involved (stat. art. (3) 4). Members are always free to leave the Fellowship and under certain circumstances may be asked to leave.

There is a process involved in exiting which respects the members, the Fellowship, and the commitment that has been made. As non-

---

[82] Cf. Chapter II, section 1.3.1.b.

Catholics are not members of the Fellowship it is the membership of Catholics in both the Lamb of God Fellowship and the Lamb of God Ecumenical Christian Community, of which it is a part, which makes the Fellowship fit into the category of ecumenical associations.

+ Rights and Duties

The rights and duties which the Lamb of God Catholic Fellowship enjoys are both specifically Catholic and ecumenical. Those specifically Catholic involve formation in the Fellowship and the Community while rights and duties touching the sphere of ecumenism involve activities with the Lamb of God Community as well as other ecumenical groups. The rights and duties aid the Fellowship in its Catholic identity as well as its ecumenical undertakings.

The Catholics of the Fellowship have the right to formation in Catholic beliefs and practices as provided by the Fellowship. Included in the formation is study of Catholic doctrine and practical Christian living. At times the Fellowship gathers for the celebration of Mass, usually members would attend in their own parishes. The basic course and ongoing teachings for the newcomers are also available to members. Members of the Fellowship gather for these times of learning and worship (stat. art. (4) 1-4).

Catholic members of the Fellowship are automatically members of the Community. With this right comes the duty to join in Community wide gatherings which the statutes guarantee will not hinder the belief of Catholic members. The beliefs of all the denominations are to be respected.

The Catholic Fellowship will seek relationships with other similar groups around the world. This is most obviously manifest by the participation of the Fellowship in the Fraternity. The Fellowship has the right to be respected by the non-Catholic groups with which it interacts.

> Such relationships are only entered into when the non-Catholic leadership with whom collaboration is envisioned is able to fully accept the necessity of Catholics to be faithful to the governance, teaching, worship and sacramental life of the Roman Catholic Church (stat. art. (6) 3).

Such a statement builds mutual respect and helps to alleviate false irenicism which undermines any true ecumenism. The rights and duties included in the statutes of the Fellowship lead to the acceptable ecumenical cooperation with the Community of which the Fellowship is a part. Once again the ecumenical character of the Fellowship is supported.

+ Governance

External Governance

External governance concerns the relationship between the association and the competent authority, in the case of Lamb of God Catholic Fellowship the local ordinary or bishop. Concerning external governance, the statutes address the relationship between Church hierarchy and the Fellowship itself, ecumenical relations, as well as approval of the curriculum for teaching and formation of Fellowship members. Since the bishops who have given approbation to the Fellowship know that it is part of a larger ecumenical community, the fact of this ecumenical involvement on the part of the Fellowship is always apparent.

According to c.305,§1, the Fellowship is subject to the supervision of competent ecclesiastical authority. The statutes require that the local ordinary will be invited to visit the Fellowship on an ongoing basis to have a first hand experience of the life of the Fellowship (stat. art. (7) 3). Elders of the Fellowship will report annually to the local ordinary informing him of the activities of the Fellowship and Community. Included in this report is to be information covering development in the areas of: 1) ecumenical activity, 2) teaching, 3) apostolic works and 4) worship (stat. art. (7) 2). The place of the bishop in both the ecumenical affairs and associations in his diocese is defined in this section of the statutes. He is not only to be informed of the situation of the Fellowship but also the Community for which he has some concern as the Catholic Fellowship takes part in its activities. The statutes are specific in recognizing four areas of interest which are to be reported to the bishop. These are listed directly after the Community is mentioned; therefore, the activities of the overall Community, in which members of the Fellowship may participate, are a part of the annual report. The statutes support the opportunity for the local ordinary to get to know the Fellowship and Community and their works. As an introduction to this section covering the relationship between the Fellowship and the diocese, the statutes read that the Fellowship is under the spiritual authority of the bishop of the diocese (stat. art. (7) 1). This particular statute acts as a summary statement for the position in which the Fellowship views its bishop.

Two important areas which affect the day to day life of the Fellowship are the teachings offered to members and the elders who serve as leaders of the Fellowship. Both of these involve governance on the part of the local ordinary. The curriculum, including teaching material and its presentation, is under the authority of the bishop or his representative (stat. art. (4) 5). The group of Catholic elders who govern the Fellowship as well as a presiding elder are all subject to the approval of the local ordinary. The statutes carefully spell out the bishop's position in these matters. He has the right of veto when a person is discerned for the position of elder. He may also demand the removal of an elder. The elder who is chosen to preside must have the bishop's approval (stat. art. (5) 5-6). Besides these areas the bishop also is consulted on any changes or developments not broadly provided for in the statutes (stat. art. (5) 4). With the pastoral care of the bishop in curriculum, leadership and new developments the Fellowship is in a good position to live out its ends in the most beneficial way possible.

The ecumenical relationships into which the Fellowship enters are mentioned numerous times in the statutes. The role of the local ordinary is also frequently mentioned. It seems evident that the bishop has a part in the ecumenical role of the Fellowship since he is the spiritual authority and has a supervisory role over the group. In fact the specific role of the bishop is stated where the statutes call the Fellowship to promote ecumenism according to the teachings of the Church and under the guidance of the local ordinary (stat. art. (6) 1).

Governance is important to the life of the Fellowship. To have a relationship with the larger ecumenical Community of which it is a part and also its own bishops put it into a position to be able to meet the call for associations to foster a more perfect life and other works of the apostolate[83]. This consideration of the external governance of the Lamb of God Catholic Fellowship reinforces its statutes as fitting into the category of ecumenical association.

Internal Governance

Areas specifically involving the internal governance of the Community which have not already been covered under other headings are the process of choosing elders, their role, significant developments and financial responsibilities. Elders who will serve the Fellowship are discerned by the ecumenical covenant Community, who submit names of possible future leaders; the persons themselves, considering family and work obligations; and those serving as elders at the present time. When these three sources agree a new elder is chosen. The process is guided by the body of elders of the covenant Community; it is their responsi-

---

[83] C.298,§1 *CIC* 83.

bility to choose a new elder (stat. art. (5) 2). This area of internal governance involves not only the Fellowship but the whole Community. Even though the bishop has the power to veto the choice of catholic elders to the Fellowship it is the ecumenical Community and its elders which discerns who will be chosen. This process for choosing the leadership of the Fellowship involving any number of persons from different religions adds to the reasons for which the Fellowship can fit the wide understanding of the definition of ecumenical associations.

It is the body of elders of the Community who review the service of the elders in their capacity of service to the Community (stat. art. (5) 3). It is clear that when the statutes speak of the body of elders they refer to the Community elders of which the Catholic elders are members. When the statutes refer specifically to the Catholic elders or the elders of the Fellowship they are named in this manner. It is possible that Catholics may serve as elders of the Community but not of the Fellowship. All Catholic elders of the Community are not automatically elders of the Fellowship (cf. stat. art. (5) 1). Again the situation of Catholic elders in the Community who are members of the Fellowship as the two bodies are linked adds to the ecumenical situation of the Fellowship.

Changes in the organization and structure of the life of the Fellowship are possible. As stated earlier when these are significant and are not broadly provided for in the statutes, the bishop is to be consulted and his approval is needed. The internal governance of the Fellowship is also involved as these changes require the consultation and assent of the publicly committed members of the Fellowship.

The last area of internal governance to be considered is finances. As the Catholic Fellowship is a part of the overall Community whose members are also members of the Community one would imagine that certain financial responsibilities exist for all members of the Community. Still the Fellowship has established finances independent of the Community (stat. art. (8) 1). A portion of any excess income is to be used as a gift for diocesan needs (stat. art. (8) 2). The point here is the separate finances for the Lamb of God Catholic Fellowship. Even though the Fellowship and Community share activities this is one of the areas where the Fellowship separates itself.

+ Conclusion

With its relationship to the Lamb of God Covenant Community the Lamb of God Catholic Fellowship certainly fits into the category of ecumenical associations. It is ecumenically involved in its ends, membership (to the Community), rights and duties, and governance. Along with the Alleluia Fellowship it makes a good example of associations which may not have non-Catholic members but are intensely involved ecumenically. Without strictly fitting the definition for ecumenical associations according to *ChL* 31 the Catholic Fellowships and the Catholic Fraternity of Charismatic Covenant Communities certainly fit a broad understanding of the term.

1.2.3 Interconfessional Communities

a) *L'Arche*

Jean Vanier founded l'Arche in 1964 when, with the cooperation of Father Thomas Philippe, he took up residence with two mentally handicapped men. This first community was founded in France at Trosly-Breuil. From that time, the community has grown and others have emerged. Today there are some one hundred l'Arche communities and over one thousand Faith and Light communities worldwide[84].

+ Ends

The vision and inspiration of l'Arche are simple: mentally handicapped persons and those who come to live with them make their home in clusters of homes in a local area. Workshops and schools may be a part of the community living situation. In the words of the founder, «In l'Arche we are discovering work, prayer, forgiveness and celebration; we minister to each other and celebrate our being bonded together, our oneness»[85].

+ Members

In many ways l'Arche started out as a Catholic organization. However, after the first, other communities were soon founded by Catholics and non-Catholics alike. Catholics and non-Catholics with mental

---

[84] J. VANIER, *Jesus the Gift of Life*, 7. Faith and Light are communities made up of persons who have family members or friends with a mental handicap. The group began in 1971 and is a sister group to L'Arche. Members of the communities do not live together as in the L'Arche Communities. They do meet periodically, building bonds of support and love, in the spirit of the gospels. In 1994 there were one thousand one hundred Faith and Light communities in sixty-four countries of the world.

[85] J. VANIER, *Jesus the Gift of Life*, 8.

handicaps live in community with those who serve them. Steve and Ann Newroth, members of the Anglican Church of Canada, founded the l'Arche community of Daybreak near Toronto in 1969. They were joined by Catholics, members of the United Church of Canada, and other churches of the reformed tradition. The first community in India was founded in 1970 by Gabrielle Einsle at Bangalore. She, a Roman Catholic, lived with mentally handicapped Indians who were Hindu[86]. So almost from the beginning l'Arche was an ecumenical, interreligious and interconfessional organization.

The organizational situation of l'Arche is different from communities or movements seeking recognition as private or public associations of the faithful. The ecumenical procedure of the l'Arche community has been to give members of each faith or denomination equal place and time. The praxis of the Apostolic See has been to allow only Catholics to be members with «full rights»; other participants are inscribed in some other manner. All persons seeking God may participate in l'Arche and Faith and Light as members with full rights. That individual members have relations with some faith is important; time is spent daily in prayer in the communities. With some desire for the spiritual mentally handicapped persons and co-workers make up the community of l'Arche. The handicapped residents of the l'Arche communities may be Catholic or non-Catholic. The co-workers who serve them are also Catholic or non-Catholic. A distinction is not made between religions as in Focolare where non-Catholic Christians are associates and non-Christians participate as collaborators.

+ Rights and Duties

Fundamentally the experience of living in a l'Arche community has been spiritually developmental for J. Vanier himself. Living with persons that have mental handicaps which are sometimes severe reveals the weakness and meaning of human flesh. The meaning of the Word made flesh and His path into weakness and vulnerability is also manifest.[87] The purpose of living in community is not just to be together but to move beyond oneself for the others[88]. Spiritual benefits are the real rights and duties of living in community with l'Arche. The ecumenical/interreligious aspect of the community gives participants a real op-

---

[86] T. VANIER, *One Bread, One Body*, 1-3.
[87] J. VANIER, *Jesus the Gift of Life*, 7.
[88] J. VANIER, *Community and Growth*, 2.

portunity to grow in unity and a spirit of unity with brothers and sisters whose beliefs draw them to serve others.

+ Governance

The ecumenical/interreligious situation of l'Arche has affected its relationship with the churches. At the beginning, Father Thomas Philippe and J. Vanier developed close links with the local bishop, Stephane Desmazières. His successor, Bishop Adolphe-Marie Hardy ordained three priests specifically for l'Arche[89]. However, as has been seen earlier, the appeal of the l'Arche communities draws persons of all beliefs. L'Arche communities are encouraged to have a religious affiliation which is considered an important element for the community and also for the individuals in it. Communities may be of one faith and, if Christian, may be a part of a particular Christian church or ecclesial community. Interdenominational and inter-faith communities are also possible[90].

> Communities are beginning to define their religious identity and although there is sometimes an understandable reluctance to do this for fear of «excluding» people, the existing community and potential new members need to be able to identify and clarify their expectations of one another. The definition of religious identity is essential, too, if we are to dialogue with local bishops and other church and religious leaders. If they are to relate to us they need to know who we are[91]!

The danger of someone feeling excluded is always present. The self-description of each community helps members to better understand what they are joining and what they can expect of the other members. Ecumenical/interreligious situations can be very sensitive especially when persons are living together and are trying to follow the teachings of their own churches and religions.

When asked about the relationship between l'Arche and the Roman Catholic Church J. Vanier responded:

> L'Arche is a Federation of communities which is inter-denominational and interreligious. So we have no juridical link with the Catholic Church.
> We have yearly meetings with the PCL, for the Unity of Christians and for Inter religious dialogue. And the PCL has accepted to ask a Bishop to be a reference for l'Arche on the international level[92].

---

[89] T. VANIER, *One Bread, One Body*, 33.
[90] T. VANIER, *One Bread, One Body*, 34.
[91] T. VANIER, *One Bread, One Body*, 34-35.
[92] J. VANIER, *Personal letter*, 6 July 1997.

While a relationship clearly exists between l'Arche and the Roman Catholic Church, the federation is not able to have a canonical status because it has no stable relationship with any particular Church. The concept of self-definition or religious belonging as written about by Thérèse Vanier is important to the identity of each individual l'Arche community. This does not exist for the federation as it is inter-denominational and interreligious.

+ Conclusion

L'Arche has a great appeal to the mentally handicapped and their families and supporters within the past thirty years. The rapid growth of both l'Arche, from one community in 1964 to over one hundred communities twenty years later, and Faith and Light, from its beginnings in 1971 it has grown to include over one thousand member communities within the span of twenty years are proof of the desire of persons for support in living with the mentally handicapped. These organizations fill a need in the Church and in society for the support of the mentally handicapped and their families.

L'Arche does not only help others; it is a means of religious transformation for all the individuals who take part in it. J. Vanier has said that persons within the communities minister to one another and celebrate their oneness. Living in community has been spiritually developmental for J. Vanier himself.

L'Arche has a concern for their own identity as a worldwide association. Besides being open to all mentally handicapped persons l'Arche at its roots a concern for all persons. This is an important spiritual challenge for members, those considerig membership and persons who are in relation with l'Arche.

The relationship that l'Arche has with the Apostolic See is particular. Because it is interconfessional there is no canonical juridical link with the Roman Catholic Church. Work toward having a bishop liaison is most promising.

1.3 *Associations Approved in a few Dioceses of the United States*

1.3.1 Ecumenical Associations with Non-Catholic Members
      According to ChL 31

a) *Mother of God Community*

Even as recognition of Mary as the Mother of God by Roman Catholics is at times a stumbling block to union for non-Catholics with the Church of Rome, there are those among the separated brethren who are not deterred by the *hyper dulia* given to Our Lady and join Roman Catholics who seek to pay her honor. This is certainly the case with the first association to be studied in this dissertation whose headquarters is located in the United States. «The name Mother of God signifies that the Community, receiving and treasuring the Word of God like Mary, is called to bring forth the life of Christ to the world» (stat. 1.2)[93]. The idea of a community began in 1966 with the meeting of two women in the Washington, DC area. Both were involved in Charismatic Renewal and felt a call to the work of renewal in the Church. By 1968, a weekly prayer group was meeting. Some participants made commitments to the Community in 1971 and in 1972 households of single members were established.

+ Ends

The ends of the Mother of God Community can detected throughout its statutes. Two sections which are particularly poignant are, «Nature and Purpose» and «Spiritual and Theological Formation». Here the statutes clearly express the ecumenical character of the Community. When not explicit this character is manifest in non-restricting language regarding membership of the baptized in general: both Catholics and Christians of various denominations. The canons being clear that the purpose and character of an association be included in its statutes[94], its statutes remark:

> Mother of God Community is a covenant community whose purpose is to glorify Jesus Christ, whose members are empowered in the Baptism in the Holy Spirit to live a life of holiness, mutual love and service to the Church in anticipation of Christ's return (stat. 1.5).

further it is stated that:

> While sharing in the common grace of baptism in the Holy Spirit which has brought Christians from all Churches to praise and worship God to-gether at Prayer Meetings and enjoy fellowship with each other, the Community encourages its members to preserve and foster their active participation in the life of their respective ecclesial communities (stat. 1.5).

---

[93] The statutes for the Mother of God Community were obtained from the Community itself and were also found on the World Wide Web at: http:/www. motherof-god.org/index.htm

[94] C.304,§1 *CIC* 83.

In respecting the different ecclesial communities to which members may belong, they are encouraged to actively participate in those same communities, while at the same time belonging to Mother of God Community. As a part of the nature of the Mother of God Community, the statutes recognize that «Christians of other traditions have been and remain integral to the charism and life of the Community» (stat. 1.4). Non-Catholics are also mentioned in the section concerning members; their mention here concretizes the ecumenical nature of the Mother of God Community. There is certainly a *communicatio in spiritualibus* at Community gatherings. The statutes refer to the grace of the baptism in the Holy Spirit as «common» to all members, fitting the definition of *communicatio in spiritualibus* as found in *AT* 25. There *communicatio in spiritualibus* is described as a sharing in the spiritual heritage which persons of diverse heritage have in common[95]. As the widespread Charismatic or Pentecostal Movement is a rather new phenomena among the Christian churches, it does have a heritage that can be shared in common.

The statutes continue to hone the ends of the Community, always with room for Catholics and non-Catholic Christians alike. Among points to which the Community aspires Christian unity is again mentioned: «With the guidance of the Spirit, the Community aspires to be a people who witness to the call to Christian unity in the Body of Christ» (stat. 1.9).

The first statute in the section, «Spiritual and Theological Formation» is another example of *communicatio in spiritualibus* in Mother of God Community. Again the Charismatic Renewal is mentioned. However, here the statutes go further:

> The spiritual and theological roots of the Community lie in the Catholic Church through its founding members and early history, and in the Charismatic Renewal. The Community has also been profoundly enriched by the spiritual heritage of other church traditions (stat. 5.1).

The guidelines in this section of the statutes continue to manifest the ecumenical character of the Community. While it is rooted in Catholic theology and spirituality as well as in the Charismatic Renewal, the statutes present the Mother of God Community as being profoundly enriched by the spiritual heritage of other ecclesial traditions. The nature of this spiritual heritage is not specifically identified in the statutes.

---

[95] Cf. Chapter I, section 8.

Respect and autonomy, which are to be enjoyed by all members, are the particular concern of spiritual and theological formation (stat. 5.3; 5.51; 5.5.2). In general, «diverse and varied opportunities for spiritual growth and development, sacramental, liturgical and other worship celebrations, individual spiritual direction and devotional activities consistent with the above» (stat. 5.5.5), are to be provided for all Community members. These would be for the whole Mother of God Community, respecting Roman Catholic sacramental discipline and the autonomy of the various traditions represented. This ecumenical statement invites Christians to share *communicatio in spiritualibus* when possible and at the same time to respect each ecclesial community and its teachings. Number thirty-six of the encyclical letter *Ut Unum Sint* is quoted as the Community's desire for Church unity is voiced in the statutes. *Ut Unum Sint* #31[96] makes the point that full communion is only possible with acceptance of the whole truth and that any false irenicism brought about by agreements must be avoided as these only create problems which will merely resurface at a later date (stat. 5.2). By citing *Ut Unum Sint*, the statutes make clear the desire of the Community to function ecumenically under the competent authority in the Catholic Church. With the ecumenical end firmly planted among the other purposes of the Community the statutes address Community membership.

+ Membership

Besides having an ecumenical end or apostolate, some associations have placed in their statutes provisions for non-Catholic Christians to be inscribed as members. This is a deeper step as various documents have called associations in particular and Catholics in general to have an ecumenical spirit[97]. The actual membership of non-Catholics in an association manifests a particular commitment to the ecumenical movement. Non-Catholic Christian membership in the Mother of God Community makes it fit the definition of ecumenical associations according to *ChL* 31.

The first statute of the section on membership clearly includes non-Catholic Christians: «The membership of the Mother of God Community, while *primarily* composed of Catholics, *is open to* baptized Christians in good standing in their ecclesial communities» (stat. 2.1;

---

[96] JOHN PAUL II, enc. lett. *Ut unum sint, AAS* 87 (1995) 921-982.
[97] ED93, 52. and *UR* 4.

emphasis added). The three stipulations found in this statute clarify membership in the Mother of God Community.

1) The Community is primarily composed of Catholics. As a private association of the Christian faithful it is established in the Archdiocese of Washington. «While enjoying its own autonomy, [the Community] is subject to the supervision and governance of ecclesiastical authority from both the diocesan bishop and the Apostolic See» (stat. 1.1). Because of its goals and because of its canonical recognition, the Mother of God Community is rooted in the Catholic Church. As stated earlier, the membership of the Community will always be composed of a Catholic majority (stat. 1.4; 2.1). This meets the stipulation in *ChL* 31.

2) Membership is open to baptized Christians (stat. 2.1). Proof of baptism can be produced by a certificate or the affidavit of witnesses. One manifestation of the bond formed among the baptized as they are incorporated into the Body of Christ is the presence of non-Catholic Christians in canonical associations of the Christian faithful.

3) Members must be in good standing in their own ecclesial communities (stat. 2.1). The statute assumes that the persons wishing to join Mother of God Community are members of some ecclesial community. It was noted earlier that these persons are encouraged toward active participation in the life of their own ecclesial communities. To be in good standing, persons are not to be involved in any irregularities that are outside the rules and regulations of their own communities[98].

The statutes continue and list requirements for persons wishing to become members of the Community (stat. 2.2-2.4). A subsection concerning the initiation process is included within the membership section (stat. 2.5-2.9). Nowhere are non-Catholic Christians limited or restricted from enjoying the full benefits of the Community.

As an ecumenical association, members participate in community functions as well as in the activities of their own ecclesial communities. As the law permits, they belong to a canonical association and also participate in ecumenical activity as encouraged by the Church.

+ Rights and Duties

Once inscribed into the Mother of God Community, members, Catholic and non-Catholic, have certain rights and duties. Included among these rights and duties are the right to be involved in Commu-

---

[98] Irregularities would seem to include divorced and remarried Roman Catholics (without an annulment) however this situation is not positively stated in the statutes.

nity activities, to receive respect, to freely make personal decisions, and to be guaranteed confidentiality. One right assures that members can «participate in the vision, inspiration and fruits of the Community's ecumenical dimension» (stat. 2.10). This statute continues to enforce the fact that the Mother of God Community is *de facto* ecumenical. Ecumenism is not the Community's only end, but is surely one which is important to the existence of the association. Duties of the members include: attending prayer meetings, active participation in community programs, free-will offerings, as well as contribution of time, talent and prayerful support of the Community and resolving conflicts in the spirit of the Gospel (stat. 2.10). The duties do not put Catholics or non-Catholics in danger of having their faith harmed.

+ Governance

External Governance

The Mother of God Community is subject to the supervision and governance of the diocesan bishop as well as the Apostolic See. At the same time the Community enjoys a legitimate autonomy (stat. 1.1). If in the ecumenical arena of the Community conflicts occur which cannot be resolved by recourse to a strict interpretation of the statutes, the diocesan bishop is to be consulted (stat. 5.4).

The leadership of the Community Council and the Spiritual Advisor are to ensure that authentic Catholic teaching as declared by the magisterium is provided for Catholic members (stat. 5.5.1). Members of diverse traditions are to enjoy respect and autonomy in relating to Community members of different traditions than their own.

Throughout the statutes, the relation between the Community and the diocesan bishop is evidenced. In fact the diocesan bishop is mentioned in each of the nine major divisions of the statutes, save one. Though he is not mentioned in the section concerning Community activities, he does receive an annual report from the Community Council which makes him aware of the activities of the Community (stat. 4.11).

Consultation is to take place with the diocesan bishop when a member of either of the governing bodies of the Community, (that is, the Community Council and the Advisory and Mediation Committee) is to be removed. It is also a duty of the Council to consult with the diocesan bishop or his representative when necessary (stat. 4.10; 4.11; 4.15.2). When a Community member has a grievance or concern involving the Community the Advisory and Mediation Committee is to provide means for reconciliation and, when appropriate to make the archdiocese aware of the situation (stat. 4.20).

The Spiritual Advisor is a priest, chosen by the Community, freely exercising a ministry in the diocese, who is approved by the diocesan bishop (stat. 5.3)[99]. Only with the authorization of the bishop will the Spiritual Advisor celebrate sacraments requiring jurisdiction or delegation, such as Matrimony and Baptism (stat. 5.6)[100]. The role of Spiritual Advisor in the Community is one which is confirmed by the bishop; he receives delegation when needed. This continues to accentuate the role of the diocesan bishop as the competent authority in the external governance of this private association.

Other areas where the bishop plays a governing role in the Community are temporal goods, dissolution and revision of the statutes. The Mother of God Community provides, through its council, an annual financial report to the bishop (stat. 7.4). A decree of the bishop is one of the ways that the Community can be suppressed (stat. 8.1.5). In order to change the statutes, revisions must be reviewed and approved by the diocesan bishop (stat. 9.4).

The Community has a very open relationship with the diocese. This relationship provides protection for all members and their faith traditions. As a private association recognized by the Church as ecumenical it is as open as possible to the supervision of the competent authority. Catholic members of the Mother of God Community are not in danger of having their faith hindered; in fact, the statutes provide for authentic Catholic teaching as proclaimed by the Magisterium. The Community is one which will provide positive ecumenical formation.

Internal Governance

The organization or internal governance of the Community consists of the Community Council and the Advisory and Mediation Committee, each having its own chairman. Any member who is elected may serve in these positions of leadership. However only «a member in good standing of the Catholic Church» (stat. 4.12) can serve in the position of chair of the Community Council. Since the chair of the Community Council is the highest position in the Community, it is certainly important to have a Catholic serve in this capacity. This person will affect the balance of the Catholic and ecumenical dimensions of the

---

[99] c. 324,§2 *CIC* 83.
[100] cc.1108, 861-862 *CIC* 83.

association. It was prudent of those who drafted the document to have added this statute. The two governing bodies play an important role in the overall and specifically spiritual welfare of the Community.

"The Community Council serves in a leadership capacity to provide for the life and development of the mission and goals that are foundational to the Community» (stat. 4.1). Some of its more important duties are:

– to provide spiritual leadership, especially through the prayer meeting;
– to foster relationships with other communities and organizations and
– to maintain open dialogue and seek Community consultation and approval regarding those decisions that affect the nature, purpose or direction of Community life and any major financial decisions (stat. 4.11).

Some of the duties of the advisory / mediation committee include:

– to pray for the Community;
– to advise the Council and
– to assist the Council in determining which decisions and issues warrant the input and/or deliberative vote of the entire Community (stat. 4.20).

The Mother of God Community is governed internally by these two bodies along with the Spiritual Advisor. The two support and complement one another well. While the Community Council leads in glorifying God in their activities, the Advisory and Mediation Committee ensures that Community-wide attention be brought to issues where necessary. Prayer for and advice given to the Council certainly are helpful for a balanced administration of the whole Community.

Even though it is not strictly administrative, the role of the spiritual advisor, whose appointment is confirmed by the diocesan bishop, is important especially to the ecumenical facet of the Community. «Along with the Council, he oversees and secures the ongoing spiritual development of all members» (stat. 5.1). Striving to do this, his duties include,

being available to Protestant and Orthodox members for support and encouragement in their life within the Community and by being a liaison, where necessary, with the ministers of their churches or ecclesial communities (stat. 5.6).

Non-Catholic Christians in the Mother of God Community play an important role for the whole association. The only position in the association which is not open to non-Catholics is that of Chair of the Community Council. All members in the Community are full members; no other titles exist for those who take part in the Community.

The ends of the Community can be met by following the statutes and engaging the supervision of competent authority. The Mother of God Community is an excellent example with which to start the study of ecumenical associations at the diocesan level in the United States of America.

+ Conclusion

The Mother of God Community is pointedly ecumenical. The *communicatio in spiritualibus* clearly present in the Community is based in the charismatic renewal, Catholic Church teaching on the ecumenical movement and the presence of non-Catholic Christians in the Community. The statutes draw these points into one when the Community recognizes that it is rooted in the Roman Catholic Church but also has been enriched by other «church» traditions. This recognition of how the Community has been enriched by other «church» traditions clarifies its ecumenism.

It may not be possible for all Christians to be inscribed into the Mother of God Community. The Community expects that non-Catholic Christians who join are in good standing with their own ecclesial communities. A respect of the ecclesial communities from which the Mother of God Community draws membership manifests the ecumenism of the Community.

The governance of the association as outlined in the statutes is an instrument which will guard the Catholicity of the association. The role of the diocesan bishop in relation with the Community is evidenced throughout the statutes. It is he who is to be consulted when doubts may arise concerning unresolved ecumenical questions. The bishop also has the final word when sacraments which are usually preformed in the parish are to held within a community setting. The statutes have been written so that a healthy balance will be kept between the governing bodies of the Community and the diocese.

b) *Magnificat*

Magnificat, a private association of the faithful, was approved by the Archbishop of New Orleans in 1986. «Magnificat ministry emanates from a desire to share with Catholic women the fruit experienced through the Roman Catholic Church and Charismatic Renewal» (stat. preamble)[101]. Even the name, like the Mother of God Community, is

---

[101] Magnificat has used the designation «constitution» for its statutes. The term «statutes» will be used when the constitution/statutes of Magnificat are cited.

quite Catholic and the group is dedicated to Mary the Mother of God. (stat. preamble) A desire is present in the Constitution to serve all women. However, leadership of Magnificat prefer it not to be considered an ecumenical association[102]. It is, in fact, at the service of the Roman Catholic Church and Catholic women in particular. The possibility of non-Catholic members belonging to Magnificat places it within the definition of ecumenical association as used in this dissertation. While the statutes[103] are considered, those particular statutes that support or allow non-Catholic members will be highlighted as well as those which solidify the Catholic roots of the association.

An interlinear commentary and historical introduction or preamble accompany the constitution. These are very useful tools in aiding persons to read the statutes. They often give canonical background, define terms, and offer information for persons not familiar with Magnificat. The next to last commentary entry states that the commentary and preamble do not belong to the Constitution itself and that they may be updated or changed by the Central Service Team, which is the governing body for all Magnificat chapters, without episcopal review or approval. This is a technical yet important point. Information found in the preamble or commentary should clarify as it explains the understanding of the constitution. Changes in the preamble or commentary should not change the understanding of the text of the constitution itself. By once again considering the ends, rights and duties, membership, and governance, a comprehensive overview of Magnificat can be obtained.

+ Ends

The objectives of Magnificat are: to live the mystery of Mary's visit to Elizabeth, to aid Catholic women in their openness to the working of the Holy Spirit in their lives, to foster growth in holiness and to sponsor the Magnificat Meal (stat. II.A.1-4). The story of the visitation found in the gospel of Luke 1:39-56 is inspirational for the association and its name and objectives:

> The essence of Magnificat is the encounter between Mary and Elizabeth. Magnificat is a woman-to-woman ministry which calls forth a lively faith in God and His actions in daily life, a love for Mary and for the Church, and deep holiness. Praying, fellowshiping [sic], reading the scriptures,

---

[102] M. QUIRK, *Personal letter*, 24 October 1996.

[103] The *Constitution for Magnificat* contains its statutes. When reference to the document is made in the body of the dissertation either term will be used.

teaching, witnessing, and serving one another constitute the principle means by which the women of Magnificat foster such holiness. (stat. preamble)

This explanation from the preamble further clarifies the purpose of Magnificat.

Some of the objectives of Magnificat are specifically Catholic while others would also appeal to women involved in Charismatic or Pentecostal ecclesial communities. Non-Catholics would obviously not be able to participate in the sacraments of the Holy Eucharist and Reconciliation or be called to have an allegiance to the Catholic Church. By these and other means, Catholic women are encouraged to grow in holiness. Most of the means promoted by the objectives in the statutes can involve non-Catholic Christian women. Some of these include: daily prayer, understanding of the vocation of Christian women and promoting unity. Examples of terminology which specifically are shared with Charismatic and Pentecostal ecclesial communities and are found in the statutes as defining the objectives of Magnificat are: commitment of lives to Jesus as Lord, sharing the good news of salvation, and experiencing the presence and power of the Holy Spirit (stat. II.A.2; B.4). This terminology does not in itself signify an ecumenical disposition for Magnificat. It does however reinforce the influence of the Charismatic Renewal in the lives of those women who founded the ministry. (stat. preamble) In fact, «it greatly appreciates the inspiration and support it has received from the Women's Aglow Fellowship»[104]. It would seem that Magnificat at least began as a Catholic form of Women's Aglow[105]. That the association has received inspiration and support from Women's Aglow connotes a relationship between the two at some point in time. There is a share in spiritual heritage as well as ends for the two groups. *Communicatio in spiritualibus* is present among Catholics and any non-Catholics who may gather at a Magnificat meal. As there are specifically spiritual areas in which Catholics and non-Catholics can share in achieving the goals of Magnificat, the community is an ecumenical association.

---

[104] M. QUIRK, *Personal letter*, 24 October 1996.

[105] Women's Aglow is a pentacostal women's group whose beginings in 1967 in Seattle, Washington, USA focused around gathering for a meal and to give praise to God, listen to speakers and support one another. Today the outreach has grown to over on thousand Fellowships and provides spiritual reading material and publishes her own magazine, «Aglow».

The Magnificat meal constitutes the essential function of the Magnificat ministry. The centrality of the meal to Magnificat can be likened to the centrality of the Eucharist to the Church. [...] Although paraliturgical, the Magnificat Meal is more than a social event; it is a means of ministry. Care must be taken to maintain an atmosphere of prayer (stat. VI.A).

Gathering for the Magnificat Meal is the objective of Magnificat that is viewed as the essential function of the ministry. The other objectives can all be achieved or begun at the meal. The presence of non-Catholics at the Magnificat Meal would not take from the objective to gather and would promote unity among believers.

The importance of the Magnificat Meal to the association is accentuated in the statutes concerning meetings. Other ministries besides the Meal may be undertaken by the association. These may include: days of renewal, retreats, «Life in the Spirit» seminars[106], and bible study groups (stat. VI.E.2, commentary). Before these are listed the statutes relate the following:

1) The local chapter should become proficient at celebrating the Magnificat Meal before sponsoring other functions.

2) The local chapter should celebrate the Magnificat Meal for at least a year before attempting to add other functions (stat. VI.E.1-2).

Thus the importance of the celebration of the meal is again manifest in the statutes as one of the objectives of the association. Other ministries may be undertaken, but the meal is always central to Magnificat.

+ Members

It is in the section concerning membership that the incorporation of non-Catholics into Magnificat is most clearly stated. This places the association in the category of ecumenical associations: for if an association is to be considered ecumenical the ability for the group to inscribe non-Catholic members must be reflected in the statutes. There are stipulations for membership to Magnificat.

The nature of membership in Magnificat is primarily spiritual. By registering women become members. Becoming a member does bring with it objective rights and duties. These will be discussed in the section specifically dealing with these areas.

---

[106] «Life in the Spirit» seminars instruct attendees concerning Charimatic/ Pentacostal spirituality especially involving Baptism in the Spirit.

The statutes describe Magnificat as: «spiritual in nature and open to all women who: 1) strive to incorporate in their lives the objectives of Magnificat, 2) agree to pray for Magnificat and its members, and 3) register with a local chapter» (stat. IV.A.1-5) All women who agree with the requirements for membership are able to join Magnificat. The only men present at the meal would be the spiritual advisor, if a male has been chosen (stat. V.I; commentary), and the speaker if a man has been asked to speak, which is rare (stat. VI.B.3 ; C; commentary). Priests who are involved in the Charismatic Renewal, especially the diocesan liaison to the Catholic Charismatic Renewal, are good choices for spiritual directors. The commentary uses both personal pronouns he and she to refer to the spiritual director; it is clear that a man or woman can serve in this capacity. The care that the statutes use when describing members as women and the option of women or men for the position of spiritual director and speaker support the understanding of all women as referring to women of different Christian communities as well as different religions. The word Catholic is obviously absent from this article of the statutes.

Potential members must meet the three listed requirements in the statutes. The first asks members to strive to make the objectives of Magnificat a part of their own lives. Any woman, if she so desires, will be able to do this; however, as reviewed above, some of the objectives are specifically aimed at Catholics. Those who are not Catholic, in their striving to make the objectives a part of their lives, are not called to do what they are not able to do: namely, they are not required to receive the sacraments of the Catholic Church or to have a deep love and loyalty for the Catholic Church. However, it seems that non-Catholics who join Magnificat would have some respect for the Catholic Church or they would not join a Catholic organization. The second, to pray for Magnificat and its members, and the third, to register with a local chapter, requirements for membership are able to be fulfilled by any woman who is willing. The statutes say nothing about presence at any meetings or participation in any ministries, save prayer. Homebound persons or those who cannot attend meetings for other reasons are able to become members. «Membership is effected by familiarizing oneself with the objectives of Magnificat and signing a request for membership form. Members' names are inscribed on the local chapter's roll, which is kept by the secretary» (stat. IV.B-C).

Even though it is clear from the statutes, especially these on membership, that non-Catholics can be inscribed into Magnificat as members the situation is further explained in the commentary:

> Since membership is open to all women, those belonging to other religions who fulfill the three conditions stated above may also become members. This openness entails no danger that Magnificat will depart from its Catholic objectives. Another statute requires that officers be practicing Catholics. Non-Catholics may also attend Magnificat functions without becoming members (stat. IV.A).

The actual number of non-Catholic members belonging to Magnificat is not documented and is believed to be small if any join at all.[107] Presently Magnificat has five chapters in the Archdiocese of New Orleans, twenty-eight others in the continental United States and chapters in Canada, Grenada, US Virgin Islands, Barbados, Tobago, Trinidad and Malta; the association is truly international[108]. With the strong Catholic objectives of Magnificat the probability of it taking an interdenominational character is slim. The statutes concerning membership are most clear in manifesting Magnificat as a canonical association which is ecumenical.

+ Rights and Duties

One of the beauties of Magnificat is its simplicity. For those who are members, the rights and duties are not overwhelming. Since any woman can attend the Magnificat Meal, attendance is not a duty or a right for those inscribed in the association. Living out the objectives required for Magnificat members is a duty as well as a right. As members of Magnificat, women have the right to be called forth by their commitment to live the obligations of belonging to the association. Women who are registered with a particular Magnificat chapter are also to pray for Magnificat and its members.

When considering the corporate nature of Magnificat, a number of rights and duties surface. Among these is the duty to have the bishop's approval for changes in the constitution, which will be covered in the section on governance. Again simplicity enables Magnificat to center its efforts on the meal and other ministries in which a particular chapter may be involved.

---

[107] J. LACOCO, *Personal letter*, 25 November 1996.
[108] J. LACOCO, *Personal letter*, 25 November 1996.

+ Governance

The study will reveal how the association interacts with competent authority and also within its own governmental structure. Contact with both the local bishop and the Central Service Team assure that the ends of Magnificat are met.

External Governance

The relationship between Magnificat and the bishop of the place where the local chapter is found is one of supervision[109]. Along with the Central Service Team, the bishop helps to preserve the integrity of Magnificat at all its local chapters. Because Magnificat has its headquarters in the Archdiocese of New Orleans, all of the Magnificat chapters through the Central Service Team maintain a special relationship with that archbishop. Any amendments to be made to the constitution, which may be suggested by the Local Service Teams to the Central Service Team, must be reviewed or approved by the Archbishop of New Orleans. Since the local bishop where a chapter of Magnificat is found must review or approve the statutes of Magnificat, any revision or change in the statutes would be presented to him for his own review or approval (stat. XI.G.2.b; V.B.2). The temporal goods of both the Central Service Team and Local Service Teams are a matter for governance. A year-end financial report is made available to the Archbishop of New Orleans or the diocesan bishop where local chapters are found (stat. XI.L.2; V.D.4.i). If for some reason a chapter or the Central Service Team is dissolved or suppressed, according to the statutes, finances left in the treasury are to be used according to the will of the donor (stat. X.D. commentary; XI.M.2)[110].

In terms of governance, the relationship between the diocesan bishops and the local chapters of Magnificat is in many ways mirrored by the Central Service Team (stat. XI.D.2; L). The previous paragraph considered external governance from the relationship of the bishop and the Central Service Team. Overlaps between the local chapters and Local Service Teams were often present. Civil incorporation and bylaws also affect both Central and Local Teams while manifesting the particularities of the different chapters and their own relationship with their diocesan bishops. While local chapters seek to have their own

---

[109] C.305, §2 *CIC* 83.
[110] C.1301 *CIC* 83.

statutes reviewed or approved[111] by the diocesan bishop, they are authorized to make minor modifications to the statutes. Bylaws are permitted to help Local Service Teams to facilitate their own Magnificat ministry; allowing each chapter to minister in the way most suited to the needs of the women it serves. However, the statutes and bylaws must be in accord with the ends of the latest revision of the Constitution of Magnificat. Bylaws of a Local Service Team involve internal and external governance. Once formulated they must be approved internally by the central service team and externally by the diocesan bishop (stat. VII.A.1-5).

Internal Governance

Before considering internal governance in particular an overview of the structure of the association will be considered. This will include the role of the Central Service Team and that of the local chapters. The Central Service Team, located in New Orleans, is the governing body for all of the local chapters of Magnificat. The Central Service Team is set up much like the Local Service Teams, but does not sponsor the Magnificat meal (stat. XI.D.2). It oversees the association as a whole. Along with the bishops of the dioceses, it strives to preserve the integrity of the Magnificat ministry (stat. XI.B).

The local chapters of Magnificat are governed in a simple manner which can expand or diminish as needed. Each chapter is governed by a Local Service Team of five or three women. They are assisted by an Advisory Team. To ensure the smooth running of the meal and other ministries, chairwomen may be charged with running the various functions of the local chapter. These chairwomen may be members of the Advisory Team. A local chapter is composed of the persons serving in the above mentioned positions along with the spiritual advisor and the members themselves (stat. V.A-B). When a Local Service Team of Magnificat is formed, it is the bishop who is called upon to appoint someone who will in turn select the first service team (stat. V.F.1-5). Even from the infancy of a new chapter, the role of the bishop is crucial since he reviews or approves the statutes.

---

[111] MAGNIFICAT, *Constitution*, III.B.2. «"Reviewing" these statutes means no more than reading them. It is equivalent to allowing Magnificat to become established within a diocese without commenting on its merits. "Approving" these statutes establishes a closer relationship between Magnificat and the diocesan bishop. Episcopal approval of these statutes can indicate an intention to make Magnificat a public Association».

Some rights of non-Catholic members are restricted as they are limited in the roles they can take in the government of Magnificat. Both levels of government within Magnificat, the Central Service Team and Local Service Team will be affected by the restrictions.

For Magnificat, internal governance takes place between the two levels of administration and within the chapters and teams themselves. The levels of administration are the Local Service Team and the Central Service Team. Much of the rapport between the two is mirrored by the relationship between the Local Service Teams and their diocesan bishops. Besides faithfulness to the goals of Magnificat, the governing tasks of the Local Service Team include running the Magnificat meal, confirming speakers with the spiritual advisor, appointing the Advisory Team and making an annual report of the activities of the Magnificat ministry to the local chapter (stat. V.B). The Local Service Team itself has a number of duties. These include regular meetings (stat. VI.F), decision making, by unanimity or at least consensus, and regular meetings with the Advisory Team and spiritual advisor (stat. VI.I-K).

Other matters of internal governance include: ministries, dissolution, the Magnificat name and Catholics as Team members. Local chapters may set up ministries run by chairwomen and members of the Advisory Team. These ministries aid the smooth running of the Magnificat meal and other works of the local chapter (stat. VIII.A-B).

The statutes have placed no restriction on those women who serve Magnificat on the Advisory Team. However, only Catholics may serve as officers on the Local Service Team (stat. V.H.1). Without some limitations on the roles in which non-Catholics are able to serve Catholic associations might struggle in maintaining their Catholicity. Without some limitations associations which are under study in this dissertation would not be able to be named ecumenical and still have the possibility to be canonically recognized by the Catholic Church. Magnificat allows non-Catholics full membership, they cannot be considered members with full rights. This praxis is also employed by the Mother of God Community in Washington, DC. Women who are on the Advisory Team serve as chairwomen for different committees which serve the Magnificat Meal. Ministries include: greeters, ticket sales, publicity, music and intercessory prayer. According to the statutes non-Catholics are not restricted from serving in these positions.

Local Service Teams themselves are able to dissolve the local chapter of Magnificat. The diocesan bishop also can dissolve the local chapter. And if a chapter does not serve a Magnificat meal for ten consecutive years the chapter is dissolved *de facto* (stat. X). Finally, it is the Central Service Team that can grant or prohibit the use of the name Magnificat and its logo by its local chapters. The name and logo are both to be registered at civil and ecclesiastical law (stat. XI.G.1; I).

+ Conclusion

Magnificat is a prime example of an ecumenical association. While Magnificat's objective is to help Catholic women be open to the work of the Holy Spirit through a commitment of their lives to Jesus, membership is open to all women. Approved by and under the supervision of the Archbishop of New Orleans the private association of the Christian faithful is canonically recognized.

The praxis, as set forth in the constitution, allows non-Catholics to be full members of Magnificat but not with full rights. The Mother of God Community has a similar praxis in which non-Catholics are limited in the role they may take in community government.

c) *The Brothers and Sisters of Charity*

The Brothers and Sisters of Charity were approved as a public association of the Christian faithful on 4 October 1995. The statutes of the community are in the form of a constitution. John Michael Talbot, the general minister, spiritual father and founder, has brought the community through a number of stages since his original vision for the group in 1971. After joining the Secular Franciscan Order himself in 1978 the community received approval to function as Secular Franciscans. The Little Portion Hermitage, where the members of the integrated[112] monastery live, was blessed by Bishop Andrew McDonald of Little Rock and the then Bishop of Springfield-Cape Girardeau, Bernard Law, on 4 October 1985. Between the years 1978-88, the community reformed and returned to using the word «charity» in its name as well as the original integrated vision where celibate men and women and families would live in community. This led to approval as a private association of the faithful in 1990 (stat. 1). Even after being erected as a public association, questions brought further changes. Where previously the association had desired to be entirely ecumenical, non-Catholics within the community today are not to be «canonical members»[113]. A consideration of the ends, members, rights and duties, and governance with

---

112 Both men and women belong to the monastery and live on the premises.
113 J.M. TALBOT, *Personal letter*, 18 December 1997.

the ecumenical orientation of the community will lead to a discussion of the praxis used in this particular situation. The 1994 edition of the General Constitution will be used as a more recent copy is not available. The founder himself says that the members of the «domestic community who are not Catholic still affiliate and enter into the community "in the same way as before", however, they are not canonical members of the canonical public association of the faithful»[114].

+ Ends

The section of the General Constitution which presents the ends of the community is the first chapter containing the basic principles and visions of the community. Pertinent paragraphs of the constitution follow.

> The Brothers and Sisters of Charity is a Catholic based, ecumenical, covenant community of singles, celibates, and families called as a monastic and domestic spiritual family into deep love relationships with and in Jesus Christ. Jesus is our primary example; the Scripture is our primary rule; our primary law is love (stat. 19).

> The primary expression of this charism of love is integration. As such, we integrate all religions from a uniquely Christian base, all Christian faiths from a uniquely Catholic base. Franciscanism is our mother, but we are a child born from this heritage in a way that is unique and new (stat. 19).

These paragraphs are important to understand the ecumenical aspect of the association. While the association is open to the participation of non-Catholics, a Catholic base is its permanent structure. Non-Catholics who become involved in the community are aware that the organization is a Catholic one.

Not mentioned in the historical introduction to this section covering the Brothers and Sisters of Charity is that the founder himself is a convert. Before his conversion he was a popular musician in the United States and continued to write, sing and play music after his conversion to Catholicism. His music is used in Catholic Churches across the country. Concerts and worship services have been offered to the public. Talbot's following is wider than members of the Catholic Church. As the structure of the Brothers and Sisters of Charity unfolded, members of other religions, churches and ecclesial communities were interested in committing themselves to the lifestyle. It is an example of *communi-*

---

[114] J.M. TALBOT, *Personal letter,* 18 December 1997. Emphasis added.

catio in spiritualibus in microcosm. The community is based on early Church monastic practices which the founder has adapted to the community. As persons have followed the spiritual conversion of the founder, they too have shared in this spirituality which is both charismatic and contemplative, combining a call to solitude with a call to community, a primary call to contemplative community with a mandate from the gospel and the apostolic action of the evangelical life (stat. 19). This unique mixture of spiritual and religious activity is that of the founder.

The association has two expressions, monastic and domestic. The base and center is the monastic expression, an integrated community. At the hermitage, (which is patterned after the classical semi-eremetical *skete* or *laura*, or the house of prayer of the *kellion*), persons may live in the single, celibate, married, clerical or lay states. The domestic expression of the association is made up of persons who generally live in their own homes with a less externally intense manifestation of intentional community (stat. 19). The core monastic expression is completely Catholic while twenty to thirty percent of the domestic expression is non-Catholic[115]. The ends of the association, with its two expressions, can well fit into the model of an association of the faithful in the Catholic Church. Considerations of membership, duties and rights and governance will demonstrate this.

+ Members

Persons seeking membership in the community must undergo a period of formation which is styled after that of institutes of consecrated life. It includes candidacy, postulancy and novitiate, leading to profession. The question of excluding non-Catholics or non-Christians is not an issue which is specifically highlighted. On the contrary they are welcomed. However the constitution does ask that «candidates must be able to profess the content and context of the Apostle's and Nicene Creeds for membership in the community» (stat. 27). It is an interesting point since baptized Christians who desire to enter into full communion with the Catholic Church are asked to make a declaration of faith which involves the recitation of the creed. Entrance into the Brothers and Sisters of Charity is certainly not to be equivocated with entrance into the Roman Catholic Church. Non-Catholics are however entering or participating in a body which is canonically recognized by

---

[115] J.M. TALBOT, *Personal letter*, 12 March 1996.

the Church. These non-Catholics, it would seem, believe many of the teachings of the Church, but are not ready to enter into full communion with the Church.

Concerning the ecumenical situation of members the constitution states:

> Non-Catholic members respect the Catholic base of the community by not entering into contention with the magisterium of the church[116] in public. However, true ecumenical dialogue is encouraged. Likewise, Catholics respect all non-Catholic religions as encouraged and guided by ordinary church teaching (stat. 27).

+ Rights and Duties

The rights and duties of Brothers and Sisters of Charity include community prayer and services, community formation, and respect for and protection of Church teaching and authority. As a public association of the faithful the Brothers and Sisters of Charity impart Christian teaching in the name of the Church[117]. Naturally this is done within the area and for the purposes for which the association has been erected[118]. Again, the ecumenical aspects of the community will be highlighted.

The community seeks to prayerfully worship God. At the monastic branch, members are inspired to seek «God alone». All are encouraged to participate in daily Mass as this is essential to the devotional life of the association. The constitution clearly states that intercommunion is not practiced with non-Catholic members (stat. 21). The devotions which are practiced by the association give special attention to the mysteries of the lives of Jesus and Mary. Additionally the saints are honored since they give example to those striving to follow Christ. The Catholic foundation and means to approach God which the community uses in prayer does speak of the belief of those participating in the life of the community. The phrase, «lex orandi, lex credendi», rings true in this situation.

Furthermore, «All devotions are guided by the wisdom of the Scriptures and the magisterium of the church» (stat. 21). The following

---

[116] The term «church» when used by the *Constitution, Rule and Directory* of the Brothers and Sisters of Charity is meant to refer to the Roman Catholic Church. In situations where this is not true, the reference to ecclesial communities or other wording will make such obvious.

[117] C.301,§1 *CIC* 83.

[118] J.L.GUTIÉRREZ, «Associations of Christ's Faithful», 247-248.

of Church teaching as a duty as well as a right includes the instruction of authentic and true teaching of the magisterium of the Roman Catholic Church to those in the association. In this way it is believed that the gospel is lived more radically (stat. 23). The official prayer of the Church, the Divine Office, is prayed by those in the monastery and the domestic families (stat. 23). As the Brothers and Sisters of Charity give praise to God they do it in a manner which is particularly Catholic.

+ Governance

The authority to which the community is subject, both internally and externally speak of the beliefs and organization of the community itself. The external governance, that is those from whom the association takes direction and supervision, will speak volumes about the desires of the association itself. Individual members joining such an association also will look to this authority for direction. The persons chosen, Catholic or non-Catholic to serve in positions of authority also speak of the overall goals of the group. Any specifications concerning these persons will be carefully noted as they help to form members of the community.

External Governance

One paragraph under the heading «Communal Life» is particularly telling. It speaks of allegiance to the Holy Father as well as the relationship with other churches, ecclesial communities, and all people.

> We are always to be united with the church Jesus founded. The Franciscan tradition, moreover, binds us to a special reverence for the pope, and complete obedience to him. According to our monastic traditions, let us show respect for each individual bishop as the successor of the apostles. Likewise, as was the desire and example of St. Francis, we give due respect to all priests, deacons, and religious. As an ecumenical community, we likewise show respect for all the various ecclesial communities which call upon Jesus as Lord. We show respect to all the people of God as members of Christ's body, all people on earth as created in God's image, and all creation as bearing traces of God. We try to bring the unity of Jesus Christ to and with all (stat. 20).

Unity with the Roman Catholic Church, reverence for the Pope and complete obedience to him is an absolutely clear indication that the association is subject to the Church and her teachings and happily accepts this situation. This is clear to all members of the association. The use of the word «respect», which certainly has a different connotation from «reverence» and «obedience», further clarifies the position of authority of the Pope and Church teaching in the life of the Brothers and Sisters of Charity.

Having taken to heart the call of the gospel to go and teach all nations, the ministerial scope of the community is international. The consent of the local bishop or his equivalent in the law, is always requested before foundations are erected or ministries are undertaken (stat. 20)[119]. The founding father envisions for the future the possibility of the community changing from diocesan to pontifical status meaning that they would be directly recognized by the Apostolic See and would cooperate with diocesan bishops where the community is operating in a way that is appropriate to the expression of the community found in the diocese. At this time a monastic branch is located in the Diocese of Granada in Nicaragua[120].

In each diocese where the community operates the bishop is respected. This is evidenced by acknowledgment of the requirement that they submit themselves to the supervision of the local ordinary[121]. The bishop of Little Rock, where the motherhouse is located, is singled out as being in authority over the association (stat. 28). It is he who confirms the successors to the spiritual father and mother of the community (stat. 117)[122]. As has been shown the spiritual father is the general minister of the community; the spiritual mother is the vicar general minister.

As a Catholic organization, unity with Rome and the local ordinary are very important to the Brothers and Sisters of Charity. Even as an ecumenical group, the relationship of Church authority toward the community is one of supervision. Confirmation of the minister general and vicar general minister by the bishop of the diocese in which the motherhouse is founded is another manifestation of the loyalty of the association to the Church. The numerous times when the paragraphs of the constitution state that the community follows the teaching of the Church reinforce that it is indeed rooted in the Catholic Church.

---

[119] C.305,§2 *CIC* 83.

[120] J.M. TALBOT, *Personal letter*, 18 December 1997.

[121] C.305,§2 *CIC* 85.

[122] This citation is from the «Directory» section of the *Rule, Constitution and Directory*.

Internal Governance

The internal governance of the community is tied to external governance which works hand in hand with Church authorities.

> Each expression of the community; the single, celibate brotherhood and sisterhood, family monastic, and domestic, exist under their own leadership and Particular Directory, but are united by one Scripture Rule, these Constitutions, and one General Leadership (stat. 20).

The highest form of authority in the community is found within the General Chapter. It is made up of the permanently professed members of the monastic and domestic expressions or their delegates. A General Chapter is usually called every five years. Other forms of governance which exist within the community are the General Council and the Plenary Council. The General Council is made up of the general minister, the vicar general minister and the elder brothers and sisters of each particular expression. Domestic brothers and sisters have consultative vote which is to be taken seriously before decisions are made. The General Council meets as often as necessary during the year (stat. 20). The Plenary Council, which meets once a year, helps to plan an annual general conference. Leadership representatives from all particular monastic and domestic expressions come together and interpret and implement the Constitutions and the decisions of the most recent General Chapter. Their decisions remain in effect until the next Plenary Council meeting (stat. 28).

In the conclusion to the section of the constitution regarding government an article states that all leaders

> must be knowledgeable of Catholic Christian doctrine and Franciscan monastic spirituality from both study and experience. The ministers will be subject to the guidance of the church, and will thus guide the brothers and sisters by both example and work (stat. 30).

It would seem improbable that a non-Catholic could fit this definition of leader. At the same time, it is not impossible that a non-Catholic fit this role. To say that a person who is not Catholic has experienced Catholic Christian doctrine and is willing to be subject to the guidance of the Roman Catholic Church is much to expect. The hinge words to this statement are «experience» and «subject». To ask a non-Catholic to guide others according to Catholic doctrine does not seem possible. What adds to making the aim of the statement questionable, as to its meaning Catholic only, is a paragraph in the «Domestic Directory» section of the *Rule, Constitution and Directory* which explicitly requires Catholics for certain leadership roles.

> Formation Assistants are to assist Regional postulants and novices, assigned to them by Regional Minister and/or Vicar, in their assigned formation studies, Rule, Constitutions, and reading list. [...] Due to the Catholic base of the community and the teaching role of formators, Formation Assistants are chosen from the Catholic membership who have the proper gifting to fulfill their role (stat. 90)[123].

It should be remembered that the «Directory» is not the law as is the «Constitution». The «Directory» gives the mode for executing or living the law. The point made here in the «Directory», which is not technically a part of the «Constitution», concerning the requirement for domestic formation assistants to be Catholics is the only time in the *Constitution, Rule and Directory* that a direct requirement concerning a person's religious affiliation is made. Other approvals and requirements are put forth but these only imply conclusions regarding ecclesial membership. One last position will be considered concerning non-Catholics in governance of the Brothers and Sisters of Charity. As a public association of the faithful the Brothers and Sisters of Charity act in the name of the Church. Non-Catholics were not to be inscribed into public associations of the faithful according to the proposed c.307,§4 sch 82[124]. This prohibition did not become law because the canon was removed by the Supreme Pontiff before the promulgation of the *CIC* 83. Still, the practice of the PCL has seemed to be (no examples are extant) not to erect associations with non-Catholic participants public juridic persons. The Brothers and Sisters of Charity follow the praxis of the PCL and do not allow non-Catholic Christians who participate to enroll as canonical members.

Overall, the internal governance of the Brothers and Sisters of Charity serves the goals of the association. The various layers of government work with the central authority: the general minister and general vicar minister either are an active part of governance or receive reports from subordinates as to existing circumstances, especially in the domestic expression. This is important as the group strives to be Catholic and ecumenical at the same time. That leaders are to have a knowledge of Catholic Christian doctrine and Franciscan monastic

---

[123] This citation is from the «Directory» section of the *Rule, Constitution and Directory*.

[124] PCCICR, *Codex Iuris Canonici: Schema Novissimum* (1982), 53.

spirituality through study and experience coupled with the requirement for formation assistants to be Catholic help the community to meet its ends.

+ Conclusion

The Brothers and Sisters of Charity are of interest to this study for several reasons. Having been approved as a canonical public association of the faithful which is ecumenical, the possibility of incorporating members who are non-Catholics eventually became a question and led to the understanding that non-Catholics would not be considered canonical members. This is the direction which the community decided to pursue. Since the community may in the future desire to transfer to a pontifical status, it was judged wise to act cautiously at this time.

Correspondence with the minister general confirmed the fact that there are differing opinions concerning the membership of non-Catholics in canonical associations[125]. The choice of the Brothers and Sisters of Charity suits their ends as they still are ecumenical in their nature and purpose. Only the status of the non-Catholics who participate in the community changes. All will participate as they had before, but are not to be considered canonical members. The Constitution of the Brothers and Sisters of Charity addresses and is a catalyst to achieving the ends of the association.

d) *Glenmary Co-Missioner Association*

The Glenmary Co-Missioner Association (Glenmary Co-Missioners) has been in existence since 1991 when the group was formed with the assistance of the Glenmary Sisters and the Glenmary Home Missioners. The Association has both civil and canonical recognition. It is a non-profit organization in the State of Tennessee and has a canonical relationship with the Diocese of Nashville as a private association of the faithful with juridic personality.

+ Ends

The Glenmary Co-Missioners work for social justice and community development in poor struggling communities of the rural Southern United States. The Co-Missioners work with local persons and together strive to better the local situation. This is done by supporting local en-

---

[125] Cf. J.M. TALBOT, *Personal letters* 12 March 1996; 18 December 1997.

deavors, recognizing the Kingdom of God where structural poverty and powerlessness seem to prevail. Co-Missioners seek to empower people to see their faith in Jesus Christ as liberating them in their own situation.[126] As poverty has no religious or denominational boundaries the Association will serve anyone in need and those to be a part of the Association who can best help in a particular site.

+ Members

Two Glenmary Co-Missioners work alongside the local community and its leadership. An Incoming Co-Missioner is from outside the area and sent by the Association's headquarters in Nashville. This person is Catholic. A Local Co-Missioner from the culture and faith tradition of the mission site works together with Incoming Co-Missioner. This person may or may not be Catholic. It is most appropriate if the Local Co-Missioner shares the faith of the poor who are being enabled and served. Both Missioners are funded by the Co-Missioner Association. As they work, they live the mission and vision of the Co-Missioners[127].

The By laws of the Glenmary Co-Missioners state, «Membership shall consist of a mixed association of laity and clergy together (c.298 CIC 83) which is open to Catholics and people of other religious traditions» (byl. III.2)[128]. All members, Catholic and non-Catholic, share in the goals and ideals of the Association. Included among the types of membership are Local and Incoming Co-Missioners, members of the Servant Leadership Team, local liaisons, which represent the different cultural groups, and members of the Servant Team. The faith of the Local Co-Missioner ought to be that of the people of the area in which the Co-Missioners serve. After three years the incoming Co-Missioner moves on to a new assignment. The Local Co-Missioner needs to be a person who will stay in the area and continue the work that has been kindled. The rural Southern United States is not an area which has a high Catholic population. The type of work which is done by the Co-Missioners is not wholly dependent on the faith of those doing apostolate. There may indeed be situations where the best choice for a Local Co-Missioner would be a non-Catholic.

---

[126] M. FAZALUDDIN, *Personal letter*, 14 October 1996.

[127] M. FAZALUDDIN, *Personal letter*, 14 October 1996.

[128] The by laws and not statutes were used for the study of the Glenmary Co-Missioners.

There are voting and non-voting members of the Association. Local Co-Missioners are voting members of the Association. This gives non-Catholics voting rights in the Association. Associates, who support the Glenmary Co-Missioners through prayer and material assistance can be non-voting members. They elect a representative who serves on the Servant Leadership Team and therefore can vote. The Glenmary Co-Missioners are open to non-Catholic members and see these persons as important to the work of the Association.

+ Rights and Duties

Members of the Glenmary Co-Missioners have the opportunity to be a part of this association of faith and culture. They can be assured of the prayers of the associates. Membership status endures for three years with an option for renewal. Participation in the Association with rights of voting and attending meetings is enjoyed by members.

+ Governance

External Governance

The Glenmary Co-Missioners have external relationships with the State of Tennessee and the Diocese of Nashville. The relationship with the state is important as the Association is non-profit and is incorporated. The members of the service team are salaried employees of the Glenmary Co-Missioners Association. The relationship with the Church is by way of its recognition as a private association of the faithful with juridic personality[129]. Local Catholic parishes which have Co-Missioners working in their area may each have one representative on the Servant Leadership Team. Even with the possibility of non-Catholic members, the relationship with the Roman Catholic Church is extensive. As has been seen the bylaws allow non-Catholic members. In no article of the bylaws are leadership positions in the Association reserved to Catholics. Likewise, the members of the Servant Leadership Team do not have to be approved by any authority. The representation of Catholic parishes accentuates the Catholic presence in this Catholic ecumenical canonical association of the faithful which has juridic personality.

---

[129] Glenmary Co-Missioners, as has been demonstrated, is a Catholic Association. The by laws are not as clear as they might be concerning the governance of the Association.

Internal Governance

The Association is governed by a board of directors which is known as the Servant Leadership Team. The Team, of five to twelve members, includes: 1) one representative from the Home Missioners of America, Inc. and one from the Home Missioner Sisters of America, Inc., 2) one representative from each of the five ethnic community groups served by the Glenmary Co-Missioners including, Native Americans, African Americans, Appalachians, Hispanics, and Native Southerners, 3) two members of the Service Team, these may not be officers nor may they participate in personnel decisions affecting service team members, 4) one candidate from each of the Catholic parishes in the locale where the Co-Missioners are working who are in contact with the work, (only one of these will attend the annual meeting), 5) and one representative of the associate members. (byl. V.4(a)-(e)) The bylaws state that, «The Servant Leadership Team endeavors to achieve a balance of culture, gender, class and lifestyle». (byl. V.4) The annual report also describes the governing board, «The Co-Missioner Governing Board is a group of people from a wide variety of backgrounds: religious and laity, women and men from various ethnic and religious backgrounds»[130]. The Servant Leadership Team does not receive a salary as do the incoming and local Co-Missioners and those who serve the corporation in capacities which warrant a salary. The same Servant Leadership Team which governs the work of the Co-Missioners is like the work itself and moves beyond denominational boundaries. There will always be a Catholic presence on the Servant Leadership Team both because the representatives of the Home Missioners of America, Inc. and the Home Missioner Sisters of America, Inc. are religious and because the candidates from the Catholic parishes will also be Catholics. The roots of the program in Glenmary and canonical relationship with the Diocese of Nashville keep the Association Catholic even as its work for justice among the poor of the Southern United States is ecumenical.

+ Conclusion

The Glenmary Co-Missioners are another group which bring diversity to the study. The Co-Missioners work for justice and community development in poor struggling communities of the rural Southern United States. The poor are encouraged to see their faith in Jesus Christ

---

[130] GLENMARY CO-MISSIONER ASSOCIATION, *Annual Report: 1995-1996*, (1996).

as liberating them in their own situation. Incoming Co-Missioners do not remain with the local community indefinitely but move on to other mission sites. A goal of the Co-Missioners is to empower the local faithful to live out their faith and to see that they can overcome where powerlessness seems to prevail.

e) *Apostolate for Family Consecration*

The Apostolate for Family Consecration was founded in 1975. In 1986 Jerome Coniker, who along with August Mauge was one of the founders of the Apostolate for Family Consecration, adopted the Eucharistic, Marian and family-centered spirituality of John Paul II for the Apostolate[131].

What makes the Apostolate for Family Consecration of interest to this study is its numerous levels of membership as well as its appeal to families. The headquarters of the Apostolate is in Bloomingdale, Ohio. There, is found the John Paul II Family Center known as Catholic Familyland. Families vacation and make retreats at this site. A set of video recordings has been made for parish and home use. Not less than forty-three bishops and cardinals are listed on letterhead as different types of auditors and council members for the group. The group is indeed Catholic. At the same time it may appeal to Protestants who are serious about family life.

There are varying degrees of membership. Sacri-state[132] Membership and First Degree Membership are open to non-Catholics while Second Degree Membership and Third Degree Membership require that persons be fully practicing Catholics. Here two examples will be highlighted as they most clearly contrast the possibility of non-Catholic members and a level of membership reserved to Catholics.

> Sacri-state members: Anyone can become a sacri-state member by offering their prayers and sacrifices for the work and mission of the Apostolate for Family Consecration.
>
> Second degree members are fully practicing Catholics who are invited to test a lay vocation as a single or married volunteer in the Apostolate for Family Consecration[133].

It is obvious from these two examples that some types of members must be practicing Catholics while other types of membership are open to anyone.

---

[131] APOSTOLATE FOR FAMILY CONSECRATION, *A Way of Life*, (1994), 1.

[132] Sacri-state means sacrifice in one's state in life.

[133] APOSTOLATE FOR FAMILY CONSECRATION, *A Way of Life*, 28 - 29.

First degree membership has no qualifications attached to it. First degree members follow the television or radio programs produced by the Apostolate or may offer the various Apostolate multi-media evangelization and catechetical tools to interested persons. Both Second and Third Degree Members are to be fully practicing Catholics. Second Degree Members make a six month renewable commitment to test a lay vocation as a single or married volunteer. They live the St. Louis de Montfort formula of total consecration to Jesus through Mary. Third Degree Members fulfill the requirements of Second Degree Members and renew their commitment every year for six years at which time the Apostolate for Family Consecration may confirm their life commitment. Besides the acceptance or not of non-Catholics another difference between the First Degree Membership to the Second Degree Membership is that Second Degree Membership and consequently Third Degree Membership is seen as a vocation to the Apostolate for Family Consecration.

+ Conclusion

The Apostolate for Family Consecration is certainly a Catholic organization. Its openness to non-Catholic members makes it an ecumenical association. Non-Catholics who take family life seriously would be the types of families who might like to join the Apostolate for Family Consecration. Again, movements which have zealous members will attract others from within and from outside of the visible boundaries of the Church.

1.3.2 Interconfessional Associations

a) *Lamb of God Community*

Among the communities that emerged as a result of the Catholic Charismatic Renewal is the Lamb of God Community in the Archdiocese of Baltimore. Beginning in 1971, the Community was officially recognized in the Archdiocese of Baltimore in 1995. The statutes describe the Community as «desiring to be erected as a private association of the Christian faithful with an ecumenical mission» (stat. introduction).

The statutes are not as descriptive or crisp as others in this study. The relationship with the diocesan bishop may allow for a certain openness in the statutes which is filled by his own supervision. The statutes are based on the *CIC* 83 and cite pertinent canons.

+ Ends

The first section of the statutes defines the association by its nature and purpose: it is a private association of the Christian faithful existing in the Archdiocese of Baltimore. The canonical terminology and relationship to the Archdiocese of Baltimore form the foundation for the Catholicity of the Community. It is interesting that the term «Catholic» does not appear in the statutes. Still the Church, as will be seen, certainly has a supervisory role over the Community. Scripture verses are used in the description of the purpose of the association, making it easily apply to all Christians:

> «The Community's aim is *to live for Jesus Christ in the power of His Holy Spirit (2 Cor. 5:15).* [...] Members strive *to support one another in living for Him (Jn. 13:34-35).* [...] The Community is committed *to share His life with others (Acts 1:8)*» (stat. I.A; B, emphasis in the original).

These points, which make up the ends or goals of the Community, are broad-based so as to accommodate its ecumenical character.

+ Members

The Lamb of God Community is open to non-Catholic members as seen in its statutes. Various examples follow.

> The Community welcomes and encourages the presence of Christians from all denominations to share its way of life [...] (stat. IV).
> A baptized Christian may become a member of the Community by being accepted according to the membership criteria [...] (stat. II.A).
> Christians of all denominations may serve in leadership in the Community providing they accept the statutes of the association [...] (stat. V).

These quotes are taken from sections covering ecumenical relationships, membership and leadership. Each reinforces the policy of open membership to all Christians who accept the statutes. The membership criteria for the Lamb of God Community are wide enough for all Christians.

> The members make a commitment to God and one another: to live for Jesus Christ in the power of His Holy Spirit; to support one another in living for Him; and to share His life with others. They desire to walk in this commitment subject to the Holy Spirit's guiding direction for their lives (stat. II.B).

Besides the general criteria quoted from the *statutes,* the Community has certain expectations of members; some are similar to the general criteria others are more specific. Among these are: 1) attendance at membership formation courses, 2) prayer, service and financial support of the Community and 3) participation in community life. After eighteen months of involvement in community life and making the public commitment of membership a candidate may make a commitment to the Community (stat. II.B).

+ Rights and Duties

The members of Lamb of God enjoy rights and duties. Many of these are couched in the membership criteria. The right to participate in community functions is coupled with the duty to be present and active. Included also is the duty to support one another as found in the nature and purpose of the association. Ecumenical relationships both within the Community and with other Christian bodies and groups bring the duty to respect those members of different faiths as they live out the beliefs of their particular denominations.

+ Governance

External Governance

One section of the *statutes* is dedicated to relations between the Community and the diocesan church.

> The Community is under the authority of the diocesan bishop, especially in matters relating to the celebration of liturgical rites and to the exercise of works of the apostolate.
> The statutes of the Community have been reviewed and recognized by the diocesan bishop (c.299,§2,3 *CIC* 83).
> Changes to the statutes must be approved by the diocesan bishop.
> The diocesan bishop or his representative will visit the Community periodically (c.305 *CIC* 83) (stat. VI).

Another norm located in the finances section of the document reinforces the governing role of the diocesan bishop obliging the Community to submit a yearly financial report to him (stat. VII.A). In the decree of recognition the archbishop stipulated that a full independent financial audit be undertaken and that such an audit be made and given to the diocesan authorities at least every second year[134]. A relationship

---

[134] W. KEELER, *Decree of Recognition*, (Archdiocese of Baltimore), 30 November 1995.

between the Community and the diocese is obviously manifested in the statutes.

Internal Governance

The internal governance or leadership of the Lamb of God Community includes a Council, Leadership Team and a Senior Leader. The Council, elected by members of the Community, is a consultative group for the Leadership Team. It is also a decision-making body. Besides support of the Community, the Council has the responsibility of reviewing the performance of the members of the Leadership Team (stat. V.A.5.f). The members of the Leadership Team are elected secretly by the Council (stat. V.A.5.g). As a body, Leadership Team members are the primary decision makers for the Community. Their responsibilities include the day to day running of the activities of the Community (stat. V.B). They «oversee Community services and ministries, e.g., prayer meetings, small groups, teaching, children's ministries, school, local outreaches, conferences, national and international missions» (stat. V.B.4.f). The Leadership Team fosters the vision and mission of the Community, provides spiritual leadership, by way of a finance committee oversees the budget, supervises the acceptance of new members and represents the Community to those outside (stat. V.B.4.b; c; d; e; g). A Senior Leader, who makes a full time commitment to oversee the life of the Community and service given by the Leadership Team, is chosen from the Leadership Team by the council and ratified by the Community. He is the chairman of the leadership team and the council (stat. V.B.2). It should be remembered that there is no requirement for the members of the Council, Leadership Team and the Senior Leader himself to be Catholic. Still the Community fits all canonical categories and follows the canons referring to private associations of the faithful. If in fact the number of non-Catholics grew so that the Community no longer had a Catholic majority, this could certainly be a topic for the annual meeting. If this case did in fact develop, the periodic visit of the diocesan bishop or his representative would become very important.

+ Conclusion

The *statutes* are written according to the *CIC* 83. Of the associations studied, the Lamb of God Community has the most open statutes: any baptized Christian may be a full member and enjoy all rights. It seems that the Senior Leader must be a male while members of the Leadership Team may be male or female. The obvious use of gender specific pronouns clarify these positions. (The Work of Mary was similar requiring a female as president and priests as vicar and vice president.) Gender specific positions limit the full use of rights by the membership, but only in a very narrow way. However, the question at hand is not gender but religious and denominational affiliation. The Lamb of God Community does not restrict non-Catholic Christians from membership or any leadership roles. Even though these non-restrictive statutes are not *contra legem,* they interestingly enough do not contain the designation, «Catholic». This is worthy of note as all other canonically recognized statutes do contain the term, «Catholic». The association will require attentive supervision and a strong relationship with the local bishop. Particular attention is suggested because the statutes do not mention a spiritual director for the group, who is mentioned by all other canonical associations. With non-restrictive statutes the Lamb of God Community does not fit the definition for ecumenical associations as found in *ChL* 31. Even though it is recognized by a Roman Catholic Bishop it is not considered an ecumenical association in this book.

The Lamb of God Community brings variety to the study. Its use of canon law is unique.

1.4 *Ecumenical Associations Existing in the United States without Official Approval*

Any number of un-official associations exist in the United States which have a large number of Catholic members along with a number of non-Catholics. These groups do not have canonical recognition, often because they have not asked to have the statutes reviewed, or the local bishop has not felt that he can recognize them. A consideration of these groups will only help to clarify the situation of those which are recognized canonical associations of the faithful. Examples follow.

1.4.1 Ecumenical Associations with Non-Catholic Members According to ChL 31

a) *People of God's Love Community*

The People of God's Love Community is a covenant charismatic association in Columbus, Ohio founded in 1977. The Community, besides offering meetings and formation for its own members, supports the Catholic Charismatic Renewal in the Diocese of Columbus.

Non-Catholics attend Community gatherings. Some of the non-Catholics are members of the Community. The presence of non-Catholics in the Community is small, perhaps five percent, but still is a presence making the group of interest to this study[135].

The relationship with the local bishop is by way of the liaison for Charismatic Renewal, Fr. Justin Reis, who has made a public (covenant) commitment to the People of God's Love and is also a founding member of the Community. In its support of the Catholic Charismatic Renewal the Community is involved in teaching, music ministry and youth work. College seminarians from the Pontifical College Josephinum and members of the Pontifical Institute for Foreign Missions retreat house are also involved in the work of the People of God's Love.

Relationships to other communities similar to their own is important to Community members. While all relationships are informal they support one another in community lifestyle. A long standing relationship exists with the People of God Community in Pittsburgh and through them with the North American Branch of the Sword in the Spirit. There is no official governmental relationship with the Sword in the Spirit, however at least one member of the People of God's Love usually attends the annual Community planning conference of the Sword in the Spirit with other senior coordinators.

While the Community sees itself becoming more involved in Catholic Charismatic Renewal activities in the diocese it is also involved in ecumenical endeavors. One senior coordinator from the People of God's Love Community is involved with local city pastors in the organization, Capitol City Association of Ministers. A member of the steering committee of the Association, he is in a unique position as a bridge between the Catholic Charismatic Renewal and the Protestant charismatics in Columbus. The People of God's Love are participating in the activities of Capitol City Association of Ministers, the local Catholic Charismatic Renewal, and the Sword in the Spirit[136].

+ Conclusion

The People of God's Love, while not a canonically recognized association of the faithful certainly do maintain a relationship with their own diocese through the liaison officer for Charismatic Renewal. They are open to non-Catholic members. If statutes of the Community were

---

[135] W. DURRANT, *Personal letter,* 30 May 1997.
[136] W. DURRANT, *Personal letter,* 30 May 1997.

to be presented to the competent authority and the Catholic integrity of the association safeguarded it, the Community would certainly be a candidate to receive status as a private association of the faithful.

1.4.2 Interconfessional Associations

a) *The Work of Christ Community*

An ecumenical Christian community is the way in which the Work of Christ Community describes itself[137]. Some ninety persons, who had been involved in Charismatic Renewal, made a formal covenant on Pentecost Sunday 1974. Since that time the Community has grown from ninety to approximately two hundred and twenty members[138].

+ Ends

Accordant to its own definition of its purpose and mission, the desire that people commit their lives to Christ and live as mature Christians is foundational to the Work of Christ. The Community and its members proclaim and defend the gospel, foster worship, love of God and live for His glory, and form personal relationships which are loving and which encourage Christian lifestyle. The work of evangelization is important as it helps others to know Christ as it spurs those evangelizing to live the gospel fully. As an ecumenical community it fosters Christian unity among Christians of different traditions through collaboration and cooperation[139].

A goal of the Work of Christ is not to become a church but to be a community of persons belonging to different Christian churches. The Community envisions active participation by its members in their own parishes and congregations. Community life is to be a common life that supports and is complementary to church membership. The purpose and mission of the Work of Christ are supported by the activities of the Community[140].

Members of the Work of Christ feel that:

Christian community can only be formed by those willing to freely embrace it. [....] Members of the Work of Christ love the churches of which

---

[137] *An Ecumenical Christian Community: The Work of Christ.* (Lansing, Michigan: The Work of Christ Community [1996]), 3.

[138] D. HIGLEY, *Personal letter*, 11 June 1997.

[139] *An Ecumenical Christian Community: The Work of Christ*, 5.

[140] *An Ecumenical Christian Community: The Work of Christ*, 5.

they are members. They want to serve their church and work for renewal within their church. They also see a need for tangible Christian community and are willing to build that life with members of other churches.

The Work of Christ has also been called to be a witness to ecumenical cooperation, and this call helped to form our decision to build community with Christians from different traditions. [....] Ecumenical Christian community provides a way to live and work together towards a common goal while we pray for greater unity[141].

The ecumenical aspect of the Community is addressed as is the reason for community to exist outside the visible boundaries of a particular church or churches. Persons who wanted to fully embrace their Christianity have done this with others who will support them in their decision. Recognizing the power of association, they gather with other like minded Christians and answer the call they have heard to live ecumenical cooperation working toward unity.

The ecumenical and Christological ends to the Community overtly manifest themselves. These suit the Community as Christ and the gospels are the areas in which the different churches and ecclesial communities can share. A study of the members, duties and rights, and governance of the Community also will bring forth the ecumenical aspect of the Work of Christ.

A Catholic fellowship exists within the Community. This group of Catholics meets at least three times a year. At meetings issues are addressed which arise in the ecumenical milieu of the Community and also education is provided for members of the Fellowship in Catholic doctrine[142]. The existence of the Fellowship indicates that the Catholic members of the Community wish to remain Catholic and develop their faith within the context of an ecumenical community.

+ Members

Persons desiring to become members of the Work of Christ need to have committed themselves to Christ, have been baptized in the Holy Spirit and be serious about living the gospel faith. Those who make a «public commitment» to the Community promise to keep the covenant as best they can. There is a process for entry into the Community as well as different levels of membership. An «underway commitment», which usually lasts about five years, is made before making the «public

---

[141] *An Ecumenical Christian Community: The Work of Christ*, 6-7.
[142] D. HIGLEY, *Personal letter*, 11 May 1997.

commitment», which is an open-ended perpetual commitment to the Community. During the formation period of the «underway commitment», persons experience community life first hand and seek God's will concerning the «public commitment». The publicly committed members pledge themselves to membership in the Work of Christ for life unless the Lord clearly calls them to service elsewhere. Persons not able to make the full commitment to the Community may join as «associates»[143].

The process by which one becomes a member of the Community is simple and not restricted by membership in any particular church. Nor is membership in the Catholic Church a requirement. All that is necessary is commitment to the Work of Christ, making an underway commitment and the making of a public commitment to live the covenant. Although baptism by water would seem to be a requisite for membership in a Christian group this is not stated in the informational handbook of the Work of Christ which only speaks of those who have been baptized in the Holy Spirit[144]. Although there is no specific mention of water baptism the fact that the members are Catholic, Luthern Evangelicals, and Orthodox supposes the necessity of water baptism. We may suppose that members received water baptism when they became members of their own churches and Baptism in the Spirit as a part of their entrance into the Community.

+ Rights and Duties

The primary right and duty of members of the Work of Christ is to the covenant lifestyle. The most telling paragraph, for these purposes, of the covenant involves ecumenism:

> We desire to be united in love and to share a common heart, mind, and purpose with our brothers and sisters in The Work of Christ Community. God has called us to be an ecumenical, charismatic, Christian community in which He gives us the strength, order, and grace to live for Him totally and to joyfully lay down our lives for one another. As an ecumenical community, we are committed to the support and encouragement of spiritual renewal among all Christian people[145].

As with the whole covenant, this paragraph encourages members towards a love for God and neighbor. Those who are a part of the

---

[143] *An Ecumenical Christian Community: The Work of Christ*, 8 - 9.
[144] *An Ecumenical Christian Community: The Work of Christ*, 8.
[145] *An Ecumenical Christian Community: The Work of Christ*, 17.

Work of Christ have the right to receive the benefits of the other members of the Community living the covenant. That the others would pray for them, assist them in their spiritual, physical and material lives, and ultimately lay down their lives for Community members are some of the benefits which ought to make a difference in the spiritual lives of the persons who are a part of the Work of Christ.

Participation in community activities is one of the benefits as well as duties which members enjoy. Activities, which are all ecumenical, include: 1) Community gatherings occurring several times each month where in the whole Community enjoys worship and praise, bible teaching and time for sharing. 2) Small groups for men and women offer prayer, support and encouragement to those living the community life. 3) Celebration of the Lord's Day includes families and singles coming together on a Saturday evening to prepare to celebrate Sunday. 4) Service teams gather to meet the different needs of the Community. Child care and intercessory prayer are two examples of this group's activities. 5) Outreach programs aimed at bringing people to Christ and Christian spiritual growth are offered for and by the Community. 6) Community courses are offered that cover such topics as child rearing and family life. Most Community events are open to the public[146]. These benefits and duties of Community members are advantageous to the Christian life. Members feel that the Community offers a true opportunity to live the corporate and communal lifestyle described in the New Testament[147].

+ Governance

External Governance

Even though members of the Community remain active in their own parishes and congregations[148], no official church organization has any role of authority over the Work of Christ. There is good but informal relationship with the Diocese of Lansing. The relationship of Catholic members of the Community with their Church is through their own parish, not the Community nor the Catholic Fellowship which exists within the Community. A priest of the Diocese of Lansing is assigned as a liaison between the Community and the Diocese[149].

---

[146] *An Ecumenical Christian Community: The Work of Christ*, 11 - 12.
[147] *An Ecumenical Christian Community: The Work of Christ*, 6.
[148] *An Ecumenical Christian Community: The Work of Christ*, 5.
[149] D. HIGLEY, *Personal letter*, 11 June 1997.

The Work of Christ Community is a member of the Sword in the Spirit, an international ecumenical association of member communities. The Catholics within the Work of Christ are members of a Catholic fellowship within the Community. The Catholic Fellowship of the Work of Christ is also a member of the Christ the King Association, an international association of Catholic communities and fellowships.[150] Neither the Sword in the Spirit nor Christ the King, which are closely related but independent organizations, are officially recognized by Catholic Church authorities. The Sword in the Spirit is on the mailing list of the PCL. This, however, gives no official standing to the organization. The Work of Christ Community and its Catholic Fellowship recognize the need for participation in a larger, wider network of communities with a call and mission similar to their own. They are members of the parent organizations for this reason.

Internal Governance

The internal governance of the Work of Christ Community involves itself in guiding community life. As an ecumenical community, the plurality of leadership is important to the members of Work of Christ. The leaders who govern the Community are called coordinators. A senior coordinator, who serves a five-year term, is the chairman to the body of coordinators[151].

At present there are three Catholics, two Protestants and one Orthodox member of the leadership team. This reflects the overall demographics of the Community: seventy-two percent Catholic, eleven percent Lutheran, ten percent Evangelical and seven percent Orthodox. The numbers speak of the ecumenical dimension of the Community[152].

The coordinators are not the only members of the Community who hold leadership positions. An Advisory Council exists to assist the decision making process in the Community. There are also leaders of groups for men and women, and heads of service groups and ministries. Those who are elected members are the coordinators and members of the Advisory Council[153]. These service posts are open to all fully committed members of the Community.

---

[150] D. HIGLEY, *Personal letter*, 11 June 1997.
[151] *An Ecumenical Christian Community: The Work of Christ*, 9.
[152] D. HIGLEY, *Personal letter*, 11 June 1997.
[153] *An Ecumenical Christian Community: The Work of Christ*, 9.

+ Conclusion

The Work of Christ is different from other groups which have been studied in that it does not maintain any relationship or interaction with the hierarchy of the Catholic Church, save the diocesan liaison with the Catholic Fellowship. A plurality in its governing body of leaders and the obvious lack of references to things Catholic also set it apart from groups which are recognized as canonical associations of the faithful. The relationship of the Community itself with the larger associations of communities which are also ecumenical will without a relation with the hierarchy makes it unique. Given these examples it can be assumed that one or more of them would be the reason why the Community is not recognized as a canonical association of the faithful in its diocese. As the relations develop at an international level between the Sword of the Spirit and the PCL it is possible that the relationship between the Catholic Fellowship in The Work of Christ also may develop. The situation is similar to that of the Alleluia Catholic Fellowship, however more levels exist for the Work of Christ which would need to be organized. Still the group is very well organized and has a large Catholic membership.

b) *The Word of God Community*

The Word of God describe themselves as an ecumenical charismatic Christian community[154]. Much like the Work of Christ they had their beginnings in the Catholic Charismatic Renewal, and have always been an ecumenical community. During its almost thirty years of existence the Community has experienced drastic fluctuation in population. The internal structure of the Community had much to do with these changes.

+ Ends

The Word of God Community strives to provide a community atmosphere for members in order that they may grow in their faith and commitment to the Lord in their everyday lives. What they had found in the Charismatic Renewal they want to share in everyday life. The Community members desire to give their whole lives to God in the power of the Holy Spirit and to be fruitful in His service.[155] Those who

---

154 WORD OF GOD, *Opportunities for Involvement*, 1.
155 R. MARTIN, «A Work In Progress», 4.

become members of the Community believe that the Community atmosphere can help them to live out their baptismal call as Christians as well as the call of John 17, 21, «that all be one».

+ Members

As an ecumenical or inter-denominational community persons of various Christian backgrounds have always been able to be full members of the Word of God Community. Full members make a covenant with the Community which is considered permanent. It is however possible to be released from this commitment. The membership of the Community has included: Orthodox, Roman Catholics, Pentecostals, Lutherans, Presbyterians, Methodists and Baptists[156]. Members attend their own churches for liturgical and sacramental worship which is not possible in the context of the ecumenical community. The membership of the Community started at two hundred ten members in 1970 and peeked at one thousand five hundred sixty-five members in 1986. Statistics released in 1996 show four hundred thirty two members in the Community. The ratio of Catholics to all other denominations has remained somewhat the same throughout the life of the Community. Catholics have always accounted for between forty-nine and sixty-eight percent of the population.

+ Governance

External Governance

The Community itself has never had any official canonical relationship with the Church because of their ecumenical status[157]. For the Word of God this has meant that non-Catholics are able to serve in leadership capacities. The Catholics who have been in leadership positions in the Community have kept in personal communication with their bishops.

External relationships have existed between the Community and a number of associations of communities. The Word of God was, as the Work of Christ is, a member of the Sword of the Spirit international association of Catholic and ecumenical communities. Since 1990 the relationship has been a fraternal connection and not a full membership. At present, the Community is not in formal relationship with any other

---

[156] P. TIEWS, *Personal letter*, 23 June 1997.
[157] P. TIEWS, *Personal letter* 23 June 1997.

grouping of communities. They do stay in contact with many communities and associations of communities around the world[158].

Currently a personal or non-territorial parish, Christ the King, has been erected by the Diocese of Lansing in Michigan, which Catholic Community members are encouraged to attend. This followed changes in the Community to be considered in the section covering internal governance. The Catholics within the Community who attend Christ the King make up about one-third of the parish population. Another third is comprised of persons who were members of the Community but are not at this time. Persons who have joined the parish without having any former involvement with the Community make up the last third of the parish population.

Internal Governance

The Community has gone through a number of different stages involving internal structure. In 1982, four congregations were formed which comprised the total membership of the Word of God Community. The Community hoped to form an «integrated ecumenical model» where members would share in community activities as one body and then in the congregations for sacraments and liturgical worship. By 1990, it was obvious that this model was not working because the ecumenical Community tended to take priority over the life of the churches. Concurrently a number of members decided to invest more completely in their own particular churches. The Community supported their decision. The present solution of a personal parish works well with the developments of the Community structure. This is evidenced by membership in the parish both of Community members and former Community members.

What becomes obvious is that non-Catholics as well as Catholics were instrumental in the formation of the Community. Thus the Community would always have an ecumenical flavor which would not have its beginning or end in Roman Catholicism. A Catholic leader or board would not have the last word about decisions. This is the reason that the Community itself it not able to be recognized by competent authority as an association. Even for the body of Catholics within whom are members of the Word of God the possibility of recognizing them as a Catholic fellowship would take a certain supervision on the part of the Church and the overall Community itself.

---

158 P. TIEWS, *Personal letter*, 23 June 1997.

+ Conclusion

The Word of God Community is similar to other charismatic communities in this study but is at the same time rather unique. As has been seen the Community has undergone a drastic change in membership as well as a change in structure. The present structure for the Catholics in the Community is a personal or non-territorial parish. Even though this does not fit the structure of an ecumenical association according to *ChL* 31 it is of interest because it is an alternative for Catholic members of interconfessional associations.

1.4.3 Atypical Ecumenical associations

The final two groups of the study are neither Catholic nor canonical. They tend to being similar to religious institutes in that they fashion themselves somewhat after ICL in the Catholic Church.

a) *The Ecumenical Order of Charity*

The Ecumenical Order of Charity was founded in 1898 by an Old Catholic bishop at Oxford, England to be an ecumenical community. The group was to witness to the whole Body of Christ. After moving to the United States in the 1960's, working for the peace and justice movement, a daughter community was founded. The mother community has gone out of existence and the daughter community has taken up where the former left off[159].

+ Ends

«For the Sake of the Kingdom» is the motto of the Ecumenical Order of Charity. It is the end toward which they work. The Order sees itself as a religious community of men and women living a vowed consecrated life directed by a common rule of life which is *The Founding Document* (FD I.1). They believe themselves:

> to be a part of the Divine Flame and that same Indwelling Life is the common factor in all life. Knowing that we are all one and that all life has value, we take seriously our responsibility for others and for all creation. Consequently, we hold that all things and events are part of an indivisible whole and that the highest law of life is to do no harm to any living creature (FD I.2).

---

[159] D. ROBERT, *Personal letter,* 17 February 1997.

Canonical associations of the Christian faithful are to follow their statutes in accordance with the law and teachings of the Church[160]. This is true especially if they wish to be recognized by the Church. The companions, members of the Ecumenical Order of Charity, are not bound together by the teaching or doctrine of a particular denomination, but are joined by their *Founding Document* (FD IV.1). The Order see themselves as ecumenical, its tradition being Christian. The model of an historical/scriptural Christ or a Cosmic Christ may be chosen to be followed by the individual companions. They believe that they give themselves less than they deserve when the companions conform to hierarchical or scriptural authority only for the sake of denominational membership (FD IV.5). As the Order is an ecumenical group which was reestablished outside the boundaries of any particular church or ecclesial Community it is not legally recognized by any ecclesial authority. Recognition would not be of value to the Order[161]. It is evident that the group is not a candidate to be recognized as a canonical association of the Christian faithful by the Roman Catholic Church.

+ Members

Members come from various Christian denominations including Roman Catholic, Episcopal and Lutheran. They remain active within their respective churches. Formation includes a postulancy and a novitiate which leads to vows and eventually permanent vows. Presently there are eight in either permanent vows or at some stage of formation[162].

+ Rights and Duties

The members are able to cooperate with one another in a community which strives to be loving and supportive. Companions may live alone, with their families, or with other companions in one of the Community houses. The one and only reference point for all, regardless of their living situation is to build together in Christ (FD V.2).

The vows taken by the companions of the Ecumenical Order of Charity are: Simplicity of Life, Purity of Heart, Obedience, Non-Violence, and Universal Citizenship. (FD VI.2) The first three vows

---

[160] Cf. c.304,§1; c.305,§§1,2; c.315; c.321 *CIC* 83.

[161] D. ROBERT, *Personal letter*, 17 February 1998.

[162] *Community, The Newsletter of the Ecumenical Order of Charity*, Summer 1997, 1.

are similar to the evangelical counsels, the last two are added as a part of *The Founding Document*. The vows are to have neither an ecclesiastical nor a legally binding status; they bind only in the heart of those who profess them. (FD VI.4) Even though the profession of vows give the members companion status, vows are lived in the heart of each of the companions.

All novices and professed Companions of the Order are to submit an annual report to the Director General. The annual report contains a summary of the novice's or companion's life in religion as well as projections for the future (FD XVIII.1). It is possible that a companion may be dismissed from the Order on the basis of an unsatisfactory annual report. Due process is followed before a final termination would take place (FD VI.8). Because of the Community structure which allows persons to live in a number of different situations the annual report becomes an important tool for communication of the experience of religious life and goals for the companions.

+ Governance

In reply to a questionnaire, the general director made it clear that the Order is not officially recognized as an association by any diocese or bishop[163]. The Order itself follows a collegial system of governance in which each member, using *The Founding Document* as his guide, is responsible for his/her own actions. The general assembly, consisting of all professed members, is the main governing body of the Order. Its responsibilities are as follows:

> To elect the Director General. To conduct official business of the Order. To make changes to The Founding Document as necessary. To review and act on agenda topics put forward by the professed Companions. To protect the charism and heritage of our Order (FD XX.4).

The internal governance of the Order is simple and organized in a fashion that the goals of the group can be met.

The director general guides the Order in a way that comes from a shared understanding of *The Founding Document*. He or she is elected every four years; there is no limit to the number of terms a general director may serve (FD XXI.2). As a closing statement concerning governance the founding document states, «In our Order there are no "superiors" or "inferiors" only friends» (FD XXI.4).

---

163 D. ROBERT, *Personal letter*, 17 February 1998.

+ Conclusion

The Ecumenical Order of Charity does not seek any recognition or approval from any church or ecclesial community. The Order prefers not to be in relation as a community but encourages its individual members to be in relation with their own churches. Since the Ecumenical Order of Charity itself is opposed to any hierarchical structure, it is not in a position to be considered an association of the faithful by the Roman Catholic Church.

b) *The Mercy of God Community*

In many ways the Mercy of God Community is similar to the Ecumenical Order of Charity. They are open to accept members from any Christian denomination. Being ecumenical, for them, means that they have no allegiance to one specific church or ecclesial community. After formation periods of candidacy and novitiate persons make final profession. All baptized Christians are eligible for membership.

The Mercy of God Community began in 1992 when it evolved from the Brothers of the Mercy of God, founded in 1988. The new group is also open to women. The Community was founded in Hartford, Connecticut and is civilly incorporated in the state of Rhode Island.

+ Ends

Members of the Mercy of God Community, «promise to live the Gospel of Jesus, "in the manner of Saint Francis and Saint Claire". To achieve this end Francis and Claire remain the principal inspiration and example by their total commitment to the Gospel»[164]. As an ecumenical community members pursue: Christian unity, a spirituality based on the teachings of Jesus, prayer and meditation. While respecting all denominational traditions they extend the gospel message beyond parochial bounds striving to be prophetic to the whole world[165]. The By-Laws of the Community further define its nature and purpose. Among the charisms and missions listed are: engaging in continuous spiritual formation, conducting Christian ecumenical worship services, helping persons to become more fully who they are, involvement in religious education and collaborating with similar non-canonical communities

---

[164] MERCY OF GOD COMMUNITY, *The Rule*, #4.
[165] MERCY OF GOD COMMUNITY, *The Rule*, #6.

(byl. 2.1; 2.2) [166]. The nature of the Community strives to follow Jesus' call in the gospel using Francis and Claire as models.

+ Members

Membership in the Community is open to any adult regardless of gender, race, nationality, ethnic origin, physical ability, affectional orientation, marital or relationship status, socioeconomic class, educational or occupational background or place of residence (byl. 5.1). There are not many restrictions to membership. The members retain their own denominational affiliation and parish membership. The Community is meant to be complimentary to parish life. At the present time membership includes: Roman Catholic, Episcopal, United Methodist, Baptist, Servant Catholic, Old Catholic, Catholic Apostolic Church in North America, Lutheran and American Catholic[167].

Besides full members, there are associates. An associate is someone who wishes to identify with the Community and provide prayerful and or material support. This is the only involvement required (byl. 5.5.1). Associates may be Christians or non-Christians. Full members proceed through formation which includes candidacy, novitiate and profession.

+ Rights and Duties

The members enjoy sharing with others in community life. The establishment of households is not a requirement as persons may belong to the Community and remain in their present living situation. All professed members attend plenary meetings of the Community. A newsletter published quarterly is sent to all members and interested persons. Members in good standing receive copies of the governing documents and other Community reports. Lists of names of members and other interested parties are considered strictly confidential. These are not shared as the privacy of persons is respected (byl. 7.5; 7.6; 7.7). Communication is important to the Community as they do not gather in residences.

+ Governance

«The Community places itself under the inspiration and authority of the Holy Spirit. Temporal Governance shall be on a collegial and

---

[166] THE MERCY OF GOD COMMUNITY, *By-Laws*, are a pamphlet taken from the Mercy of God Handbook.

[167] B. KETCHAM, *Personal letter*, 17 March 1997.

democratic basis» (byl. 5.1). As the Community looks to God for inspiration it has a government which serves its members. The leader is called a president and Brother/Sister Servant. This person is assisted by officers and a council. The council holds regular meetings, at least three each year. (byl. 6.1) Elections are held for all positions every three years. All professed members are eligible to vote.

At this time there is a retired Anglican Bishop who acts as an ecumenical advisor to the Community. A Roman Catholic advisor would also be desirable. According to the president this does not seem probable in the near future[168].

+ Conclusion

Presently it does not seem possible for the Mercy of God Community to be canonically recognized as an association of the Christian faithful. In order to be so recognized, an association must be willing to accept the supervision of competent ecclesiastical authority as well as that of the Apostolic See. By placing itself solely under the authority of the Holy Spirit, the Community expresses its autonomy from any particular Church or ecclesial community.

1.5 *Summary of Associations Studied*

The question of ecumenical associations was brought about by the *lacuna* or aperture found in canons 298-329 of the *CIC* 83 which does not forbid non-Catholics from becoming members of associations of the Christian faithful. The charge of *ChL* 31 supported the openness of the canons. While the charge of *ChL* 31 to the PCL and PCPCU to draw up a list of conditions with which ecumenical associations can be recognized, approved or erected has not yet been met, a review of the present praxis will provide examples of relationships which presently exist between international associations and the PCL. Examples are helpful to local churches where bishops seek to erect, approve or recognize ecumenical associations. By reviewing the canonical praxis of the Apostolic See with international ecumenical associations and then the canonical praxis between the dioceses of the United States of America and ecumenical associations existing within their jurisdiction, this summary will attempt to present a praxis which exists at the level of the Apostolic See and the diocesan level in the United States of America.

---

[168] B. KETCHAM, *Personal letter*, 17 March 1997.

1.5.1 Types of Associations Studied

Before a review of the praxis, an overall presentation of the nineteen associations studied is undertaken. Of greatest interest to the dissertation are the associations which are canonically recognized by the Apostolic See or one of the one hundred seventy-six Latin rite dioceses located in the United States of America. Thirteen of the nineteen groups in the study are canonically recognized. These will be highlighted in the section on praxis. Other associations which are not canonically recognized have been included in the study as they give insight into reasons canonical recognition may or may not be given as well as examples of various types of ecumenical associations which are in existence.

Section one of chapter two describing the method employed categorized the associations into: 1.2) international associations approved by the Apostolic See or in direct connection with it 1.3) associations approved in the dioceses of the United States of America, and 1.4) ecumenical associations in the United States of America without official approval.

The particular needs of each diverse association (sections 1.2; 1.3; and 1.4) can be met through the different levels of canonical recognition. The systematization of the various associations under study here is unique. This comes about as the consideration of the status of these groups both international and in the United States brings together associations which fit into the structures of the *CIC* 83 as well as associations which are *praeter legem* but not necessarily *contra legem*. Further distinctions will now be identified. Each of the three categories will be reviewed.

All of the international associations (section 1.2) save the two fellowships which participate in larger interconfessional communities are on the address list of the PCL. All of the international associations except the Lamb of God Catholic Fellowship are private associations of the Christian Faithful recognized by the Apostolic See at the PCL. Two other exceptions are the Alleluia Catholic Fellowship and Chemin Neuf which are private and public associations of the faithful respectively with juridic personality approved in their dioceses.

The eight international associations reviewed in the dissertation were further categorized into: 1.2.1) ecumenical associations with non-Catholic members according to *ChL* 31, 1.2.2) ecumenical associations comprised of only Catholic members that participate in interconfessional communities and 1.2.3) interconfessional communities. Each of the associations fits into its respective categorical section which brings definition to the Associations itself. Still there are differences between each which reaffirms the fact that each of the Associations is unique and has unique needs.

L'Arche is mentioned here as it is in a category of its own (1.2.3). It is international and ecumenical but is not canonically recognized. Its status is made clear in the letter of the founder; because of its ecumenical/interreligious approach it is not canonically recognized by the Apostolic See.

Once the diocesan level has been engaged, the dissertation focuses on associations found in the United States. These associations are further divided into those approved (1.3) and those without official approval (1.4). These subsections each are further divided into: ecumenical associations with non-Catholic members according to *ChL* 31 (1.3.1; 1.4.1) and interconfessional associations (1.3.2; 1.4.2). Interestingly enough one of these associations, the Apostolate for Family Consecration is on the address list of the PCL. There is an interest on the part of the Apostolate to be officially recognized by the PCL[169]. Participation in the Apostolate for Family Consecration certainly is international making it a candidate for recognition by the PCL. Both the Work of Christ and the People of God's Love Communities have a relationship (in the case of the People of God's Love this is not official) with the Sword of the Spirit, an unofficial interconfessional community of communities. The Sword of the Spirit also appears on the address list of the PCL. Even though appearance on the address list of the PCL does not put the association into a canonical relation with the Apostolic See the importance of some working relationship or even communication between the listed association and the PCL is to be noted.

The interconfessional associations, as was L'Arche which is ecumenical and interreligious, are a special situation. They are ecumenical but do not follow *ChL* 31. Again, *ChL* 31 concerns the Roman Catholic presence in an ecumenical association. This concern specifically includes the number of non-Catholics in the association and therefore the leadership positions. The interconfessional associations in the study have a strong Catholic majority, but may not have restrictions in place or may not wish to recognize that *ChL* 31 does bring restrictions. Among the interconfessional Associations in the United States only the Lamb of God is officially recognized by its diocese.

---

[169] J. CONIKER, *Personal letter*, 1 August 1997.

The last two groups in the study are atypical ecumenical Associations (1.4.3). In a number of ways they resemble institutes of consecrated life. They are ecumenical but may be too open to certain teachings which are not acceptable to the magisterium. Any relation which might exist between the atypical ecumenical associations and individual Roman Catholics would not be of an official nature.

This overview ought to help bring into focus the associations under study by this dissertation. As the next section of the summary studies the praxis between the hierarchy and the recognized associations it will be good to keep in mind the categories of each particular association.

1.5.2 Praxis between Church Hierarchy and Associations of the Faithful

The praxis or relationship between the ecumenical associations and the Church authority by whom they are recognized, approved or erected can be clarified by two questions. These involve membership of non-Catholics in the associations. The questions are as follows: 1) How are non-Catholic Christians permitted to inscribe in canonically recognized associations of the faithful, as members or in some other manner? 2) What rights are enjoyed by members and by those inscribed in some other manner? The summary will review these questions for the Apostolic See and the dioceses of the United States of America.

a) *Praxis at the Level of the Apostolic See*

Two of the three associations which have a decree of approval from the PCL assign another title to non-Catholics who inscribe in the association. Focolare names those non-Catholic Christians who make up a part of the association, «associates», and non-Catholic non-Christians, «collaborators». Emmanuel names its non-Catholic Christian participants «associate brothers». *La Fraternité Chrétienne Intercontinentale des Personnes Malades Chroniques et Handicapées Physiques* does not name non-Catholics inscribed differently than the Catholics who belong to the association. It would seem that the change in praxis here from Focolare and Emmanuel may reflect the status of the members as chronically ill and physically handicapped. Still the PCL is open to non-Catholics in *La Fraternité Chrétienne Intercontinentale des Personnes Malades Chroniques et Handicapées Physiques*. Besides the Fraternity, the praxis of the other two groups is clear: non-Catholics may not belong to associations of the faithful as full members but may be aggregated under some other title.

Full rights are enjoyed by Catholics in all of the three associations studied, save in Focolare where the positions of the president, vice-president/vicar restrict rights by gender and vocation. The statutes of all three associations limit the rights of non-Catholic members as these participants are not able to serve in all of the governing roles of the associations to which they belong. The praxis of the Apostolic See recognizes that the difference in name or mode of belonging to the association is related to the rights one enjoys as a person who is inscribed into the association. The Apostolic See is open in certain situations to non-Catholic members to participate in associations of the faithful as full members. However, non-Catholics never have full rights in an association.

Chemin Neuf is a special case in this dissertation. In *Chemin Neuf* non-Catholics do not have a different title or name from the Catholics. In fact they are called members. However, while they are full members they are not members *pleno iure*. The non-Catholics will not have all the rights and duties that Catholics have in an association of the Christian faithful which is canonically recognized by the Roman Catholic Church. Here the Community and the Archdiocese of Lyon use the same praxis as the Apostolic See, by restricting the rights of non-Catholics to serve the association by playing a role in its governance.

b) *Praxis at the Level of the Dioceses of the United States of America*

Of direct import to this section of the summary are the associations of the Christian faithful in the United States of America which are at least recognized by their local bishop. The Alleluia Catholic Fellowship is used as an example of the way statutes define the membership of an association. It is clearly stated in the statutes that only Catholics can be members of the Fellowship: «Membership in the Fellowship is open to baptized Roman Catholics who are active members of the Alleluia Community [...] Its membership consists of Catholic single lay men and lay women...» (stat. II.A; B)[170]. This is just as important for associations which allow non-Catholic members. The same two questions used to summarize the praxis at the level of the Apostolic See will be used here.

---

[170] Cf. c.304,§1 *CIC* 83.

The ecumenical associations found in the United States of America which are a part of this study including The Mother of God Community, Magnificat and Glenmary Co-Missioners are taken together since they generally use the same praxis. The Lamb of God Community is treated differently since its praxis is different. The prior three associations all at least approved by their bishop call the non-Catholics and Catholics who are inscribed members. The praxis of the dioceses involved allow non-Catholic Christians to be full members equivalent to the Catholics in these canonical associations of the Christian faithful. However, similar to the praxis at the Apostolic See, the non-Catholic Christian members do not have full rights. None of the associations limit the non-Catholic Christians from all positions of service and authority, but there are some limits made in the statutes of each of the associations as can be observed in the detailed studies of the statutes. While the statutes of these associations allow all Christians to inscribe as full members only the Catholics have full rights to serve in the government of the associations.

The Lamb of God Community has a praxis which is different: all Christians are able to be full members and all members have full rights. There is no restriction on which positions in the government of the Lamb of God Community are able to be filled by Catholics or non-Catholics; all positions are open to all members. While the other canonical associations studied are at least approved by the diocesan bishop, the Lamb of God Community is simply recognized meaning that its statutes have been reviewed without the bishop giving his approval or recommendation to the association. The Lamb of God Community, while offering full rights to all members, places itself under the authority of the diocesan bishop. The last two points mentioned, recognition and full rights to all members (Catholics and non-Catholics are able to have full membership), make The Lamb of God Community unique to this study. The Brothers and Sisters of Charity in their desire to maintain their status as a public association of the faithful have removed the non-Catholics from canonical membership. Even though not necessary, this may have been a wise decision as it more closely follows the praxis of the Apostolic See as it has dealt with private associations. The association is also different from the others because it desires to eventually have a Pontifical status.

c) *The Difference in Praxis between the Apostolic See and that of the Dioceses of the United States of America*

The differences, as well as similarities, in praxis between the Apostolic See and the dioceses of the United States of America concerning membership of non-Catholics in associations of the Christian faithful is rather simple. Differences in praxis include use of the word member and the canonical status applied to (private reviewed, private approved, private with juridic personality or public) associations of the Christian faithful. As will be presented, the two are related.

The point where the praxis differs is the membership of non-Catholics in the associations. The Apostolic See in most cases limits the use of the title «member» to Catholics. The inscribing of members is related to the rights which a person possesses in the association. The dioceses of the United States freely inscribe both Catholics and non-Catholics as members. All baptized Christians are considered full members even though the rights of non-Catholics are limited. The limitation of rights does not affect membership. The practice in the United States is that persons can be full members, they can be given the same name as members *pleno iure,* without having full rights. Neither the Apostolic See nor the dioceses of the United States give non-Catholics full rights. The question of membership is dealt with differently by the Apostolic See and the dioceses studied in the United States. The Apostolic See most often limits the term members to Catholics inscribed in ecumenical associations. These associations which have non-Catholics inscribed in some manner are assigned juridic personality. The Work of Mary, Emmanuel and the International Christian Fraternity are private juridic persons in the Roman Catholic Church.

A praxis used by the approved associations studied is that non-Catholics do not serve in all roles of service and governance within associations of the Christian faithful which are approved at the level of the Apostolic See or at the diocesan level in the United States of America. The particular positions which are limited to Catholics vary from association to association. The distribution of roles of governance and service is left to the judgment of the competent authority.

Three different praxes are evident. The first two are different at the Apostolic See and the United States Dioceses and the third is similar. They have just been identified and discussed, but are mentioned here as they will be important to the next chapter concerning the canonical background of ecumenical associations. The three practices are: 1) the use of the term member, 2) the use of categories of associations (private reviewed, private approved, private with juridic personality or public), and 3) the rights enjoyed by the non-Catholics who take part in the association. Chapter III is the specifically canonical study.

2. Conclusion

After a study of *ChL* 31 and c.307,§4 sch 82 and before the summary of the associations and their praxis nineteen associations were studied. These formed the heart of the chapter as real living examples of associations with many different canonical links to ecclesiastical authority were presented. A consideration of a number of different contemporary associations gives a true example of how the Apostolic See and the dioceses of the United States of America are presently interpreting the *CIC* 83 in its canons covering associations. The study helps associations which are presently writing statutes and also the Apostolic See as it prepares guidelines according to *ChL* 31. Also aided are the individual dioceses themselves as they create procedures for recognizing associations in their dioceses.

His Holiness John Paul II certainly supports ecumenical associations. The work of *ChL* 31 makes this eminently clear. This is not a support which will cease but in fact one which the Pope assigned to pontifical councils to research further. There is no question as to the existence of ecumenical associations, they are active within the Church.

Even since the promulgation of the *CIC* 83 the Holy Father has supported ecumenical associations. His suppression of c.307,§4 sch 82 manifests his desire not to forbid the associations as the *CIC* 17 had. From this point in time ecumenical associations had canonical support to serve the people of God through participating in the mission of the Church.

The development of the *CCEO* 90 as reported in *Nuntia* is telling for the position of non-Catholics and ecumenical associations. The statement was made that even if it seemed better for non-Catholics to be excluded from associations because of disharmony which would occur this prohibition would not become law for ecumenical reasons. The importance of ecumenism to the Church is manifest in this discussion.

The types of ecumenical associations in existence are varied. The diversity of the associations which are presented in the second chapter manifests this fact. The variety of associations now in existence encourages the completion of the work by the PCL and PCPCU. The task of the PCL is mammoth as it oversees the EMNC. The importance of a canonical foundation upon which the associations can build increases as the number and variety of EMNC continues to climb.

CHAPTER III

**The Development of the Notion of Ecumenical Associations
of the Christian Faithful: *CIC* 17 – *CIC* 83**

1. Introduction

The purpose of this chapter is to explore the development of ecumenical associations since the *CIC* 17 until the *CIC* 83. This study will trace their gradual development in the Roman Catholic Church. Furthermore, differences in the systems of the *CIC* 17 and the *CIC* 83 will be identified since the changes in the codal system do open the way for the ecumenical associations of the faithful. While the first juridical possibilities for their formation came with the drafting of the *CIC* 83 these possibilities themselves were prompted by the Second Vatican Council at which ecumenical and ecclesiological developments, both theological and pastoral, took place thereby opening the doors to truly ecumenical associations. The chapter will begin with the decided «no» initially given to ecumenical associations by the *CIC* 17, and will proceed to the contemporary openness of the *CIC* 83. In conclusion, the more amicable configuration of ecumenical associations of the Christian faithful within the Roman Catholic Church will be presented.

2. A Clear «No» and then Silence: c.693, §1 *CIC* 17

Here the study of c.693,§1 *CIC* 17 is continued[1]. Because c.693,§1 *CIC* 17 initiated the particular canonical practice of not allowing non-Catholics to inscribe into associations of the Christian faithful, the pre-

---

[1] The canon which did not allow non-Catholics to become members of associations of the Christian faithful has been discussed in Chapter I, section 2.1., «Non-Catholic Members of Associations of the Faithful».

sent section will make a deeper study of the fonts and commentators of the *CIC* 17.

2.1 *Fonts*

The fonts of c.693,§1 *CIC* 17 are threefold[2]. The first is a response to an inquiry made to the Sacred Congregation for the Propagation of the Faith in which it was asked if a warning ought to be issued against the practice of the bishops of the United States accepting non-Catholics as honorary members of the Society of St. Vincent de Paul. The response stated that in general non-Catholics ought not be allowed to participate as honorary members. Even if these same non-Catholics had spontaneously given alms, which could be accepted, their participation was not permitted[3]. As the only font which directly addresses non-Catholics, it does not discuss membership of non-Catholics in associations of the Christian Faithful as a whole, but simply honorary membership. Yet, the response as a source for 693,§1 *CIC* 17 makes the prohibition eminently clear: if non-Catholics are not even able to become merely honorary members, their membership in associations of the Christian faithful is out of the question.

The other two fonts are in the form of letters written by Pius IX. Both letters address the evils of Freemasonry[4]. While the first, *Quamquam* (1873), cites letters of his predecessors who pronounced Freemasonry anathema[5], the second letter and third font, *Exortae* (1876), reminds the reader of the pontiff's previous warnings and calls Freemasonry a damnable sect[6]. Pius IX continues his pronouncement against the Freemasons by noting that they are trying to infiltrate the Christian army and that they are in no way to enter any Church sodalities[7]. It needs to be remembered that at the time non-Catholics Christians were viewed as either heretics or apostates, and possibly also schismatics. Some of the same disdain for the Masons would have been shared for those persons who had left the Church as well as those from other religions. For non-Catholic Christians, this would change only with the Second Vatican Council. *UR* 3 stated that non-Christians who were

---

[2] P. GASPARRI – J. SERÉDI, *Codicis Iuris Canonici Fontes,* III, 198.

[3] SACRA CONGREGATIO DE PROP. FEDE (C. G.). 19 September 1867, in GASPARRI, P. – SERÉDI, J., ed., *Codicis Iuris Canonici Fontes,* VII, 406.

[4] Cf. PIUS IX, lett. *Quamquam,* 70-72; PIUS IX, lett. *Exortae,* 99-101.

[5] Cf. PIUS IX, lett. *Quamquam,* 70-71.

[6] PIUS IX, lett. *Exortae,* 99.

[7] PIUS IX, lett. *Exortae,* 99.

faithful to their own beliefs were not to be held responsible for the sins of their ancestors.

The Pontiff's letters against members of Freemasonry were a certain foundation for forbidding members of condemned sects, those punished by censor and in general held to be public sinners, from inscribing in associations of the faithful[8]. And the response of the Sacred Congregation for the Propagation of the Faith serves well as a font for the prohibition against non-Catholics inscribing in associations of the Christian faithful[9].

2.2 Commentaries

Of the commentators consulted[10] only a few commented on the prohibition against non-Catholics. Most gave attention to the meaning in law of condemned sects, persons notoriously punished by censor and public sinners in general. Abbo and Hannan, and Conte a Coronata both include in their definitions of non-Catholics: heretics, apostates and schismatics[11]. Cappello and Blatt also include these three titles in their definition of non-Catholics which at the time would have included those separated from the Roman Catholic Church as a result of the Reformation. The commentators who did write concerning non-Catholics made it clear that non-baptized persons as well as baptized non-Catholics were not able to be inscribed into associations of the Christian faithful[12]. Non-Catholic baptized persons, Protestants and Orthodox, fit into the category of those not able to join associations since they were considered to be either heretics or apostates and possibly schismatics. As stated above, this juridical situation changed due to the ecclesiological and ecumenical developments of the Second Vatican Council.

2.3 Placement

The *CIC* 17 treats of ecclesiastical associations, that is associations guided or organized by the Church hierarchy. One may ask why these

---

[8] C.693,§1 *CIC* 17.

[9] C.693,§1 *CIC* 17.

[10] The following were consulted: Abbo and Hannan, Augustine, Blat, Bouscaren and Ellis, Cappello, Lydon, Conte a Coronata, Jone, Wernz and Vidal, and Stanislaus Woywod.

[11] Cf. Chapter I, section 2.2.

[12] F. CAPPELLO, *Summa Iuris Canonici*, II, 123; A. BLAT, *Commentarium*, 637.

ecclesiastical associations are located in the third part of book II of the *CIC* 17, *De Personis*, which is entitled *De laicis*. The first two parts of the book are titled *De clericis* and *De religiosis*. Because the associational configurations presented in the *CIC* 17 are ecclesiastical, it would make sense that they appear in one of the parts concerning clergy or religious. However, the organization of book two has itself been the subject of commentary among doctors. Amos commented that the arrangement of book II, «Concerning Persons», reveals a hierarchical image of the Church. To further his view, he made two points concerning the *CIC* 17. First, the parts on clergy and religious preceded those on laity, leading one to understand that official energy flowed from the top down. Second, he wrote that the organization also would lead one to understand that associations of the faithful could only be peopled by laity, which he also dubbed an incorrect suggestion.[13] Meanwhile Pagé noted that of the forty-four canons in part III of book II of the *CIC* 17, «Concerning the Laity», forty-two dealt with associations of the faithful[14]. Perhaps the author is questioning the small number of canons concerning the laity as Church members, since baptized Catholics have certain rights and duties with regard to associations and separate from them. Only two canons in part III concern the laity apart from their relation to associations. The *CIC* 83 would contain a large number of canons which include all the baptized under the heading *Christifideles*.

2.4 *Ecclesiological view of persons from CIC 17 to CIC 83*

In the ecclesiology which the *CIC* 17 utilized when it considered persons in the Church, the Church was composed of two groups of persons: clergy and laity. These two were the division made directly as one sought to organize the types of baptized persons who are members of the Roman Catholic Church. The view of the Second Vatican Council and the *CIC* 83 is that the Church is principally composed of the Christian faithful, a unifying rather than a distinctive definition. The concept is not radically different from that of the *CIC* 17, but the emphasis is placed on the *Christifideles* and only then the fact that both the clergy and laity make up the *Christifideles*.

Jone anticipated the conciliar view and described *fideles* as both laity and clerics. According to him, associations are treated in part III,

---

[13] J. AMOS, «A Legal History», 281.
[14] R. PAGÉ, «Associations in the Church», 167.

De laicis because the laity often make up the major part of these associations and in this way often fill the roles of governance in the association. Jone is rather progressive in his thought: instead of the hierarchy which places clergy above the laity he first notes that all faithful can be either laity or clerics[15]. This is to reaffirm that fundamentally persons are members of the Church through baptism.

It is to be recalled that the associations recognized in the *CIC* 17 are ecclesiastical, that is they are either erected or approved by the hierarchy of the Roman Catholic Church[16]. Thus even though the associations are occupied in large part by lay persons, they are called ecclesiastical. Associations neither erected nor approved by the Supreme Pontiff or the local ordinary but doing some pious work with the ends of the Church in mind are not ecclesiastical. They are lay and may be simply commended by the hierarchy. These distinctions will be discussed in detail in the next section.

3. Associations of the Faithful in the *CIC* 17

An association of the faithful as recognized by the *CIC* 17 is:

> A freely chosen society or a free union of the faithful, constituted by the approbation of ecclesiastical authority to promote a more perfect Christian life among the members or for the practice of some works of piety or charity or for the increase of public manifestations within the life of the members[17].

The definition of an association of the faithful as set forth by the commentators Wernz and Vidal is rooted in cc.684; 686,§1; and 685 *CIC* 17. Here two essential elements unite which are the foundation for an ecclesiastical association. These are: 1) erection by or at least the approbation of ecclesiastical authority, and 2) a religious finality[18]. These two elements will also form the foundation for associations in the *CIC* 83[19].

---

[15] H. JONE, *Commentarium in Codicem Iuris Canonici*, 606.

[16] C.686,§1 *CIC* 17.

[17] F. WERNZ – P. VIDAL, *Ius Canonicum*, 503. «Societas voluntaria seu libera unio fidelium cum approbatione auctoritatis ecclesiasticae constituta ad perfectiorem vitam christianam inter socios promovendam vel ad aliqua pietatis aut caritatis opera exercenda aut ad incrementum publici cultus citra vitam communem sociorum».

[18] F. WERNZ – P. VIDAL, *Ius Canonicum*, 503.

[19] Religious finality, c.685 *CIC* 17 is a direct font for c.298,§1 *CIC* 83. The canons concerning approbation of associations of the faithful are dispersed throughout

The associations of the *CIC* 17 were encouraged by Wernz because in his mind there was hardly another more effective media for fostering and preserving a flourishing Christian life in the parishes than the care on the part of the pastor and other priests to erect, direct and preserve associations. In the life of a parish active associations whether generic (open to all parishioners) or particular (for single classes such as men, women, teenagers, or boys or girls) made a great contribution. Through the apostolate of associations much could be obtained for divine worship which, in turn, contributes much to faith and piety[20]. Catholics were praised for joining associations which were erected or at least recommended. They were also warned against inscribing in associations which were covert, condemned or strove to withdraw from the legitimate supervision of the Church[21]. Strong associations, like the EMNC of today, built up the Church. As Wernz points out, they could make a great contribution to the faith and piety of those inscribed. As the associative element in the *CIC* 17 is studied, the structure of associations will be given special attention. Along with what might be considered a *lacuna* concerning non-Catholic members[22] and abrogation of the prohibition of the inscription of non-Catholics in associations[23], the actual structure as found in the *CIC* 83 is more open to ecumenical associations than was the *CIC* 17.

3.1 *Arrangement of the Canons*

Part three of book II of the *CIC* 17, *De laicis*, includes two titles: title XVIII, *De fidelium associationibus in genere* and title XIX, *De fidelium associationibus in specie*. Title XVIII is a general norms section for part three and title XIX describes categories into which all associations recognized by the Church would be arranged.

3.1.1 In General

The general norms title expresses the meaning of ecclesiastical associations and therefore aids in the understanding of associations which are not ecclesiastical but lay. The canons which manifest these

---

the canons as their composition and organization change considerably from the *CIC* 17 to the *CIC* 83.

[20] F. WERNZ – P. VIDAL, *Ius Canonicum*, 504.

[21] C.684 *CIC* 17.

[22] Cf. c.316,§1 *CIC* 83; c.307,§4 sch 82.

[23] Cf. C.693,§1 *CIC* 17.

differences, namely cc.684; 686,§1 *CIC* 17 will be studied in section 3.2, «Ecclesiastical and Lay Associations of the Faithful: A Comparison».

3.1.2 In Particular

Title XIX lists the types of associations as: third orders secular, confraternities and pious unions[24]. A hierarchy is also given to them: 1) third orders secular, 2) archconfraternities, 3) confraternities, 4) primary unions, and 5) pious unions[25]. Third orders follow the spirituality and are under the guidance of an ICL. When it comes to establishing sodalities of tertiaries, they are under the supervision of the local ordinary. Finally, their rule must be approved by the Holy See[26]. The relationship between the Church and a third order is the closest which exists between an association and the hierarchy as a result of the relationship which the sodality has as an extension of the first order with which it is affiliated.

Confraternities are established only by a formal decree of erection of the competent authority; pious unions may be erected but require merely the approval of the ordinary. The formal decree of erection which the confraternities or pious unions (which may also be approved without receiving juridic personality) receive invests them with juridic personality, making them legal persons; the approval sometimes given to pious unions makes them capable of obtaining spiritual favors and in particular indulgences[27]. In the order of hierarchy, the confraternities outrank the pious unions because the former always have juridic personality. Nevertheless, both are recognized by the Church and are called ecclesiastical associations. Confraternities and pious unions are able to aggregate or affiliate with themselves other associations of the same type. When this is done these are named archconfraternities or primary unions[28]. Detailed information concerning these aggregates of associations is found in the third chapter of title XIX, *De archiconfraternitatibus et primariis unionibus*[29]. In the heirarchical order archconfraternities outrank confraternities and primary unions outrank pious unions. The hierarchy which existed for associations in the *CIC* 17 is

---

[24] C.700 *CIC* 17.
[25] C.701,§1 *CIC* 17.
[26] Cc.702,§1; 703 *CIC* 17.
[27] C.708 *CIC* 17.
[28] C.720 *CIC* 17.
[29] Cf. Cc.720-725 *CIC* 17.

of importance as it will be compared to the hierarchy as found in the *CIC* 83.

Before clarifying the differences between ecclesiastical and lay associations in the *CIC* 17, the notion of juridic personality bears comment. A juridic person in the Church is a corporation of persons or things, enjoying its own personality apart from that of its individual members. Besides the moral persons of the Catholic Church and the Apostolic See[30], which were instituted by the authority of our Lord Himself, other lesser juridic persons were instituted by ecclesiastical law for some religious end either by the law itself or by decree[31]. Juridic persons are by nature perpetual. Since juridic personality is distinct from that of physical persons, the juridic person continues even after its members may have departed, such that *ipso iure* the juridic person exists for one hundred years after its last member has departed, unless suppressed by lawful authority[32]. Since it is created by public authority it can be extinguished only by public authority[33].

3.2 *Ecclesiastical and Lay Associations of the Faithful: A Comparison*

At the beginning of this section (3) it was noted that ecclesiastical associations are always in need of formal erection or at least require the approbation of ecclesiastical authority and must have a religious finality *ex natura rei*. After reading cc.684; 686,§1 *CIC* 17 which distinguish various types of associations, three classes of associations of the faithful may be identified. C.686,§1:

> No association in the Church is recognized which has not been erected or at least approved by legitimate ecclesiastical authority[34].

manifests two types of associations that are recognized by the Church. These are associations erected by or at least approved by the legitimate ecclesiastical authority. The third type of association, recommended by the Church, has its reference in c.684:

---

[30] In the *CIC* 17 the terminology, «moral person» was used for all corporations which had juridic personality. In the *CIC* 83 only the Church and Apostolic See are named moral persons, other corporations with juridic personality are called juridic persons.

[31] C.100,§1 *CIC* 17.

[32] C.102,§§1;2 *CIC* 17.

[33] T.L. BOUSCAREN, *Canon Law A Text and Commentry* 88.

[34] C.686 *CIC* 17 «Nulla in Ecclesia recognoscitur associatio quae a legitima auctoritate ecclesiastica erecta vel saltem approbata non fuerit».

The faithful are to be commended, if they give their names to associations erected or at least recommended by the Church; however, they should be on their guard against secret, condemned, seditious or suspect associations as well as those which aim to remove themselves from the legitimate vigilance of the Church[35].

The situation is outlined in the first half of the canon. Unlike c.686,§1 the associations themselves are not the grammatical subject of the canon. Persons who join the associations are the subject. They are to be praised when they join associations of the faithful which are erected, a term also seen in c.686,§1, or at least recommended. The term recommended is not used again in reference to associations of the faithful. C.686,§1 clarifies the standing of recommended associations in the Church. They may in fact be associations of Catholics who gather for religious ends; however, they have neither canonical nor juridical standing in the Church unless they are erected or at least approved by the Apostolic See or the local ordinary[36].

One major division between types or levels of associations as identified in the *CIC* 17 is that of ecclesiastical associations and those which are not, referred to as lay associations. Canonically, however, the distinction between the two types of ecclesiastical associations is also rather large. An association which has juridic personality has a much different standing within the Church than one which does not. A juridic person in the *CIC* 17 was the subject of rights distinct from the physical persons who are inscribed in the association[37]. This needs to be seen in contrast to associations that are merely approved yet ecclesiastical, which do not have rights as juridic persons, though the individual members gathering in the association each maintain their rights as physical persons. The rights and the perpetual nature belonging to juridic persons differentiates them substantially from those associations merely approved in the *CIC* 17.

Commentators on the *CIC* 17 shed much light on the differences between the three types or levels of associations found in the Piobenedictine Code. Even though erected and approved associations are grouped under the same heading, «ecclesiastical associations», Conte a

---

[35] C.684 *CIC* 17. «Fideles laude digni sunt, si sua dent nomina associationibus ab Ecclesia erectis vel saltem commendatis; caveant autem ab associationibus secretis, damnatis, seditiosis, suspectis aut quae studeant sese a legitima Ecclesiae vigilantia subducere».

[36] C.686,§3 *CIC* 17.

[37] C.99 *CIC* 17.

Coronata points out a difficulty in identifying the differences between approved associations and associations which are merely commended which do not fit in this same category[38]. As a means of defining the diverse types of associations differences will be identified. First the lay associations will be compared to those recognized by the *CIC* 17 as ecclesiastical, i.e., the differences between associations merely recommended and those which are approved or erected. Then, the differences between associations which were juridic persons and those not enjoying such status will be noted.

3.2.1 Lay Associations compared to Ecclesiastical Associations

Conte a Coronata made the valid point that the differences between associations merely recommended and those approved may at times be confused. The question would lead to the famous case of the Society of St. Vincent de Paul in the Diocese of Corrientes in Argentina. A review of the case will take place in a following section (3.3). The distinctions will now be identified between associations erected or approved, called «ecclesiastical», and those merely commended, called «lay», under the system of the *CIC* 17.

Even as Conte a Coronata found recommended and approved associations rather close in comparison, Wernz made the point that simple commendation differs from real approbation. Commendation is given to associations which come together for some pious purpose and, even though they do not possess ecclesiastical approbation, are commendable because of obvious good works and fruits. If an association is not involved in some pious or religious work, if its scope is only temporal, it is not able to even be commended. It must be remembered that commended associations did not fall under the *CIC* 17 as did associations which were approved or erected. The activities of the commended association would be viewed as undertaken by the individual members of the association[39].

Cappello also made the point that there were associations which were not ecclesiastical, but called lay. They were however answerable to the ordinary of the place where they were located. These associa-

---

[38] M. CONTE A CORONATA, *Institutiones Iuris Canonici*, I, 890. The difficulty in distinguishing approved and commended associations will be more clearly seen and discussed in Chapter III, section 3.3 covering the Societies of St. Vincent de Paul in the Diocese of Corrientes.

[39] F. WERNZ – P. VIDAL, *Ius Canonicum*, 503-4.

tions may have been either profane or pious. Only those with a pious end could be recommended[40].

Jone was rather progressive in his thought; drawing distinctions between ecclesiastical and lay associations, he called commended associations «private» regardless of praise, pious ends or reception of indulgences[41]. As these associations are not persons within the Church, they are the initiative of lay persons and are not canonically recognized as moral persons apart from their membership. The use of the term «private» is interesting as it would be officially adopted in the *CIC* 83.

Abbo and Hannon[42], and Woywod also speak of three types or levels of associations in the *CIC* 17. Within these three divisions is found the separation between lay and ecclesiastical associations. Among the commentators on the *CIC* 17, it has been seen that there are indeed associations named ecclesiastical and others named lay. Those referred to as lay received this label because they are not ecclesiastical. The name had nothing to do with the status of the members in the Church. These lay associations were called «recommended» in the *CIC* 17[43]. The identification of the various levels of associations in the *CIC* 17 will be helpful in recognizing levels in the *CIC* 83 and the ecumenical possibilities for associations of the Christian faithful.

3.2.2 Associations with Juridic Personality and those without it

This section will reinforce the differences between associations with juridic personality and those which have not been erected juridic persons. This division takes place between the two levels of ecclesiastical associations: erected associations and those which are at least approved. Wernz gave a succinct explanation of the differences between erected and approved associations: following c.687 *CIC* 17, he pointed out that erection made by formal decree gives the association a juridical personality which merely approved associations lack. At the time of its erection an association of the faithful obtains from an ecclesiastical authority the character of an ecclesiastical corporation erected as a true juridical person[44]. The erected association of the faithful is not able to be destroyed by votes nor by the departure of a great number of the

---

[40] F. CAPPELLO, *Summa Iuris Canonici*, II, 117.

[41] H. JONE, *Commentarium*, 606.

[42] J. ABBO, *The Sacred Canons*, 693; S. WOYWOD, *A Practical Commentary*, I, 303.

[43] Cf. c.684 *CIC* 17.

[44] F. WERNZ – P. VIDAL, *Ius Canonicum*, 506.

members. The normal ways that a juridic person ceases to exist are two: 1) suppression by the competent authority, usually the same authority by whom it was erected or 2) if it has not had members or activity for one hundred years[45].

Cappello also drew clear distinctions between approved and erected associations.

> Between an *approved* and *erected* association a great distinction exists. An erected association is a real moral person and therefore posses a juridic personality fully distinct from the collective personality of the individual members; on the other hand the approved association is merely a collective person in no way distinct from the union of the individual members but is publicly recognized and is strengthened by ecclesiastical authority[46].

Cappello underlined that the juridic personality of the erected association is distinct from the collective personality of its individual members, while the approved association is merely a collective person in no way distinct from the aggregate of the individual members but is publicly recognized and is strengthened by ecclesiastical authority.

The distinctions clarified by both Wernz and Cappello will also be useful in considering differences in the types of associations in the *CIC* 83. Before studying the associations of the *CIC* 83 the «Resolution of 13 November 1920» concerning the St. Vincent de Paul Society will be explored.

3.3 *The Status of the St. Vincent de Paul Society in the* CIC *17*

Only three short years after the *CIC* 17 was promulgated, the watershed rescript for private associations of the faithful was written. This is the only rescript which serves as a font for what would be a new chapter in the *CIC* 83. It is cited by commentators making reference to recommended associations[47]. The letter dealt with a group that was in ex-

---

[45] C.102 *CIC* 17.

[46] F. CAPPELLO, *Summa Iuris Canonici*, II, 117. «Inter associationem *approbatam* et *erectam* datur magnum discrimen. Haec est vera persona moralis ideoque iuridica personalitate gaudet, e personalitate collectiva singulorum membrorum plane distincta; illa, contra, est persona mere collectiva, ab unione singulorum membrorum nullatenus distincta, at publice recognita et ecclesiastica auctoritate firmata». Emphasis in original.

[47] Among these commentators are: F. CAPPELLO, *Summa Iuris Canonici*, 117; M. CONTE A CORONATA, *Institutiones Iuris Canonici*, 883; H. JONE, *Commentarium*, 606; F. WERNZ – P. VIDAL, *Ius Canonicum*, 505.

istence but questioned if and how this society could fit into the categories of associations set up by the *CIC* 17.

The Sacred Congregation of the Council received a letter from the Bishop of Corrientes, Argentina, written on September 8, 1919. Abuses in action and in government, as well as things harmful to morals and religion on the part of the St. Vincent de Paul Society had been brought to the attention of the bishop. These difficulties, which were not described in the rescript, led him to question the status of the association which seemed to him to be a pious union according to c.707 *CIC* 17[48]. Before considering the question, the legislation, and the reply contained in the rescript, it will be worthwhile to consider the two bodies involved, the Sacred Congregation of the Council and the St. Vincent de Paul Society.

The Sacred Congregation of the Council was established by Paul IV on 30 December 1563 shortly after the close of the Council of Trent on 4 December 1563. As a branch of the Roman Curia the task of the Congregation was the accurate application of the decrees of the Council. Throughout its more than four-hundred years of existence its purpose was revised. Since at least the time of the *CIC* 17 until 1967, when it was suppressed, the Congregation governed all pious sodalities except third orders, secular institutes, and Catholic Action associations. The Congregation was replaced by the Congregation for Clergy under Paul VI by his Apostolic Constitution, *Regimini Ecclesiae Universae*[49].

Ozanam founded the St. Vincent de Paul Society in 1833 at Paris. Soon a rule based on the writings of Saint Vincent de Paul was adopted, and the name was changed from Conference of Charity to Conference of Saint Vincent de Paul. Within twenty years the society boasted over two thousand members[50]. By 1855 there were two thousand eight hundred fourteen conferences or groupings throughout the world[51]. In 1933 the society had grown so that 12,500 conferences existed worldwide and had an overall membership of 250,000 men[52]. Along with its growth in numbers of participants the presence of the Society spread throughout the world. Also by 1933 the St. Vincent de Paul Society was present in twenty countries of the world, including the United States, Mexico, Canada and a number of countries in

---

[48] SACRA CONGREGATIO CONCILII, *Resolutio 13 November 1920*.

[49] PAUL VI, apost. const. *Regimini Ecclesiae universae, AAS* 59 (1967) 908.

[50] H. HUGHES, *Frederick Ozanam*, 11.

[51] T. AUGE, *Frederick Ozanam and His World*, 25.

[52] H. HUGHES, *Frederick Ozanam*, 161-162.

Europe and South America[53]. Its phenomenal growth can be attributed to the dedication of its founder and also the zeal of the laity who were members of the organization.

From the beginning, the society had developed as a lay organization and approbation of ecclesiastical authority was not sought, nor were conferences erected by the act of religious superiors. Pope Gregory XVI formally approved the lay character of the society and granted it indulgences. There was no mention of erection or approval by ecclesial authority. Pius IX also desired that the society retain its character as lay or non ecclesiastical. The members viewed their lay status as connoting faithfulness, not an independence from the Church[54].

3.3.1 The Rescript from the Sacred Congregation of the Council

a) *Dubium*

The Bishop of Corrientes, Argentina, asked the Sacred Congregation of the Council to solve the doubt, «regarding the dependence of Conferences of St. Vincent de Paul on the power of the Ordinary»[55]. Since the Conferences were not ecclesiastical either by erection, and therefore not juridic persons, or even by approval, the bishop had good reason to inquire about his authority in this matter since these particular conferences were in his diocese. The rescript praised the society and recognized that never had approbation of ecclesiastical authority been required for the statutes nor for the internal organization and never had particular conferences been erected through an act of an ecclesiastical superior or even with his approbation. Conferences had been instituted by the private agreement of pious faithful who gathered themselves together to exercise the esteemed works of charity and had been incorporated into the society by means of admission given by the general council. The Congregation went on to state specifically, «therefore it has been raised and has been promoted as a lay society that is not ecclesiastical, that is not having its existence from an act of ecclesiastical authority»[56].

---

[53] D. McCOLGAN, *A Century of Charity,* I, 46.

[54] SACRA CONGREGATIO CONCILII, *Resolutio 13 November 1920,* 138.

[55] SACRA CONGREGATIO CONCILII, *Resolutio 13 November 1920,* 135; «circa dependentiam Conferentiarum S. Vincentii a Paulo a potestate Ordinarii».

[56] SACRA CONGREGATIO CONCILII, *Resolutio 13 November 1920,* 137. «Orta ergo est et propagata tamquam societas laica i. e. non ecclesiastica seu non habens esse ab actu auctoritatis ecclesiasticae».

The rescript cited two letters of Pope Gregory XVI, one in which he indeed granted indulgences to councils or conferences instituted by the approval of the general council of the Society of St. Vincent de Paul[57]. The other addressed individuals who gave alms to the Society of St. Vincent de Paul. This document is not specifically cited; however, a date is given[58]. In the first instance the pontiff not only supported the society in general but in particular its own internal governance, i.e. conferences erected or approved by the general council. In the second instance, he lauded persons who aided the Society by means of alms. Indulgences were conceded in a third example to two persons who supported the society with their offerings[59].

The previous support of Pope Pius IX was also noted. An excerpt from a book on the life of Ozanam gave more support to the internal governance.

> Clearly it was easy to understand that the spiritual union would have been immediately broken if each bishop had organized associations in his own diocese and compiled their rule in a manner which he believed most convenient[60].

Here the international nature of the organization was again recognized and indeed not questioned. The society never made it a priority to obtain juridic personality in the Church. Meanwhile, it did take the time to obtain juridic personality from the civil authority in order to be legally capable of receiving bequests and other donations[61].

The Society of St. Vincent de Paul was very successful in its service of the poor and it grew at a surprising rate all the while enjoying the support of the Church, laity, priests, bishops, and popes alike. What helped its relationship with ecclesiastical authority remains so positive even without the associations having attained ecclesiastical approbation or erection was that the society maintained from the beginning an intimate connection with the clergy and Church authority. The Congregation noted that even though the pastor did not preside over the Vin-

---

[57] GREGORY XVI, apost. lett. *Romanum decet Pontificem*, 375-376.

[58] Cf. SACRA CONGREGATIO CONCILII, *Resolutio 13 November 1920*, 138.

[59] SACRA CONGREGATIO CONCILII, *Resolutio 13 November 1920*, 138.

[60] Quoted from «Vita di Ozanam, scritta dal canonico suo fratello: versione italiana», p. 109, as found in SACRA CONGREGATIO CONCILII, *Resolutio 13 November 1920*, 138: «Era facile a capire che l'unione di spirito sarebbe stata immediatamente rotta, se ogni vescovo avesse organizzato le conferenze della propria diocesi e compilato il loro regolamento, nel modo ch'egli avesse creduto più conveniente».

[61] SACRA CONGREGATIO CONCILII, *Resolutio 13 November 1920*, 138.

centian Councils, nevertheless he in effect did preside for the sake of honor, or in his absence through another pious priest. Always there was some priest who served as spiritual leader, who for the Vincentian Councils, as the groupings were known, was a true ecclesiastical assistant[62].

b) *Reply*

The Vincentian Conferences were recognized as lay, not because of their ends, but because they had no canonical standing in the Church. It is interesting that the *CIC* 17 did no more than mention associations which are commended; the commentators called them «lay» associations. The question still remained for the Society of St. Vincent de Paul where they fit into the *CIC* 17. Conte a Coronata was cited earlier in the dispute about differences between approved and commended associations: he affirmed commended associations while commenting that they were hard to distinguish from those which were approved[63]. The Sacred Congregation simply stated:

> Therefore in addition to strictly ecclesiastical associations that are erected and directed by ecclesiastical authority, there exist other unions of the faithful that are also founded for a pious purpose but are constituted by the power and government of lay persons. But these are merely approved or commended by ecclesiastical authority and are undertaken for the benefit of the neighbor in need of help[64].

The St. Vincent de Paul Society was a union of the faithful which was not ecclesiastical. Any approval was a form of praise[65]. These associations did not necessarily have to be subject to the power of the Ordinary as far as existence, constitution, organization of their statutes, and internal government were concerned. The Sacred Congregation

---

[62] SACRA CONGREGATIO CONCILII, *Resolutio 13 November 1920*, 138.

[63] Cf. M. CONTE A CORONATA, *Institutiones Iuris Canonici*, I, 890.

[64] SACRA CONGREGATIO CONCILII, *Resolutio 13 November 1920*, 139. «Dantur ergo praeter consociationes stricto sensu *ecclesiasticas*, quae ab auctoritate ecclesiastica eriguntur et diriguntur, aliae fidelium uniones etiam ad finem pium excitatae, sed sub potestate et regimine laicorum constitutae, ab auctoritate vero ecclesiastica mere probatae seu laudatae, quae suscipiuntur in utilitatem proximi auxilio indigentis». Emphasis in original.

[65] Use of the term «*probatae*» from p. 139 of the resolutio must be contrasted with «*approbata*» of c.686,§1 *CIC* 17. The «*approbata*» in the *CIC* 17 is stronger. These terms are different as «*probatae*» does not refer to a «canonical approval» found in the *CIC* 17.

openly distinguished pious societies as St. Vincent de Paul from societies approved or erected by the Church which were covered in the canons of *CIC* 17. However citing c.336,§2 *CIC* 17, the Congregation reviewed the authority and competence of the bishop in whose diocese a council of St. Vincent de Paul may have been located.

> Indeed it can be said unreservedly that, just as the individual faithful are under the jurisdiction of the bishop so they remain subject to his jurisdiction when they are united in societies: because, although the bishop from this fact alone cannot direct a society by the power of his jurisdiction just as he directs societies and confraternities that are properly ecclesiastical nevertheless he has the right and the obligtion to be vigilant (lest abuses creep in) or the faithful because of their association fall into perdition[66].

Even though the Society of St. Vincent de Paul may have established itself, governed itself, approved its own statutes and amendments to these nevertheless, as are all individual members of the Church, the individual member is subject to the jurisdiction of the bishop. This jurisdiction on the part of a bishop exists in the territory of his own diocese. As an international group the society had to remember the relationship between the bishop and the flock of his diocese. Leo XIII in his encyclical, *Humanum Genus*[67], asked the bishops of the world, in combating the problems of freemasonry, to support and encourage sodalities and associations of lay persons. The Society of St. Vincent de Paul was mentioned in particular by the pontiff.

c) *Legislation*

The third section of the resolution concerned the law of the *CIC* 17. It clearly delineated associations erected by the competent Church authority from other associations. Other associations had to be approved in order to be recognized by the Church. The St. Vincent de Paul Society was mentioned as being commended, and had been neither erected nor approved. Only associations erected by the Church

---

[66] SACRA CONGREGATIO CONCILII, *Resolutio 13 November 1920*, 140. «Immo absolute potest vere dici, quod sicut singuli fideles iurisdictioni Episcopi subsunt, ita manent huius iurisdictioni subiecti, quando in Societates uniuntur. Quamquam enim Episcopus ex hoc solo facto societatem vi suae iurisdictionis dirigere nequit, quemadmodum societates propie ecclesiasticas et confraternitates dirigit, *ius tamen habet et obligationem* INVIGILANDI, ne abusus irrepant neve fideles occasione societatum ruinam salutis incurrant» (Cfr. Cod., can. 336 § 2). Emphasis in original.

[67] LEO XIII, Enc. lett. *Humanum Genus, ASS* 16 (1883-84) 431.

gained juridic personality and only those approved or erected were considered ecclesiastical. The statutes of these associations must have been approved either by the Holy See or the Ordinary of the place[68]. The associations of the Society of St. Vincent de Paul would be considered recommended[69].

The ultimate resolution simply stated that the Bishop in this case had the right and duty of vigilance over the society. He was not to allow the society to stand against faith and custom. And in the case of abuses he was obliged to correct and repress them. The rescript was approved and confirmed by Pope Benedict XV and signed by I. Mori, Secretary[70].

d) *Terminology*

The difficulty of terminology identified by Conte a Coronata persists as the roots of private associations are unearthed. *CIC* 17 uses the term erection (*erigere*) consistently to mean associations erected by the Church and, therefore, having juridic personality. The question of one or two other types of associations as recognized by the Church remained, because of the continued use of the words to commend (*commendare*) and to approve (*approbare*). It was not clear how commended associations fit into the *CIC* 17. The Sacred Congregation in its rescript to the Bishop of Corrientes stated that the Society of St. Vincent de Paul is not an ecclesiastical association but a lay one[71]. At the same time the Congregation seems to have said that the *CIC* 17 refers to the situation of the Society of St. Vincent de Paul, and had placed the association into the non-ecclesiastical sphere of recommended associations[72]. If the Congregation had been referring to the relationship of the bishop with the associations within his diocese, confusion would have been reduced, but this does not seem likely since this relationship was never discussed in section III of the rescript. C.684 uses «commended» to refer to associations which the faithful were praised for joining (the faithful were also praised for joining associations erected by the Church). However c.686 *CIC* 17 recognized no association in the Church unless it had been either erected or at least

---

[68] SACRA CONGREGATIO CONCILII, *Resolutio 13 November 1920*, 141.
[69] C.684 *CIC* 17.
[70] SACRA CONGREGATIO CONCILII, *Resolutio 13 November 1920*, 144.
[71] Cf. SACRA CONGREGATIO CONCILII, *Resolutio 13 November 1920*, 138.
[72] Cf. SACRA CONGREGATIO CONCILII, *Resolutio 13 November 1920*, 140.

approved by the competent authority. Here the *CIC* 17 used the word, «approved». The St. Vincent de Paul Societies met the criterion to be included in the category of recommended associations of the faithful. They were not ecclesiastical but lay. The bishop would not relate canonically to the society as much as to the individual members who made up the society.

The following excerpt from a commentary on title XVIII, «Associations of the Faithful in General», by Woywod, brings some clarity to the question of the types of associations covered by the canons but not what might be considered controversial wording, (commended - approved).

> In the following Canons, the Code treats exclusively of associations which are strictly ecclesiastical, and which are, therefore, subject to the jurisdiction of the Church in all their actions as an ecclesiastical organization. Other societies of Catholic laymen or women organized for the purpose of Christian charity are private affairs of Catholics, just as societies of a literary, artistic, or social character. Consequently, such societies are not subject to the ecclesiastical authorities, except in so far as the Church, in her capacity of the divinely appointed authority and guardian of the faith and morals of her subjects, has always a claim on their obedience. The whole question of the difference between ecclesiastical societies and other societies of Catholic laymen or women was discussed in the *Acta Apostolicae Sedis* in connection with the case of the St. Vincent de Paul Society in the Diocese of Corrientes in Argentina.[73]

e) *Implications*

The resolution concerning the Saint Vincent de Paul Society brings some clarity to the question of how associations are classified as «ecclesiastical» or «non-ecclesiastical». The Society received support from all levels of the hierarchy. Positive comments were received from pastors and also popes. Support and positive comments did not affect their status as ecclesiastical or non-ecclesiastical. They had not been erected and had not asked for approval from the competent authority. The Society of St. Vincent de Paul did not fit into the *CIC* 17 as an association of the faithful. Where do associations of its nature find themselves in the canons of the law of the Church? Were the Code absolutely clear, the rescript would not have had to be written. When it appeared in the *Acta Apostolicœ Sedis,* the rescript, a particular adminis-

---

[73] S. WOYWOD, *A Practical Commentary,* I, 302.

trative act, set an example, recognizing the right of the laity to form commended associations which would be non-ecclesiastical but still under the jurisdiction of the bishop. As the rescript was used as a footnote and tool to manifest the rights of the laity to form associations, it was truly a guideline waiting to be incorporated into the revised Code of Canon Law.

4. Associations of the Christian Faithful in the *CIC* 83

This section of chapter three presents associations in the *CIC* 83 and basically follows the format used in section 3 which studied associations in the *CIC* 17. Subsections will treat: 1) the arrangement of the canons, 2) the development of associations of the Christian faithful in the *CIC* 83 at the Second Vatican Council, 3) the transition from the *CIC* 17 to the *CIC* 83, 4) the particular configuration and comparison of the different types of associations themselves and 5) points which move toward the presence of ecumenical associations in the Church. Numbers 2) and 3) cover the important underpinnings of the changes found in the *CIC* 83 as well as offer a comparison of associations in the two codes of law. These do not parallel the format used in section three for the *CIC* 17.

4.1 *Arrangement of the Canons*

As the *CIC* 83 developed the whole title concerning associations of the Christian faithful was moved. The shift did not take place «within the very last weeks before promulgation of the 1983 Code»[74] but prior to 25 March 1982 and was a part of the sch 82 which was presented to the Holy Father on 22 April 1982, a full eight months before the *CIC* 83 was promulgated[75]. The transfer involved placing section III, «Concerning Other Associations of the Christian Faithful» located in part III, «Concerning Associations in the Church» of book II of the sch 80 to book II, part I, «Concerning the Christian Faithful» in sch 82. Both schemata (sch 80 and sch 82) book II, «Concerning the People of God», included three divisions[76]: 1) «Concerning the Christian Faithful», 2) «Concerning the Constitutional Hierarchy of the Church», and

---

[74] E. KNEAL, «Associations of the Christian Faithful», 243.

[75] *Comm.* 28 (1996) 192, and F. D'OSTILIO, *La Storia*, 110.

[76] The term «division» is used here to avoid confusion. Sch 80 used the term «section» for the canons concerned with associations of the faithful, while the sch 82 placed these canons under the division «title».

3) «Concerning Associations in the Church», (sch 80) or «Concerning Institutes of Consecrated Life and Societies of Apostolic Life», (sch 82). The name of the third division was changed when the canons specifically concerned with associations of all the Christian faithful were moved to the first division. The change reveals the view of the associations by the *PCCICR*. The name given to the heading for ICL, SAL and Other Associations of the Christian Faithful, «Concerning Associations in the Church», in sch 80 may give the impression that ICL and SAL are associations similar to the others of section III. This confusion is avoided by the change in position of the canons relating specifically to the canons under study. After having been grouped with ICL (secular institutes are included here) and SAL, the associations which are the topic of study were placed beside three other divisions: 1) «Concerning the Rights and Duties of All the Christian Faithful», 2) «Concerning the Rights and Duties of the Lay Christian Faithful» and 3) «Concerning Sacred Ministers or Clerics». Personal prelatures were added to the first part of book II after the sch 82 was presented to the Holy Father. By being moved to the first part of book II the division concerning associations is not equated with ICL and SAL as it may have been had it not been moved. Section III in sch 82 had been named, «Associations in the Church» placing ICL, SAL, and associations of the Christian faithful under the same heading. In the broad sense of the term, ICL and SAL are associations. Because they are distinct from ICL and SAL[77], it seems wise that the canons concerning associations of all the Christian faithful were placed under part I. This repositioning gives them a certain autonomy, whereas in the previous ordering they may have seemed to have had some association with ICL and SAL even though the canons named them as distinct[78].

Most important in a study of the canons is the present code itself. Turning to the arrangement of the canons in the *CIC* 83 two views will be considered. First a study of the types of associations as manifested by the chapters of the title is undertaken. Secondly a study of other possible ways of dividing the canons, which are less connected with the different chapters of title V will be presented. A presentation of the more important divisions that will affect ecumenical possibilities will conclude the section.

---

[77] C.298,§1 *CIC* 83.
[78] Cf. E. KNEAL, «Associations of the Christian Faithful», 243.

4.2 *By Chapter*

There are four chapters found under title five, «Associations of the Christian Faithful», of the first part, «Concerning the Christian Faithful», of book two, «Concerning the People of God», of the *CIC* 83. The four chapters are: 1) «Common Norms», 2) «Public Associations of the Christian Faithful», 3) «Private Associations of the Christian Faithful», and 4) «Special Norms for Lay Associations». There are thirty-two canons in the title, but when one considers the paragraphs and numbers which also make up the canons the total number rises to fifty-eight[79].

The common norms chapter provides the general norms to be used for all associations in this title. The majority of the canons pertain to all associations of the Christian faithful. The canons at times specifically make reference to «*omnes christifidelium consociationes*»[80]. Along with providing general norms for associations of the faithful the chapter touches on other minor characteristics of associations which make them unique. All associations in the *CIC* 83 are either public or private. Other types of associations presented in the first chapter, which are either public or private are: those which use the title «Catholic» in their name, clerical associations and third orders. Even though not necessarily true in all cases the associations treated in this study choose to use the title Catholic only when all members of the association were to be Catholics. Of the associations included in the research for this study only the fellowships which are members of the Catholic Fraternity of Charismatic Covenant Communities and Fellowships, as well as the Fraternity itself, use the term Catholic in their titles. The Fraternity includes c.300 in its statutes (stat. 1.1), as does the Lamb of God Catholic Fellowship (stat. 2.), while the Alleluia Catholic Fellowship (stat. VI.A; B) uses the term Catholic in its title without directly citing the canon. The signature of the bishop approving the statutes is enough to give approval for the use of the term. Clerical associations would not be open to non-Catholics because they only inscribe Catholic clerics.

---

[79] The precise number becomes important when comparing types of associations and the fonts.

[80] Two canons, cc. 304 and 305 *CIC* 83 use the terminology «all associations of the Christian faithful». Four canons cc. 298, 306, 307, and 309 *CIC* 83 refer to all without specifically stating such. Cc. 299 and 310 *CIC* 83 concern private associations and c. 301 *CIC* 83 makes reference to public associations of the faithful. Other canons in the chapter deal with: using the title «Catholic», c. 300 *CIC* 83; clerical associations, c. 302 *CIC* 83; third orders, cc. 303 and 311 *CIC* 83 and dismissal from an association, c. 308 *CIC* 83.

The third orders follow the legislation found in the *CIC* 83[81]. The first chapter remains general while the second and third speak specifically to public and then private associations of the faithful.

The second chapter concerns public associations of the faithful. It covers the associations, erected by competent ecclesiastical authority, which are empowered to act in the name of the Church. A number of the canons in this chapter which will now be identified can affect the presence of non-Catholics in public associations. The Holy See, bishops' conference and diocesan bishop have the authority to establish public associations within their spheres of competence[82]. A public association is granted juridic personality by the decree which establishes it. Here it also receives the mission to pursue its ends which are contained in its approved statutes[83]. The final pertinent canon lists reasons that persons may not join public associations[84]. Not included among these prohibitions are non-Catholics and non-Catholic Christians. Since non-Catholics are not barred from inscribing in public associations of the Christian faithful, it seems possible that the decision to admit or bar them would be made by those competent to establish them. Other issues and opinions will be considered as the study continues.

Private associations of the faithful are the concern of the third chapter. Most associations which are ecumenical are private. The present study identifies only two ecumenical associations which are public. Because private associations are the initiative of the Christian faithful who direct and moderate them[85] membership is the determination of those who form the statutes. It is then the task of the competent authority to review[86], approve[87] or assign juridic personality[88] to the private association wishing to be recognized in some manner by the Church. Even with a certain autonomy private associations are subject to the supervision and governance of ecclesiastical authority[89]. Between the canons in the chapter and the attention that private associations are given in the common norms chapter, the rights of Catholics to

---

[81] Cc.303, 311 *CIC* 83.
[82] C.312 *CIC* 83.
[83] Cc.313, 314 *CIC* 83.
[84] C.316 *CIC* 83.
[85] C.321 *CIC* 83.
[86] C.299,§3 *CIC* 83.
[87] C.322,§2 *CIC* 83.
[88] C.322,§1 *CIC* 83.
[89] C.323,§1 *CIC* 83.

found and regulate associations according to the needs they see as present in the Church are satisfied. At the same time the role of the Church is manifested. The right of the laity and in fact of all the Christian faithful to gather in associations in the Church is clearly set forth in this chapter on private associations.

The final chapter of the title has as its focus associations which are specifically lay. The chapter is not so much a canonical treatment of associations which are lay but an exhortation of persons belonging to these associations[90]. No new canonical information is contained in the chapter. The canons themselves do not define lay associations. It is not specifically stated that only lay persons are eligible to inscribe into lay associations. That the canons refer only to laity is inferred by comparison to c.298,§1 *CIC* 83 which mentions associations of clergy, laity and clergy and laity together. Mixed and associations of only clergy have been presented. This fourth chapter presents associations composed only of laity. This treatment does not balance with the divisions in the rest of the title. Three types of associations are mentioned in c.298§1 *CIC* 83. Clerical associations and associations comprised of both clerics and lay are covered under the first three chapters. They do not have a chapter of their own. The presence of a chapter covering the special situation of lay associations, even if it is primarily exhortative, seems to encourage and give a special place to them. All canonists do not agree with this position. One example is Kneal who points out what he sees as awkwardness in the presentation and placement. He writes that the three canons manifest a stratified ecclesiology and a seemingly pejorative stance[91].

The different types of associations displayed by the headings of title five of book two of the *CIC* 83 include public and private associations and lay associations. The seemingly unbalanced treatment ought to be seen as bringing attention to associations which are composed exclusively by lay persons. Other types of associations have also been identified.

4.2.1 Other divisions

There are certainly more types of associations than may be located in the headings and even canons of the *CIC* 83. To those that have been

---

[90] J.L. GUTIÉRREZ, «Associations of Christ's Faithful», 261.

[91] E. KNEAL, «Associations of the Christian Faithful», 245. The position of this thesis does not agree with the view of Kneal.

identified: public and private, lay or clerical, and laity and clerics together, third orders and associations which use the title Catholic in their names, and associations which do not, a number will be added. Some of these will be studied in this section while others will be explained later under another heading. Among these are diocesan, national and international or universal associations[92].

Again the purpose of considering the different types of associations of the Christian faithful in the Church is to aid in recognizing the possibilities of the great variety of associations, specifically those which inscribe non-Catholics and are described as ecumenical associations. Diverse types of public and private associations of the faithful will not be covered here, as they will be included in a later section of this chapter (4.5), which will compare and contrast the two. Further discussion will be undertaken in the sections covering public and private associations because juridic personality is integral to the associations' status as either public or private, as well as to their ends and relationship with ecclesiastical authority. Associations which have and do not have juridic personality as well as ecumenical associations as a type in the *CIC* 83 will now be presented.

One of the most important characteristics distinguishing associations whether public or private is whether or not they enjoy juridic personality. To understand all that having juridic personality means for an association it is necessary to review the canons in book one of the *CIC* 83 which cover juridic persons. Pertinent characteristics of juridic persons are that they: 1) are aggregates of persons or things, 2) are directed to a purpose befitting the Church's mission, 3) transcend the purpose of the individuals who may be a part of them[93], 4) are constituted through a provision of the law itself or by a special concession given in the form of a decree by the competent authority[94], 5) and are by nature perpetual[95]. Juridic persons like associations of the Christian faithful may be either public or private. Both public and private juridic persons cease to exist when lawfully suppressed by competent authority or are inactive for one hundred years. Private juridic persons also cease to exist when according to the statutes: the association is to be dissolved or in the judgement of the competent authority the founda-

---

[92] C.312,§1 *CIC* 83.
[93] C.114,§1 *CIC* 83.
[94] C.114,§2 *CIC* 83.
[95] C.120 *CIC* 83.

tion itself has ceased to exist[96]. Public associations always have juridic personality while private associations may be established as juridic persons with approval and upon request.

It is possible for associations of the Christian faithful, both private and public to inscribe non-Catholic Christians. The particulars will be discussed in the sections of this chapter covering such associations (4.5) and the ecumenical possibilities for associations of the Christian faithful (5). The varied types of associations identified continue to clarify the fact that under the *CIC* 83 the number of possibilities of associative types is great. The particular discussion of private and public associations will be undertaken after the discussion of the development of associations in the *CIC* 83 (especially based in the Second Vatican Council) and the transition from the *CIC* 17 to the *CIC* 83 (which highlights the canonical developments). These two sections are sandwiched here naturally as they make the logical connections between the various types of associations which exist, their relationship with the competent authority, as well as their particular ends.

4.3 *Associations of the Christian Faithful at the Second Vatican Council: effects in the CIC 83*

Since theological shifts made at the Second Vatican Council were to be foundational to the *CIC* 83 they will be reviewed at this point. Without the input of the Council the new code might have been merely a new collection of laws.

4.3.1 Background

The announcement of John XXIII on 25 January 1959 at the Basilica of Saint Paul outside the Walls of a synod for the Diocese of Rome, an ecumenical council and a renewed code of canon law[97] came twenty-four years before the *CIC* 83 would be promulgated. Once the Second Vatican Council had begun, the *PCCICR*, which had been created on 23 March 1963 decided on 12 November 1963 that it was best for its own work to await the completion of the Council. In this way the decisions of the Council could be better integrated into the new code of law. The principal reason for the new code after the Pontiff's call for its complete revision was that the Council requested it[98]. In his

---

[96] C.120,§1 *CIC* 83.
[97] JOHN XXIII, all. *Questa festa, AAS* 51 (1959) 68.
[98] JOHN PAUL II, apost. const. *Sacrae disciplinae leges, AAS* 75 (1983) VII-VIII.

allocution at a solemn session of the *PCCICR* on 20 November 1965 publicly inaugurating its work, Pope Paul VI, while laying the foundation for the work gave the commission two principles to guide the entire project. The first was that the revised code be not merely a new collection of laws. Rather, it ought to reform the law in keeping with contemporary ways of thinking (the Johannine «aggiornamento»), while continuing to hold to the foundation of the law which had been passed down. The second principle was that in revising the code, attention was to be continually given to the letter and the spirit of the Second Vatican Council[99]. As was shown in chapter one of this dissertation the documents of the Second Vatican Council had a great impact on the eccesiological and ecumenical situation of the Roman Catholic Church[100]. Because the universal Catholic Church formally committed itself to participation in the ecumenical movement.

4.3.2 An Ecumenical and Ecclesiological Foundation

John Paul II, in the Apostolic Constitution *Sacrae disciplinae leges* by which he promulgated the *CIC* 83, supports both the ecclesiology and ecumenism of the Second Vatican Council. He calls the *CIC* 83 a grand work of putting the ecclesiological teaching of the Second Vatican Council into canonical language. As far as possible the *CIC* 83 is to be related to the Council's image of Church as its primary pattern. The Code was to express structurally as much as possible the nature of the image of the Church as it had been described by the Second Vatican Council[101]. The Holy Father continues and refers to the *CIC* 83 as a complement to the Council's authentic teaching in particular its dogmatic and pastoral constitutions[102]. Before moving on to the ecumenical influence on the *CIC* 83, via the Council, John Paul II punctuates the fact that while remaining true to the Church's legislative tradition the newness of the *CIC* 83 is found in its ecclesiological teaching[103].

Considering the teaching found in *LG* 8 and *LG* 15 alongside *LG* 14 which identify non-Catholics who are baptized with the same intent as the Catholic Church as not fully incorporated into the Church of Christ which subsists in the Roman Catholic Church, it is clear that there is some level of incorporation. This ecclesiological teaching of *LG* 8

---

99 PAUL VI, all. *Singulari cum animi, AAS* 57 (1965) 988.
100 Cf. Chapter I, section 4.
101 JOHN PAUL II, apost. const. *Sacrae disciplinae leges*, XI.
102 JOHN PAUL II, apost. const. *Sacrae disciplinae leges,* XII.
103 JOHN PAUL II, apost. const. *Sacrae disciplinae leges,* XII.

which recognizes «elements of sanctity and truth» in other churches and ecclesial communities is important to this study. The ways that this teaching is transposed into canonical language, especially as it concerns associations, will be of great importance to this work and will be treated later in the chapter. Here it is enough to say that the recognition on the part of the council fathers in *LG* 15 that the Roman Catholic Church is joined in many ways to baptized persons who are honored with the name Christian, is one of the first steps in inviting non-Catholic Christians to become members of associations of the Christian faithful. It must be well noted that this specifically ecclesiological point, that not only Roman Catholics belong to the Church of Christ, is also ecumenical: baptized non-Catholic Christians are in communion with the Church of Christ which subsists in the Roman Catholic Church. They are not however fully incorporated into the Roman Catholic Church. The Holy Father calls the Church to devote a certain diligence to its ecumenical efforts, to explore, identify and share those areas of the faith in which Catholics are one with their separated brethren[104]. The *mens legislatoris* is that the ecumenical movement as defined by the Council[105] would be partially realized through the structures of the *CIC* 83.

4.3.3 Fonts

The provenance of the fonts of the canons on associations obviously is telling. Those which are from the Second Vatican Council in particular would follow the ecclesiology of the Council and are of interest for that reason.

Because one of the goals of the chapter is to study the configuration of the canons covering associations of the faithful in each of the codes, the fonts of the *CIC* 83 which are from the documents of the Second Vatican Council will be identified. The fonts of the *CIC* 83 are generally four: 1) the *CIC* 17, 2) the Second Vatican Council, 3) papal statements, and 4) other documents of the Roman Curia. There are fonts upon which individual paragraphs and numbers as well as the canons themselves are constructed. Of the four chapters, those entitled «Common Norms» and «Special Norms for Lay Associations» have a large number of their fonts in Conciliar documents[106].

---

[104] JOHN PAUL II, apost. const. *Sacrae disciplinae leges,* XII.

[105] Cf. *UR* 3-4.

[106] In the first chapter «Common Norms», seven canons, paragraphs or numbers have fonts which are from the Second Vatican Council. The seven canons, para-

The Council document cited as a font more than any other is *AA*. *AA* 24 which concerns relations between associations and the hierarchy itself is cited five times in the «Common Norms» chapter. *AA* 20 which discusses Catholic Action is cited twice in the second chapter, «Public Associations of the Christian Faithful». The Council documents are not cited again in the second chapter. *AA* 19, concerning the variety of types of group apostolate is cited twice in the third chapter, «Private Associations of the Christian Faithful». *CD* 17 which is also cited in this chapter, directs bishops to encourage various forms of the apostolate and to watch over and coordinate them. Associations are encouraged especially those which have some evangelical end such as: 1) achieving a more perfect life, 2) announcing the gospel to all, 3) promoting Christian doctrine or public worship, and 4) pursuing social goals or practicing works of piety or charity[107]. The ecclesiology of the Second Vatican Council, which stresses the universal call to holiness arising from baptism[108] and therefore accentuates fundamental equality in the apostolate of the Church, is reflected in the activity in which the faithful are encouraged to engage as members of the Church. Thus, the bishops themselves are to encourage those persons involved in associations in their own particular churches.

The chapter presenting the private associations has among its fonts the Decree of the Sacred Congregation of the Council to the Bishop of Corrientes (13 November 1920). As has been shown the decree reinforces the right of laity in the Church to form lay associations and thus serves as a forerunner to the Second Vatican Council and its ecclesiological view of Church composed of all the baptized. This model of the Church as composed of all the baptized does not make such a pronounced division between the laity and the clergy (as in the *CIC* 17).

The Decree also supports the canons which state that the Christian faithful direct and moderate private associations[109]. These private associations are subject to the supervision of ecclesiastical authority[110] and

graphs or numbers include citations from forty articles of the documents of the Council.

In the fourth chapter, «Special Norms for Lay Associations» there are three canons. Two of the canons have fonts from the Second Vatican Council. Between the two canons sixteen articles from the Council are cited. These are organized into appendix III.

[107] *CD* 17. Also cf. c.298,§1 *CIC* 83.

[108] *LG* 10, 39-42.

[109] C.321 *CIC* 83.

[110] C.323,§1 *CIC* 83.

each association may designate its own moderator and officers[111]. When the Decree appears as a font to the common norms chapter it refers specifically to: 1) encouraging persons who join associations which are in some way recognized by the competent ecclesiastical authority[112], 2) the right of the Christian faithful to establish and run (private) associations[113], 3) situations in which associations are to be public and therefore established by competent authority[114], and 4) the subjection of all associations, both public and private, to the competent ecclesiastical authority be it at the level of the local or the universal Church[115]. When the Decree is not being used to directly support private associations of the Christian faithful, it is used to clarify the differences between public and private associations and to reinforce the call of all associations to be subject to competent ecclesiastical authority.

Articles 19 and 24 of *AA* are of special interest here because both proclaim the right of the laity to found and direct associations. The Decree of the Sacred Congregation of the Council to the Bishop of Corrientes is cited in both articles. As was affirmed in the previous section, the decree issued by the Sacred Congregation for the Council to the bishop of Corrientes in Argentina stated that the laity do have the right to form associations with spiritual ends. And it is this basic right of the Christian faithful which brings us closer to the question of ecumenical associations. Once the right to gather persons together for a common end or purpose is recognized, the questions regarding types of associations and membership in them arise.

To conclude this section covering the major documents of the Second Vatican Council which were as fonts for the canons which refer to associations of the Christian faithful, three points are highlighted. These are followed by a glance towards the next section. The first point is the right of the laity to gather in associations[116]. This leads to the second which is the importance of a relationship between the lay apostolate which would include associations and ecclesiastical author-

---

[111] C.324,§1 *CIC* 83.

[112] C.298,§2 *CIC* 83.

[113] C.299,§1 *CIC* 83.

[114] C.301,§§1; 2 *CIC* 83. Even as these paragraphs define public associations the differences between public and private associations become pronounced.

[115] C.305,§§1; 2 *CIC* 83.

[116] Cf. *AA* 19.

ity[117]. The third point is the inclusion of non-Catholic Christians as in-corporated into the Church of Christ. A review of other fonts follows.

4.3.4 Other Fonts and Chapters

To complete the study of the fonts of the Second Vatican Council in the *CIC* 83 it is necessary to compare and contrast the various fonts found in the chapters of title five.

The font most oft cited in the title is the *CIC* 17 appearing forty times in thirty-three canons, paragraphs or numbers. In seven of the canons the *CIC* 17 serves as a source more than once. Of the thirty-three canons where the *CIC* 17 is a font, twenty-nine are in the first two chapters. The common norms chapter at times uses the *CIC* 17 to draw out the differences between public and private associations of the Christian faithful[118]. Other instances relate to canons concerned with ends of the associations, admission of members, statutes and submission to competent authority.

Likewise, the second chapter concerning «Public Associations of the Faithful» is widely dependent upon the legislation of the *CIC* 17. This makes sense because the public associations of the *CIC* 83 are all juridic persons. The third orders and erected associations (confraternities and archconfraternities) were juridic persons in the *CIC* 17. Pious unions may or may not have had juridic personality. The relationship between Church hierarchy and the erected associations of the *CIC* 17 is similar to the relationship which exists today between Church hierarchy and the erected associations of the *CIC* 83.

4.4 *The Transition from/and Comparison of the CIC 17 to the CIC 83*

The understanding of associations in the *CIC* 83 is both similar and dissimilar to that in the *CIC* 17. The Second Vatican Council and the use of the *CIC* 17 as fonts to the *CIC* 83, which have been reviewed, are the transitional stepping stones from the *CIC* 17 to the new code. This section will complete the picture by comparing the *CIC* 17 and the *CIC* 83. The ways in which the two codes are similar will first be presented, including considerations of the purpose and types of associations. To balance the study, differences between treatment of associa-

---

[117] Cf. *AA* 23, 24, 25 and *CD* 17 which can be juxtaposed with Cc. 298,§2; 299,§§2, 3; 300; 301,§§1, 2, 3; 302; 305,§§1, 2; 312,§§1, 2; 313; 314; 317,§1; 320,§§1, 2; 322,§§1, 2; 323,§1; 324,§2; and 325,§1 *CIC* 83.

[118] Cf. cc.301,§§1; 2 *CIC* 83.

tions in the two codes will also be presented. The presentation of the differences will include considerations of the ordering of the canons and the names given to the types of associations by the two codes of law. As with anything which undergoes change there will be some consistent qualities as well as some elements which are different.

4.4.1 Similarities Between Associations of the Faithful in the *CIC* 17 and the *CIC* 83

The overall purpose and goal of associations of the faithful in the two codes remain the same, c.298,§1 *CIC* 83 being built squarely on c.685 *CIC* 17. Both codes contain the triple goal of associations of the Christian faithful: 1) working toward a more perfect Christian life among the members, 2) promoting public worship (*CIC* 83 adds Christian teaching), and 3) engaging in works of piety and charity, (*CIC* 83 adds works of the apostolate, like evangelization and those which animate the temporal order with the Christian spirit). This consistency is not surprising because these goals also apply to physical persons who are members of the Church of Christ or who are fully incorporated into the Roman Catholic Church, as well as to members of ICL or SAL. While the consistency is not surprising the additions are significant. Inviting associations to engage Christian teaching and works of the apostolate like evangelization draws them more profoundly into the Church's mission. The category «associations of the faithful» is clearly differentiated from religious institutes in both the *CIC* 17 and the *CIC* 83[119]. This perimeter places a certain consistency between the two codes of law. With an equal purpose which is differentiated from religious institutes, the essence of associations is consistent from the *CIC* 17 to the *CIC* 83.

Some of the categories of associations remain the same, bringing further consistency to the transition to the *CIC* 83. The names used to categorize associations have changed and for this reason canonical principles and terms will be used to make reference to the consistent categories of the codes. Ghirlanda divides the categories into three different classes. Firstly, both codes canonically recognize associations which are juridic persons and those which are not. Secondly, among the associations which do not have juridic personality both codes canonically recognize a class of associations that have received approval from ecclesiastical authority. And finally, there is a third class

---

[119] C.685 *CIC* 17; c.298,§1 *CIC* 83.

of associations which do not have a canonical standing as corporate body in the Church. For Ghirlanda the public associations of *CIC* 83 are the same as the ecclesiastical associations which had been erected juridic persons by a formal ecclesiastical decree. He cites cc.686, 687 *CIC* 17 and c.301 *CIC* 83 to justify his position. In the second class Ghirlanda compares approved ecclesiastical associations without juridic personality from c.686 *CIC* 17 with approved private associations without juridic personality as described in cc.299§1 and 322 *CIC* 83. Thirdly he identifies the «lay» or recommended associations of the *CIC* 17 with private associations of c.299 *CIC* 83[120]. While these have canonical rights and duties according to *CIC* 83 they did not have them according to *CIC* 17.

Ghirlanda makes the point that some bishops believe that associations which existed before the *CIC* 83 are obliged to suppress them according to their old canonical status and re-erect, re-approve or re-recommend them according to the norms of the *CIC* 83. Schulz seems to come from this same mindset. He saw all canonical legislation regarding lay associations from the *CIC* 17 to have fallen completely to the side[121]. Ghirlanda sees the suppression and reformation by the bishops as unnecessary since the associations continue according to their proper nature[122]. This point is certainly valid and is followed in this thesis where the standing of associations is evaluated by their canonical relationship with ecclesiastical authority. The juridic personality of erected associations certainly would endure as would ecclesiastical approval or an agreement among members of the Church. Leaving aside the bishops whom Ghirlanda mentions in his article, most of the persons who write on the development of associations from the *CIC* 17 to the *CIC* 83 dwell on the differences in the treatment of associations between the two codes of law.

4.4.2 Differences Between Associations of the Faithful in the *CIC* 17 and the *CIC* 83

While the purpose of associations of the Christian faithful as well as the canonical underpinnings of juridic personality, approval or recommendation basically remain the same, *CIC* 83 is wider and more open to various possibilities of different types of associations than its prede-

---

[120] G. GHIRLANDA, «Questioni irrisolte», 89.
[121] W. SCHULZ, «La posizione giuridica», 130.
[122] G. GHIRLANDA, «Questioni irrisolte», 88.

cessor. In a number of ways the associations themselves are different from the *CIC* 17 to the *CIC* 83. It will be asserted that the organization of the canons, as well as the canons themselves, indicate and identify the openness of the *CIC* 83 to associations of the Christian faithful which incorporate non-Catholic members. First the actual configuration of the canons will be mentioned, followed by a consideration of the relevant naming of the types of associations in each code.

At the same time that it reorganized the law regarding them, the *CIC* 83 profoundly restructured associations of the faithful[123]. The configuration of sections covering associations of the faithful are drastically different in the two Codes. The divisions of *CIC* 17[124] show one type of differentiation while the *CIC* 83 works from one which is a newer development and therefore a rethought schematic. Some ideas from the *CIC* 17 are certainly present in the *CIC* 83, but are categorized differently. Differences are not only present on the surface, that is in the organization of the titles and chapters which contain the canons, but within the description of the various types of associations and their relationships with the competent ecclesiastical authority.

The way that the associations are categorized is very different in the two codes, manifesting a new development of associative life in the Church. The *CIC* 17 makes divisions according to the ends of the associations (third orders, confraternities and pious unions) while the *CIC* 83 makes divisions according to relationship with the ecclesiastical authority (public associations of the Christian faithful and private associations of the Christian faithful). The *CIC* 17 had a relationship with associations recognized by canon law. The associations of the *CIC* 17 even though not divided in the code according to relations to ecclesiastical authority fit into certain categories of relationship or they would be without rights and duties under the law. The great number of options for associative life discussed and encouraged by both *AA* 19 and *CD* 17 replace the confraternities and pious unions[125] which categorized the types and ends of associations in the *CIC* 17. This is a huge difference between the two codes of law. While the *CIC* 17 outlines both the ends of the associations, through the naming of the associations, and the relation with ecclesiastical authority, through cc.684, 686,§1, the new code, outlines the relationship the associations have

---

[123] S. RECCHI, «Gli stadi evolutivi», 363.

[124] Cf. Chapter III, section 3, «Associations of the Faithful in the *CIC* 17».

[125] Third orders were a special case, because the title is retained, but the *CIC* 83 is also open to new terminology for these associations.

with ecclesiastical authority distinguishing them by the names public or private, and its openness to various types of associations by the ends listed in c.298,§1 *CIC* 83. The view that the *CIC* 17 based its division of association on ends and the *CIC* 83 on relation with ecclesiastical authority is a good comparitive foundation. C.301,§1 *CIC* 83 tempers the dichotomy because it associates competent ecclesiastical authority with associations which intend to impart Christian teaching in the name of the Church promote public worship or achieve other ends reserved to ecclesiastical authority. The *CIC* 83 here does not include ends in classification. This relation between ends and classification does not occur outside of the realm of competent ecclesiastical authority[126].

Both codes of law start with a general norms section on associations, followed by the presentation of types of associations. The *CIC* 83 attaches three canons which focus on the laity and which do not balance what has gone before. This imbalance may seem strange, but further encourages the laity to inscribe in associations of the Christian faithful.

Beyond the division of third orders secular, confraternities, and pious unions and their conglomerates in the *CIC* 17, a central distinction is between ecclesiastical and lay associations[127]. This distinction though certainly real was more evident in the system of the *CIC* 17 than in the canons themselves. These lay associations were neither identified by this name nor described as such in the Pio-benedictine Code. They were in fact associations not approved or erected by ecclesiastical authority and therefore not ecclesiastical associations[128], nor were they associations which are secret, condemned, seditious, suspected or those which aim to remove themselves from the legitimate ecclesiastical vigilance. These associations were those which had been merely recommended by the Church[129]. Their position became more stable in law after the letter of the Sacred Congregation of the Council to the Bishop of Corrientes on 13 November 1920. Again the term lay is used to identify associations not erected or approved but merely recommended by ecclesiastical authority in the *CIC* 17.

---

[126] G. GHIRLANDA, «Questioni irrisolte», 84.

[127] Cf. Chapter III, section 3.2.1, «Lay Associations compared to Ecclesiastical Associations».

[128] C.686,§1 *CIC* 17.

[129] C.684 *CIC* 17.

It is an interesting usage which could have led to confusion[130] because the two titles in the *CIC* 17 which present the Church's law on associations are found under part three of book two, *«De laicis»*, which refers to persons who are neither clerics nor religious. Parts one and two of book two are dedicated to just these two groups of persons. It seems as if the associations described in the titles only inscribe lay persons. In fact under the system of the *CIC* 17 there were associations of clergy and associations to which both clergy and laity belonged. So, in the *CIC* 17 the term «lay» is used for the title of the third part of book two and also to categorize associations which were not ecclesiastical.

The *CIC* 83 has a more straightforward meaning of the term. At the beginning of title five c.298,§1 *CIC* 83 clearly states that associations may be composed of clergy, laity, or clergy and laity together. The last three canons of the title are the fourth chapter, which is dedicated to associations which have only lay members. The lay associations in the *CIC* 83 can be either public or private. Both have rights and duties in the Church. It is certainly a change for lay associations since those in the *CIC* 17 had no rights or duties as a canonical body in the Church. As has been seen differences in the use of the term lay is one example of the differences in organization between the *CIC* 17 and the *CIC* 83.

Within the system of the *CIC* 17 another important distinction was identified among those associations considered ecclesiastical. This distinction was between associations with juridic personality (erected by competent ecclesiastical authority) and those without (merely approved by ecclesiastical authority)[131]. There is no division in the *CIC* 83 among associations formed by Church authority, which for the most part are formed through the initiative of private persons. The *CIC* 83 adds another category of associations which are established by the private initiative of the Christian faithful yet are granted juridic personality by the competent authority. This last category is the private initiative of physical persons in the Church, not of the competent ecclesiastical authority, even though a private association with juridic personality is a juridic person in the Church.

As a consideration of the names and ends of the associations are set forth they will be used as a means to draw out differences between associations in the *CIC* 17 and the *CIC* 83. After the complexity of the

---

[130] J.L. GUTIÉRREZ, «Associations of Christ's Faithful», 245.

[131] Cf. Chapter III, section 3.2.2, «Associations with Juridic Personality and those without Juridic Personality».

associational organization in the *CIC* 83, the differences in classification of the associations and specific naming will be studied.

The general division according to type between the two codes into categories of associations of the faithful which is clear in the presentation in the canons is the types of associations. The *CIC* 17 devotes three specific chapters to the five types of associations it recognizes canonically. The first chapter of title XIX covers third orders, the second chapter, confraternities and pious unions, and the third chapter archconfraternities and primary pious unions. These are contrasted with those of the *CIC* 83, public associations of the Christian faithful and private associations of the Christian faithful. Each of the three general ends of associations which have remained in the *CIC* 83 are represented by one of the three basic types of associations in the *CIC* 17. So the associations in the *CIC* 17 were categorized or named by their ends[132]. Such a naming certainly gives focus to the associations and their purpose. This cannot be said for the *CIC* 83 because the three goals for associations are not associated with the divisions of public and private associations. In fact the goals as found in the *CIC* 83 have been widened to include Christian teaching and evangelization, two areas which might warrant juridic personality because associations engaged in these pursuits may be viewed as acting in the name of the Church. Since associations in the *CIC* 83 are not foundationally categorized by their ends, one wonders how they are classified. The answer is that they are generally classified by their relationship with the competent ecclesiastical authority. Therefore the purposes of the associations no longer distinguish the types of associations, but the persons who erect or establish them. The ends of the association are not without importance because the ends will at times determine whether the associations are to be erected as public or established by the people themselves as private.

Shifting the weight of classification of associations from their ends to their relationship with competent authority drastically opens the field of possible types of associations. Provost points out that associations are formed for specific purposes[133]. These would not be limited to the titles as had been in the *CIC* 17. Amos, citing *AA* 19 posits that *CIC* 83 does not supply the terminology to establish a perfect correspondence between ends and kinds of associations and that the new code

---

[132] Cf. Chapter III, section 4.3.1.
[133] J. PROVOST, «The Realization», 761.

does not limit ends for associations[134]. For Amos these two factors make the organization of associations in the *CIC* 83 complex. Possibilities of various types of associations in the *CIC* 83 abound as is manifest by the absence of titles which are associated with the purpose and ends of the associations. A number of authors comment in a way that recognizes the openness of the *CIC* 83 to new forms of associative life.

In a broad stroke Boni views the proposed scope of the *CIC* 83 as difficult to realize because it melts theology and law, doctrine and norm, life and discipline into one harmony[135]. Even as Boni writes concerning the *CIC* 83 and is concerned with religious life, his view touches the openness of the *CIC* 83 to various types of associative life in the Church.

In his commentary on c.298,§1 *CIC* 83, Gutiérrez comments specifically on reasons why associations might be constituted. He states that the objects for which associations are begun are all related to the supernatural mission of the Church. The objects, according to Gutiérrez are described generally and loosely[136]. A less than specific description is open to a variety of possibilities.

In Feliciani's work on the People of God he comments on the different treatment of associations in the *CIC* 17 and the *CIC* 83. He recognizes that in the *CIC* 17 types of associations were named according to their ends. Associations in the *CIC* 83 are full of ends. Their existence is truly personal and individual to each association[137].

Feliciani and the other just mentioned authors reinforce the openness of the new associations to the variety of religious purposes. This openness to a plethora of types of associations finds its roots in the Second Vatican Council as evidenced in the titles of the types of associations in the *CIC* 83. Associations with non-Catholic members is merely one of the possibilities among the wide field which is present.

The canonically recognized associations under the system of the *CIC* 17 were all established by ecclesiastical authority. This is true whether the associations were erected as juridic persons or simply given approval. Their relationship with competent superiors was therefore assumed. Classifying associations according to their ends makes sense because the issue of their task in the visible church is more easily seen.

---

[134] J. AMOS, *Associations of the Christan Faithful* (1986), 189.
[135] A. BONI, «La vita religiosa», 523.
[136] J.L. GUTIÉRREZ, «Associations of Christ's Faithful», 246.
[137] G. FELICIANI, *Il popolo di Dio*, 146.

In the *CIC* 83 the names and structures assigned to confraternities and pious unions were no longer used. Only third orders retained their title and this was not without exception[138]. The *CIC* 83 while not renouncing the past remains open to the novelty of the future[139].

To make a definitive comparison of the types of associations in the two codes of law is not simple because authors differ in their views of types of associations, and on which groupings of persons they would include in a list of associations according to the law. Examples of lists of two authors are presented in the appendix.

4.5 *The Configuration of Associations of the Christian Faithful in the CIC 83*

4.5.1 Introduction

An effort has been made to present the *CIC* 83 in somewhat the same manner as the *CIC* 17 was presented. Still, the previous two sections of the work have been a tangent in order to demonstrate the developmental changes from the *CIC* 17 through the Second Vatican Council which influenced the *CIC* 83. Now the configuration of the associations as found in the *CIC* 83 itself will be studied.

Even as this attempt is made to follow the system used to study the *CIC* 17 the differences between the two codes will continue to be manifest. The section (3) covering the *CIC* 17 first highlighted the systematic organization of the canons in the code and secondly the biggest division among the associations in the system of the *CIC* 17, even though this division is not listed in the code itself. The division and differences between ecclesiastical and lay associations are different from public and private and to use these to make a comparison is not really helpful except to point out that the categories have a different purpose[140].

After considering the great variety of associations which abound under the system of the *CIC* 83, differences between public and private

---

[138] Third orders are specifically mentioned in c.303 *CIC* 83 (Tertii ordines dicuntur aliove congruenti nomine vocantur) as associations which share in the spirit of some religious institute under the direction of the same institute. This institute naturally has a male first order and a female second order depending on the first. When there is not a second order it may be called by another name.

[139] T. VANZETTO, «Commento a un canone», 384.

[140] The differences between ecclesiastical and lay associations and public and private associations have been studied in Chapter III, section 3.2.1.

associations and a study of the characteristics of the two types will take place. Juridic personality and actions made in the name of the Church will also be covered. A number of points identifying ecumenical possibilities will complete the section.

The change in the canonical composition of associations of the Christian faithful from the *CIC* 17 to the *CIC* 83 must not be underestimated. The canons were not developed so as to distinguish one type of association from another[141] as had been done in the *CIC* 17, but to determine the intervention on the part of the ecclesiastical authority[142]. Possibilities for different types of associations abound. Using c.312,§1 *CIC* 83, Amos identifies universal (international), national and diocesan associations. From c.298,§1 *CIC* 83 he identifies associations made up of priests, laity, and priests and laity together. The ecclesiastical authority to which the first group relates is found in the canon. The second group, according to Amos, has dicasteries at the Apostolic See which are competent in respect to them[143]. It must be remembered that these associations can be erected or approved and then supervised all by the local bishop if they exist at a diocesan level. Different specific types of public or private associations will not be listed here because they will be identified when the characteristics of public and private associations are studied. The six types which Amos identifies are not confined by the headings public and private confirming the point that the categories public and private, refer to the relationship between the associations and the competent ecclesiastical authority and not to the ends of the associations[144].

4.5.2 Public vs. Private Associations of the Faithful

A new style of approaching the canons on associations has begun with the advent of public and private associations of the faithful in the Church. Here the idea of associations which are either public or private will be considered. The actual comparison and individual study will take place in the next part.

The actual origin of the concept of public and private associations is beyond the scope of the present work. However it would be good to

---

[141] W. SCHULZ, «Posizione giuridica delle associazioni», 115.

[142] G. GHIRLANDA, «Questioni irrisolte», 88; *Comm*.18 (1986), 386.

[143] J. AMOS, *Associations of the Christan Faithful* (1986), 185.

[144] Cf. P. GIULIANI, *La distinzione*, 181-188; and L. MARTINEZ-SISTACH, *La Asociaciones de Fieles*, 49-68, 85-107.

note that Beyer writes that at the time of the compilation of the *CIC* 17, the distinction between public and private associations was rejected[145]. Schulz points to the influence of Belgian civil law on Onclin who had been the secretary to the *PCCICR*. Schulz views the distinctions public and private as modes of addressing the tension in associations between autonomy and the relationship with authority[146]. So while Beyer notes the rejection of the terminology, Schulz points to its practicality at a time that the Church was striving to encourage lay involvement. Amos identifies the fundamental distinction between the two as coming from the preparatory schema on associations of the faithful[147] which never became part of the official conciliar documents[148]. From whatever source it came the distinction is present.

Schulz's identification of public and private associations as a means to resolve the tension between the liberty or autonomy of associations and the bond or relationship with Church authority can lay the groundwork for an overview of the associations be they private or public. As scholars critique the division of associations, a number of ecclesiological views are manifest. These views range from autonomy, where one would find an emphasis on the invisible Church, to a heavy dependence on the bond with ecclesiastical authority and the visible hierarchical Church. This range includes scholars who do not believe that the distinctions public and private are necessary to those who find them integral to associations in the Church at the end of the twentieth century.

The first view to be presented is that of Beyer. Making the claim that all ecclesial life is public he states that it is hard to make a distinction between public and private. Continuing, the point is made that a group in the Church is always public, that it comes together as «a gift made to the Church» and not simply a private initiative which appeals to the principle of subsidiarity. His ideas concerning associations come together as he expresses his idea that in the Church one cannot be outside the Church. He equates this to the possibility of a citizen of a certain country living outside of that country. In the Church one always lives under the direction of Peter, his successors and the bishops[149].

---

[145] J. BEYER, «La Vita Associativa nella Chiesa», 311.

[146] W. SCHULZ, «Posizione giuridica delle associazioni», 116.

[147] *Acta et Documenta Concilio Oecumenico Vaticano II Apparando, Series II, vol. III, pars I*, 420.

[148] J. AMOS, *Associations of the Christan Faithful* (1986), 190.

[149] J. BEYER, «La vita associativa», 311.

The sense of the word private as Beyer sees it would seem to be contrary to the nature of the Church[150].

Corecco questions the division between public and private associations in the *CIC* 83. In the Church there are more private associations than public and according to him this situation creates a distorted ecclesiology[151].

Montan moves slightly away from Beyer by recognizing the differences in the ideas of public and private. He reinforces the basic concept that the relationship between the association and the ecclesiastical authority will determine its status as public or private. He also recognizes the openness of the ends in the *CIC* 83[152]. Still he identifies the ends of associations as being in line with the Church[153] while at the same time calling pastors to a just equilibrium between a prudent vigilance and recognition of a true autonomy of private associations[154]. He calls for a healthy tension between vigilance and autonomy.

While accepting the basic difference between public and private associations Schulz rejects the idea that they divide the associations of the *CIC* 83 into two big categories. These are based on canonical legislation and not just the creative freedom of the laity. Even as the concepts public and private are in the law the associations are based on the theological idea of *communio*[155]. There are many ways to live *communio* in the Church and no one person or association has the answer. Schulz accepts the canonical divisions of public and private but challenges the Church not to accept only these but also the diversity of associations spoken of in both the Council and the *CIC* 83.

Ghirlanda brings together both the theological and canonical dimensions of associations. As has been presented he follows the roots of the associations from the *CIC* 17[156]. He views all associations with spiritual ends as being in ecclesial communion with the Church. In fact public and private associations are two manifestations of this reality of communion. These associations have an ecclesial character[157]. As a Christian is a person for others so in the Church the good of individuals

---

150 J. BEYER, *Il Codice del Vaticano II*, 80.
151 Cf. E. CORECCO, «I laici nel nuovo Codice», 97.
152 A. MONTAN, «Le associazioni», 331.
153 A. MONTAN, «Le associazioni», 328.
154 A. MONTAN, «Le associazioni», 338.
155 W. SCHULZ, «Posizione giuridica delle associazioni», 130.
156 Cf. Chapter III, section 4.4.1.
157 G. GHIRLANDA, «Questioni irrisolte», 86.

is always seen as the good of the Church, the good of the community and in fact the good of all[158]. In the review of private associations Ghirlanda's idea will be presented. Here it is seen that both the law and theology are used to understand associations in the Church. An ample amount of both is needed for associations to be well understood.

A fundamental definition or explanation of the terms public and private is that they speak of the relationship between the associations and the ecclesiastical authority[159]. Ghirlanda however further emphasizes the importance of the ends of associations. He writes that it is also by reason of the ends that associations are public or private[160]. An association which desires to teach Catholic doctrine in the name of the Church or train others for the purpose of formation for ministry in the Church ought to be erected by the competent ecclesiastical authority as a public association of the faithful. If such an association were to start as private it would be wise that the private nature of the work of the association be made clear to its members. Molano proposes that the division of associations into public and private comes from the means by which the ends, common for the Church, will be achieved[161]. Associating the means with the names public and private brings out another nuance of achieving the ends assigned to the Church. In fact the ends may be reached in a number of ways. These authors bring a richness to the meaning of the terms.

At the other end of the spectrum from the idea that all ecclesial life is public making private associations irrelevant is the importance of the distinctions which are found in the *CIC* 83. Kneal in his commentary on the canons calls the dichotomy between public and private associations critical. His position rests on the difference between the erection of public associations which are able to act in the name of the Church and those associations which do not act in the name of the Church[162]. To further support his position he accentuates the intensity of supervision of public associations by competent authority comparing it to the autonomy of private associations.

The viewpoints of associations of the faithful are quite varied among scholars. They range from the very theological to those which are solely rooted in the canons. The present day praxis of associations

---

[158] G. GHIRLANDA, «Questioni irrisolte», 86.
[159] L. NAVARRO, *Diritto di associazione*, 141.
[160] G. GHIRLANDA, «Questioni irrisolte», 84.
[161] E. MOLANO, «Juridic Persons», 136-137.
[162] E. KNEAL, «Associations of the Christian Faithful», 245.

is somewhere in between the two. The Church must have the ability to supervise if an association is to in any way associate itself with the visible hierarchical Roman Catholic Church.

4.5.3 Public and Private Associations: An Explanation and Comparison

If the two types of associations were mirror images with different ways of manifesting themselves a comparison could easily be made. If they were simply different types of associations which came together for different purposes similar to the third orders, confraternities and pious unions of the *CIC* 17, a comparison would be relatively simple. However the situation for the two styles of association is complex.

a) *Public Associations of the Christian Faithful*

Among the characteristics which make public associations of the faithful unique and different from those which are private, two stand out. The first is that public associations are erected by competent ecclesiastical authority having a strong bond with the authority which erected them. Secondly, they act in the name of the Church.

Public associations of the Christian faithful as described in the canons are erected by the competent ecclesiastical authority, and not only act under its vigilance but also under its superior direction. The statutes of the public association must be approved by the competent ecclesiastical authority[163]. It is not until the moment that the association is erected by the ecclesiastical authority that it becomes a public association of the Christian faithful in the Roman Catholic Church. The act of erection is constitutive for these associations[164]. Associations erected by the hierarchy become corporations of public law and receive a mission in which the ends of the association presuppose a participation in the mission received at baptism by all Christians. These associations are submissive in all governance of the sacred pastors[165]. When a public association of the Christian faithful is erected it automatically becomes a public juridic person with public juridic personality in the Church. The association is therefore permanent and has rights and duties in the Church.

---

[163] These characteristics of public associations come from cc.301,§1; 305,§1; 315; 314 *CIC* 83.

[164] L. NAVARRO, *Diritto di associazione*, 142-3.

[165] G. GHIRLANDA, «Questioni irrisolte», 84.

The group of study of the *PCCICR* made it clear that when teaching Christian doctrine, even when this is done in the name of the Church, is not a magisterial function to such associations. The function in fact does not treat of a canonical mandate received but of a mission that remains developmentally generic[166]. All Roman Catholics participate in the mission of the Church and are called to represent the Church as members of the Body of Christ. This includes all Catholic members of associations whether public or private. In fact, to transmit Christian doctrine ought not to be considered a work reserved to the authority but corresponding to each member of the Church. Associations established for the purposes of teaching Christian doctrine in the name of the Church or promoting public worship must be public (c.301,§1 *CIC* 83)[167]. The competent authority can also erect public associations according to c.301,§2 *CIC* 83 for spiritual ends not adequately provided for in private associations. Any association erected according to the norm of c.301,§2, in that it is public, is a public juridic person (c.116,§1) and always acts in the name of the Church in virtue of the erection itself effected by ecclesiastical authority. As far as it is required, *quatenus requiritur*, according to c.313 *CIC* 83, a public association receives a mission to speak in the name of the Church. The particular activity of the association is in a formal way representative of the activity of the Church[168]. The association officially acts on behalf of the Church in matters for which it has been erected. If the competent ecclesiastical authority which erects an association wishes for it to act in the name of the Church for some specific purpose, the statutes as well as the decree of erection ought to reflect this.

b) *Private Associations of the Christian Faithful*

Private associations have a much different relationship with the competent authority than that of public associations. Private associations are never founded by ecclesiastical authority but by individuals in the Church. The competent ecclesiastical authority may or may not recognize their existence according to the law. Even though they may not have legal standing under the law they can exist. The recommended associations of the *CIC* 17 fit this category in the *CIC* 83.

---

166 *Comm.* 12 (1980), 94-95.
167 J.L. GUTIÉRREZ, «Associations of Christ's Faithful», 248.
168 A. MCGRATH, «Associations of Christ's Faithful», 173.

The variety of expressions of private associations of the Christian faithful in the Church fills a spectrum of possibilities. It goes from *de facto* associations, which exist without any official recognition, to those with juridic personality. According to at least one author the latter may act in the name of the Church in specific situations, if authorized to do so by competent authority[169]. Because the associations in the *CIC* 83 are not systematized directly according to their ends as were those of the *CIC* 17, the possibility for the existence of various types of associations excedes those which are described in the *CIC* 83[170]. Even associations which lack statutes may exist legitimately even though they cannot be recognized as private associations of the Christian faithful by the review of statutes[171].

As presented above, associations which are not legally recognized in the *CIC* 83 may exist[172]. In the system of the *CIC* 83 these are sometimes referred to as *de facto* associations. The healthy tension which has been noted between autonomy and governance[173] brings into question associations which are not canonically recognized in the Church but are rather visible to the Catholic faithful, but may not have their statutes reviewed[174]. The variety and autonomy of associations in the *CIC* 83 makes their formation foreseeable and legitimate. As members of the Roman Catholic Church or a Roman Catholic organization one would think that the association would want to have a link with the ecclesiastical authorities. This may not always be true. Amos lists a number of reasons that associations may be merely praised or recommended, recognized or unrecognized by ecclesiastical authority. His reasons included: 1) associations which have ends only loosely tied to the Church's goals, 2) associations which may need to prove themselves before they may be approved by the competent ecclesiastical authority, 3) the need to prepare workable statutes, 4) time for reflection or experimentation, 5) group stability and 6) associations which

---

169 E. MOLANO, «Juridic Persons», 136-137. However, we recognize that the association remains private even if it acts in the name of the Church if its mandate to act is valid only in certain situations. But if acting in the name of Church constitutes the end for which the association exists a public association must be erected.

170 L. NAVARRO, *Diritto di associazione*, 78.

171 L. NAVARRO, *Diritto di associazione*, 78-79; Cf. W. SCHULZ, «Posizione giuridica delle associazioni», 122.

172 C.299,§3 *CIC* 83.

173 See Chapter III, section 4.5.2.

174 E. KNEAL, «Associations of the Christian Faithful», 243.

may want to distance themselves from ecclesiastical authority[175]. The last point is an interesting one because it is in direct opposition to c.684 *CIC* 17. It never was put into any positive light as the question of non-Catholic participation in associations of the Christian faithful had been. Like the prohibition of non-Catholics, those who would try to remove themselves from legitimate ecclesiastical authority are not mentioned in the *CIC* 83[176]. These points are important to this work because ecumenical associations in general and associations which accept non-Catholic members in particular do fit into these categories. To recognize where an association stands canonically in relation to competent ecclesiastical authority is important for the association if it wishes to have its statutes reviewed, to be approved or to eventually acquire juridic personality by decree from that same authority.

Schulz practically doubled the types of associations he lists[177] by recognizing the use of the title «Catholic» as a differentiation of type among associations. Comments on the use of this title range from a simple decision of the competent authority to signifying that an association represents the Church in some manner[178]. It will not affect the present work because the system of the canons themselves provide the framework for the relationship with the competent ecclesiastical authority.

While *de facto* associations need no comment or evaluative statement from ecclesiastical authority associations which are praised or recommended do[179]. Some documented comment of the competent authority would suffice. No official document would be required because these associations have no rights or duties before the law, Nor have they had their statutes examined by competent authority[180]. Still the comment of the competent ecclesiastical authority does in a particular way guarantee associations which have been praised or recommended[181].

---

[175] J. AMOS, *Associations of the Christan Faithful* (1986), 181-182.

[176] Amos makes a small list of associations which do not have canonical recognition in *Associations of the Christan Faithful* (1986), 182.

[177] Cf. appendix I.

[178] Cf. A. MONTAN, «Le associazioni», 333; E. KNEAL, «Associations of the Christian Faithful», 245.

[179] Cc.298,§2; 299,§2 *CIC* 83.

[180] C.299,§3 *CIC* 83.

[181] G. GHIRLANDA, «Questioni irrisolte», 87.

Associations whose statutes have been reviewed represent another type of private association in the *CIC* 83[182]. These associations make an important step in having their statutes reviewed by the competent ecclesiastical authority. The review of the statutes intends to show that the statutes of the association are in harmony with Church doctrine and universal law[183]. This is the first level of association where the fact and or recognition of persons gathering in association is brought together with a consideration of the statutes of the association. The examination of the statutes of such associations was foreseen by the canonical norm[184]. Statutes describe the association's 1) purpose or social objective, 2) place of headquarters, 3) governance and 4) conditions of membership[185]. Recommendation or praise may come with the review of the association's statutes even when all three are individual steps.

The review of the statutes is important because the statutes represent the association canonically to the competent ecclesiastical authority. An association is canonically recognized in the Church only after its statutes have been reviewed[186]. Those wishing to be granted juridic personality must have their statutes approved[187]. The statutes also represent the juridic person when no physical persons are left in an association. The step of reviewing the statutes which separates an association from others which are merely *de facto* associations or have been recommended or praised is important. It is the review of the statutes which puts an association into the position in which it may eventually have its statutes approved and acquire the status of a juridic person in the Church.

Recognition in the Church is not easy to interpret as it is used in c.299,§3[188]. This canon underlines the importance of the bond between an association and its own statutes within the canonical order in the Church. The identification of associations recommended, praised or *de facto* does not call for statutes. Accepting the fact that they can indeed be recognized as individual types of associations, it seems best for the purposes of this work to group praised and recommended under asso-

---

[182] C.299,§3 *CIC* 83.

[183] J.L. GUTIÉRREZ, «Associations of Christ's Faithful», 246; L. NAVARRO, *Diritto di associazione*, 83.

[184] W. SCHULZ, «La posizione giuridica», 122.

[185] C.304,§1 *CIC83*.

[186] C.299,§3 *CIC* 83.

[187] Cc.314; 322,§2 *CIC* 83.

[188] C. REDAELLI, «Alcune questione pratiche», 348; E. KNEAL, «Associations of the Christian Faithful», 245.

ciations referred to as *de facto*. This will form a category of associations with attributes similar to the lay or recommended associations of c.684 *CIC* 17.

The approval of the statutes is a different step from mere review. Where approval would signify that the competent ecclesiastical authority is ready to erect the association to the level of juridic person, with all the ramifications which accompany juridic personality, a simple review of the statutes does not. It would seem that an association may ask for both approval and juridic personality, but two separate steps or points would always be involved. The statutes would be approved by the competent ecclesiastical authority and the association would be erected a juridic person.

The difference between associations whose statutes have been reviewed and those whose statutes have been approved is not always clear. The question or problem ought to be clearly stated. Is there a difference between these two types of private associations of the Christian faithful? The question will be answered in two phases. The first will consider: 1) the part of the competent ecclesiastical authority making the recognition, 2) the action taken by the authority and 3) the effect which the particular recognition has on the association. The second will involve: 1) the canons concerned with associations, 2) the pertinent terms of the canons covering associations found in other areas of the *CIC* 83, and 3) the *recognitio statutorum*.

The first phase answers will compare the relation of the above noted points and the two types of associations. If they are the same it will be noted, if they are different this also will be identified. Both positive and negative answers will receive elaboration. The competent ecclesiastical authority which is able to review and or approve the statutes of a private association of the Christian faithful is the same. The different groups of authority are: the Apostolic See, the conference of bishops in its own territory and the diocesan bishop[189]. The action taken by the competent ecclesiastical authority to recognize the statutes of an association as either reviewed or approved would most often be the same, but may be different in certain cases. The exception to this rule would be when an association is having its statutes approved and is being erected as a juridic person in the same document. Approval in this case would be directly linked to the granting of juridic personality. The effects which a decree of review of the statutes by competent authority

---

[189] Cf. c.312 *CIC* 83.

would have on the associations signifies that the statutes of the association are not in opposition to official Church teaching. Approval signifies that competent authority supports the association and its statutes. Neither brings juridic personality: but while an association whose statutes are approved can be erected to juridic personality by the competent authority, associations whose statutes are reviewed are merely recognized by the Church. Competent authority may not praise or recommend the association but still acknowledge that there is nothing wanting in the statutes so that it may be recognized by the Church.

The second phase includes a more in depth study. Four canons aid us in appreciating the difference between associations whose statutes are reviewed and those whose statutes have been approved. The canons are: Cc.299,§3; 302; 314; 322,§2 *CIC* 83. C.299,§3 *CIC* 83 states:

> No private association of Christ's faithful is *recognized / (acknowledged)* in the Church unless its statutes have been *reviewed* by the competent authority[190].

The meaning of neither of the pertinent terms is explained[191]. The verb *recognoscere* is found only in this canon of title five. The use of the term refers to the lowest level of recognition of an association by the Church. This is in contrast to the highest level of recognition for a private association of the Christian faithful which would occur when a private association by a formal decree of the competent ecclesiastical authority acquires juridic personality[192].

C.299,§3 *CIC* 83 also contains the term *agnoscere* which will classify three types of associations. Associations recognized by the Church are those: 1) whose statutes have been reviewed, 2) whose statutes have been approved and 3) which have been designated juridic persons. *Agnosco, agnoscere* is a level of recognition of associations only as it encompasses the three mentioned possibilities. The same term *agnoscere* is utilized in c.302 *CIC* 83 concerning clerical associations.

> Associations of the Christ's faithful are called clerical when they are under the direction of clerics, presuppose the exercise of sacred orders, and are *recognized / (acknowledged)* as such by the competent authority[193].

---

[190] C.299,§3 *CIC* 83 «Nulla christifidelium consociatio privata in Ecclesia agnoscitur, nisi eius statuta ab auctoritate competenti recognoscantur». Emphasis added.

[191] E. KNEAL, «Associations of the Christian Faithful», 245.

[192] Cf. c.322,§1 *CIC* 83.

[193] C.302 *CIC* 83 «Christifideles consociationes clericales, eae dicuntur, quae sub moderamine sunt clericorum, exercitium ordinis sacri assumunt atque uti tales a

The term even though it is the same has a different technical sense in the two canons. Its significance in c.302 *CIC* 83 is different because it is linked to clerical associations which like lay associations can be public or private. If a clerical association is private it may exist at any of the different levels of canonical recognition which have been identified. Whereas the significance of the term *agnosco, agnoscere* in c.299,§3 *CIC* 83 relates to three specific levels of canonical representation, c.302 *CIC* 83 relates to all possibilities of association by clerics. C.302 *CIC* 83 refers less to the association's relationship with the competent authority and more to the recognition or acknowledgment on the part of the authority that all of the members of the association are clerics[194].

C.314 *CIC* 83 reads:

> The statutes of any public association require the *approval* of the authority of which, in accordance with can. 312 §1, is competent to establish the association; this approval is also required for a revision *(recognition)* of, or a change in, the statutes[195].

The required approval of the statutes as well as the *recognitio vel mutatio* of this canon reminds one that they are in chapter two concerning public associations of the Christian faithful. Even though private associations also need to be approved before they can obtain juridic personality, the Latin is slightly different. It seems strange and unnecessary to use a different word when the meaning is the same[196]. It is granted that public and private juridic persons are different, as their designation makes clear. Approval for both private and public associations comes with the possibility of juridic personality. For public associations this is automatic[197]. Another difficulty with the canon is its

---

competenti auctoritate agnoscuntur». Emphasis added.

[194] The English translation of the term, *agnosco, agnoscere*, is consistently «recognized» between cc.299,§3 and 302 *CIC* 83 in the translation approved by the NCCB. The translation approved by the Episcopal conferences of Australia, Canada, England and Wales, India, Ireland, New Zealand, Scotland and Southern Africa translates *agnosco, agnoscere* as «recognized» in c.299,§3 and as «acknowledged» in c.302 *CIC* 83.

[195] C.314 *CIC* 83 «Cuiuslibet consociationis publicae statuta, eorumque recognitio vel mutatio, approbatione indigent auctoritatis ecclesiasticae cui competit consociationis erectio ad normam can. 312,§1». Emphasis added.

[196] W. Schulz notes that the Latin in this canon is not clear. W. SCHULZ, «Statutengenehmigung», 1-3.

[197] The reason for the use of *approbatio* and *probatio* and not the same term is unclear.

redundancy or its mistranslation. It would seem that three things require the approval of the competent ecclesiastical authority: 1) the statutes themselves, 2) the recognition of the statues and 3) a change in the statutes. This is a most literal translation of the Latin. The two English translations[198], the Italian[199], the Spanish[200], French[201] and German[202] all use the word «revision» and not the words found in Cassell's Latin Dictionary[203]. Cassell's offers: a reviewing, inspection, examining. It is intriguing that the translations of the *CIC* 83 use revision because this in not found in the dictionary. The canon itself would be redundant if the dictionary offerings were used. This is true because the canon calls for the approval of the statutes as well as an approval of their recognition (here the translators have used «revision») or change. The use of the word *recognitio* does not seem to be clear. The development of c.314 *CIC* 83 included no major changes from the third session of the groups of study concerning the laity through the sch 82 and the *CIC* 83. The term *approbatio* was used since the third session at which a list of canons was discussed, *recognitio* was used since the fourth session and *mutatio* since the fifth. Only minor changes were made in the schemata from sch 80 to sch 82[204]. An examination of the development of the canon reveals the desire to use the terminology even though it does not help in clarifying the different types of associations presented in the *CIC* 83.

The *approbatio* which was used in c.314 *CIC* 83 for public associations is related to the *probata* and *probatio* of c.322,§2 *CIC* 83 for private associations which reads:

> No private association of Christ's faithful can acquire juridical personality unless its statutes are approved by the ecclesiastical authority mentioned in can. 312 §1. The approval of the statutes does not, however, change the private nature of the association[205].

---

[198] CSLA, *Code of Canon Law*, 110-111; THE CANON LAW SOCIETY OF GREAT BRITIAN AND IRELAND, *The Code of Canon Law*, 53.

[199] T. BERTONE, ed., *Codice di Diritto Canonico*, 242-243.

[200] A. BENLLOCH POVEDA, ed., *Código de Derecho Canónico*, 169.

[201] J. PASSICOS, *Code de Droit Canonique*, 53.

[202] *Codex Iuris Canonici. Codex des kanonischen Rechtes*. Lateinisch-deutsche Augsgabe, 135.

[203] D. SIMPSON, *Cassell's Latin Dictionary*, 504.

[204] A comparison of the canons which were discussed at the sessions of the groups of study and the schemata are presented in an organized manner in the appendix of, L. NAVARRO, *Diritto di associazione*, 218-281.

[205] C.322,§2 *CIC* 83. «Nulla Christifidelium consociatio privata personalitatem

Uses of the term speak of the approval of the statutes of the associations.

This review of the pertinent canons exposes the idea of approval in cc.314; 322,§2 *CIC* 83, the idea of acknowledgment or recognition in cc.299,§3; 302 *CIC* 83, the idea of review also in c.299,§3 *CIC* 83 and recognition (or revision) in 314. A polarity between approval and simple review or acknowledgment is manifest as the pertinent canons of the title are studied.

A study of the terms[206] as they appear elsewhere in the *CIC* 83 supports this polarity and therefore the fact that the review and the approval of the statutes of an association of the faithful are two different canonical acts. Other canons which incorporate the terms, *approbatio*, *probatus/a* or *probatio* concern such situations as approval by formal decree, approval by Apostolic See for ecclesiastical universities or faculties, proofs in tribunal cases or persons approved for certain offices in the Church. From a comparison with the use of the term in the *CIC* 83 the statutes of an association *recognoscantur* by the competent authority. Different than an approval which tends to have an all encompassing positive seal, the review centers on the statutes and their proper construction[207]. Review is a step towards approval, but not approval itself. Review does not mean that the competent authority supports all that an association is and does but more precisely that nothing concerning the statutes is *praeter legem* or *contra legem*. *Agnosco, agnoscere* and *recognitio* (even though it has the strange use in c.314 *CIC* 83) convey a recognition or acknowledgment on the part of the competent authority of the association and its statutes. Springing from c.299,§3 *CIC* 83 the idea of recognition of only associations with statutes which have been reviewed, a new concept in the canonical system was born. This leads to the views concerning these types of associations.

The system of the *CIC* 83 uses the terminology *recognitio statutorum* to encompass associations whose statutes have been reviewed by competent ecclesiastical authority as well as those whose statutes have been approved by competent ecclesiastical authority. The *recognitio*

---

iuridicam acquiere potest, nisi eius statuta ab auctoritate ecclesiastica, de qua in can. 312, §1, sint probata; statutorum vero probatio consociationis naturam privatam non immutat». Emphasis added.

[206] X. OCHOA, *Index Verborum* and H. ZAPP, *Codex Iuris Canonici: Lemmata*, are very helpful in researching words and themes in the *CIC* 83.

[207] Cf. 304,§1 *CIC* 83.

statutorum verifies that the statutes of the association conform to the law and that there may be nothing present contrary to the faith, to custom, and to ecclesiastical discipline. The recognition further verifies that the ends are permitted or allowed and that the ends are included in the limits as posted in cc.215; 298,§1 *CIC* 83. Finally the recognition establishes that the means or methods as proposed in the statutes are generally speaking adequate to the ends and to social activities[208]. Specific to the statutes the *recognitio statutorum* is different from granting juridic personality to an association. This recognition or examination is one way of obtaining a *nihil obstat* for the statutes. This act of the authority is truly an act of control of guardianship or of legality[209]. It is important to remember that the association which receives *recognitio statutorum* is a private association of the Christian faithful without juridic personality. As a corporate body these associations have no rights or duties in the Church[210]. As a body the private association does not act in the name of the Church but in its own name or in the name of the single members of the association.

When authors speak of associations with statutes which have been reviewed or of those whose statutes have been approved they are in support of the position which holds for these two levels of associations whose statutes have been recognized. The closest relation with ecclesiastical authority for private associations is obtained by those with juridic personality.

Navarro clearly describes private associations of the Christian faithful with juridic personality using a number of points. First, he recognizes that the association as a juridical person, is institutionalized, giving life to the new body which is diverse from the sum of the individuals who compose it. Secondly, such bodies continue to have a private nature and develop an ecclesiastical task but do not carry out their functions in the name of the Church. Thirdly, the granting of the personality is not a constituent act or component of the association as it is for public associations of the faithful[211], since the constitution of the

---

[208] L. NAVARRO, *Diritto di associazione*, 83.

[209] L. NAVARRO, *Diritto di associazione*, 82.

[210] C.310 *CIC* 83.

[211] It needs to be remembered that public associations have diverse and developing functions in the name of the Church which are not always necessarily hierarchical functions. (Cf. C.301,§2 *CIC* 83) The teaching of Christian doctrine is not a hierarchical function in as much as it springs from baptism and so is included in both private and public associations (c.298,§1 *CIC* 83). Public associations accomplish this task in the name of the Church with a special mission in which the ecclesiastical

private association arises from autonomous initiative of the Christian faithful. Lastly, Navarro writes that such bodies are not incorporated into the structure of the Church or Church organization[212]. Nevertheless this non-incorporation is not the view of all authors[213]. The new private juridic persons of the *CIC* 83 are a great step forward for the rights of the layperson and for all Christian faithful in the Church. Previously in the Church no private juridic personality was granted to any corporation of persons, however now persons have a greater opportunity to participate in the ministry of the Church as members of private associations of the faithful. Most often they will not normally act in the name of the Church; work of this nature is left to public associations.

A final level of private associations of the faithful in the Roman Catholic Church is found when they act in the name of that same Church. The example involves private associations of the Christian faithful which have been granted juridic personality. Private associations act on the behalf of their members or of the association if the association has juridic personality. The question is, «can a private association ever act in the name of the Church»? Three points will bring us to our answer. First, it ought to be remembered that some scholars question the distinction between public and private associations of the Christian faithful. Jean Beyer in particular believes that the terms private and public do not represent the Church. In his mind there is nothing private in the Church[214]. Secondly, while scholars hold that private associations act in their own name and never in the name of the Church[215], an opening in which they may has been proposed. In the case of a private association with juridic personality there is the possibility of acting in the name of the Church.

> The competence to create public juridic persons is the province of ecclesiastical authority (116,§1), while the constitution of a private juridic person is the result of private initiative. It is possible, however, for a private juridical person to receive from ecclesiastical authority a mandate which entrusts it with an undertaking to be carried out in the name of the Church[216].

---

community is directly involved. (Cf. G. GHIRLANDA, «Questioni irrisolte», 87-8; *ChL* 29.)

[212] L. NAVARRO, *Diritto di associazione*, 95.

[213] Private associations are inserted into the organization of the Church at different levels. (Cf. E. MOLANO, «Juridic Persons», 137.

[214] Cf. Chapter III, section 4.5.2.

[215] J.L. GUTIÉRREZ, «Associations of Christ's Faithful», 258.

[216] E. MOLANO, «Juridic Persons», 137. Cf. Chapter III, section 4.5.3.

The third point is that other scholars have not made much of private associations acting in the name of the Church. It is certainly not accepted as common. However, nothing forbids it and it is the prerogative of the local bishop to erect juridic persons and grant juridical personality. It is also the right of the bishop to assign a mandate to those whom he wishes to undertake some task or mission in the Church[217].

These special cases or exceptions to the rule continue to clarify the openness to the possibly large number of different types of associations which may exist. These all find expression in the *CIC* 83.

The levels of private associations of the faithful addressed in this dissertation have been selected because their relationship with competent ecclesiastical authority is closely connected with the recognition of the statutes by that same authority. The statutes are truly the heart of the association. After *de facto* associations are identified, the associations with statutes which have been reviewed or approved and associations which are endowed with private juridic personality propose to reach ecclesial ends and manifest varying degrees of ecclesiality[218]. This is a wider view than that of the system of the *CIC* 17 which used the term ecclesial to refer to associations constituted by Church authority.

Summarizing and clearly defining the similarities and differences between associations in the *CIC* 17 and the *CIC* 83 clarifies the possibilities of ecumenical associations. After remembering the similarities between associations in the two codes of canon law, among these that persons gather in associations which are not ICL or SAL and that they gather for at least one of the following purposes: 1) achieving a more perfect life, 2) announcing the gospel to all by promoting Christian doctrine or public worship, and 3) pursuing social goals, or practicing works of piety or charity, differences are identified. Distinctions concerning types of associations within each of the codes themselves manifest much about what the associations themselves are able to do. Distinctions in the *CIC* 17 include ecclesiastical and lay associations, but also associations which are erected juridic persons and those which are not. Confraternities always had juridic personality while pious unions may or may not have had it. The erection of an association as a juridic person involves a juridical act. This makes the distinction concerning juridic personality in the *CIC* 17 one between the associations

---

[217] Cf. c.229,§3 *CIC* 83.

[218] Cf. L. NAVARRO, *Diritto di associazione*, 70; G. GHIRLANDA, «Questioni irrisolte», 87.

and the competent authority. There also is a distinction in the *CIC* 83 between associations which have juridic personality and those which do not. The associations without juridic personality are not recognized as a corporate body before the law. Still the most notable distinction among the associations in the *CIC* 83 is between public and private associations of the Christian faithful. An association is public or private depending on the manner in which it does its ecclesial ministry. The ministry of the association may be done in the name of the Catholic Church, in which case the association will be public, or ministry may be done by an association in its own name in which case it would be private. Ecumenical associations have the spread of the faith as an apostolate even as they are open to inscribing members of different faiths in a specifically Catholic association. The particular configuration of the associations in the new code manifests a focus on the manner in which an association does its ministry. This shift is another movement away from obligations of the *CIC* 17 towards the concentration on rights in the *CIC* 83, or the, «no» of the *CIC* 17 to the openness of the *CIC* 83 to ecumenical associations.

5. Consequences for Ecumenical Associations

Though the arguments in support of non-Catholic membership in ecumenical associations are substantiated by several points, the principal basis will be discussed under two headings: 1) the current codal provisions, and 2) the supervisory role of the diocesan bishop. The latter are to be found in the *CIC* 83, among the stated guidelines of the codal reform and within the documents of the Second Vatican Council. Specific possibilities for the existence of ecumenical associations will be presented.

5.1 *Current Codal Provisions*

5.1.1 Canon 215 *CIC* 83

The fundamental right of the Christian faithful to associate is stated in the *CIC* 83[219]. The right is based on both natural law and the very nature of the Church into which the faithful are incorporated by means of baptism.

After natural law first recognizes the instinct for self preservation and then the inclination toward conjugal union, which along with

---

[219] Cc.215; 299,§1 *CIC* 83.

bearing and educating children forms the first community of humanity there is also the tendency to communicate and to form various kinds of associations. Since human beings are social beings natural law also contains solidarity and work[220]. When persons work together the power and the gift of cooperation are made visible. Because what one person is able to accomplish is multiplied exponentially when there is collaboration toward a common purpose.

CIC 17 does not explicitly pronounce on the right of association found in natural law. The *CIC* 17 centered more on the obligations of Christians than on their rights: rights were more central to the Second Vatican Council an the *CIC* 83. But rights always imply duties, so that *CIC* 17 and *CIC* 83 are not contradictory but rather have different emphases. Natural law implies human participation in eternal law. The eternal law that is the eternal mind of God and orders all things to the end for which they were created. Documents written during the period between the two codes constructed a bridge between the natural law and the right of association. Among these are Pope John the XXIII's encyclical *Pacem in Terris* and other papal encyclicals which treat labor or the social aspects of mankind. Two documents of the Second Vatican Council, *AA* 19b, d and *DH* 3, 4a specifically serve to bridge natural law and its manifestation in the Church. While *AA* 19 supports the human rights of persons to associate, *DH* 3 specifically indicates that the highest form of human activity is found in obedience to the divine law. *DH* 4a makes a particular link between the right to association as found in natural law and also in the Church. The right of individuals to freedom from religious coercion must also be affirmed when they act in community. Religious communities as well as other types of associations are required by individuals as well as by humanity and indeed by religion itself[221]. This natural right to gather applies to all persons because natural law is not limited by any one religion. Therefore full or incomplete communion with the Catholic Church does not affect the right to association. When the Second Vatican Council treated the right to association and its basis in natural law it was not only speaking to Christians in full communion with Rome but also to

---

[220] J. HERVADA, *Introduzione*, 144.

[221] Cf. *AA* 19b, d; *DH* 3, 4a; G. FELICIANI, «Il diritto di associazione», 314-315. Other encyclicals which Feliciani cites to support the point are: *Rerum novarum*, 15 May 1891, *ASS* 23 (1890-1) 665; *Quadragesimo anno*, 15 May 1931, AAS 23 (1931) 204; *Sertum laetitiae*, 1 November 1939, *AAS* 31 (1939) 643; *Mater et magistra*, 15 May 1961, *AAS* 53 (1961) 416.

other Christians. Although proper to everyone the right to association applies particularly to Roman Catholics and to all other validly baptized Christians. *LG* 10 and 11, rooted in *LG* 15, acknowledge the communion, even though partial, which exists between Roman Catholics and other baptized Christians.

The communion into which persons enter when they receive the sacrament of Baptism confirms the right of persons to gather founded on the social nature of human beings[222]. This right of the faithful to form associations springs from Baptism and not from the concession of authority. It corresponds with the *communio* which the Church embodies among all those who believe in Christ[223].

In summary: this treatment of the right to association is based on c.215 *CIC* 83 when the Lord called people to gather He promised to be in their midst[224]. The right to association is not simply a subjective right that is conceded, but is proper to all human beings. Human authority does not give this right but rather recognizes it as intrinsic to every human being.

5.1.2 Canons 298-329 CIC 83

The terminology used in the *CIC* 83 itself is another support for ecumenical associations. The precise use of the term «Catholic» in the *CIC* 17 and the *CIC* 83 on one hand, compared to its absence in title five of book two, «Associations of the Christian Faithful», on the other, opens the way for a wider interpretation of who may and may not become members of associations of the faithful. Even though some may reject the use of the terminological question as a means of proving that non-Catholics may be inscribed into associations of the Christian faithful according to cc.298-329 *CIC* 83, it is hoped that the possibility for confusion which does exist in the *CIC* 83 will be evident. When comparing the canons of *CIC* 17 which are clear in forbidding non-Catholics from becoming members of associations of the faithful, as well as those with precise adjectival usage, to the canons of *CIC* 83 which are less clear and do not use limiting terminology, the intent of the *PCCICR* and the Holy Father himself to allow the possibility of ecumenical associations or at least to leave the question open becomes evident.

---

[222] W. SCHULZ, «La posizione giuridica», 120.
[223] G. GHIRLANDA, *Il diritto nella Chiesa*, 237.
[224] Mt. 18,19-20.

When c.693,§1 *CIC* 17, which clearly forbade non-Catholics from membership in associations of the faithful, is compared to cc.307 and 316 *CIC* 83 which leave the question of membership to the statutes of each particular association, a manifest difference in wording with a concordant juridical consequence emerges. The *CIC* 83 is not restricting the membership of associations of the faithful only to Catholics. Because the *CIC* 17 clearly forbade the inscription of non-Catholics, persons publicly known to be under ecclesiastical censure[225], which would include apostates, heretics and schismatics, the careful wording of the canons, is very important. The fact that cc.298-329 *CIC* 83 neither offer hospitality nor deny it to non-Catholics, including baptized non-Catholics and others is interesting especially in light of the prohibitions of the *CIC* 17. When the work of the *PCCICR* is taken into consideration it is even more intriguing[226]. The motives of the Supreme Pontiff in removing c.307,§4 sch 82 without any clarification concerning our separated brethren, members of other religions and persons of good will remain a mystery. If the removal had not taken place, the issue of terminology would not be so vital. When the situation of non-Catholics in associations was addressed all was clear. Now when an answer is sought on a query of non-Catholics in associations, the further question of who are the *Christifideles* may also be asked. Without c.307,§4 sch 82 the rights of ecumenical associations in the Roman Catholic Church are at times unclear.

Another example of the inclusive and open use of terminology within title five compared with other canons of the *CIC* 83 appears in the canons regarding the sacraments. Here it is stated that baptized persons are able to receive communion if they are not forbidden by law[227]. The introductory norms section concerning sacraments specifically identifies Catholic ministers as the administrators of the sacraments to Catholic members of the Christian faithful[228]. If further distinction is necessary persons are directed to later paragraphs as well as other canons[229]. The canons make clear when non-Catholics may and may not participate in the sacraments. Thus, it is plain that the canons themselves do not often make any distinction between Catholics and non-Catholics when using the term *Christifideles*, an omission which ap-

---

[225] Cf. c.693,§1 *CIC* 17.
[226] Cf. Chapter II, section 3.1.
[227] C.912 *CIC* 83.
[228] C.844,§1 *CIC* 83.
[229] Cc.844,§2,3,4; 861,§2 *CIC* 83.

pears intentional rather than accidental. Interpreting the law, one is bound to follow the legal maxim: where the law does not distinguish, neither should we. The openness of cc.298-329 to ecumenical associations is manifest by the absence of specific language which would bar non-Catholics from becoming members of such associations.

5.1.3 Canon 204,§1 *CIC* 83

C.844 *CIC* 83 uses the term, «*christifideles catholici*». The adjective «Catholic» found in Catholic Christian faithful or Catholic members of the Christian faithful indicates that the current code uses the term «Christian faithful» to encompass all Christians. «Catholic» here identifies a subgroup within the larger group of Christian faithful. This distinction is supported by c.204,§1 *CIC* 83 which uses the term «*Christifideles*» without the limiting adjective «*catholici*». The distinction made in c.844 *CIC* 83 supports ecumenical associations of the faithful as cc.298-329 *CIC* 83 refer to the Christian faithful and not specifically to Catholic Christian faithful. The lack of specific wording as used in c.844 *CIC* 83 is another support of non-Catholic membership in canonical associations of the faithful.

It is interesting to note the number of times that some of these terms appear in the *CIC* 83. The term *Christifidelis, is* appears over four times as often as the term *Catholicus, i* or *Catholicus, a, um*. The Christian faithful are mentioned one hundred twenty-eight times, while the term Catholic is used only twenty-eight times[230]. One of the few times they appear together is in the canons covering sacraments which were just discussed. This does not add to the clarity of the *CIC* 83 whose canons concern only the Latin Rite of the Roman Catholic Church.[231] The wide use of the term Christian faithful in the *CIC* 83 is not helpful. The term was not used in the *CIC* 17.

A canon which seems to have an effect on the openness of the *CIC* 83 to ecumenical associations is c.204,§1 *CIC* 83 which describes the Christian faithful. The canon tells us that all baptized Christians are incorporated into Christ and form part of the people of God. C.204,§1 *CIC* 83 states:

> Christ's faithful are those who, since they are incorporated into Christ through baptism, are constituted the people of God. For this reason they participate in their own way in the priestly, prophetic, and kingly office of

---

[230] X. OCHOA, *Index Verborum*, 67, 68, 77, 78.
[231] C.1 *CIC* 83.

Christ. They are called, each according to his or her particular condition, to exercise the mission which God entrusted to the Church to fulfill in the world[232].

Non-Catholic Christians who are members of ecumenical associations are also a part of the Church of Christ even though they are not fully incorporated members of the Roman Catholic Church.[233] The words of the canons themselves give us a juridic definition and not merely a description of the *Christifideles*. The canons which follow speak of the Roman Catholic Church as: the entity in which the Church of Christ subsists, having members in full communion through the profession of faith, the sacraments and ecclesiastical governance, and being in special relationship with catechumens[234]. It must be admitted that the term *Christifideles* is used to refer to Catholics in the *CIC* 83. C.204,§2 CIC 83 itself begins to hone the definition of *Christifideles* from (the wider theological definition which includes all the baptized) to the stricter canonical use. Many of the canons of title one, «The Obligations and Rights of all the Christian Faithful», which includes cc.208-223,§2 are addressed to Catholics specifically. The wording of the canons makes this obvious since they refer to union with the Church, the duty to show Christian obedience to pastors and the right to be assisted by the reception of the sacraments[235]. However, the words of c.204,§1 *CIC* 83 do not make such distinctions which direct the meaning of Christian faithful to Catholics only. This is possible to see because the following paragraph and canon both develop and hone the description of Christian faithful found in c.204,§1 *CIC* 83. One would think that Christian faithful at times refers to all Christians. This idea is based on the Apostolic Constitution *Sacrae disciplinae leges* in which the Supreme Pontiff stated that the *CIC* 83 required the prior work of the Second Vatican Council. John Paul II went on to write that the *CIC* 83 was to translate the conciliar ecclesiological teaching into canonical terms[236].

---

[232] C.204,§1 *CIC* 83. «Christifideles sunt qui, utpote per baptismum Christo incorporati, in popolum Dei sunt constituti, atque hac ratione muneris Christi sacerdotalis, prophetici et regalis suo modo participes facti, secundum propriam cuiusque condicionem, ad missionem exercendam vocantur, quam Deus Ecclesiae in mundo adimplendam concredidit».

[233] *LG* 15.

[234] Cf. cc.204,§2; 205; 206,§1 *CIC* 83.

[235] Cf. Cc.209,§§1,2; 210; 212,§§1,2,3; 213; 214.

[236] Cf. Chapter III, section 3.2.2.

There is a certain amount of confusion since members of the *PCCICR* disagreed on the meaning of the term and did not clarify its significance for the *CIC* 83, particularly in c.204 *CIC* 83[237]. Because the term is not clearly defined it can be understood in both a wider or stricter sense, depending on the context. If the term *Christifideles* is taken in the stricter sense limitations are present, as identified in the previous paragraph. When all the baptized are included they would be able to be members of associations of the faithful based on c.204 *CIC* 83. The wider sense of the term is used theologically in the documents of the Second Vatican Council.

In the plenary session of the *PCCICR* in 1981 the relator responded to a *non placet* made concerning the then c.201 sch 80. One father believed that the canon was too open as it stood and gave examples of other texts which would be clearer. These included c.1 sch 77 «The People of God» (based on c.87 *CIC* 17) and c.6 sch *LEF*. These canons unlike c.201 sch 80 had qualifying terms which would make it clear that the canon did not refer to all baptized Christians, but only those in full communion with the Apostolic See[238]. The relator to the plenary responded that the text could remain as it was because even though the term *Christifideles* included all baptized Christians in the theology of the Second Vatican Council, in the *CIC* 83 it included only the Roman Catholics. Three points seem very strange about this statement: 1) to say that the term has one meaning in theology and another in canon law is in direct opposition to the call of the Supreme Pontiff that the *CIC* 83 put into canonical terms the ecclesiology of the Second Vatican Council, 2) he uses the term *Christifideles catholici* in his explanation even though he himself has said that the term *Christifideles* is clear by itself in canonical parlance, and 3) even though he felt that the understanding of the term was clear it was not or a *non placet* would not have been raised and the issue would have been mute after the first discussion of the term[239].

5.1.4 Canon 11 *CIC* 83

C.11 *CIC* 83 states:

Merely ecclesiastical laws bind those who were baptized in the catholic Church or received into it, and who have a sufficient use of reason and,

---

[237] Cf. *Comm.* 14 (1982), 157; *Comm.* 12 (1980), 59-63.
[238] C.6 LEF; c.1 sch 77 *schema canonum Libri II De Populo Dei*.
[239] *Comm.* 12 (1980), 59-63.

unless the law expressly provides otherwise, who have completed their seventh year of age[240].

The canon does not exclude non-Catholics from membership in associations of the Christian faithful because their right to belong does not involve merely ecclesiastical law, but also natural law. By codal disposition, baptized non-Catholics are not subject to ecclesiastical law. However, this does not forbid them from voluntarily submitting to at least some of the canons contained in the Code. Inscribing in an association of the faithful is one example. Persons who are non-Catholics and enter associations as members would need to agree with the statutes of the association and follow Church teaching and the desires of the competent authority who has recognized or at least reviewed the statutes of the association.

5.1.5 Canon 1 *CIC* 83

Canons 1 - 6 provide the limits for the *CIC* 83. C.1 begins by stating that the *CIC* 83 addresses only the Latin Church,

The canons of this Code concern only the Latin Church[241].

This limitation does not mean that the *CIC* 83 never refers to persons who are not members of the Latin Church. In fact, significant provisions are made for the Eastern Ritual Churches, particularly regarding baptism and relationship to rite. The object of c.1 *CIC* 83 is to establish that the *CIC* 83 does not abrogate the apostolic letters addressed to the Eastern Rites by Pius XII. The canon also foresaw the promulgation of the *CCEO* 90, a code written specifically for the Eastern Rite Churches of the Roman Catholic Church.

5.1.6 Juridic Persons and Individual Members

The membership status of individual participants in associations of the Christian faithful is not affected by the particular Christian denomination to which they belong. This is true because: 1) as baptized Christians they are members of the Church of Christ, 2) the associations of the faithful to which they belong (a juridic person here) is a

---

[240] C.11 *CIC* 83. «Legibus mere ecclesiasticis tenentur baptizati in Ecclesia catholica vel in eandem recepti, quique sufficienti rationis usu gaudent et, nisi aliud iure expresse caveatur, septimum aetatis annum expleverunt».

[241] C.1 *CIC* 83. «Canones huius Codicis unam Ecclesiam latinam respiciunt».

corporate body separate from the individuals who are members of the association, and 3) the individual members of public associations do not act in the name of the Church; only the juridic person *per se* of which the members are a part, does this.

In the case of associations which are not juridic persons, the juridic relationship exists between the ordinary and the individual members of the association. Non-Catholic baptized Christians would not be barred from entering associations in this situation. Their relationship with the hierarchy would be the same as for non-members of the association. No *de facto* juridic relationship exists between non-Catholic Christians and the Church hierarchy. The Roman Catholic Church does not demand obligations or duties from these persons. No law forbids the non-Catholic baptized Christian from following the teachings of the Supreme Pontiff or those of the diocesan bishop. Here a person uses free will and possibly fullfills a desire to enhance his or her knowledge of the Roman Catholic faith both intellectually and spiritually by freely joining an association and following its statutes. Alternately, the individual may wish to engage in an activity, even a spiritual one, which the association sponsors or promotes and which his own ecclesial body lacks, thus being the ground for a *communicatio in spiritualibus*.

Again the point is made: the law permits non-Catholics to be members of canonical associations of the Christian faithful. When addressing the possibility of an ecumenical association in his diocese the bishop ought to note whether persons are baptized Christians or not. If non-baptized were to enter an association it should properly be named interreligious. Discussion at the *PCCICR* was open to interreligious associations[242]. The primary concern of this work is ecumenical associations, but the acceptance of non-baptized members has not proven to be *contra legem* or even *praeter legem*. Because the baptized are a part of the Church of Christ there is a greater possibility for sharing in beliefs between them and the Roman Catholic Church and thus an openness to a legitimate *communicatio in spiritualibus*. While baptized non-Catholics enter into ecumenical relations with the Roman Catholic Church, non-baptized enter into interreligious dialogue. It would seem that a bishop would be more likely to approve an ecumenical association of the faithful in his diocese than an interreligious one.

---

[242] *Comm.* 18 (1986), 219.

6. The Supervisory Role of the Diocesan Bishop

6.1 The Bishop's Authority Over Associations

The bishop always has authority over any associations which exist in his diocese[243]. With regard to ecumenical associations he answers his call to care for all who are living in his diocese[244] by recognizing and providing supervision for the associations[245].

6.2 The Bishop's Authority Over Ecumenical Affairs

The bishop's charge to oversee and promote ecumenical affairs in his diocese is made both in the documents of the Second Vatican Council and the *CIC* 83[246]. If the bishop were to see the need and benefit of non-Catholics belonging as members to an association of the faithful in his diocese he has the authority to erect, approve, or review the association and/or its statutes. The decision to allow non-Catholics to become members of canonical associations of the faithful in his hands. This right of the bishop is clear from examination of both the documents of the Second Vatican Council and the *CIC* 83.

6.3 The Guiding Principles of Codal Reform

The fifth guiding principle of codal reform agreed upon by the *PCCICR* was subsidiarity or a healthy decentralization. This puts into the hands of the local bishop whatever can be done by him without disrupting the unity of the universal Church. As each diocese has a different ecumenical situation, it makes sense that the decisions about non-Catholics entering associations of the Christian faithful as members be handled by the local bishop. If he believes it advantageous for all involved, non-Catholics can be enrolled. In particular non-Catholic Christians, because they are not fully incorporated in the Catholic Church are not able to be members with full rights. These are not non-Catholics acting as if they were Catholics, but Christians sharing in the benefits of belonging to the people of God and Church of Christ, sharing in the same mission received at baptism.

---

[243] C.305,§§1; 2.

[244] *CD* 11, 16, 17; *UR* 8.

[245] The bishop's support and supervision of associations in his diocese also helps to fulfill the second section of c.1752 that the supreme law of the Church is the salvation of souls.

[246] Cf. *UR* 8; *CD* 13; c.383,§3.

Questions which are resolved for at a higher level ought to be dealt with at the lowest level, as close to those who will be affected by the decisions as possible. The silence of the code on the matter, besides possibly being a *lacuna* in the law, grants permission. The old adage is recalled which states, «he who is silent is understood to consent».

7. Ecumenical Associations in the United States of America

The United States of America is not and never has been a Catholic country. Even from the time when it was settled by Europeans the aboriginal persons who had lived in the territory which became the United States did not have a religion which continued to have a great effect on the newcomers to the infant nation. Throughout its development the young nation strove to protect the religious freedom of her inhabitants. This created a unique situation in the United States: as a result many fled to her shores to escape religious persecution, Catholics and Protestants alike. This is not to say that the country under study ought to have ecumenical associations of the faithful while others do not. Or, even that other countries do not have situations that warrant such associations. The point being made is simply that the situation in the United States of America is ripe for ecumenical associations. Along with the openness of the *CIC* 83 to ecumenical associations the situation of ecumenical associations in the United States is quite natural and within the limits of the law.

The praxis of the PCL differs from the recommendation here. In associations of the faithful with ecumenical participation the most oft used praxis is that only Catholics are named members even though this is not always the case[247]. The point of this dissertation is not to favor one praxis over another, but simply to show the possibility of ecumenical associations and that such associations do exist following their statutes while operating under the supervision of the local bishop or Apostolic See.

A number of ecumenical associations of the Christian faithful took part in the meeting of the Holy Father with EMNC in Rome for Pentecost 1998. Among these were: Opera di Maria (Focolare), L'Arche, Faith and Light, Chemin Neuf, Charismatic Renewal and Emmanuel. The EMNC in this list were part of an article reporting information

---

[247] *La Fraternité Chrétienne Intercontinentale*, a private association of the faithful with juridic personality and non-Catholic members, received its decree from the PCL. Cf. Chapter II, section 5.3.

concerning groups which were present. The article was found in a special section to *L'Osservatore Romano* covering the Pentecost event. Over fifteen percent of EMNC listed fit the categories of the dissertation as ecumenical associations[248]. The support of the Supreme Pontiff for the EMNC ws evidenced by the gathering itself. Use of the term «ecclesial» instead of «ecclesiastical» when referring to the EMNC gives a sense of their task as not just within the Roman Catholic Church closely collaborating with the hierarchy, but as a mission which involves all the Christian faithful in education of persons, culture, work, charity, justice and ecumenism[249]. The coverage of the events of Pentecost 1998 speaks of the dedication of the Apostolic See to EMNC. If pictures do speak louder than words the photographs of the Holy Father meeting with members of EMNC speak volumes. It was encouraging to see that Jean Vanier of l'Arche was pictured not once but twice[250]. Recalling that l'Arche does not have a canonical relationship with the Apostolic See, the support of his ecumenical and interreligious work is evident. The event of Pentecost 1998, the meeting of the Holy Father with EMNC, was not specifically canonical. However, his will was certainly once again manifest concerning ecumenical associations as groups of this nature even if not canonically recognized received the praise and support of the Bishop of Rome.

8. The best Methods of Praxis for Ecumenical Associations in Dioceses and at the Pontifical Council for the Laity

As the two major supports for ecumenical associations of the Christian faithful are the canons themselves and the competence of the bishop of the diocese over associations and ecumenism, these are key to the best praxes for the ecumenical associations. Communication between the ecumenical association and the local bishop will allow for the most productive juridic situation. The needs of the diocese could be served while members of the associations strove to perfect their own lives, promote public worship, or carry out works of piety, charity or mercy.

The *CIC* 83 as law is made up of structures and actions. For associations these are spelled out in cc.298-329. For those who moderate ecumenical associations to strive to follow these would prove most

---

[248] «L'incontro del Santo Padre», 9-15.
[249] Cf. F. VALIANTE, «La missione», 4.
[250] Cf. «L'incontro del Santo Padre», 10; F. VALIANTE, «Il grande compito», 7.

profitable for the well being of the association. Following the law of the Church manifests docility as well as openness to the work of the Holy Spirit on the part of the association and a commitment to the good order of the ecclesial *polis*. The associations ought to follow the law as it is written, and therefore be open to non-Catholic members if this fits within the objectives of their statutes.

As the hierarchy and the officers of the association work on the status of an association deciding whether its statutes ought to be recognized/praised, reviewed, approved or the association should be erected into a juridic person, much care ought to be taken. By moving slowly from one level of recognition to the next a maturation process can take place for the association and its members.

An ideal time for the ecumenical association to evaluate its own goals and relationship with the local competent authority is during the preparation time for the quinquennial report and the *ad limina* visit of the diocesan bishop. This time would also be most opportune for the competent authority to consider its own relationship with the association. Often statutes of associations require that meetings between the hierarchy and association officials take place at least annually. The more opportunities for communication to take place between a bishop and associations existing in his diocese, the greater chance of maintaining good relations between them. The present praxis of the PCL is the best for the international associations. Each association is unique, therefore each one is treated individually. Recall *La Fraternité Chretiénne Intercontinentale Des Personnes Malades Chroniques et Handicapées Physiques*[251] which allows non-Cathlics to be inscribed as members. Even though in the majority of the cases non-Catholics who inscribe in associations are not assigned the label «members», it is possible that this term be used.

With the study complete, the differences between the praxis at the universal level and that of the United States of America are present. Even though non-Catholics are able to enter associations of the faithful as members, it is the decision of the competent authority to decide whether to allow these in a diocese or universally if these are to be approved by the PCL. As recognized in the dissertation, the *CIC* 83 does not forbid and therefore allows non-Catholics to enter associations of the Christian faithful as members. Such associations do exist and are able to meet the goals for which they were formed. The canonical rela-

---

[251] Cf. Section 5.1.1 c.

tionship with the competent authority is vital if the organization is to be recognized as an association in law. The right of the Catholic Christian faithful to be joined by the Christian faithful in associations is encouraged by the ecclesiology found in the documents of the Second Vatican Council, where bishops are assigned a supervisory role over associations and ecumenical affairs in their respective dioceses. These same duties and rights have been identified in the *CIC* 83. The Supreme Pontiff, John Paul II, has shown support for ecumenical associations throughout his pontificate in a number of ways: first by the removal of c.307,§4 sch 82 from the *CIC* 83, then specifically by his promotion of ecumenical associations in *ChL* 31, and finally through his over all support of a developing ecumenism within the Romn Catholic Church. His encouragement of EMNC, a number of which are ecumenical, at Pentecost 1998 only reinforces the positive attitude he has held toward ecumenical associations.

9. Conclusion

This chapter has presented the development of the notion of ecumenical associations of the Christian faithful from the *CIC* 17 to the *CIC* 83. A development certainly has taken place. Under the *CIC* 17 ecumenical associations were not possible while under the *CIC* 83 they are blooming. The «no» of c.693, §1 *CIC* 17 to the guarded openness of c.307,§4 sch 82 is a clear manifestation of this development. Implied by the change is the legal right of the existence of ecumenical associations under the *CIC* 83.

The recognition of the existence of lay associations which did not have official Church approval or erection gave groups formed by the laity strength as bodies existing within the Roman Catholic Church. The rescript from the Sacred Congregation of the Council to the Bishop of Corrientes in Argentina recognized the legal existence of these associations. The strength of association brought to groups by the rescript supported the formation of associations through the empowerment of the laity.

The Second Vatican Council was instrumental in the promotion of ecumenical associations. It encouraged both ecumenism at a grass roots level and various types of group apostolate. Ecumenical associations specifically answer this call of the council.

Chapter three showed the importance of the naming of the types of associations listed in the *Codex Iuris Canonici*. The associations of the *CIC* 17 were named according to their ends while those of the *CIC* 83 were named generally by their relationship with the competent ecclesiastical authority. This accented the openness of goals and ends to which the associations of the *CIC* 83 might view as purposes for their existence and means by which they could contribute to the mission of the Church and the goals proposed in c.298,§1 *CIC* 83.

Differences and similarities were identified between public and private associations. While differences point out unique relationships with ecclesiastical authority, similarities show the possibility of a share in the same ecclesiastical mission and the proposed goals for associations. Citing the opening canon of the title on associations c.298,§1 *CIC* 83 the purpose of associations can be viewed as an aid to living the baptismal right together for the fulfillment of the baptismal vocation.

The bishop is the authority competent to supervise associations in his own diocese. The *CIC* 83 and the Second Vatican Council both support the bishop's role in ecumenical affairs and in the support and supervision of associations. C.312,§1 *CIC* 83 recognizes competencies for establishing public associations and for assigning juridic personality to private associations of the Christian faithful. The bishop in his own diocese following the praxis of the Apostolic See governs and or supports associations of the Christian faithful in his own diocese. It is his decision whether to be canonically aware of ecumenical associations which may exist within his diocese.

The final summary point will turn to the more amicable configuration of associations of the Christian faithful in the Roman Catholic Church. Associations of the faithful ought to follow the canons, cc.298-329 *CIC* 83, and also the praxis used at the Apostolic See as well as that of their local bishop. The real examples of associations presented in chapter two which are recognized canonically give credence to the importance of relations between the associations and the competent ecclesiastical authority. The better relations are between associations and ecclesiastical authority, the better the mission of the Church will be accomplished.

GENERAL CONCLUSION

The general conclusion includes more than fifteen points. Each will be presented accompanied by an example and an implication.

The shift from the Pio-benedictine to the John-pauline code of law opens the possibility for the existence of ecumenical associations of the Christian faithful which will canonically participate in the mission of the Roman Catholic Church. In a wide sense all associations which are mentioned in the *CIC* 83 and/or are recognized (*recognitio statutorum*) by the Church participate in her mission because they have an ecclesiastical character. With the promulgation of the *CIC* 83 the *CIC* 17 was abrogated[1]. One of the goals of the new code was to modify the legislation of the *CIC* 17. Its abrogation made room for the innovations of the Second Vatican Council. The *CIC* 17 forbid non-Catholic to join third orders, confraternities and pious unions, in effect all of the associations of the faithful outlined by the code. The *CIC* 83 simply does not place any such restriction on the rights of non-Catholics or of such associations.

The *CIC* 83 has raised the statutes of canonically recognized associations to a higher level of importance. To know whether an association is able to be ecumenical or interreligious, that is to admit non-Catholic members, its statutes must be consulted[2]. C.304,§1 *CIC* 83 lists «conditions of membership» as one of the items which the statutes are to enumerate. The law itself puts the decision concerning diversity of membership into the hands of those who establish or erect such associations.

The supervision of associations is a constant. In a similar way to the care a bishop has for the flock in the diocese he serves, he is charged with providing supervision for the associations which are established

---

[1] C.6,§1 *CIC* 83.
[2] Cc.304; 314; and 321 *CIC* 83.

or erected in his diocese. These situations include associations both public[3] and private[4] having juridic personality, private associations whose statutes have been approved or reviewed[5], and *de facto* associations. Associations in the Catholic Church will always have some pastoral supervision either as a corporate body or as individuals. Ecumenical associations will not be unsupervised. There should be no danger to the faith of Catholics who are inscribed in these associations.

John Paul II and the Second Vatican Council have both endorsed a wider range of types of associations in the Roman Catholic Church. As consultor to the Council for the Laity, Cardinal Karol Wojtyla presented the situation in Poland. Levels of apostolate were recognized by the bishops of Poland for the parish, the family and individual professionals. His work on the Council for the Laity brought the future John Paul II into contact with many diverse modes of lay involvement in the Church[6]. The Second Vatican Council in its decree *AA* 19 expounds on the great diversity found among associations. The endorsement of different types of associations in the Roman Catholic Church is certainly a new development. Ecumenical associations are an important part of this development in the Catholic Church in which subsists the wider Church of Christ.

In *CIC* 83 the Vicar of Christ as supreme legislator in the Catholic Church removed any hindrances to ecumenical associations in the *CIC* 83. The Holy Father and the experts who helped him in the personal examination of the sch 82[7] removed c.307,§4 sch 82 from the *CIC* 83. Since this canon related directly to non-Catholic members of associations at a number of levels, the supreme pontiff's intervention in this regard shows his interest in the matter and his own desire for the further development of ecumenical associations.

John Paul II clarified his support for ecumenical associations by means of his post-synodal apostolic exhortation *ChL*,which specifically calls for the recognition by the PCL of ecumenical associations. Associations with non-Catholic members are not simply mentioned by the pontiff; he describes them and assigns their further definition and approval to specific pontifical councils. Here Pope John Paul II renews

---

[3] C.301,§§1; 2; and 3 *CIC* 83.

[4] C.322,§1 *CIC* 83.

[5] Cc.299,§3; 305,§1*CIC* 83.

[6] R. GOLDIE, *From a Roman Window*, 121.

[7] U. BETTI, «In margine», 628.

his support for ecumenical associations and continues to point the way for their development within the Roman Catholic Church.

The great jubilee of the year 2000 is being used by the Pope to further his ecumenical agenda for the Roman Catholic Church. His concern for ecumenism and interreligious dialogue is manifest in the apostolic letter «*Tertio Millennio Adveniente»,* specifically numbers 24, 34, 37, 41 and 54[8]. The Pope's specific support for ecumenism and interreligious dialogue as a part of the jubilee, the preparation for which he views as a hermeneutical key to his pontificate, continues the development of work with other Christian faiths and religions which was encouraged at the Second Vatican Council.

Ecumenical associations are highlighted by the Pope's praise of them. At the World Congress of Ecclesial Movements in Rome, 27-29 May 1998, John Paul II encouraged the movements as the fruit of the springtime announced by the Second Vatican Council[9]. Among the associations upon whom the Supreme Pontiff showered praise were a number of ecumenical associations. Because of their status some were only able to participate as observers. The Pope's support for ecumenism, interreligious dialogue, associations and their combination was manifest once again at this showcase of the EMNCs.

The role of the bishop concerning ecumenism has witnessed some development. The relationship which began to unfold between the Roman Catholic Church and the Protestant communities prior to the Second Vatican Council was at the level of the Apostolic See. At the Council the bishops were called to have a certain care for all persons in their dioceses. Separated brethern were included[10]. In the past the Apostolic See set the tone for ecumenical relations for the universal Church. Now the bishop follows the guidelines set forth by the Church (ED 93) but has much more responsibility in his own diocese. Non-Catholics who belong to Catholic associations of the Christian faithful are members of organizations controlled by the bishop in his own diocese.

The bishop is the competent authority to approve associations in his own diocese and therefore is instrumental in the variety of membership of the associations under his supervision. The *CIC* 83 assigns the

---

[8] JOHN PAUL II, Apost. lett. *Tertio millenio adveniente, AAS* 87 (1995) 19, 26, 29, 32, 37.

[9] JOHN PAUL II, Alloc./address «Ringraziamo sempre», 27 May 1998, *OR,* 28 May 1998, 6.

[10] *CD* 16.

bishop the power to establish associations in his own jurisdiction[11] and to write letters of consent for associations established elsewhere to exist within his territory[12]. It is the bishop's role to approve associations and their statutes[13], in this way shaping the associational and ecumenical development of his diocese. It is at the level of associations that much true ecumenism will take place. This a most appropriate place because the supervision of the bishop is foreseen in the *CIC* 83.

Even though bishops have an expanded role in the two spheres of ecumenism and associations, they still look to the Apostolic See for direction. The ecumenical directories published from the Vatican are universal guidelines to be followed by all of the particular Churches. The *CIC* 83 and any guidelines from the PCL are also to be followed by bishops concerning associations of the Christian faithful. Diocesan bishops make decisions concerning ecumenical associations and those associations with non-Catholic members according to the particular needs of their diocese only in light of their own competent authority.

Attitudes and practices of the Roman Catholic Church towards ecumenism and interreligious cooperation have changed in recent years, opening vistas not imagined in the past. Before the Second Vatican Council Catholics would not have been encouraged to participate in services of other ecclesial communities or churches; today this is allowable. Whereas in former days Catholics were not to stand as witness at the weddings or baptisms of Protestants, it would be accepted today. In the spirit of ecumenism non-Catholics are much more welcome to attend Catholic services and to be present at the reception of sacraments by Catholics. This attitude and change in practice opens the Church to welcoming non-Catholics who are willing to follow Church law which would affect them as inscribed members of Roman Catholic associations of the Christian faithful.

Such associations are an excellent way for the Catholic laity to concretely live out the call of the ecumenical directories. Communities like *Chemin Neuf* in Lyon, France live and participate in an association which is ecumenical and has an excellent rapport with its bishop, enjoying canonical recognition in the diocese. The community also has

---

[11] C.312,§1 *CIC* 83.

[12] C.312,§2 *CIC* 83. Written consent does not seem to be required by the *CIC* 83 for private associations.

[13] Cf. C.322,§§1,2 *CIC* 83.

ties with the Apostolic See. Ecumenical associations are fertile ground for the unity of Christians to be concretely evidenced[14].

The unfortunate use of some terms in the *CIC* 83 adds to the confusion concerning associations of the faithful. One example is the leaving of the explanation of *Christifideles* at the level of the *PCCICR* plenary session. This may have been fine for the overall sense of the term in the *CIC* 83. It may however be a source of confusion for c.204,§1 *CIC* 83 as well as for the situation of non-Catholic baptized persons and the possibility of their inscription into associations of the Christian faithful as described in the *CIC* 83. The implication here is simply the importance of clarity in the use of words.

Ecumenical associations studied here exist at all levels and are in accord with the *CIC* 83. All the levels (public, and the four types which are private: *de facto*, reviewed, approved and juridic persons) are represented by associations which exist in particular dioceses. These associations have their headquarters within a particular diocese and fall into one of the categories of associations found in the *CIC* 83. All of the four associations which are recognized by the PCL are private with juridic personality. The practice of the Apostolic See is somewhat different than that of the dioceses at this point in time. Individual dioceses utilize the different types and levels of association because they have specific situations which are able to be addressed by a smaller group in the diocese. One diocese may have a large number of non-Catholics while another may be predominantly Catholic. The way that these decisions are dealt with by individual dioceses and the Apostolic See will be different. The *CIC* 83 presents competent authority with a number of different ways to handle these situations, conveying an openness to a wealth of ways to associate. The variety of associations which do exist and are in relation with the competent authority manifests the presence of ecumenism and interreligious dialogue in the sphere of associations. The question may arise whether it is better for an ecumenical association to be public or private even though the *CIC* 83 permits both. It would seem that private ecumenical associations are preferable because these do not act in the name of the Church. Ecumenism is better served where the non-Catholic can contribute to the effort something it would be difficult to do in a public association which acts in the name of the Church. For a non-Catholic to act in the name of the Church would be difficult.

---

[14] ED93 27.

The fundamental right of persons to gather in associations and the divine right of persons to search for God must always be affirmed by the Church. These points in themselves do not constitute reason for the existence of ecumenical associations under the supervision of the Catholic Church. All that has been said in this conclusion rests on these truths. The *CIC* 17 concentrated on obligations, while the *CIC* 83 has greater focus on the rights of individuals. This does not mean that obligations are not also present in the *CIC* 83. C.215 *CIC* 83 guarantees the right of associations to the faithful. Nowhere is the right for non-Catholics forbidden. It is in fact allowed and is practiced throughout the Catholic world.

The part which non-Catholic members of Catholic associations may play will advance the call for unity[15]. As ecumenism and interreligious dialogue continue to develop, the situation in the associations will also flower. In order for associations to remain Catholic the moderator and chaplain must be Catholic, leadership positions in the association would be held by Catholics. The population of the association must always have a Catholic majority[16]. By following guidelines found in the law and the statutes of the association, great progress will be made for unity in the truth.

The rights and obligations of non-Catholics who are inscribed in ecumenical associations are similar to those of non-Catholics not inscribed. Only those rights particular to the association and not restricted by Church law are open to non-Catholic members. These rights might include pursuing apostolic ends, attendance at meetings or certain spiritual benefits, like prayers and support of other members of the association. Rights restricted by Church law would include reception of the sacraments. Since initiation into the Church involves the sacraments non-Catholics are constricted in having full rights in a Catholic association.

Even though non-Catholics cannot be forced to follow Roman Catholic Church teaching it is logical that those who wish to be fully inscribed in a Catholic association would respect the Church and her representatives. Examples from statutes of communities studied show acceptance and indifference toward Church teaching. In order for non-Catholics to participate they must be willing to freely embrace obligations required for participation in the association. Because the right of

---

[15] John 17,21.
[16] *ChL* 31.

assembly is a natural right it ought not to be refused to human beings desiring to be inscribed and who are willing to accept the obligations of inscription.

The strict definition of ecumenical association is that of *ChL* 31. Interreligious or interconfessional associations can fit into a wider definition of ecumenical associations. However, they are not the same. Interconfessional associations have non-Catholic members who are also in leadership positions. The ratio of Catholics to non-Catholics does not have a majority requirement. They do not follow the guidelines of *ChL* 31 and are not recognized as a body by the Roman Catholic Church. Interrreligious associations have non-baptized members but otherwise follow *ChL* 31. These are not forbidden by the *CIC* 83 but are a rarity within the confines of the present study. Theologically it is difficult to present a case for non-baptized to be full members of associations of the Christian faithful in the Catholic Church. Since they are not members of the Church of Christ there is a question as to their being members of an association of the Christian faithful. They may be able to enter an association as guests, or under another title other than member.

The continual work of the Holy Spirit in the Church calls all believers to unity, to become one in God. The existence of the associations themselves is in place, but the situation of the associations in the Church (both particular and universal) continues to unfold. Once the work of the PCL and PCPCU is completed the situation will be much clearer[17]. The status of ecumenical associations in the Roman Catholic Church continues to develop.

---

[17] *ChL* 31.

APPENDICIES

1. Appendix I: Associations in *CIC* 17 and *CIC* 83

Associations in the *CIC* 17

I. Confraternities (1)
    A. Archconfraternities (2)
        1. all are ecclesiastical
        2. all have juridic personality
II. Pious Unions (3)
    A. Primary Unions (4)
        1. all are ecclesiastical
        2. some (with) have juridic personality
        3. some (without) do not have juridic personality
III.Third Orders (5)
    A. all are ecclesiastical
    B. all are attached to some religious order
    C. if a third order is divided into several associations the legitimately established branch is a sodality of tertiaries
IV. Associations mentioned but without rights and duties in canon law
V. Recommended associations (6)
VI. Negative associations (not to be supported by Catholics) — secret, condemned, seditious, or suspect, and associations which strive to remove themselves from the legitimate supervision of the Church[1]

Figure 1: Associations in the *CIC 17* as described by Amos.

---

[1] J. AMOS, *Associations of the Christan Faithful* (1986), 26-34.

For the purposes of this work only the associations numbered 1-6 are used. The associations identified in number VI, while recognized by the *CIC* 17 as types of associations, are used as examples of negative associations which persons ought not to join.

Winfried Schulz outlined the associations in the *CIC* 83 in the following manner:

I.   Private associations

A.   Private associations not recognized
    1. De facto associations (1)
        a. without the attribute «Catholic association»
        b. with the attribute «Catholic association»
    2. Non-recognized associations toward whom action has been taken by the ecclesiastical authority
        a.   with statutes examined according to the norm of canon 299,§3 *CIC* 83 (2)
            i. without the attribute «Catholic association»
            ii. with the attribute «Catholic association»
        b.   associations not recognized but praised by ecclesiastical authority
            i. without the attribute «Catholic association»
            ii. with the attribute «Catholic association»
        c.   associations not recognized but recommended by ecclesiastical authority
            i. without the attribute «Catholic association»
            ii. with the attribute «Catholic association»

(Here the author would place approved associations not erected private juridic persons. Schulz does not identify these as a type in his schema.) (3)

B. Private associations recognized, erected with private juridic personality (4)
    1. Private associations recognized and praised
        a.   without the attribute «Catholic association»
        b.   with the attribute «Catholic association»
    2. Private associations recognized and recommended
        a.   without the attribute «Catholic association»
        b.   with the attribute «Catholic association»
II. Public association erected with public juridic personality in the Church (5)
A. by work of the law
B. through formal decree on the part of the competent authority[2]

Figure 2: Schulz's outline of associations according to CIC 83.

---

[2] W. SCHULZ, «La posizione giuridica delle associazioni», 129.

According to Schulz's chart there are fourteen different types of associations in the *CIC* 83. He distinguishes them according to whether the name Catholic appears in their name. This almost doubles the number of types of associations which Schulz recognizes in the law. For the purposes of this dissertation the associations on Schulz's list which are numbered 1 - 5 will be used as the types which exist in law. The greater number of types of associations in the *CIC* 83 and Schulz's particular division between associations using the term Catholic in their name and those which do not opens the possibilities of various types of associations in the *CIC* 83. Other ways of dividing the canons are reviewed in section (4.5) of the paper which compares and contrasts public and private associations of the Christian faithful.

2. Appendix II: Associations in this Dissertation and Their Juridic Status

Associations of the Christian Faithful *headquaters*	Public or Private *Date of Approval*	Juridic Personality	Comments
Alleluia Catholic Fellowship *Savannah, GA*	private, does exist outside diocese *approval letter of 29 January 1992 from diocesan bishop of Savannah*	yes	Catholic membership only
Apostolate for Family Consecration *Bloomingdale, OH*	—	—	specific information not available
Brothers and Sisters of Charity *Little Rock AR*	public *erected on 4 October 1993 by diocesan Bishop of Little Rock*	yes	non-Catholic participants not considered canonical members
Catholic Fraternity of Charismatic Covenant Communities and Fellowships *Rome, Italy*	private *universal, approved by decree of 30 November 1990, renewed on 27 November 1995*	yes - erection by PCL	Catholic communities and fellowships are members
Chemin Neuf *Lyons, France*	public *diocesan with universal outreach, approved on 20 April 1984 by Archbishop of Lyons*	yes	Catholic and non-Catholic members
Ecumenical Order of Charity *Vancouver, WA*	—	—	no canonical recognition
Emmanuel *Rome, Italy*	private *universal, approved on 8 December 1992*	yes - erection by PCL and the Archbishop of Paris	catholic membership, non-Catholics participate as associate brothers
Glenmary Co-Missioners *Nashville, TN*	private *diocesan regional, approved 9 April 1992, by Bishop of Nashville*	yes	Catholic and non-Catholic members

La Fratémite Chrétienne Intercontinentale Rome, Italy	private universal, approved in September 1989, renewed in February 1995	yes - erection by PCL	Catholic and non-Catholic Christian members
Lamb of God Catholic Fellowship Christchurch, New Zealand	Catholic national approved or recognized by dioceses in New Zealand *see fn. 81 p. 135.	no	all Catholic members
Lamb of God Community Baltimore, MD	private, diocesan statutes reviewed on 30 November 1993 by Archbishop of Baltimore	no	membership is open to baptized Christians
L'Arche Cuise-la Motte, France	—	—	open membership
Magnificat New Orleans, LA	private, diocesan, international approved on 8 August 1986 by Archbishop of New Orleans	no	membership open to all women
Mercy of God Community Chesapeake, VA	—	—	—
Mother of God Community Washington, DC	private approved on 14 February 1997 by Archbishop of Washington, DC	no	membership is open to Christians
Opera di Maria (Focolare) Rome, Italy	private approved with decree of 29 June 1990, modifications to statutes approved 25 October 1994	yes - erection by PCL	membership open to Catholics others participate at various levels
People of God's Love Community Columbus, OH	—	—	membership open to Christians
Word of God Community Ann Arbor, MI	—	—	membership open to Christians
Work of Christ Community Lansing, MI	—	—	membership open to Christians

3. Appendix III: Fonts of cc.298-329 CIC 83 – Fonts for Chapter One

1983 Code of Canon Law	1917 Code of Canon Law	Rescript to the Bishop of Corrientes	Papal and Magisterial Documents	Vatican II Documents
298 §1	685		Pius XI, Enc. *Ubi Arcano*, 23 Dec 1922; Pius XI, Ep. *Dilecte Fili*, 7 Nov 1929	CD 17; OT 2; GE 6, 8; AA 5-8, 11, 18-19; PO 8
298 §2	684	SCConc Resol. 13 Nov 1920	SCSO Resp., 8 July 1927; Pius XII, Constit. Ap. *Bis Saeculari*, 27 Sep 1948; SCSO Monitum, 28 July 1950	AA 21
299 §1		SCConc Resol, 13 Nov 1920		AA 19, 24
299 §2				AA 24
300				AA 24
301 §1	686§1	SCConc Resol, 13 Nov 1920	Pius XI, Ep. *Dilecte Fili*, 7 Nov 1929; Pius XII, All., 4 Sept 1940	AA 24
301 §2	686§1	SCConc Resol, 13 Nov 1920	Pius XI, Ep. *Dilecte Fili*, 7 Nov 1929	AA 24
303	702		ES I, 35; REU 73 §3	
304 §1	689 §1; 697			
304 §2	688			
305 §1	336 §2; 690 §1	SCConc Resol, 13 Nov 1920	Pius XI, Enc. *Maximam gravissimamque*, 18 Jan 1924	
305 §2	394 §1; 690 §2	SCConc Resol, 13 Nov 1920	ES I, 35; SA Normae, Nov 1969	
306	692		CI Resp I, 4 Jan 1946; SSCon Ind, 24 May 1950	
307 §1	694 §1		SSConc Resp, 18 Mar 1941	
307 §2	693 §2			
307 §3	693 §4			
308	696 §1			
309	697 §1			
311			ES I, 35	

Fonts for Chapter Two

1983 Code of Canon Law	1917 Code of Canon Law	Rescript to the Bishop of Corrientes	Papal and Magisterial Documents	Vatican II Documents
312 §1, 1	686 §1-2		Coetus Sanctae Romanae Ecclesiae Cardinalium Resp. III, 2 SA Normae, Nov 1968	
312 §1, 2	686 §1-2		SCE Rescr., 28 Jun 1969 SCGE Rescr., 26 Nov 1978	
312 §1, 3	686 §2, §4			
312 §2	686 §3			
313	687		Pius XI, Ep. *Dilecte Fili*, 6 Nov 1929 Pius XI, Ep. Ap. *Ex Officiosis Litteris*, 10 Nov 1933 Pius XI, Enc. *Firmissimam Constantiam*, 28 Mar 1937 ES I, 35	AA 20
314	689			
315			Pius XI, Ep. *Dilecte Fili*, 6 Nov 1929 Pius XI, Ep. Ap. *Ex Officiosis Litteris*, 10 Nov 1933 Pius XI, Enc. *Firmissimam Constantiam*, 28 Mar 1937 ES I, 35	AA 20
316 §1	693 §1			
316 §2	696 |2			
317 §1	698 §1			
317 §2	698 §1			
317§4			Pius XI, Ep. *Dilecte Fili*, 6 Nov 1929 Pius XI, Ep. *Dobbiamo intrattenerla*, 26 April 1931 Pius XI, Enc. *Non Abbiamo Bisogno*, 29 Jun 1931	
318§2	698 §3			
319 §1	691 §1			
319 §2	691 §5			
320 §1	699 §2			
320 §2	699 §1			

Fonts for Chapter Three

1983 Code of Canon Law	1917 Code of Canon Law	Rescript to the Bishop of Corrientes	Papal and Magisterial Documents	Vatican II Documents
321		SSConc Resol., 13 Nov 1920		
322 §1	100 §1			
323 §1	336 §2 690 §1	SSConc Resol., 13 Nov 1920		
323 §2				CD 17 AA 19
324 §1		SSConc Resol., 13 Nov 1920		AA19
326 §2	1515 §1			

Fonts for Chapter Four

1983 Code of Canon Law	1917 Code of Canon Law	Rescript to the Bishop of Corrientes	Papal and Magisterial Documents	Vatican II Documents
327	686		Pius XII, All., 5 Oct 1957	LG 31 AA 2, 7, 19
328			Pius XII, All., 12 Oct 1952 Pius XII, All., 11 Jan 1953	
329				IM 15 LG 35 AA 4, 28-32 DH 14 AG 26 GS 43, 72

* Canons which are not listed do not have fonts.

ABBREVIATIONS

§ / §§	Paragraph / Paragraphs
AA	CONCILIUM OECUMENICUM VATICANUM II, *Apostolicam Actuositatem* [Decree on the Aposolate of Laity]
AAS	*Acta Apostolica Sedis*
AG	CONCILIUM OECUMENICUM VATICANUM II, *Ad Gentes* [Decree on the Missionary Activity of the Church]
AkathKR	*Archiv für katholisches Kirchenrecht*
all.	allocution
Ant.	*Antonianum*
Apoll.	*Apollinaris*
apost.	apostolic
art.	article(s)
arts./artt.	Articles
AS	*Acta Synodalia Sacrostancti Concilii Oecumenici Vaticani Secundi*, Città del Vaticano 1974-1978
ASS	*Acta Sanctae Sedis*
AT	SECRETARIATUS AD CHRISTIANORUM UNITATEM FOVENDAM, *Ad Totam Ecclesiam* [The Directory Concerning Ecumenical Matters: Part One]
byl.	bylaws
c./cc.	canon/canons
CCEO	*Codex Canonum Ecclesiarum Orientalium*
CD	CONCILIUM OECUMENICUM VATICANUM II, *Christus Dominus* [Decree on the Pastoral Duty of Bishops]
cf.	confer
C. G.	*General acts of the Congregation of the Society for the Propagation of the Faith.* These were before Gratian.
ChL	JOHN PAUL II, *Christifidelis Laici*
CI	Pontificia Comissio ad Codicis Canones Authentice Interpretandos
CIC 17	*Codex Iuris Canonici* 1917
CIC 83	*Codex Iuris Canonici* 1983

CLSA	Canon Law Society of America
Comm.	PONTIFICIA COMMISSIO CODICI IURIS CANONICI RECOGNO- SCENDO, *Communicationes*
const.	constitution
CS	PIUS XII, *Clerici Sanctitati*
DH	CONCILIUM OECUMENICUM VATICANUM II, *Dignitatis Humanae* [Declaration on Religious Freedom]
Dir.	*Direzione*
Ed.	Editor/s
ED93	PONTIFICIUM CONSILIUM AD UNITATEM CHRISTIANORUM FOVENDAM, *Ecumenical Directory 1993*
EJCan	*Ephemerides Iuris Canonici*
EMNC	Ecclesial Movement(s) and New Community(s)
EN	PAUL VI, *Evangelii Nuntiandi*
enc.	encyclical
Ep.	Epistula
ES	PAUL VI, Motu proprio *Ecclesiae Sanctae*
exh.	exhortation
FD	*The Founding Document* of the Ecumenical Order of Charity
fn.	Footnote
GE	CONCILIUM OECUMENICUM VATICANUM II, *Gravissimum Educationis* [Declaration on Christian Education]
GS	CONCILIUM OECUMENICUM VATICANUM II, *Gaudium et Spes* [Pastoral Constitution on the Church in the Contemporary World]
ICL	Institute(s) of Consecrated Life
ICO	International Catholic Organization(s)
IM	CONCILIUM OECUMENICUM VATICANUM II, *Inter Mirifica* [Decree on Instruments of Social Communication]
Ind.	Indultum
Irén.	*Irénikon*
LEF	Lex Ecclesiae Fundamentalis
lett.	letter
LG	CONCILIUM OECUMENICUM VATICANUM II, *Lumen Gentium* [Dogmatic Constitution on the Church]
NCCB	National Conference of Catholic Bishops (United States of America)
OE	CONCILIUM OECUMENICUM VATICANUM II, *Orientalium Ecclesiarum* [Decree on the Catholic Eastern Churches]
ORSup	*L'Osservatore Romano. Supplemento*
OT	CONCILIUM OECUMENICUM VATICANUM II, *Optatam Totius* [Decree on Priestly Formation]

p.	page
PCCICOR	Pontificia Commissio Codici Iuris Canonici Orientalis Recognoscendo, *published in Nuntia.*
PCCICR	Pontificia Commissio Codici Iuris Canonici Recognoscendo, *published in Communicationes.*
PCPCU	Pontifical Council for Promoting Christian Unity
PCL	Pontifical Council for the Laity
PO	CONCILIUM OECUMENICUM VATICANUM II, *Presbiterorum Ordinis* [Decree on the Ministry of Priests]
QDE	*Quaderni di diritto ecclesiale*
Rescr.	Rescriptum
Resp.	Responsum
REU	PAUL VI, Apost. Const. *Regimini Ecclesiae Universae*
SA	Supremum Tribunal Signaturae Apostolicae
SAL	Society (s) of Apostolic Life
SCCon	Sacra Congregatio Concilii
SCE	Sacra Congregatio pro Episcopis
SCGE	Sacra Congregatio pro Gentium Evangelizatione
Sch	Schema
SCSO	Sacra Congregatio Sancti Officii
Ses	*Session*
SPUC	Secretariat for the Promotion of the Unity of Christians (SPUC was named a pontifical council in *Pastor Bonus:* PCPCU)
Stat. 90	Opera di Maria, *Statuti Generali*, 1990.
Stat. 95	Opera di Maria, *Statuti Generali*, 1995
Stat.	Statutes from association of the section in which the citation is found
StCan	*Studia canonica*
TG/DC	Tesi Gregoriana, serie Diritto Canonico
TG/Teol	Tesi Gregoriana, serie Teologia
TS	*Theological Studies*
UNDA	The Catholic Association for Radio and Television
UR	CONCILIUM OECUMENICUM VATICANUM II, *Unitatis Redintegratio* [Decree on Ecumenism]
UECI	Unione Editori Cattolici Italiani
vs.	versus
Vol.	volume
Vols.	volumes
WCC	World Council of Churches

BIBLIOGRAPHY

1. Ecclesiastical Documents

Acta et Documenta Concilio Oecumenico Vaticano II Apparando, Series II, Vol. III, Pars I, Città del Vaticano 1969.

Acta Synodalia Sacrosancti Concilii Oecumenici Vaticani II, Vol. II, Pars I, Città del Vaticano 1975.

CANADIAN CONFERENCE OF CATHOLIC BISHOPS, *Recognition of National Catholic Associations,* Ottawa 1992.

Codex Canonum Ecclesiarum Orientalium auctoritate Ioannis Pauli promulgatus, *AAS* 82 (1990) 1061-1363.

Codex Iuris Canonici auctoritate Ioannis Pauli PP. II promulgatus, *AAS* 75 (1983) 1-317.

Codex Iuris Canonici. Codex des kanonischen Rechtes. Lateinisch-deutsche Augsgabe, ed. Deutsche Bischofskonferenz – al., Kevelaer 1994[4].

Codex Iuris Canonici Pii X Pontificis Maximi iussu digestus Benedicti Papae XV auctoritate promulgatus, AAS 9 (1917) 3-521.

CONCILIUM OECUMENICUM VATICANUM II, *Constitutio Dogmatica de Ecclesia «Lumen gentium»,* 21 November 1964, *AAS* 57 (1965) 4-71.

——, *Declaratio de libertate religiosa «Dignitatis humanae»,* 7 December 1965, *AAS* 58 (1966) 929-946.

——, *Decretum de Apostolatu laicorum «Apostolicam actuositatem»,* 18 November 1965, *AAS* 58 (1966) 837-864.

——, *Decretum de Ecclesiis Orientalibus Catholicis: «Orientalium ecclesiarum»,* 21 November 1964, *AAS* 57 (1965) 76-89.

——, *Decretum de Oecumenismo «Unitatis redintegratio»,* 21 November 1964, *AAS* 57 (1965) 90-112.

——, *Decretum de Pastorali Episcoporum Munere in Ecclesia «Christus Dominus»,* 28 October 1965, *AAS* 58 (1966) 673-701.

GREGORY XVI, Apostolic letter *Romanum decet Pontificem,* 10 January 1845, in *Acta Gregorii Papae XVI,* III, Città del Vaticano 1902, 375-376.

————, Letter *Libenti sane animo,* 27 May 1846, in *Acta Gregorii Papae XVI,* III, Città del Vaticano 1902, 538.

JOHN XXIII, Apostolic letter/motu proprio *Superno Dei nutu,* 5 June 1960, *ASS* 52 (1960) 433-337.

JOHN PAUL II, Allocution/address *Ad eos qui plenario coetui Secretariatus ad Unitatem Christianorum fovendam interfuerunt coram admisos,* 5 February 1988, *AAS* 80.2 (1988) 1202-1203.

————, Allocution/address «Ringraziamo sempre», 27 May 1998, O*R* 28 May 1998, 6.

————, Allocution/address «To the Eighth International Meeting of the Catholic Fraternity of Charismatic Covenant Communities and Fellowships», 1 June 1998, O*R* 4 June 1998, 6.

————, Apostolic constitution *Sacrae disciplines leges,* 25 January 1983, *AAS* 75 (1983) VII-XXX.

————, Apostolic exhortation *Christifideles Laici,* 14 April 1989, *AAS* 81 (1989) 393-521.

————, Apostolic letter *Tertio millennio adveniente,* 10 November 1994, *AAS* 87 (1995) 5-41.

————, Prefatio *Codex Iuris Canonici, AAS* 75 (1983) i-xxx.

————, Encyclical letter *Ut unum sint,* 25 May 1995, *AAS* 87 (1995) 921-982.

LEO XIII, Apostolic letter *Amantissimae Voluntatis,* 14 April 1865, *ASS* 27 (1894-95) 583-593.

————, Encyclical letter *Annum Sacrum,* 25 May 1899, *ASS* 31 (1898-99) 646-651.

————, Apostolic letter *Apostolicae Curae,* 13 September 1896, *ASS* 29 (1897) 193-203.

————, Encyclical letter *Cartitas Studium,*25 July 1898, *ASS* 31 (1898-99) 6-14.

————, Encyclical letter *Divinum Illud,* 9 May 1897, *ASS* 29 (1897) 644-658.

————, Encyclical letter *Humanum Genus,* 20 April 1884, *ASS* 16 (1883-84) 166-179.

————, Apostolic letter *Praeclara Gratulationis Publicae,* 20 June 1894, *ASS* 26 (1893-94) 705-717.

————, Apostolic letter *Provida Matris,* 5 May 1895, *ASS* 27 (1894-95) 645-647.

LEO XIII, Encyclical letter *Satis Cognitum*, 29 June 1896, *ASS* 28 (1895-96) 708-739.

———— Encyclical letter *Tamesti Futura*, 1 November 1900, *ASS* 33 (1900-1901) 273-285.

————, Letter *Testum benevolentiae*, 22 January 1899, *ASS* 31 (1898-99) 470-479.

PAUL VI, Allocution *Duc hic praesentes*, 18 March 1974, *AAS* 66 (1974) 743-749.

————, Allocution *Singulari cum animi*, 20 November 1965, *AAS* 57 (1965) 985-989.

————, Apostolic constitution *Regimini Ecclesiae Universae*, 15 August 1967, *AAS* 59 (1967) 885-928.

————, Apostolic exhortation *Evangelii Nuntiandi*, 8 December 1975, *AAS* 68 (1976) 5-76.

PIUS IX, Letter *Quamquam*, 29 May 1873, in GASPARRI, P. – SERÉDI, J., ed., *Codicis Iuris Canonici Fontes*, III, Roma 1935, 70-72.

————, Letter *Exhortae*, 29 April 1876, in GASPARRI, P. – SERÉDI, J., ed., *Codicis Iuris Canonici Fontes*, VII, Roma 1935, 99-101.

PIUS X, Encyclical letter *Singulari Quadam*, 2 September 1912, *AAS* 4 (1912) 652-656.

PIUS XI, Allocution to the Italian University Catholic Federation, 10 January 1927, *Irén.* 2 (1927) 20-21.

————, Encyclical letter *Mortalium animos*, 6 January 1928, *AAS* 20 (1928) 5-16.

————, Encyclical letter *Rerum Orientalium*, 8 September 1928, *AAS* 20 (1928) 277-288.

PIUS XII, Apostolic letter *Clerici sanctitati*, 11 June 1957, *AAS* 49 (1957) 433-603.

————, Encyclical letter *Humani Generis*, 12 August 1950, *AAS* 42 (1950) 561-578.

————, Encyclical letter *Mystici Corporis*, 29 June 1943, *AAS* 35 (1943) 193-248.

PONTIFICIA COMMISSIO CODICI IURIS CANONICI AUTHENTICE INTERPRETANDO, *Codex Iuris Canonici*, Città del Vaticano 1989

PONTIFICIA COMMISSIO CODICI IURIS CANONICI ORIENTALIS RECOGNOSCENDO, *Nuntia*, vols. I, V, XII, XIII, XV, XVIII, XXXI, Città del Vaticano 1975-1990.

PONTIFICIA COMMISSIO CODICI IURIS CANONICI RECOGNOSCENDO, *Communicationes*, vols. I, XII, XIV, XV, XVII, XVIII, XXVIII, Città del Vaticano 1969-1996.

PONTIFICIUM CONSILIUM AD UNITATEM CHRISTIANORUM FOVENDAM, *Directoire pour l'application des Principes et des Normes sur l'œcuménisme,* 25 March 1993, *AAS* 85.2 (1993) 1039-1119 [Directory for the Application of Principles and Norms on Ecumenism].

SACRA CONGREGATIO CONCILII, *Resolutio 13 November 1920, AAS* 13 (1921) 135-144.

SACRA CONGREGATIO DE PROPAGANDA FIDE (C. G.), 19 September 1867, in GASPARRI, P. – SERÉDI, J., ed. *Codicis Iuris Canonici Fontes,* VII, Roma 1935, 406.

SECRETARIATUS AD CHRISTIANORUM UNITATEM FOVENDAM, *Directorium de re oecumenica: Ad totam Ecclesiam,* 14 May 1967, *AAS* 59 (1967) 574-592.

SUPREMA SACRA CONGREGATIO S. OFFICII, Decretum *De participatione catholicorum societati ad procurandum christianitatis unitatem,* 4 July 1919, *AAS* 11 (1919) 309-316.

———, Dubium *De Conventibus (quos dicunt) ad procurandam omnium Christianorum unitatem,* 8 July 1927, *AAS* 19 (1927) 278.

———, Instruction *Ecclesia Catholica,* 20 December 1949, *AAS* 42 (1950) 142-147.

SUPREMAE S. ROMANAE ET UNIVERSALIS INQUISITIONIS, *Ad Quosdam Puseistas Anglicos,* 8 November 1865, *AAS* 11 (1919) 312-316.

———, *Epistola ad omnes Angliae Episcopos,* 16 September 1864, *AAS* 11 (1919) 310-312.

2. Books and Articles

ABBO, J. – HANNAN, J., *The Sacred Canons: A Concise Presentation of the Current Disciplinary Norms of the Church,* I, St. Louis, MO 1957.

AMOS, J., «A Legal History of the Associations of the Christian Faithful», *StCan* 21 (1987) 271-297.

———, «Associations of the Christian Faithful: History, Analysis and Evaluation», in *Proceedings of the Fiftieth Annual Convention, Canon Law Society of America 1989,* Washington, DC 1989, 129-138.

———, *Associations of the Christian Faithful in the 1983 Code of Canon Law: A Canonical Analysis and Evaluation,* Washington, DC 1986.

AQUINAS, T., *Summa Theologiae,* New York 1974.

AUBERT, R., *Le Saint-Siege et l'union des Églises,* Bruxelles 1947.

AUBERT, R., «Stages of Catholic Ecumenism from Leo XIII to Vatican II», in *Renewal of Religious Structures*, ed. K. Shook, Montreal 1968.

AUGE, T., *Frederick Ozanam and his World*, Milwaukee 1966.

AUGUSTINE, C., *A Commentary on the New Code of Canon Law*, St. Louis, MO 1919.

BARRETT, R.J., «The Non-Recognized Association and Its Capacity to Act in Court», *Periodica* 86 (1997) 677-711.

BAUM, G., *That They May be One: A Study of Papal Doctrine, Leo XIII - Pius XII*, London 1985.

BELL, G., ed., *The Stoc kholm Conference 1925*, London 1926.

BENLLOCH POVEDA, A., *Código de Derecho Canónico: edición bilingüe, fluentes y comentarios de todos las cánones*, Valencia 1993.

BERTONE, T., ed., *Codice di Diritto Canonico: Testo ufficiale e versione italiana*, Roma 1984.

BETTI, U., «In margine al nuovo Codice di Diritto Canonico», *Ant.* 58 (1983) 628-647.

BEYER, J., *Il Codice del Vaticano II. Dal Concilio al Codice*, Bologna 1984.

———, *Il Rinnovamento del diritto e del laicato nella Chiesa*, Milano 1994.

———, «La vita associativa nella Chiesa», *QDE* 3 (1990) 308-312.

BLAT, A., *Commentarium Textus Iuris Canonici, Liber II*, Roma 1934.

BOFFA, C., *Canonical Provisions for Catholic Schools (Elementary and Intermediate)*, Washington, DC 1939.

BONI, A., «La vita religiosa nella struttura concettuale del nuovo Codice di Diritto Canonico», *Ant.* 58 (1983) 523-627.

BONNET, P. – GHIRLANDA, G., *De Christifidelibus: De eorum iuribus, de laicis, de consociationibus*, Roma 1983.

BOUSCAREN, T.L. – ELLIS, A., *Canon Law: A Text and Commentary*, Milwaukee 1946.

BOUSCAREN, T.L., «Cooperation with non-Catholics: Canonical Legislation», *TS* 3 (1942) 475-512.

———, *Canon Law Digest*, III, Milwaukee 1954.

THE CANON LAW SOCIETY OF GREAT BRITIAN AND IRELAND, *The Code of Canon Law: in English translation*, London 1983.

CAPPELLO, F., *Summa Iuris Canonici*, Roma 1962.

CAPRILE, G., *Il Sinodo dei Vescovi 1987*, Roma 1989

CLARK, S., *Building Christian Communities*, Notre Dame 1973.

CLARKE, T., *Parish Societies*, Washington, DC 1943.

CONTE A CORONATA, M., *Institutiones Iuris Canonici*, Torino 1950.

CORDES, P., *Born of the Spirit: Renewal Movements in the Life of the Church*, South Bend, IN 1992.

————, *Call to Holiness: Reflections on the Catholic Charismatic Renewal*, Collegeville, MN 1997.

CORECCO, E., «Istituzione e carisma in referimento alle strutture associative», in *The Associational Element in the Church*. Proceedings of the VIth International Congress of Canon Law, ed. W. Aymans – K.-T. Geringer –H. Schmitz, St. Ottilien 1989, 79-98.

————, «I laici nel nuovo Codice di diritto canonico», in *Il nuovo codice di dirritto canonico*, Leumann (To) 1985,

CSLA, *Code of Canon Law: Latin-English Edition*, Washington DC 1983.

CURTIS, G., «P. Couturier», in *Ökumenische Profile*, I, 347-353.

D'OSTILIO, F., *La storia del nuovo Codice di Diritto Canonico: revisione – promulgazione – presentazione*, Roma 1983.

————, *Prontuario del Codice di Diritto Canonico*, Roma 1994.

DENZINGER, H. – HÜNERMANN, P., ed., *Enchiridion Symbolorum*, Bologna 1996.

DRAZEK, C., «Le radici del magistero di Giovanni Paolo II sui laici», *ORSup* 29 May 1998, 5-6.

FAVALE, A – al., ed., *Movimenti ecclesiali contemporanei: dimensioni storiche, teologico-spirituali ed apostoliche*, Roma 1991.

FELICIANI, G., «Il diritto di associazione dei fedeli dal Concilio al Codice», *QDE* 3 (1990) 313-323.

————, *Il popolo di Dio*, Bologna 1991.

FRERE, W., *Recollections of Malines*, London 1935.

GALLAGHER, J., *A Woman's Work: Chiara Lubich*, London 1997.

GASPARRI, P., *Codex Iuris Canonici, Prefatione, Fontium Annotatione et Indice Analytico-Alphabetico*, New York 1918.

GASPARRI, P. — SERÉDI, J., ed., *Codicis Iuris Canonici Fontes*, I-IX, Roma 1926-1939.

GEROSA, L., «La consacrazione episcopale: punto sorgivo dell'unità e carisma nella Chiesa?», in *The Associational Element in the Church*. Proceedings of the VIth International Congress of Canon Law, ed. W. Aymans – K.-T. Geringer – H. Schmitz, St. Ottilien 1989, 119-135.

GHIRLANDA, G., *Il diritto nella Chiesa mistero di comunione: compendio di diritto ecclesiale*, Roma 1993^2.

GHIRLANDA, G., «Movements within the Ecclesial Communion and the Rightful Autonomy», *Laity Today* 32-33 (1989-1990) 46-71.

――――, «Questioni irrisolte sulle associazioni di fedeli», *EJCan* 49 (1993) 73-102.

GIULIANI, P., *La distinzione fra associazioni pubbliche e associazioni private dei fedeli nel nuovo Codice di Diritto Canonico,* Roma 1986.

GOLDIE, R., *From a Roman Window: Five Decades: The World, The Church, and the Catholic Laity,* Blackburn, Australia 1998.

GOTI-ORDEÑANA, J., «El Derecho de Asociación y el Pluralismo en la Iglesia», in *The Associational Element in the Church*. Proceedings of the VIth International Congress of Canon Law, ed. W. Aymans – K.-T. Geringer – H. Schmitz, St. Ottilien 1989, 61-72.

GREEN, T., «Persons and Structures in the Church: Reflections on Selected Issues in Book II», *Jurist* 45 (1985) 24-94.

GUILDAY, P., *The Life and Times of John England,* I-II, New York 1927.

GUTIÉRREZ, J.L., «Associations of Christ's Faithful», in *Code of Canon Law Annotated,* ed E. Caparros – M. Thériault –J. Thorn, Louiseville, Quebec 1993, 242-319.

HARDON, J., *Christianity in the Twentieth Century,* Garden City, NY 1971.

HEINEMANN, H., «Die Mitgliedschaft Nichtkatholischer Christen in Kirchlichen Vereinen», *AKathKR* 153 (1984) 416-426.

HENDRICKS, J., «Le associazioni dei fedeli e i loro statuti», *QDE* 3 (1990) 365-376.

HEREDIA, C. *La naturaleza de los movimentos eclesiales en el derecho de la Iglesia,* Buenos Aires 1994.

HERVADA, J., *Introduzione critica al diritto naturale,* Milano 1990.

HOLLENWEGER, W. J., «From Azusa Street to the Toronto Phenomenon: Historical Roots of the Pentecostal Movement», *Concilium* 1996/3 (1996) 3-14.

HUGHES, H., *Frederick Ozanam,* London 1933.

«L'incontro del Santo Padre con i movimenti Ecclesiali e le nuove Comunità», *ORSup,* 29 May 1998, 9-15.

«Joint Working Groups. I. The Roman Catholic Church and the WCC», in SPUC, *Information Service,* 1967/1, 3-4.

JONE, P., *Commentarium in Codicem Iuris Canonici,* Paderborn 1950.

JOZWIAK, L., *Marriage Encounter as a Private Association of the Christian Faithful,* Washington, D.C. 1991.

KNEAL, E., «Associations of the Christian Faithful»,in *The Code of Canon Law: A Text and Commentary*, ed. J. Coriden – T. Green –D. Heintschel, New York 1985, 243-257.

LENOIR, F., *Les commautés nouvelles: interviews des fondateurs*, Paris 1988.

LORIT, S. – GRIMALDI, N., *Focolare after Thirty Years*, Brooklyn, NY 1976.

LYDON, P.J., *Ready Answers in Canon Law*, New York 1937.

MACRÉAMOINN, S., *The Synod on the Laity: An Outsider's Diary*, Dublin 1987.

MARTIN, R., «A Work in Progress», *Faith and Renewal* (January/February 1993) 3-8.

MARTINEZ-SISTACH, L., *Las asociaciones de fieles*, Barcelona 1994[3].

MATTEI, G., «Un grande evento ecclesiale in preparazione al Giubileo del 2000», *ORSup*, 29 May 1998, 3.

MCAVOY, T., *The History of the Catholic Church in the United States of America*, Notre Dame, IN 1969.

MCCOLGAN, D., *A Century of Charity, The First One Hundred Years of the Society of St. Vincent De Paul in the United States*, I, Milwaukee 1951.

MCDONNELL, K. – MONTAGUE, G., ed., *Fanning the Flame*, Collegeville, MN 1991.

MCDONNELL, K., ed., *Open the Windows: The Popes and the Charismatic Renewal*, South Bend, IN 1989.

MCGRATH, A., «Associations of Christ's Faithful», in *The Canon Law: Letter and Spirit*, ed. G. Sheehy– R. Brown – D. Kelly – A. McGrath – F. Morrisey, London 1995, 115-209.

MCMANUS, F., «The New Code of Canon Law And Ecumenism», *Ecumenical Trends* 13 (1984) 17-19.

MOLANO, E., «Juridic Persons», in *Code of Canon Law Annotated*, ed. E. Caparros – M. Thériault – J. Thorn, Louiseville, Quebec 1993, 133-140.

MONTAN, A., «Le associazioni dei fedeli nel Codice di Diritto Canonico», *QDE* 3 (1990) 324-344.

MORRISEY, F., *Papal and Curial Pronouncements: Their Canonical Significance in Light of the Code of Canon Law*, Ottawa 1995.

———, «The Right of Association as a Basic Right of the Faithful», in *The Associational Element in the Church*. Proceedings of the VIIth International Congress of Canon Law, ed. W. Aymans – K.-T. Geringer – H. Schmitz, St. Ottilien 1989, 7-24.

«I movimenti e le nuove comunità presenti all'incontro con il Papa», *ORSup* 29 May 1998, 9-15.

MOYNIHAN, J., *The Life of Archbishop John Ireland,* New York 1953.

MÜLLER, H., «Das konsoziative Element in seiner Bedeutung für die Ökumene», in *The Associational Element in the Church.* Proceedings of the VIth International Congress of Canon Law, ed. W. Aymans – K.-T. Geringer – H. Schmitz, St. Ottilien 1989, 243-266.

NAVARRO, L., *Diritto di associazione e associazioni di fedeli,* Milano 1991.

NOLAN, H., ed., *Pastoral Letters of the United States Catholic Bishops.* I. *1792-1940,* Washington, DC 1984.

OCHOA, X., *Index Verborum as Locutionum Codex Iuris Canonici,* Roma 1894.

OLIVER, R., *The Vocation of the Laity to Evangelization. An Ecclesiological Inquuiry into the Synod on the Laity (1987), «Christifideles Laici» (1989) and Documents of the NCCB (1987-1996),* TG/Teol. 26, Roma 1997.

PAGÉ, R., «Associations in the Church», *The Jurist* 47 (1987) 165-203.

PASSICOS, J., *Code de Droit Canonique: Texte officiel et traduction français,* Paris 1984.

PIVONKA, L., «The Revised Code of Canon Law: Ecumenical Implications», *The Jurist* 45 (1985) 521-548.

POSPISHIL, V., *Eastern Catholic Church Law,* New York 1996.

PROVOST, J., «The Realization of Ecclesiastical Purposes through and in Associations of Secular Law», in *The Associational Element in the Church.* Proceedings of the VIth International Congress of Canon Law, ed. W. Aymans – K.-T. Geringer – H. Schmitz, St. Ottilien 1989, 751-769.

RECCHI, S., «Gli stadi evolutivi dell'associazione: dal gruppo all'istituto di vita consacrata», *QDE* 3 (1990) 441-453.

REDAELLI, C., «Alcune questioni pratiche riguardanti le associazioni di fedeli nel contesto italiano», *QDE* 3 (1990) 345-355.

«Report on the Plenary Meeting of the PCPCU: Relations with the WCC, Including Faith and Order», in PCPUC, *Information Service,* n. 91 (1996/I-II) 45-51.

ROCCA, G., «Le nuove comunità», *QDE* 3 (1992) 163-176.

ROUSE, R. – NEILL, S., *A History of the Ecumenical Movement,* Norwich 1967.

SCHULZ, W., «Cristiani non-cattolici come membri di associazioni cattoliche», *Studi in onore di Lorenzo Spinelli,* Modena 1989, 1065-1076.

SCHULZ, W.,«Can. 314», in *Münsterische Kommentar zum Codex Iuris Canonici*, ed. K. Lüdicke, Essen 1984-, Losenblattwerk May 1989.

———, «La posizione giuridica delle associazioni e la loro funzione nella chiesa», *Apoll.* 59 (1986) 115-130.

———, «Le norme canoniche sul diritto di associazione», *Apoll.* 50 (1977) 149-171.

SEMBENI, G., *Direttorio Ecumenico 1993: svilluppo dottrinale e disciplinare*, TG/DC 19, Roma 1997.

SHEERIN, J.P. – HOTCHKIN, J.F., ed., *Addresses and Homilies on Ecumenism 1978-1980*, Washington, DC 1981.

SIMPSON, D., *Cassell's Latin Dictionary*, London 1993.

SOKOLICH, A., *Canonical Provisions for Universities and Colleges: A Historical Synopsis and a Commentary*, Washington, DC 1956.

STELTEN, L., *Dictionary of Ecclesiastical Latin*, Peabody, MA 1995

SUDBRACK, J., «Discipleship in Religious Life», *Theology Digest* 43 (1996) 23-27.

TAVARD, G., *Two Centuries of Ecumenism: The Search for Unity*, Notre Dame 1960.

URQUHART, G., *The Pope's Armada*, London 1995.

VALIANTE, F., «La missione dei movimenti ecclesiali alle soglie del nuovo millennio», *OR*, 29 May 1998, 4.

———, «Comunione e unità per vivere la missione della Chiesa», *OR*, 30 May 1998, 5.

———, «Il grande compito dell'Unità da vivere nella testimonianza», *OR*, 31 May 1998, 7.

VAN ELDEREN, M., «Editorial», *The Ecumenical Review* 49 (1997) 303.

VANIER, J., *Community and Growth*, London 1996.

———, *Jesus the Gift of Love*, London 1988.

———, *La sfida dell'arca*, Roma 1984.

VANIER, T., *One Bread, One Body: The Ecumenical Experience of L'Arche*. Leominister 1997.

VANZETTO, T., «Commento a un canone: l'irradiarsi di un carisma oltre l'istituto di vita consacrata», *QDE* 3 (1990) 384-393.

VERCRUYSSE, J., *Introduzione alla Teologia Ecumenica*, Casale Monferrato 1992.

VROMANT, G., *De Fidelium Associationibus*, Louvain 1955.

VISCHER, L., *A Documentary History of the Faith and Order Movement 1927-1963*, St. Louis, MO 1963.

WERNZ, F., – VIDAL, P., *Ius Canonicum*, Roma 1933.

WOOLF, H. – *al.*, ed., *Webster's New Collegiate Dictionary*, Springfield, MA.

WOYWOD, S., *A Practical Commentary on the Code of Canon Law*, New York 1925.

ZADRA, B., *I movimenti ecclesiali e il loro statuti*, TG/DC 16, Roma 1997.

ZAMBONINI, F., *Chiara Lubich: A Life for Unity*, London 1992.

ZAPP, H., *Codex Iuris Canonici Lemmata*, Freiburg 1986.

3. Materials Concerning Associations Reviewed in the Dissertation

3.1 *Alleluia Catholic Fellowship*

ALLELUIA CATHOLIC FELLOWSHIP, *Statutes*, Alleluia Christian Service Center, Augusta, GA 1992.

ALLELUIA COMMUNITY, *Alleluia Community Covenant*, Alleluia Christian Service Center, Augusta, GA 1997. (http://www.csra.net/alleluia/).

———, *Alleluia Protestant Fellowships*, Alleluia Christian Service Center, Augusta, GA 1997. (http://www.csra.net/alleluia/).

———, *Frequently asked Questions*, Alleluia Christian Service Center, Augusta, GA 1997. (http://www.csra.net/alleluia/).

CLARK, D., *Personal letter*, 6 August 1997.

LESSARD, R., *Personal letter*, 29 January 1992.

MASAK, A., *Personal letter*, 18 February 1997.

3.2 *Apostolate for Family Consecration*

APOSTOLATE FOR FAMILY CONSECRATION, *A Way of Life*, Headquarters of Apostolate for Family Consecration, Bloomingdale, OH 1994.

CONIKER, J., *Personal letter*, 1 August 1997.

3.3 *Brothers and Sisters of Charity*

BROTHERS AND SISTERS OF CHARITY, *Rule, Constitution and Directory*, Little Portion Hermitage, Eureka Springs, AR 1994.

MCDONALD, A., *Decree*, Diocese of Little Rock, AR 1993.

———, *Personal letter*, Diocese of Little Rock, AR 1993.

TALBOT, J.M., *Personal letter*, 12 March 1996.

———, *Personal letter*, 18 December 1997.

3.4 *Catholic Fraternity of Charismatic Covenant Communities and Fellowships*

Catholic Fraternity Newsletter (Brisbane, Austrlia) November 1994.

CATHOLIC FRATERNITY OF CHARISMATIC COVENANT COMMUNITIES AND FELLOWSHIPS, *Statutes,* Emmanuel Covenant Community, Brisbane, Australia 1996.

CATHOLIC FRATERNITY OF CHARISMATIC COVENANT COMMUNITIES AND FELLOWSHIPS, *Statutes,* City of the Lord, Phoenix, AZ 1995.

INTERNATIONAL BROTHERHOOD OF COMMUNITIES, *Charter,* Emmanuel Covenant Community, Brisbane, Australia 1987.

PONTIFICIUM CONSILIUM PRO LAICIS, 1585/90/S-61/B-50, Città del Vaticano.

————, *Decree,* Pontificium Consilium Pro Laicis, 27 November 1995, 1266/95/S-61/B-53, Città del Vaticano.

3.5 *Chemin Neuf*

«Chemin Neuf Community and Communion», *Tychique,* Supplement, 103 (May 1993) 2-7.

«Communauté et Communion du Chemin Neuf», *Tychique,* Supplément, 88 (November 1990) 1-31.

DECOURTRAY, A., *Decree,* Archdiocese of Lyon, France 1984.

FABRE, L., *Personal letter,* 2 August 1997.

TURBAT, O., *Spending the World Youth Day with the Chemin Neuf Community,* International Secretariat, Paris 1996.

3.6 *Ecumenical Order of Charity*

Community: The Newsletter of the Ecumenical Order of Charity (Vancouver, WA) Summer 1997.

ECUMENICAL ORDER OF CHARITY. ASSOCIATE COMPANION PROGRAM, Charitist Communications, Vancouver, WA 1995.

ECUMENICAL ORDER OF CHARITY, *An Ecumenical Religious Order for Men and Women,* Ecumenical Order of Charity, Vancouver, WA 1997.

ECUMENICAL ORDER OF CHARITY, *The Founding Document,* Charitist Communications, Vancouver, WA 1995

ROBERT, D., *Personal letter,* 17 February 1997.

————, *Personal letter,* 28 July 1997.

3.7 *Emmanuel*

COMMUNAUTÉ DE L'EMMANUEL ET DE LA FRATERNITÉ DE JESUS, *Statuts,* Headquarters of the Communauté, Paris 1992.

PONTIFICIUM CONSILIUM PRO LAICIS, 1560/92/S-61/B-45/b, Città del Vaticano.

3.8 *Glenmary Co-Missioners*

FAZALUDDIN, M., *Personal letter,* 14 October 1996.

————, *Personal letter,* 14 November 1996.

GLENMARY CO-MISSIONER ASSOCIATION, *Annual Report 1994-1995,* Corporate Office, Nashville, TN 1995.

————, *Annual Report 1995-1996,* Corporate Office, Nashville, TN 1996.

————, *A Partnership of Faith and Cultures,* Corporate Office, Nashville, TN 1996.

————, *By Laws,* Corporate Office, Nashville, TN 1991.

KMIEC, E., *Decree,* Diocese of Nashville, Nashville, TN 1993.

NIEDERGESES, J., *Decree,* Diocese of Nashville, Nashville, TN 1992.

VILLATORO, M., «The Patience of a Cautious People», *Co-Missioner News* (Nashville, TN), Spring 1995.

————, «The Summer of Our Discontent», *Co-Missioner News* (Nashville, TN), Autumn 1995.

————, «The Triumph of Friends», *Co-Missioner News* (Nashville, TN), Winter 1995.

————, «Keysville, Georgia--Reflections», *Co-Missioner News* (Nashville, TN), Summer 1996.

3.9 *La Fraternité Chrétienne Intercontinentale Des Personnes Malades Chroniques et Handicapées Physiques*

FRATERNITÉ CHRÉTIENNE INTERCONTINENTALE DES PERSONNES MALADES CHRONIQUES ET HANDICAPÉES PHYSIQUES, *Statuts,* Headquarters of the Fraternity, Verdun 1995.

3.10 *Lamb of God Catholic Fellowship*

BROWNE, D., *Decree,* Diocese of Hamilton, New Zealand, 15 February 1996.

DUNN, P., *Decree,* Diocese of Auckland, New Zealand, 29 November 1996.

HUMPHRIES, D., *Personal letter,* 12 December 1996.

LAMB OF GOD CATHOLIC FELLOWSHIP. *Statutes,* Lamb of God Center, Christchurch, New Zealand 1989.

MEEKING, B., *Decree,* Diocese of Christchurch, New Zealand, 11 August 1989.

WILLIAMS, T., *Decree,* Archdiocese of Wellington, New Zealand 12 November 1990.

3.11 *Lamb of God Community*

KEELER, W., *Decree of Recognition,* Archdiocese of Baltimore, 1993.

LAMB OF GOD COMMUNITY, *Statutes,* Headquarters of the Lamb of God Community, Baltimore 1994.

NODAR, D., *Personal letter,* 17 February 1997.

3.12 *L'Arche*

VANIER, J., *Personal letter,* 6 July 1997.

3.13 *Magnificat*

AMOS, J., *Personal letter,* 12 December 1995.

———, *Personal letter,* 29 January 1997.

LACOCO, J., *Personal letter,* 25 November 1996.

MAGNIFICAT, *Constitution,* Magnificat Central Service Team, New Orleans 1996.

———, *List of Chapters and Coordinators,* Magnificat Central Service Team, New Orleans 1996.

QUIRK, M., *Personal letter,* 17 October 1996.

———, *Personal letter,* 24 October 1996.

SKONEKI, W., *Personal letter,* 10 December 1995.

3.14 *Mercy of God Community*

Footsteps: Newsletter of the Mercy of God Community (Providence, RI), April-May 1997.

KETCHAM, B., *Personal letter,* 17 March 1997.

MERCY OF GOD COMMUNITY, *By-Laws,* Mercy of God Community, Providence, RI 1996

———, *Information,* Mercy of God Community, Providence, RI 1997.

MERCY OF GOD COMMUNITY, *Living the Rule. Praying the Rule,* Mercy of God Community, Providence, RI 1996.

————, *The Rule,* Mercy of God Community, Providence, RI 1996.

3.15 *Mother of God Community*

GILLIS, J., «The Believers Next Door», *The Washington Post Magazine,* 13 April 1997, 10-12.

————, «Paradise Lost», *The Washington Post Magazine,* 20 April 1997, 16-18.

GRESKO, G., *Memorandum on behalf of the Mother of God Community: Ecumenical Membership: the Spiritul Advisor,* Cleveland, OH, 1 July 1996.

LEONARD, M., «Mother of God Community Series Evokes Strong Emotions», *Catholic Standard-Archdiocese of Washington,* 24 April 1997, 3.

MOTHER OF GOD COMMUNITY, *Statutes,* Corporate Offices, Gaithersburg, MD 1997. (http:/www.motherofgod.org/index.htm)

————, *1995 Reorganization,* Corporate Offices, Gaithersburg, MD 1997. (http:/www.motherofgod.org/index.htm)

ZIMMERMAN, M., «A Community Divided», *Catholic Standard – Archdiocese of Washington,* 24 April 1997, 2.

3.16 *Opera di Maria*

OPERA DI MARIA, *Statuti Generali,* Opera di Maria, Roma 1990.

————, *Statuti Generali,* Città Nuova, Roma 1995.

PONTIFICIUM CONSILIUM PRO LAICIS, 900/90/S-61/A-23, Città del Vaticano.

————, 900/94/S-61/A-23, Città del Vaticano.

3.17 *People of God's Love Community*

DURRANT, W., *Personal letter,* 30 May 1997.

3.18 *Word of God Community*

TIEWS, P., *Personal letter,* 23 June 1997.

WORD OF GOD, *1996 Membership Statistics,* Word of God Community, Ann Arbor, MI 1997.

————, *Opportunities for Involvment,* The Word of God Community, Ann Arbor, MI 1997.

Word of God Newsletter (Ann Arbor, MI), February 1997.

Word of God Newsletter (Ann Arbor, MI), April 1997.
Word of God Newsletter (Ann Arbor, MI), May/June 1997.

3.19 *Work of Christ Community*

An Ecumenical Community: The Work of Christ, The Work of Christ Community, Lansing, MI 1996.
HIGLEY, R., *Personal letter,* 11 June 1997.
UCO Missions Newsletter (East Lansing, MI), Spring 1997.
UCO Missions Newsletter (East Lansing, MI), Summer 1997.
Work of Christ Newsletter (Lansing MI), 19 May 1997.
Work of Christ Newsletter (Lansing MI), 2 June 1997.

4. Materials Concerning Other Associations

4.1 *Bread of Life Catholic Fellowship*

BREAD OF LIFE CATHOLIC FELLOWSHIP, *Statutes,* Servants of Jesus Community, Concord West, Australia 1997.

BREAD OF LIFE FELLOWSHIP, *An Association of Catholics within the Ecumenical Servants of Jesus Community,* Servants of Jesus Community, Concord West, Australia: 1996.

CHIRCOP, J., *Personal letter,* 4 February 1997.

SERVANTS OF JESUS COMMUNITY, *Breaking Down Barriers Between Christians,* Servants of Jesus Community, Concord West, Australia 1996.

4.2 *City of the Lord*

JONES, J., *Personal letter,* 4 March 1996.
O'BRIEN, T., *Decree,* Diocese of Phoenix, AZ 1 November 1994.
City Life Newsletter (Phoenix) January 1996.

4.3 *Sword of the Spirit*

Community and Mission News: Sword of the Spirit, Christ the King Association, UCO Missions, North American Edition (Lansing, MI), Spring 1997.

4.4 *Pontifical Council for the Laity*

PONTIFICIUM CONSILIUM PRO LAICIS, *Liste D'Adresses (mailing list) des Associations internationales de fidèles avec lesquelles le Conseil Pontifical pour les laïcs est en relation*, Città del Vaticano, March 1994.

——, *Liste D'Adresses (mailing list) des Associations internationales de fidèles avec lesquelles le Conseil Pontifical pour les laïcs est en relation*, Città del Vaticano, January 1996.

PONTIFICIUM CONSILIUM PRO LAICIS, *Liste D'Adresses (mailing list) des Associations internationales de fidèles avec lesquelles le Conseil Pontifical pour les laïcs est en relation*, Città del Vaticano, July 1997.

——, *Liste D'Adresses (mailing list) des Associations internationales de fidèles avec lesquelles le Conseil Pontifical pour les laïcs est en relation*, Città del Vaticano, August 1997.

INDEX OF AUTHORS

GENERAL INDEX

TESI GREGORIANA

Since 1995, the series «Tesi Gregoriana» has made available to the general public some of the best doctoral theses done at the Pontifical Gregorian University. The typesetting is done by the authors themselves following norms established and controlled by the University.

Published Volumes [Series: Canon Law]

1. RUESSMANN, Madeleine, *Exclaustration. Its Nature and Use according to Current Law*, 1995, pp. 552.

2. BRAVI, Maurizio Claudio, *Il Sinodo dei Vescovi. Istituzione, fini e natura. Indagine teologico-giuridica*, 1995, pp. 400.

3. SUGAWARA, Yuji, *Religious Poverty. From Vatican Council II to the 1994 Synod of Bishops*, 1997, pp. 412.

4. FORCONI, Maria Cristina, *Antropologia cristiana come fondamento dell'unità e dell'indissolubilità del patto matrimoniale*, 1996, pp. 200.

5. KOVAČ, Mirjam, *L'orizzonte dell'obbedienza religiosa. Ricerca teologico-canonica*, 1996, pp. 368.

6. KAKAREKO, Andrzej, *La riforma della vita del clero nella diocesi di Vilna dopo il Concilio di Trento (1564-1796)*, 1996, pp. 248.

7. KUBIAK, Piotr, *L'assoluzione generale nel* Codice di Diritto Canonico *(Cann. 961-963) alla luce della dottrina del Concilio di Trento sull'integrità della confessione sacramentale*, 1996, pp. 212.

8. AMENTA, Pietro, *Partecipazione alla potestà legislativa del Vescovo. Indagine teologico-giuridica su chiesa particolare e sinodo diocesano*, 1996, pp. 272.

9. LORUSSO, Luca, *Gli strumenti di comunicazione sociale nel diritto ecclesiale. Aspettative, problematiche e realizzazioni alla luce dell'insegnamento magisteriale*, 1996, pp. 272.

10. PÉREZ DÍAZ, Andrés, *Los vicarios generales y episcopales en el Derecho Canónico actual*, 1996, pp. 336.

11. ZEC, Slavko, *La tossicodipendenza come radice d'incapacità al matrimonio (Can. 1095). Scienze umane, dottrina canonica e giurisprudenza*, 1996, pp. 288.

12. SERRES LÓPEZ DE GUEREÑU, Roberto, *«Error recidens in condicionem sine qua non» (Can. 126). Estudio histórico-jurídico*, 1997, pp. 232.

13. MINGARDI, Massimo, *L'esclusione della dignità sacramentale dal consenso matrimoniale nella dottrina e nella giurisprudenza recenti*, 1997, pp. 320.

14. MARGELIST, Stefan, *Die Beweiskraft der Parteiaussagen in Ehenichtigkeitsverfahren*, 1997, pp. 226.

15. D'AURIA, Andrea, *L'imputabilità nel diritto penale canonico*, 1997, pp. 240.

16. ZADRA, Barbara, *I movimenti ecclesiali e i loro statuti*, 1997, pp. 200.

17. MIGLIAVACCA, Andrea, *La «confessione frequente di devozione». Studio teologico-giuridico sul periodo fra i Codici del 1917 e del 1983*, 1997, pp. 336.

18. SERENO, David, *Whether the Norm Expressed in Canon 1103 is of Natural Law or of Positive Church Law*, 1997, pp. 292.

19. SEMBENI, Giulio, *Direttorio Ecumenico 1993: sviluppo dottrinale e disciplinare*, 1997, pp. 260.

20. KAMAS, Juraj, *The Separation of the Spouses with the Bond Remaining. Historical and Canonical Study with Pastoral Applications*, 1997, pp. 360.

21. VISCOME, Francesco, *Origine ed esercizio della potestà dei vescovi dal Vaticano I al Vaticano II. Contesto teologico-canonico del magistero dei «recenti Pontefici» (*Nota Explicativa Praevia 2*)*, 1997, pp. 276.

22. KADZIOCH, Grzegorz, *Il ministro del sacramento del matrimonio nella tradizione e nel diritto canonico latino e orientale*, 1997, pp. 276.

23. MCCORMACK, Alan, *The Term «Privilege». A Textual Study of its Meaning and Use in the 1983 Code of Canon Law*, 1997, pp. 444.

24. PERLASCA, Alberto, *Il concetto di bene ecclesiastico*, 1997, pp. 428.

25. ZVOLENSKÝ, Stanislav, *«Error qualitatis dans causam» e «error qualitatis directe et principaliter intentae». Studio storico della distinzione*, 1998, pp. 264.

26. GARZA MEDINA, Luis, *Significado de la expresión* nomine Ecclesiae *en el Código de Derecho Canónico*, 1998, pp. 192.

27. BREITBACH, Udo, *Die Vollmacht der Kirche Jesu Christi über die Ehen der Getauften. Zur Gesetzesunterworfenheit der Ehen nichtkatholischer Christen,* 1998, pp. 292.

28. ZANETTI, Eugenio, *La nozione di «laico» nel dibattito preconciliare. Alle radici di una svolta significativa e problematica,* 1998, pp. 404.

29. ECHEBERRIA, Juan José, *Asunción de los consejos evangélicos en las asociaciones de fieles y movimientos eclesiales. Investigación teologico-canonica*, 1998, pp. 274.

30. SYGUT, Marek, *Natura e origine della potestà dei vescovi nel Concilio di Trento e nella dottrina successiva (1545-1869)*, 1998, pp. 356.

31. RUBIYATMOKO, Robertus, *Competenza della Chiesa nello scioglimento del vincolo del matrimonio non sacramentale. Una ricerca sostanziale sullo scioglimento del vincolo matrimoniale*, 1998, pp. 300.

32. BROWN J. Phillip, *Canon 17 CIC 1983 and the Hermeneutical Principles of Bernard Lonergan*, 1999, pp. 436.

33. BAFUIDINSONI, Maloko-Mana, *Le* munus regendi *de l'évêque diocésain comme* munus patris et pastoris *selon le Concile Vatican II*, 1999, pp. 280.

34. POLVANI, Carlo Maria, *Authentic Interpretation in Canon Law. Reflections on a Distinctively Canonical Institution*, 1999, pp. 388.

35. GEISINGER, Robert, *On the Requirement of Sufficient Maturity for Candidate to the Presbyterate (c. 1031 § 1), with a Consideration of Canonical Maturity and Matrimonial Jurisprudence (1989-1990)*, 1999, pp. 276.

36. VISIOLI, Matteo, *Il diritto della Chiesa e le sue tensioni alla luce di un'antropologia teologica*, 1999, pp. 480.

37. CORONELLI, Renato, *Incorporazione alla Chiesa e comunione. Aspetti teologici e canonici dell'appartenenza alla Chiesa*, 1999, pp. 456.

38. ASTIGUETA, Damián G., *La noción de laico desde el Concilio Vaticano II al CIC 83. El laico: «sacramento de la Iglesia y del mundo»*, 1999, pp. 300.

39. OLIVER, James M., *Ecumenical Associations: Their Canonical Status, with Particular Reference to the United States of America*, 1999, pp. 336.